Blackstone's Guide to the

FAMILY LAW ACT 1996

Blackstone's Guide to the

FAMILY LAW ACT 1996

Second Edition

Tina Bond, LLB, Solicitor
Senior Lecturer in Law, University of Northumbria

A. Jane Bridge, LLB, Barrister

Paul Mallender, LLB, Barrister

and

Jane Rayson, LLB, Barrister

BLACKSTONE
PRESS LIMITED

First published in Great Britain 1996 by Blackstone Press Limited,
Aldine Place, London W12 8AA. Telephone 0181-740 2277

© T. Bond, A. J. Bridge, P. Mallender, J. Rayson, 1996

First edition, 1996
Second edition, 1999

ISBN: 1 85431 865 9

British Library Cataloguing in Publication Data
A CIP catalogue record for this book is available from the British Library.

Typeset by Montage Studios Limited, Horsmonden, Kent
Printed by Ashford Colour Press, Gosport, Hampshire

Contents

Preface

This book is intended to provide a statutory guide for legal practitioners and for all those who work in the area of family law. The Family Law Act 1996 is really a combination of two statutes rolled into one. The Family Homes and Domestic Violence Bill which foundered in 1995 gained a new lease of life when it was added to the Family Law Bill early in 1996. After much heated Parliamentary debate the Bill eventually received Royal Assent on 4 July 1996.

The new Act will revolutionise the way in which divorce takes place and it will streamline the various remedies available to deal with domestic violence. We hope that we have written a book which is 'user-friendly' and helpful. In particular, the various precedents contained in the Appendix will, we hope, prove invaluable to the busy practitioner.

Part I of the Act, which deals with the general principles governing the implementation of the statute, and Part III, which deals with the availability of legal aid for mediation, came into force on 21 March 1997. Part IV of the Act, which covers the orders available to regulate occupation of the the family home and deal with domestic violence, came into force on 1 October 1997. The latest information indicates that Part II of the statute is likely to come into force early in the year 2000. Various pilot schemes are taking place to test the new procedures envisaged by the Act and the implementation of Part II will only be possible once those schemes have been properly evaluated and the results of them put into effect.

We have endeavoured to paint the picture as it appears in January 1999, and any mistakes, omissions or faults are ours alone.

We are grateful to our families and colleagues for their support during the writing process, and to the staff at Blackstone Press for their unstinting help and for their tactful co-ordination of four busy practitioners (a task which cannot have been easy).

Tina Bond
Jane Bridge
Paul Mallender
Jane Rayson
January 1999

Chapter One
Introduction to the Act

1 Background

The Family Law Act 1996 received the Royal Assent on 4th July 1996.

The Act is an amalgam of two distinct but related areas of law and it is worth knowing a brief outline of its history.

Parts I, II and III deal with the reform of the law of divorce and related matters. Part IV regulates the law relating to occupation of the family home and provides a regime for protection of a party from domestic violence.

The provisions of Part IV of the Act were originally contained in separate legislation, the Family Homes and Domestic Violence Bill, which was withdrawn in late October 1995 following objections from a number of Members of Parliament who believed that the Bill failed to make what they regarded as an appropriate distinction between the position of married parties on the one hand and cohabitants on the other.

Lord Irvine of Lairg summarised the circumstances leading to the withdrawal of the Bill as follows: 'I can only suppose that the attitude of that uninformed minority was based upon what a tabloid newspaper, the 'Daily Mail', claimed about the Bill and not on what the noble and learned Lord's Bill provided. That minority obviously thought, because that is what they said, that the Bill for the first time would afford legal protection to mistresses and somehow, as a result, undermine the institution of marriage.' (Hansard, 30th January 1996, vol 568, no 34, col 1398).

The former Lord Chancellor, Lord Mackay of Clashfern, introduced the Family Law Bill into the House of Lords on 16th November 1995 and confirmed that not only did it contain proposals for the reform of the law of divorce but that it also incorporated the provisions of the withdrawn Bill. It is important to be aware, however, that significant amendments were made following withdrawal of the Bill. These are discussed fully in Chapter 19, but suffice it to say that they seek to reinforce at various points the distinction between married parties and cohabitants in terms of duration of an occupation order but most notably in the matters to be considered by the court. Section 41 provides that where the court is required to consider the nature of the parties' relationship and the parties are cohabitants or former cohabitants, the court is 'to have regard to the fact that they have not given each other the commitment involved in marriage': s. 41(2). In explaining this provision, the former Lord Chancellor stated 'I hope that this will emphasise the important general message that marriage is special in a way that no other relationship is' (Hansard, 30th November 1995, vol 567, col 700).

2 The need for reform

2.1 Reform of the law of divorce

In 1988 the Law Commission issued a Discussion Paper 'Facing the Future: A Discussion Paper on the Ground for Divorce' (Law Com No 170). In this Paper the Law Commission acknowledged that there were concerns as to the effectiveness of the present divorce law set out in the Matrimonial Causes Act 1973. Although the sole ground for divorce was that the marriage in question had irretrievably broken down, for a divorce to be obtained quickly, adultery or 'unreasonable behaviour' had to be alleged and it was felt that this led to acrimony and bitterness between the parties and had an adverse effect on the children concerned. In consequence, opportunities for reconciliation were lost and many marriages which might have been saved were dissolved.

The alternative basis for divorce, relying on 2 years' separation with the consent of the respondent, was frequently not available to parties on lower incomes because separation may be impossible without substantial resources — hence the law was discriminatory in its operation.

The Law Commission demonstrated that the present law failed in its object to enable a marriage to be brought to an end with minimum bitterness, distress and humiliation. It endorsed the comments made to the Booth Committee on Procedure in Matrimonial Causes (1985) that 'divorce should be truly and not merely artificially based on a no-fault ground and that the concepts of guilt and innocence which have ruled our divorce laws, and consequently our divorce proceedings, since 1857 should no longer have a part to play'.

The Law Commission concluded by stating that reform was urgently needed and offering alternative divorce models.

The Discussion Paper was followed by the Law Commission's 1990 Report 'Family Law: The Ground for Divorce' (Law Com No 192).

The Report repeated the criticisms of the present law, namely that it is confusing and misleading, discriminatory and unjust, distorts the parties' bargaining positions, provokes hostility and bitterness, is bad for children and crucially does nothing to save the marriage (Part II, pp. 5–9).

After analysing the various divorce models, the Law Commission recommended that irretrievable breakdown of marriage should remain the sole ground for divorce and that divorce should no longer be seen as a single event but should be a process over time culminating in a divorce order.

This would provide the parties with an opportunity to determine whether the marriage had in fact irretrievably broken down, to face up to the consequences of divorce and to make practical arrangements for the future.

The former government responded to the Law Commission Report by issuing its own Consultation Paper in December 1993, 'Looking to the Future: Mediation and the Ground for Divorce' (Cm 2424). Whilst the Law Commission had recognised the value of conciliation and mediation 'as a way of resolving disputes without resort to traditional adjudication' (Law Com No 192, para. 5.30), the former government made the role of mediation one of the central planks of its Consultation Paper and this was reinforced in its subsequent White Paper 'Looking to the Future: Mediation and the Ground for Divorce' (Cm 2799), published in April 1995.

In both its Consultation Paper and later White Paper, the former government accepted the criticisms of the present divorce law, stating its principal recommendation for reform at para. 2.34 as follows:

> The Government proposes … that it should be possible to obtain a divorce in England and Wales on the sole ground that the marriage has irretrievably broken down. The breakdown of the marriage should be demonstrated by the passing of a period of time for reflection and consideration in order for the couple to address what has gone wrong in the marriage, whether there is any hope of reconciliation and in the event that the breakdown is irretrievable, to make proper arrangements for living apart before a divorce order is made. The Government proposes that the minimum period for reflection and consideration should be twelve months.

2.2 Reform of the law relating to domestic violence and occupation of the family home

Speaking in the case of *Richards* v *Richards* [1984] AC 174 Lord Scarman observed:

> The statutory provision is a hotchpotch of enactments of limited scope passed into law to meet specific situations or to strengthen the powers of specified courts. The sooner the range, scope and effect of these powers are rationalised into a coherent and comprehensive body of statute law, the better.

Regrettably, Lord Scarman has had to wait 12 years for the statute law, the provisions largely coming into force on 1st October 1997.

Following the publication in 1989 of a Working Paper 'Domestic Violence and Occupation of the Family Home' (Working Paper No 113), the Law Commission reviewed the present state of the law in its 1992 Report 'Family Law: Domestic Violence and Occupation of the Family Home' (Law Com No 207).

It identified a number of anomalies and inconsistencies principally stemming from the fact that different courts offered different remedies applying different criteria. The form and scope of orders available were considered to be outdated, failing to provide adequate or appropriate remedies.

Further, no protection was available to former cohabitants and others falling outside specific categories. Such individuals had to invoke the often inadequate remedies offered by the law of torts.

In making its recommendation, the Law Commission advocated that all courts should have the same jurisdiction to make non-molestation orders and occupation orders, that each order should have its own criteria but the orders should be capable of combination with one another and with other family remedies in appropriate cases (Law Com No 207, May 1992, paras 7.1 and 7.18).

It also recommended that a wider range of applicants should be able to seek orders from the court. It introduced the concept of 'associated persons' (see Chapter 17) and recommended the retention of ex parte orders and the improvement in methods of enforcement with the court being required to attach a power of arrest in certain circumstances rather than having a discretion to do so as had previously been the case (Law Com No 207, paras 7.21, 7.22, 7.23 and 7.24).

Further, it recommended that the power to transfer tenancies then contained in the Matrimonial Homes Act 1983 should be extended to cohabitants (Law Com No 207, para. 7.28) and it proposed changes to the powers of the court in making an emergency protection order under s. 44 of the Children Act 1989 (Law Com No 207, para. 7.32 and 7.33).

3   The objects of the Act

The former Lord Chancellor summarised the objects of the legislation at the Second Reading on 30th November 1995. He confirmed that the ground for divorce would remain irretrievable breakdown. He went on to state, 'I see no merit, either moral or intellectual or practical, in retention of the requirement to make allegations of fault in order to establish breakdown ...' (Hansard, 30th November 1995, vol 567, col 701). He went on 'It is of course vitally important that marriages are not dissolved if they could be saved and therefore important that the mechanism used for testing breakdown is one which we are satisfied will do just that. The provisions in the Bill are that breakdown would be established by the passage of an absolute period of time without that period being abridged in any circumstances' (Hansard, 30th November 1995, vol 567, col 702).

Turning to what is Part IV of the Act, the Lord Chancellor confirmed that this dealt with domestic violence and occupation of the family home. He explained that the Bill was designed to provide a consistent set of remedies, eligibility for such orders being based on the concept of 'association' (Hansard, 30th November 1995, vol 567, col 705).

4   Implementation of the Act

The Lord Chancellor's Department made it clear from the outset that the provisions of the Act would be phased in, the Lord Chancellor predicting that it would be at least 2 years before the Act came into force (Hansard, 22nd January 1996, vol 568, no 29, col 839). This is because pilot studies were to be carried out on a number of the new features of divorce law including, inter alia, information meetings and mediation.

In consequence, in March 1997 the Lord Chancellor announced the establishment of a range of marriage support services, including funding for such services and legal aid for mediation. Part I, s. 22 and Part III of the Act were therefore brought into force on 21st March 1997 (Family Law Act 1996 (Commencement No. 1) Order 1997, SI No. 1077).

Commenting on the progress made in this area, Geoff Hoon MP, the Parliamentary Secretary to the Lord Chancellor's Department, stated:

> Phase 1 of the Legal Aid Mediation Pilots and research relating to these pilots is well under way.
>
> The government has a keen interest in ensuring high quality mediation services as an important step in the successful implementation of ... the Act.
>
> The government therefore very much welcomes the fact that the UK College of Family Law Mediators was formally launched in Autumn 1997 and has published ... its first directory of mediation services. (*Family Law*, March 1998)

The importance attached to some of the novel features of the new divorce law was highlighted in a press release issued by the Lord Chancellor's Department on 11th March 1997: 'It is vitally important that the information sessions should be in place and working before substantive changes in the divorce law are brought into force.'

In June 1997 the Lord Chancellor's Department announced the establishment of five pilot studies to be carried out 'to determine the best system for delivery of information meetings which divorcing couples will be required to attend before commencing proceedings'.

The pilot studies began in June 1997 and were conducted in five different areas of the country. They lasted for 9 months and are currently being evaluated. Additional pilot schemes, testing different models for information meetings, were launched in the spring and summer of 1998, including two run by law firms in Merseyside and the Isle of Wight.

Much of the legislation is skeletal in form and new law will be found in statutory instruments which are unlikely to be promulgated until the pilot studies are completed, the results analysed and the views of the advisory committee obtained. The Lord Chancellor refused to be drawn on a number of practical issues, insisting that he would be guided by what the pilot studies revealed.

By contrast, and emphasising the discrete nature of these provisions, Part IV of the Act came into force on 1st October 1997. The exception was s. 60 which was not implemented. Section 60 allows rules of court to be made authorising a prescribed person ('a representative') to act on behalf of victims of domestic violence.

The Consultation Paper on Part IV of the Family Law Act 1996 (Lord Chancellor's Department, March 1997) explained that it was the view of the Lord Chancellor's Department that 'it is appropriate to allow the courts, the police and practitioners to become familiar with the new law and to gain experience in its operation before considering the introduction of unaccustomed procedures and responsibilities of this nature'. Again, it is likely that a pilot scheme will be used before the procedure and forms are finalised.

5   Miscellaneous points

5.1   Training of mediators

It is acknowledged that intensive recruitment and training of mediators is necessary if sufficient numbers are to be available to fulfil the role planned for them in the Act. Baroness Young summed up the demands to be placed on mediators as follows:

> The faith that one is going to pin on the mediator! He is the all-wise man or woman who will divide up the assets, deal with the acrimony and who will know the very moment at which to say to the couples 'You should seek reconciliation'
> (Hansard, 23rd January 1996, vol 568, no 29, col 933.)

5.2   Preparation for marriage

It seems unfortunate to the authors that a piece of legislation entitled *Family Law* Act and having in its general principles section a requirement 'that the institution of marriage is to be supported' fails to provide for marriage preparation. This is all the more regrettable in light of the fact that in its own White Paper the former government proposed that existing initiatives to prepare couples for marriage should be reviewed to see if they could be developed to prepare couples for marriage (Cm 2799, para. 3.7).

It should be noted that the present government published a Consultation Document on 4 November 1998, setting out its plans to strengthen family life. The proposals include setting up a National Institute for Parenting and the family to offer, *inter alia*, preparation courses for marrying couples. Such preparation would include couples being given a 'statement of rights and responsibilities' before marrying. Further, a new role would be created for registrars who would offer pre-nuptial counselling as well as providing marriage preparation packs.

6   The future

The Act radically reforms major areas of family law: the principles on which lawyers have practised for the last 25 years will largely disappear. A fascinating and demanding future lies ahead.

Chapter Two
General Principles

1 General principles which apply to Parts II and III of the Act

The general principles governing the operation of Parts II and III of the Act are set out in Part I (s. 1). Parts I and III came into force on 21st March 1997. The general principles set out in Part I construct the framework within which the court and all others who use the Act *must* operate. They are that:

    (a)   the institution of marriage is to be supported;

    (b)   the parties to a marriage which may have broken down are to be encouraged to take all practicable steps, whether by marriage counselling or otherwise, to save the marriage;

    (c)   a marriage which has irretrievably broken down and is being brought to an end should be brought to an end —

        (i)   with the minimum distress to the parties and to the children affected;

        (ii)   with questions dealt with in a manner designed to promote as good a continuing relationship between the parties and any children affected as is possible in the circumstances; and

        (iii)   without costs being unreasonably incurred in connection with the procedures to be followed in bringing it to an end;

    (d)   that any risk to one of the parties to a marriage, and to any children, of violence from the other party should, so far as reasonably practicable, be removed or diminished.

2 Disapplication of general principles in Part I to Part IV of the Act

The general principles do not, however, govern the operation of Part IV of the Act which deals with issues of domestic violence. The former Lord Chancellor explained the reason for this as being that Part IV deals with different subject matter to that of Parts II and III. In Part IV, emphasis of the importance of marriage is made by s. 36 which requires the court to consider the difference in the commitment made by married people as compared with unmarried people respectively, when contemplating whether to make an order (Hansard, 22nd February 1996, vol 569, no 48, col 1155). The other general principles would be difficult to apply where domestic violence has occurred. Take, for example, s. 1(b), which encourages spouses to concentrate on saving the marriage. Although the objective of saving the marriage is important, the immediate objective so far as it concerns Part IV of the Act is to provide protection for the parties from violence. The former Lord Chancellor believed that these objectives might be seen to be in conflict.

3 Supporting the institution of marriage

One of the factors motivating the former government to bring forward this Act was the very grave concern about marriage breakdown and the need for greater emphasis on and support for marriage (Hansard, 30th November 1995, vol 567, col 700). It is impossible to look at marriage and divorce in isolation from each other. The former government expressed a wish to play a role in supporting the services available to help not only those whose marriage is in difficulty but also those considering entering marriage. In pursuance of this, s. 22(1) provides for the Lord Chancellor, with the approval of the Treasury, to make grants in connection with:

(a) the provision of marriage support services;
(b) research into the causes of marital breakdown;
(c) research into ways of preventing marital breakdown.

The provision of such grants may be made subject to such conditions as the Lord Chancellor considers appropriate (s. 22(2)). The former Lord Chancellor has said that it is important for marriage counselling to be available at as early a stage as possible when a marriage encounters difficulties, and to ensure that it is not skewed towards the end rather than the beginning of a marriage (Hansard, 22nd February 1996, vol 569, no 48, col 1185). Section 22 came into force on 21st March 1997, so that grant aid can now be made available for qualifying organisations. Systems will be put in place to monitor the utility of the various services, so that public money is given only to those who are providing the service to satisfactory standards and whose results justify the giving of further money.

Provision of marriage counselling is dealt with specifically in s. 23, which states that during the period for reflection and consideration the parties to a marriage which has broken down will be encouraged to take all practicable steps to save it by counselling or otherwise. Entry into counselling is to be voluntary on the part of both parties. The Lord Chancellor, or a person appointed by him, has the power to attach conditions to the funding of marriage counselling. This will ensure that service standards can be set and maintained, for example by imposing conditions in relation to the standard of training or other qualifications that must be met before a person could provide marriage counselling for the parties. The services would be focused on marriage counselling and not on any other form of counselling that does not have the couple's possible reconciliation as a primary objective (Mr Gary Streeter, Hansard, 17th June 1996, vol 279, no 117, col 538). See Chapter 6 for further details about marriage support services.

4 Saving marriages wherever possible: reconciliation

One of the expressed objectives of the legislation is to save marriages wherever possible and to leave the door open to reconciliation even after divorce proceedings have commenced. Before making the statement of marital breakdown which initiates the divorce process, the party wishing to do so must first attend an information meeting (s. 8; see Chapter 5) at which they will be provided with details of all the services available to them, including marriage support services, mediation, and independent legal advice. There will then be a 'cooling-off' period of 3 months within which neither party will be able to make a statement initiating the divorce process. This aims to encourage the parties to attempt reconciliation before taking any further steps towards starting the divorce process. Furthermore, once the period for reflection and consideration has started running the parties will still be able to 'stop the clock' by jointly informing the court of their wish to attempt a reconciliation (s. 7(7) and (8)). Those who have the test of formulating the new procedures will consider whether the form of the initial statement of marital breakdown should ask whether attempts at reconciliation have been made since attendance at the information meeting, with the query put in such a way that the answer would be a simple yes or no; it would be made clear that it was not a condition of making a statement that reconciliation must first have been attempted, since in some circumstances attempts at reconciliation might seem rather hollow (Hansard, 29th February 1996, vol 569, no 52, col 1691). However, this procedure would at least direct the parties' minds to the issue of reconciliation.

In addition, duties will be placed on mediators and legal representatives to keep the possibility of reconciliation continually under review in their dealings with the parties (see paragraphs 9 and 10 of this chapter). Provision is made for the Lord Chancellor to make rules requiring legal representatives to inform the parties about the availability of marriage support services, to give them names and addresses of people qualified to help to effect a reconciliation and to certify whether or not they have complied with those requirements (s. 12(2)(a)–(c)). Likewise, before the Legal Aid Board can enter into a contract for the provision of mediation services it must ensure that the provision made by the contract as to the conduct of the mediation includes provision requiring the mediator to have arrangements designed to ensure that 'the possibility of reconciliation is kept under review throughout mediation' (s. 27(6)–(9): see Chapter 9, paragraph 3).

5 Minimising distress to the parties and children

The removal of fault from the divorce process is hoped to minimise the distress caused to the parties and their children, thus helping to attain the objective set out in s. 1(c)(i). At least the process will not exacerbate an already difficult situation. A major theme running through the legislation is that it is important to avoid children being brought into the arena of conflict surrounding their parents' divorce and, furthermore, that children should maintain as good a relationship as possible with both parents, notwithstanding the divorce. However, the substantive matters concerning the welfare of the children are subject to the provisions of the Children Act 1989.

6 Promoting a good relationship between the parties and their children

Section 1(c)(ii) specifically requires anyone exercising functions under Parts II and III of the Act to deal with questions arising in relation to the proposed separation or divorce 'in a manner designed to promote as good a continuing relationship between the parties and any children affected as is possible in the circumstances'. In particular, specific duties are placed on mediators and on legal advisers to ensure that the parties continue to bear in mind the welfare and interests of their children during the course of the marital proceedings. Before the Legal Aid Board may enter into a contract for the provision of mediation, it must ensure that the contract governing the way in which the mediation is to be conducted includes a provision that the mediator has arrangements designed to ensure that the parties are encouraged to consider 'the welfare, wishes and feelings of each child', and whether and to what extent each child should be given the opportunity to express his or her wishes in the mediation (Legal Aid Act 1988, s. 13B(8), as inserted by s. 27). Provision is made for the Lord Chancellor to make rules imposing similar duties on legal representatives, and requiring them to certify whether or not they have complied with those duties (s. 12(2)(a)–(c)).

As a last resort, a party could apply to the court under s. 10(2) for an order to prevent or postpone the granting of a divorce order if:

(a)   the dissolution of the marriage would result in substantial financial or other hardship to the other party or to a child of the family; or
(b)   it would be wrong, in all the circumstances (including the conduct of the parties and the interests of any child of the family) for the marriage to be dissolved.

7   Saving costs

The continuing rise in the cost of matrimonial legal aid was one of the factors behind the moves to reform the structure of divorce law. In its proposals 'Looking to the Future' the government said that it 'believes that the costs of dissolving a marriage, like those of forming one, should be borne by a couple themselves. This recognises the responsibility of individuals; it also provides appropriate disincentives against wasteful disputes which merely dissipate a couple's assets' (White Paper, Cm 2799, 1995, para. 6.1, p. 47). Hence the invocation, as a 'general principle' that costs should not be unreasonably incurred. The former government's view was that the proposed new system should provide a better service at lower cost than the present one. The use of mediation as a method of resolving issues between couples is seen as being cheaper than litigating through the courts. Legal aid will be available for mediation provided that parties meet the criteria governing eligibility for legal aid. During the House of Commons Standing Committee debates the former government said that the figures it had available showed that where parties elect to resolve issues relating to children-only mediation, the current cost is about £250 per couple. In all-issues mediation, the current average cost is between £700 and £800 per couple. These figures compare favourably with the average cost per *party* in proceedings litigated through the courts, which in 1996 was £1,500 (Mr Jonathan Evans, House of Commons, Standing Committee E, 14th May 1996, col 271).

8   Diminishing the risk of violence to the parties and their children

The purpose of this provision is to ensure that all persons exercising any function under Parts II and III of the Act are obliged to take into account, as one of the guiding principles of the legislation, the need to remove or diminish any risk to one of the parties, or to their children, of violence from the other party (Hansard, 17th June 1996, vol 279, no 117, col 600). The potential for domestic violence will be present for some people at a number of points in the divorce or separation process, in particular when parties attend information meetings or mediation sessions. The inclusion of this provision reflects the concerns of various interest groups which were anxious that there was a need to remove or diminish, so far as reasonably practicable, the risk of domestic violence during the divorce process.

9   Duties placed on legal representatives

Great emphasis is placed upon the need for parties to have access to information to all of the various services available to help them during the separation and divorce process, to be encouraged to consider reconciliation, and to take into account the welfare, wishes and feelings of their children in the decisions and arrangements they make for the future.

In order to help achieve these objectives, s. 12 enables the Lord Chancellor to make rules requiring a person who is the legal representative of a party to a marriage with respect to which a statement has been, or is proposed to be, made:

(a)   to inform that party, at such time or times as may be specified—

   (i)   about the availability to the parties of marriage support services;

   (ii)   about the availability to them of mediation; and

   (iii) where there are children of the family, that in relation to the arrangements to be made for any child the parties should consider the child's welfare, wishes and feelings;

(b)   to give that party, at such time or times as may be specified, names and addresses of people qualified to help—

   (i)   to effect a reconciliation; or

   (ii)   in connection with mediation; and

(c)   to certify, at such time or times as may be specified—

   (i)   whether he has complied with the provision made in the rules by virtue of paragraphs (a) and (b);

   (ii)   whether he has discussed with that party any of the matters mentioned in paragraph (a) or the possibility of reconciliation; and

   (iii) which, if any, of those matters they have discussed.

The word 'specified' in s. 12(1) and (2) means determined under or described in the rules (s. 12(3)).

10   Duties placed on mediators

For full details of the code of practice which mediators must adopt in order to be able to enter into a contract with the Legal Aid Board for the provision of mediation services see Chapter 9, paragraph 3.

Chapter Three
The Procedure for Separation and Divorce

1 The ground for divorce

The ground for divorce is the irretrievable breakdown of the marriage as demonstrated by the sole fact of a period for reflection and consideration (s. 5(1)).

1.1 Meaning of 'marital breakdown'

A marriage will *only* be taken to have broken down irretrievably if (s. 5(1)):

   (a)   a statement has been made by one (or both) of the parties that the maker of the statement (or each of them) believes that the marriage has broken down;

   (b)   the statement complies with the requirements of s. 6 (see Chapter 7);

   (c)   the period for reflection and consideration fixed by s. 7 has ended (Chapter 8); and

   (d)   the application for a separation or divorce order under s. 3 is accompanied by a declaration by the party making the application that —

     (i)   having reflected on the breakdown, and

     (ii)   having considered the requirements of Part II of the Act as to the parties' arrangements for the future,

the applicant believes that the marriage cannot be saved.

The statement and the application for a separation or divorce order do not have to be made by the same party (s. 5(2)). No application for a separation or divorce order can be made with reference to a particular statement if:

   (a)   the parties have jointly given notice (in accordance with rules of court) withdrawing the statement (s. 5(3)(a)); or

   (b)   a period of 1 year ('the specified period') (or such further period as shall, having regard to the presumption that the divorce process should ordinarily be concluded within 2½ years, appear to the court in all the circumstances to be just) has passed since the end of the period for reflection and consideration (s. 5(3)(b)).

However, any period during which an order preventing divorce is in force will not count towards the 'specified period' mentioned in s. 5(3)(b): s. 5(4).

Section 5(6) will apply if, before the end of the 'specified period', the parties jointly give notice to the court that they are attempting reconciliation but require extra time: s. 5(5).

Section 5(6) provides that the 'specified period':

(a)   stops running on the day on which the notice is received by the court; but

(b)   resumes running on the day on which either of the parties gives notice to the court that the attempted reconciliation has been unsuccessful.

If the 'specified period' is interrupted by a continuous period of more than 18 months, any application by either of the parties for a divorce or separation order must be by reference to a new statement received by the court at any time after the end of 18 months (s. 5(7)).

See Chapter 7 for further information about the statement, and in particular paragraph 7 of Chapter 7 for details of when a statement will 'lapse' and when the 'lapse time' might be extended by the court. See Chapter 13, paragraph 1, for further details as to the jurisdiction of the court to entertain marital proceedings, and Chapter 13, paragraph 2 for the definition of 'marital proceedings'.

2   Steps to separation or divorce

(a)   One or both of the parties attend an *information meeting*. They are encouraged to attend marriage counselling.

(b)   At least 3 months later, a *statement of marital breakdown* is lodged with the court, and served by the court on the other party (unless it has been made jointly).

(c)   The period for reflection and consideration commences 14 days after the statement has been lodged with the court. This will last for a minimum of 9 months. It may be extended by one further period of 6 months in certain circumstances.

(d)   The parties may formally notify the court that they wish to 'stop the clock' in relation to the period for reflection and consideration in order to attempt reconciliation. If the period is suspended for more than 18 months, then a new statement must be lodged before an application for a separation or divorce order can be made.

(e)   When the period for reflection and consideration expires, either or both parties may apply to the court for a separation or divorce order. The statement will lapse if the application for an order is not made within 1 year of the end of the period for reflection and consideration (unless the lapse period has been extended).

(f)   A divorce or separation order will be granted only if the court is satisfied as to the parties' arrangements for the future.

(g)   An order preventing divorce may be made in certain circumstances.

3   Bar on commencing divorce process within first year of marriage

The Act provides that it will not be possible to commence the process which would lead to divorce within the first year of marriage (s. 7(6)), nor will it be possible for a separation order which is made before the second anniversary of the marriage to be converted into a divorce order until after the second anniversary (s. 4(1) — as to which see Chapter 5, paragraph 5). This is intended to act as a brake on couples rushing into and out of marriage.

4 No bar on commencing process for a separation order within the first year of marriage

It will be possible to commence within the first year of marriage the process which would lead to a separation order, by attending an information meeting and then waiting for 3 months before lodging a statement of marital breakdown. The party applying for the separation order would then have to wait for a further period of 9 months for reflection and consideration before the order itself could be made. Therefore, one cannot obtain a separation order in less than 1 year because it takes 1 year to obtain it.

No separation order made before the second anniversary of the marriage can be *converted* into a divorce order until after the second anniversary of the marriage (s. 4(1)). For details of the procedure for converting a separation order into a divorce order, see Chapter 4, paragraph 7.

5 Attendance at an information meeting

A person wishing to initiate proceedings for separation or divorce must first attend a compulsory information meeting before the period of time starts to run which might lead to divorce (s. 8). The former Lord Chancellor said that 'This will not only mark the seriousness of the step being taken but also ensure that essential information is conveyed to people contemplating divorce in the most effective way possible. Information provided will include information about the various services available to help people, including marriage guidance, mediation and legal services . . . It will also deal with alternative options to divorce and the consequences of divorce for the parties and their children' (Hansard, 30th November 1995, vol 567, col 702).

See Chapter 5 for detailed consideration of the form and content of information meetings.

6 'Cooling-off' period

Having attended an information meeting, the party initiating the separation or divorce must wait for a 'cooling-off' period of 3 months before lodging with the court a statement of marital breakdown ('the statement') (s. 8(2)). It is hoped that when the party has considered the information given at the information meeting, and has perhaps undergone marriage counselling and taken such legal advice as is appropriate to the particular circumstances of the marriage, the party concerned will have second thoughts about taking the serious step of filing a statement of marital breakdown and may decide not to proceed. It gives 'pause for thought'.

7 Lodging the statement of marital breakdown

The receipt of the statement by the court starts the clock running for the 9 months (or 15 months, where one party has applied for an extra 6 months pursuant to s. 7(13)) period of reflection and consideration (s. 20(1)).

The statement is intended to be neutral in the sense that it 'does not make allegations and does not, at that early stage, state that the marriage has already irretrievably broken down and that the maker of the statement wants a divorce. The spouse or spouses making the statement would be required to declare that he, she or they believe the marriage to have broken down and declare that they understand that the purpose of the period which will follow before an application to the court can be made for either a separation or a divorce order, will be for reflection on whether the marriage can be saved and consideration of the arrangements for the future, should the divorce be proceeded with' (The former Lord Chancellor, Hansard, 30th November 1995, vol 567, col 702). See Chapter 7 for more detail about the statement itself.

8 Period for reflection and consideration

The divorce can be obtained following a period of 9 months for reflection and consideration. In reality, the total waiting period will be 12 months as the party wishing to make a statement must attend an information meeting no less than 3 months before lodging the statement with the court. During those first 3 months the party may not make a statement of marital breakdown. When the 3-month period has passed, the party may make a statement of marital breakdown if he or she so wishes, and 14 days after this has been lodged with the court the remaining period of 9 months for reflection and consideration (as specified in s. 7(3)) will start to run.

If there is a child of the family who is under 16 s. 7(11) and (13) provides that the period for reflection and consideration is automatically extended by 6 months, unless the conditions in s. 7(12) satisfy the court that the divorce should not be delayed (see below).

If one, or both, of the parties wish for further time to consider their future arrangements (s. 7(10)), then they may apply under s. 7(13) for the period for reflection and consideration to be extended by 6 months (making a total of 15 months for reflection and consideration). The party applying for the extension must make the application within the prescribed period (s. 7(10)(a)) and the requirements of s. 9 must be satisfied (s. 7(10)(b)).

However, the court will *not* allow an extension if (s. 7(12)):

(a)   at the time when the application for the divorce order is made, there is an occupation order or a non-molestation order in force in favour of the applicant, or of a child of the family, made against the other party; or

(b)   the court is satisfied that delaying the making of a divorce order would be significantly detrimental to the welfare of any child of the family.

During the period for reflection and consideration the parties will be expected to reflect on whether the marriage has broken down and to consider the consequences of separation or divorce before proceeding to take any irreversible decision. The 6-month extension to the period has a specific purpose. 'It is intended to provide additional time for parties to reconsider the step that they are taking to divorce where one party does not consent, or where they have children under 16. It is not simply an extra six months to enable parties to reach decisions on their future arrangements ...' (Mr Gary Streeter, Hansard, 17th June 1996, vol 279, no 117, col 604).

At any time during the period for reflection and consideration the parties may formally notify the court that they both wish to 'stop the clock' in order to attempt reconciliation. The clock starts ticking again as soon as one of the parties notifies the court that the attempt has failed. If the period is suspended for more than 18 months, then the parties must lodge a new statement with the court before an application can be made for a separation or divorce order (see Chapter 8, paragraph 3).

If at the end of the period for reflection and consideration one or both parties so wish they may apply for a separation or divorce order on the ground that the marriage has irretrievably broken down, provided that they have satisfied the requisite conditions (s. 3(1)).

The passage of 9 months (plus an extra 3 months between attending the information meeting and filing a statement of marital breakdown) is an absolute period of time, with no provision for it to be abridged in any circumstances (s. 7(1)). It is hoped that this will provide a degree of certainty as to the length of the separation or divorce process for those who are undergoing it.

See Chapter 8 for detailed discussion of the period for reflection and consideration.

9   Arrangements for the future

Those who were consulted about the length of the period for reflection and consideration felt in general that 'a sufficient period of time should elapse in order to demonstrate quite clearly that the marriage had irretrievably broken down. The period should be sufficiently long to give parties a realistic timescale within which to reflect on whether the marriage could be saved but also a realistic time within which the practical questions about children, home and finances could be resolved' (The former Lord Chancellor, Hansard, 30th November 1995, vol 567, col 702).

During the Second Reading of the Bill in the House of Lords the former Lord Chancellor said that 'A very important requirement in the Bill is the requirement that parties decide all arrangements relating to their children, finance and home before a separation or divorce order can be made.... The Bill provides for certain narrow exceptions to the requirement that all arrangements should be decided before the divorce, such as those who are sick, disabled or being prevented from making arrangements by vindictive and obstructive spouses, and also to protect the children of such parties' (Hansard, 30th November 1995, vol 567, col 703). See Chapter 10 for a detailed consideration of arrangements for the future, the requirements for which are set out in s. 9.

10   The hardship bar

The Act gives the court power to postpone or bar altogether a divorce where one party can show that the dissolution of the marriage would result in substantial financial or other hardship (s. 10). The court can take into account all the circumstances of the case, including the conduct of the parties when considering such a bar. The bar is available in all cases, rather than just in 5-year separation cases as was the position under the old legislation. See Chapter 12 for detailed consideration of the hardship bar.

Chapter Four
Separation and Divorce Orders

1 What orders may the court make?

Under the new system established by the Act, the court may make:

(a) a divorce order — which dissolves a marriage (s. 2(1)(a)); or
(b) a separation order — which provides for the separation of the parties to a marriage (s. 2(1)(b)).

2 Divorce orders

No application may be made for a divorce order within the first year of the marriage (s. 7(6)). When a divorce order is made then it has the effect of dissolving the marriage (s. 2(1)(a)).

3 Separation orders

After a good deal of consideration, the Law Commission came to the conclusion that separation orders should be retained within the framework of the new legislation. The conditions for the grant of a separation order are the same as those for an order of divorce, except that separation orders may be obtained at the end of the first year of marriage (see further Chapter 3, paragraph 4 for further details). The bar on making an application within the first year of marriage applies only to applications for divorce orders (s. 7(6)).

The former Lord Chancellor explained that one of the reasons for retaining separation orders was that 'for religious or conscientious objections some people would not wish to have a divorce. I wish to keep open every possibility of accommodating every form of religious belief that exists in relation to this matter' (Hansard, 11th January 1996, vol 568, no 24, col 299).

He explained that another of the reasons was because 'notwithstanding that the relationship had broken down irretrievably, and was seen as such at the time, living apart in the conditions that had been arranged might demonstrate to the parties that they were better off [as] they were before. Having a separation order would preclude their entering into any other marriage relationship — they might have other relationships but not marriage. Therefore, it was thought possible that people in that situation might well be able to be reconciled after a while' (Hansard, 11th January 1996, vol 568, no. 24, col 299).

A further reason for retaining separation orders was that some people might not want to divorce because 'they wanted to keep open the possibility of access to a pension under the arrangements for marriage' (The former Lord Chancellor, Hansard, 11th January 1996, vol 568, no 24, col 300).

4   When do divorce and separation orders come into force?

Divorce and separation orders come into force on being made (s. 2(2)).

A separation order remains in force —

(a)   while the marriage continues (s. 2(3(a)); or
(b)   until cancelled by the court on the joint application of the parties (s. 2(3)(b)).

5   In what circumstances will a separation or divorce order be made?

If one or both of the parties make an application to the court under s. 3 for a separation or divorce order, then the court can make the order only if the following conditions are satisfied:

(a)   the marriage has broken down irretrievably (s. 3(1)(a))(for the meaning of 'marital breakdown', see Chapter 3, paragraph 1.1);
(b)   the requirements of s. 8 in relation to information meetings have been met (s. 3(1)(b): as to which see Chapter 5);
(c)   the requirements of s. 9 in relation to the parties' arrangements for the future have been met (s. 3(1)(c): as to which see Chapter 10); and
(d)   the application has not been withdrawn (s. 3(1)(d)).

It is important to note that (a) above requires the parties to make a statement that the marriage has broken down irretrievably, both in relation to a divorce order *and* in relation to a separation order. While under the old divorce law 'irretrievable breakdown' was always a condition that had to be fulfilled before a divorce could be obtained, it was never a condition precedent to the grant of a decree of judicial separation. Under the old law the court was not concerned to decide whether the marriage had broken down irretrievably; it merely had a duty to inquire so far as it reasonably could into the facts alleged by the petitioner (and the respondent if he had filed an answer).

Clearly, no order for divorce can be made if an order preventing divorce is in force by virtue of s. 10 (the hardship bar — see Chapter 12): s. 3(2).

6   Applications for a separation order and a divorce order in relation to the same marriage

If the court is considering an application for a divorce order *and* an application for a separation order in relation to the *same* marriage, then it will proceed as if it was considering only the application for a divorce order *unless*:

(a) an order preventing divorce is in force with respect to the marriage (i.e., under the hardship bar in s. 10) (s. 3(3)(a)); or

(b) the court makes an order preventing divorce under s. 10 (s. 3(3)(b)); or

(c) s. 7(6) or (13) applies. This covers two situations:

(i) where the statement has been made before the first anniversary of the marriage to which it relates and is therefore ineffective for the purposes of any application for a divorce order (s. 3(3)(c) and s. 7(6)); and

(ii) where the court has extended the period for reflection and consideration by a period of 6 months, s. 3(3)(c) ensures that parties cannot circumvent that extension by obtaining a separation order after 9 months and immediately applying to convert it into a divorce order (see s. 7(13));

(d) the period for reflection and consideration in respect of the divorce order has been extended by 6 months (s. 3(3)(d)). However, in this event the court could still proceed with the separation order and could permit financial provision and property adjustment orders to take effect.

7 Conversion of separation order into divorce order

The rules about the conversion of separation orders into divorce orders are to be found in s. 4 and are as follows:

A separation order which has been made before the second anniversary of the marriage cannot be converted into a divorce order until after that anniversary (s. 4(1)).

A separation order cannot be converted into a divorce order at any time while:

(a) an order preventing divorce is in force under s. 10 (the hardship bar) (s. 4(2)(a)); or

(b) s. 4(4) applies.

Section 4(4) applies (subject to s. 4(5)) if:

- there is a child of the family who is under 16 when the application under s. 4 is made or
- the application under s. 4 is made by one party and the other party applies to the court (before the end of such period as may be prescribed by rules of court) for time for further reflection.

However, s. 4(4) does *not* apply if:

- at the time when the application under s. 4 was made there is an occupation order or a non-molestation order in force in favour of the applicant, or of a child of the family, made against the other party (s. 4(5)(a))
- the court is satisfied that delaying the making of a divorce order would be significantly detrimental to the welfare of any child of the family (s. 4(5)(b)).

Section 4(4) *ceases* to apply:
- at the end of the period of 6 months beginning with the end of the period for reflection and consideration by reference to which the separation order was made (s. 4(5)(c)(i)) or

- if earlier, on there ceasing to be any children of the family to whom s. 4(4)(a) applied (s. 4(5)(c)(ii)).

Note that the above provisions bring the time periods of s. 4 in line with those in s. 7. It ensures that parties cannot circumvent the 6-month extension by obtaining a separation order after 9 months and immediately applying to convert it into a divorce order.

Otherwise, if a separation order is in force and an application for a divorce order:

(a)   is made under s. 4 by either or both of the parties to the marriage (s. 4(3)(a)), and
(b)   is not withdrawn (s. 4(3)(b)),

the court *must* grant the application for the divorce order, provided that the requirements in relation to s. 11 (the welfare of the children) have been met (s. 4(3)).

8   Withdrawal of an application for a separation or divorce order

The withdrawal of an application for a separation or a divorce order (for the purposes of Part II of the Act) refers to the position where the application for a separation or divorce order was made jointly by both parties, but a notice of withdrawal of the application is given:

(a)   jointly by both parties (s. 24(2)(a)); or
(b)   separately by each of them (s. 24(2)(b)).

When either (a) or (b) above occurs then the divorce application is withdrawn altogether, since it is clear that neither of the parties wishes to proceed with it.

However, where the application for a separation or divorce order is made jointly by both parties, but only *one* party gives notice of withdrawal, then the application for the separation or divorce order is to be treated as if it had been made by the other party *alone* and it will proceed accordingly (s. 24(3)).

Chapter Five
Information Meetings

1 Compulsory attendance before making a statement of marital breakdown

A party who wishes to make a statement of marital breakdown must (except in prescribed circumstances) have attended an information meeting not less than 3 months before making the statement (s. 8(1)). The object of this provision is to ensure that before taking the serious step of making a statement the parties have received details of the various marriage support services, mediation services and legal services which are available to help them, as well as details of the divorce process itself.

The subsequent period of 3 months is intended to enable them to absorb the information and to encourage them to take any steps they wish towards seeking marriage guidance, or other help, to try to save the marriage before finally deciding to make a statement. In Standing Committee Mr Paul Boateng explained the rationale of this effectively: '... it is likely that, once a statement has been filed and the process — which has at its heart the purposes of securing and settling arrangements for finance and for children — begins, it will be all too difficult to carve out a space for reconciliation; it is likely that attitudes will have hardened, and that process will drive inexorably to the dissolution of the marriage' (Hansard, Standing Committee E, 7th May 1996, col 123).

2 Person to conduct the information meeting

The information meeting will be conducted by a person who:

    (a) is qualified and appointed in accordance with prescribed provisions (s. 8(7)(a)), and

    (b) will have no financial or other interest in any marital proceedings between the parties (s. 8(7)(b)).

2.1 Qualifications

Mr Jonathan Evans said: 'Information meetings must be conducted by a person who has satisfied certain qualification and training criteria, to be set in regulations. ...' (Hansard, Standing Committee E, 7th May 1996, col 155). The exact qualifications will therefore not be known until the regulations have been drafted and come into force. He also said that '. . . as currently drawn, the Bill will allow a clerk from the local citizens advice bureau to speak to people' (Hansard, Standing Committee E, 7th May 1996, col 160). In relation to the concern which had been expressed that the parties would merely be shown a video he said 'That is not the context of the information meeting that I want. It is important that the person has counselling skills. That is the best way to put it. I do not wish to be more specific' (Hansard, Standing Committee E, 7th May 1996, col 160).

2.2   Requirement of no financial or other interest in the marital proceedings

During the House of Commons Standing Committee debates great emphasis was placed on the need for the person conducting the information meeting to be neutral, with no financial or other interest in the proceedings between the parties (Mr Jonathan Evans, Hansard, Standing Committee E, 7th May 1996, col 155). The object of this is to avoid the person conducting the information meeting from promoting a bias towards any particular service or solution for the parties. The role of the information provider is simply to make full information available in relation to all of the relevant services and the mechanics of the separation and divorce process itself.

3   Pilot schemes

The importance attached to some of the novel features of the new divorce law was highlighted in a press release issued by the Lord Chancellor's Department on 11th March 1997: 'It is vitally important that the information sessions should be in place and working before substantive changes in the divorce law are brought into force'. The Lord Chancellor's Department therefore organised pilot schemes to test out various methods of providing divorce information, both in one-to-one and group meetings attended by at least 10 people. The information will be available in different forms, including information packs, leaflets, videos, inter-active CD-Roms and other training materials. The first phase of the pilot schemes began in June 1997. The schemes were initially conducted in five different areas of the country and lasted for 9 months. They are currently being evaluated and research into them is being undertaken by the Newcastle Centre for Family Studies. Additional pilot schemes, testing different models for information meetings, were launched during 1998 and will be extended during the course of 1999.

In the House of Commons Standing Committee debates much time was spent discussing whether or not the proposed models for information meetings would cater properly for people from various cultural, religious and ethnic backgrounds, since it is important that people 'be able to feel at home with the information they receive and the people from whom they receive it' (Mr Peter Bottomley, Hansard, Standing Committee E, 7th May 1996, col 162). In response, Mr Jonathan Evans said that cultural, religious and ethnic factors would be taken into account in the provision of information and that 'the Lord Chancellor's Department intends that the information will be available in the main ethnic languages' (Hansard, Standing Committee E, 9th May 1996, col 165).

The former Lord Chancellor appointed an advisory board to advise on the design, establishment and implementation of pilot schemes relating to the Act, to monitor the schemes' progress, to receive and consider a report by a pilot evaluation team that will advise the Lord Chancellor on recommendations. The advisory board will also monitor the operation of the Act and report to the Lord Chancellor on issues arising from the Act's implementation. For further details about the advisory board, see Chapter 6, paragraph 6.

4 Who will attend the information meeting?

Different information meetings must be arranged with respect to different marriages (s. 8(3)).

For example, it would not be possible for Mr A and Mrs B (who wish to marry one another), to attend the same information meeting with a view to commencing separation or divorce proceedings against their existing spouses, Mrs A and Mr B. Instead, Mr A and Mrs B must attend separate information meetings in order to be in a position to start divorce proceedings against Mrs A and Mr B respectively.

4.1 Statement made by both parties

Where *both* parties intend to make a statement of marital breakdown they can choose whether to attend separate meetings or the same meeting (s. 8(4)).

This enables people to be able to attend information meetings on a one-to-one basis if they so wish. In particular, where one of the parties has been subjected to domestic violence during the course of the marriage, it should be possible for him or her to be able to attend the meeting without the other party being present (Mr Paddy Tipping, Hansard, Standing Committee E, 30th April 1996, col 84).

4.2 Statement made by only one of the parties

Where only *one* party has made a statement then the other party must (except in prescribed circumstances) attend an information meeting before —

(a) making any application to the court —
    (i)   in relation to a child of the family (s. 8(5)(a)(i)); or
    (ii)   of a prescribed description relating to property or financial matters (s. 8(5)(a)(ii)); or
(b) contesting any such application (s. 8(5)(b)).

The purpose of this provision is to ensure that before launching into litigious proceedings in response to receiving a statement of marital breakdown, the party receiving the statement or responding to an application made by the other party in connection with the statement, must first attend an information meeting. At the meeting the party will be told about all the available marriage support services, mediation services and legal services which might be able to provide assistance. It is hoped that this will motivate the party concerned to explore alternative avenues for resolving any disputes before resorting to litigation.

5 Where will information meetings be held?

The pilot schemes are testing different formats for the location in which information meetings are to be held. It will be part of the remit of the advisory board described in paragraph 3 above to consider the physical venue and surroundings in which information meetings are to take place. The time and place at which information meetings are to be held will be set out in regulations in due course (The former Lord Chancellor, Hansard, 23rd January 1996, vol 568, no 30, col 994). The former Lord Chancellor said 'I should like to provide a system in which the information sessions are conducted in circumstances as congenial as possible' (Hansard, 23rd January 1996, vol 568, no 30, col 993).

6   What information will be given to the parties?

Regulations will provide, in due course, for the type and format of the information which must be given to the parties during the meeting (s. 8(6), (8), (9), (10), (12)). The purpose of such regulations is to ensure that the Lord Chancellor can set and maintain the standards and quality of information-giving (Mr Gary Streeter, Hansard, 17th June 1996, vol 279, no 117, col 624). Although s. 8(9) contains a list of such matters, it must be made clear that 'The list in primary legislation of the information that must be provided is not exhaustive and the Lord Chancellor has the power to add other provisions in regulations' (Mr Gary Streeter, Hansard, 17th June 1996, vol 279, no 117, col 624). The pilot schemes have used different forms of information, including information packs, leaflets, inter-active CD-Roms and other training materials.

6.1   Marriage counselling

The person conducting the information meeting will be required to offer the couple the opportunity to meet with a marriage counsellor, and to encourage them to take it up (s. 8(9)(a)). Names and addresses of marriage support organisations which are in receipt of government grants will be given to the parties. However, marriage counselling will not be compulsory. During the House of Commons Standing Committee debates Mr Jonathan Evans said 'In my view, counselling will not work if it is compulsory ... Compulsory counselling would also divert [to marriages in relation to which attempts at reconciliation are hopeless] what might well be valuable marriage counselling resources' (Hansard, Standing Committee E, 7th May 1996, col 153). He also said '... the initial meeting with the marriage counsellor, as a result of the information meeting would be state funded. For some parties that meeting would therefore be free, but others may have to make a contribution. It is envisaged that the eligibility criteria will be the same as for mediation, although marriage counselling cannot be paid for out of the legal aid fund, as the matters being considered by the couple and the counsellor are not justiciable issues' (Hansard, Standing Committee E, 7th May 1996, col 155). Thus, a person who would not be required to make any contribution towards mediation provided for him or her under Part IIIA of the Legal Aid Act 1988 will not be required to make any contribution towards the cost of a meeting with a marriage counsellor arranged for him or her as a result of the information meeting (s. 8(12)). Section 23(3) of the Act states that marriage counselling may only be provided under that section during the period for reflection and consideration for persons who would not be required to make any contribution towards the cost of mediation provided for them under Part IIIA of the Legal Aid Act 1988. People who are provided with marriage counselling under s. 23 are not to be required to make any contribution towards the cost of the counselling (s. 23(4)).

A meeting with a marriage counsellor arranged under s. 8(9)(a) must:

(a) be held in accordance with prescribed provisions (s. 8(11)(a)); and

(b) be with a person qualified and appointed in accordance with prescribed provisions (s. 8(11)(b)).

See Chapter 6 for further information about marriage support services.

6.2 Welfare of the children

Section 8(9)(b) requires the person conducting the meeting to emphasise to the parties the importance to be attached to the welfare, wishes and feelings of the children. One of the general themes of the new legislation is that 'it is absolutely essential that we do what we can to preserve the relationship between children and both parents' (The former Lord Chancellor, Hansard, 29th February 1996, vol 569, no 52, col 1699). Where the parties express concern about their children then appropriate information will be provided, for example, the names and address of people qualified to help. Where the safety of a child is of concern then parties can be told how to report those concerns to the NSPCC or to the social services.

6.3 Helping the children to cope with the breakdown of the marriage

The person conducting the meeting must give the parties information as to how they may acquire a better understanding of the ways in which children can be helped to cope with the breakdown of a marriage (s. 8(9)(c)). This may include drawing the attention of the parties to leaflets and books which might assist them, and giving the names and addresses of counsellors, support groups or organisations who may be able to help. The former Lord Chancellor said 'children should be informed about what is happening to them, what will happen to them in the future and what they can do about it. The pilot of the information meetings may well help us to see how that can best be done ... the requirements of children in respect of information are quite delicate and different. It would be difficult to envisage satisfactory arrangements in all cases. This is therefore an area that the pilot studies can test for us' (Hansard, 29th February 1996, vol 569, no 52, col 1700).

6.4 Financial matters

Section 8(9)(d) requires the person conducting the meeting to explain to the parties the nature of the financial questions that may arise on divorce or separation, and services which are available to help them. This could include information about legal advice and assistance, the Child Support Agency, names and address of accountants, debt counsellors, citizens advice bureaux, estate agents, property valuers and so forth.

For further details about the financial arrangements to be made between the parties before a divorce can be granted, see Chapter 10. For a discussion of the various types of court order available for financial provision between the parties, see Chapter 11.

6.5 Domestic violence

The person conducting the meeting must give the parties information about protection against violence and how to obtain advice and assistance in connection with such problems (s. 8(9)(e)). This could include information about injunctive procedures under Part IV of the Act, how to get legal advice and assistance to institute the relevant proceedings, the addresses of women's refuges, the names and addresses of counsellors who specialise in such problems and books and leaflets setting out useful information to help anyone who may be the victim of violence.

A serious problem which must be addressed is the protection at information meetings of people who are victims of domestic violence. Mr Paddy Tipping said: 'The more radical women's groups have many reservations about how abused women will approach information sessions. They may be worried about their safety or reluctant to attend such sessions by themselves because the former abusing partner will be there. Clearly ... they could attend those meetings individually, but they need to be reassured that they can go safely, will be protected while they are there and will find a safe way back. They need to be reassured that during the session they can disclose to the counsellor that they are the victims of domestic violence ... At an information session they need to be told that there are refuges and that follow-on housing is available' (Hansard, Standing Committee E, 30th April 1996, col 84).

Section 8(2) and (4) provides for a party to be able to attend the meeting on his or her own, without the other spouse being present (see paragraph 4 above).

6.6   Mediation services

The person conducting the meeting will explain to the couple the availability of mediation as a method of resolving issues between them in relation to their separation, children and financial arrangements (s. 8(9)(f)). Names and addresses of mediators with whom the Legal Aid Board enters into contracts for mediation services will be made available to the parties. These mediators will not be 'approved' by the Lord Chancellor as such, but the parties will have the security of knowing that in order for the Legal Aid Board to enter into contracts with mediators for the provision of mediation services, the mediators must first abide by a statutory code of practice set out in regulations (which have yet to be promulgated, but which are likely to reflect much of the current code of practice under which the United Kingdom College of Mediators operates). They will be required to have in place arrangements to ensure that the issue of reconciliation is kept under continual review throughout the mediation, that the parties are encouraged to consider the wishes, feelings and welfare of any children of the family, and that each party is informed about the availability of independent legal advice (s. 27(7)(d)).

See Chapter 9 for further details about mediation.

6.7   Availability of legal advice and representation

The person conducting the information meeting is required by s. 8(9)(g) to give the parties full information about the availability of independent legal advice and representation. This could include the names and addresses of solicitors dealing with family work, solicitors on the child care panel, and information about legal aid (see paragraph 6.8 below).

6.8   Availability of legal aid

The person conducting the information meeting is also required by s. 8(9)(h) to explain to the parties the principles of legal aid and where they can go to get advice about obtaining legal aid. It will be pointed out that legal aid may be available in appropriate cases. The government has made it clear that green form legal advice will continue to be available to people in certain circumstances, and that legal aid under the Legal Aid Act 1988 will continue to be available to parties who are contemplating divorce, provided that they satisfy the eligibility criteria. However, since the whole structure of legal aid and the way that advice is delivered is currently under review by the Lord Chancellor's Department, the government has not been able to confirm or deny whether legal representation will also be made available (Mr Jonathan Evans, Hansard, Standing Committee E, 9th May 1996, col 177).

6.9 The separation and divorce process

The person conducting the information session will give the parties information about the separation and divorce process itself (s. 8(9)(i)). The procedures, time limits, documentation required and so forth will be clearly explained to them. In due course, leaflets and other written material will probably be made available for the parties to take home and read at their leisure (s. 8(8)(b)). Other methods of distributing the information may well include the use of pre-recorded videos explaining the process and the various services available (The former Lord Chancellor, Hansard, 22nd February, vol 569, no 48, col 1184).

7 What happens if a person cannot attend an information meeting?

There may be circumstances in which a party is unable to attend an information meeting at the prescribed location, for example, where a person is housebound, disabled, in custody, or when going to a particular place might put them at risk of violence. In such cases regulations will provide for other ways in which the requisite information may be conveyed to them (s. 8(8)(c)) (The former Lord Chancellor, Hansard, 23rd January 1996, vol 568, no 30, col 983).

Chapter Six
Marriage Support Services

1 General principles

During the parliamentary debates in relation to this Act great emphasis was placed upon the need for improved access for married couples to marriage support services. Formerly, the Home Office did provide funds for marriage guidance through Relate. Responsibility was transferred to the Lord Chancellor's Department at about the time the White Paper was issued but no statutory power to that effect was granted. Hence, this is the first statute to give authority for grants for services in support of marriage. The Lord Chancellor has taken over the funding of these services in order to provide the best possible integration of the policy on supporting marriage with that on divorce law (Mr Roger Freeman, The Chancellor of the Duchy of Lancaster, Hansard, 25th March 1996, vol 274, no 76, col 745). Section 22(1) of the Act, which came into force on 21st March 1997, provides for the Lord Chancellor, with the approval of the Treasury, to make grants in connection with:

(a) the provision of marriage support services;
(b) research into the causes of marital breakdown;
(c) research into ways of preventing marital breakdown.

A grant may be made subject to such conditions as the Lord Chancellor considers appropriate (s. 22(2)). See paragraph 5 of this chapter.

2 Provision of marriage support services generally

'The Government are endeavouring to provide the basis for a continuum of information and services for couples at all stages in their relationship. That provision will cover not only couples who may, sadly, be considering divorce, but couples who are deciding to marry, as well as assistance early during a problem in a marriage — before the difficulty becomes a crisis' (Mr Gary Streeter, Hansard, 17th June 1996, vol 279, no 117, col 537).

In pursuance of this aim, s. 22(3) provides that in exercising his power to make grants in connection with the provision of marriage support services, the Lord Chancellor is to have regard in particular to the desirability of services of that kind being available when they are first needed. 'Such services could include marriage preparation initiatives, work at major turning points in a couple's relationship, such as the birth of a first child, and information about services provided at places where people might otherwise go for information, so that take-up of marriage support services can be encouraged' (Mr Gary Streeter, Hansard, 17th June 1996, vol 279, no 117, col 537–8).

3 Provision of marriage support services during the period for reflection and consideration

3.1 When will marriage counselling be provided?

The statutory framework governing the provision of marriage counselling during the period for reflection and consideration is to be found in s. 23 of the Act. Marriage counselling may only be provided under this section when a period for reflection and consideration:

(a) is running in relation to the marriage (s. 23(2)(a)); or
(b) is interrupted under s. 7(8) (i.e., when the parties stop the clock running to attempt reconciliation), but that interruption must not be for a continuous period of more than 18 months (s. 23(2)(b)).

3.2 Who will be entitled to marriage counselling under the Act?

Marriage counselling may only be provided under s. 23 for people who would not be required to make any contribution towards the cost of mediation provided for them under Part IIIA of the Legal Aid Act 1988 (s. 23(3)). Such persons are not to be required to make any contribution towards the cost of the counselling (s. 23(4)). Thus, the provision of marriage counselling under s. 23 will be state funded for those who satisfy the eligibility criteria 'although marriage counselling cannot be paid for out of the legal aid fund, as the matters being considered by the couple and the counsellors are not justiciable issues' (Mr Jonathan Evans, Hansard, Standing Committee E, 7th May 1996, col 155). The eligibility criteria themselves will be the same as for mediation (as to which see Chapter 9). Of course, those who are not eligible for legal aid for mediation will have to pay for marriage counselling themselves.

3.3 How will marriage counselling be funded?

The Lord Chancellor will provide grants for those marriage support services which fulfil the relevant criteria for the provision of marriage counselling. The relevant grants will be for services in support of marriage and not for services in support of other types of relationships (Hansard, 4th March 1996, vol 570, no 54, col 61). The former Lord Chancellor felt that it was preferable to use grant-aid for organisations who qualify under the grant-aiding provisions rather than to impose a system of regulation imposed by the government (The former Lord Chancellor, Hansard, 22nd February 1996, vol 569, no 48, col 1185). His wish was to retain as much flexibility as possible.

It will be important for those seeking funding to demonstrate the effectiveness of their work. The level of grant support will depend on this from year to year and therefore it will be important for there to be provision for monitoring the utility of the service.

The former government took the view that marriage counselling should not be skewed towards the end rather than the beginning of a marriage, and that it should be available as early as possible when a marriage gets into difficulties (The former Lord Chancellor, Hansard, 22nd February 1996, vol 569, no 48, col 1185). The former Lord Chancellor said that he wished to consult the various bodies working in this field before framing the regulations governing the provision of grant-aid.

3.4 At what stage in the process will marriage counselling be offered?

The Act imposes a 3-month 'cooling off' period between the attendance of a party at an information meeting and the making of a statement of marital breakdown (s. 8(2)). At the information meeting, the opportunity of a meeting with a marriage counsellor will be offered and the party or parties attending the information meeting will be encouraged to take up that offer (Mr Jonathan Evans, Hansard, Standing Committee E, 7th May 1996, col 155). However, as has been previously stated, there will be no compulsion to attend a meeting with a marriage counsellor, since the former government took the view that the process would not work if it were made compulsory. The former government did not want an appointment with a marriage counsellor to be viewed as a hurdle that had to be cleared at an early stage in order to achieve a divorce order. It wished, rather, that people might 'keep alive, throughout the process, the possibility of achieving a reconciliation' (Mr Jonathan Evans, Hansard, Standing Committee E, 7th May 1996, col 151).

3.5 Who will inform the parties about the availability of marriage counselling?

3.5.1 Person conducting information meeting The person conducting the information meeting with the parties will be required to offer the couple the opportunity to meet with a marriage counsellor, and to encourage them to take it up (s. 8(9)(a)). Names and addresses of marriage support services which are in receipt of government grants will be given to the parties.

3.5.2 Legal representatives It is envisaged that the Lord Chancellor may use his powers under s. 12 to make rules requiring the legal representative of a party to a marriage in whose respect a statement is, or is proposed to be made to inform parties about the availability of marriage support services, to give the names and addresses of people qualified to help to effect a reconciliation, and to certify whether or not he has complied with the requirements (see s. 12(2) and Mr Jonathan Evans, Hansard, Standing Committee E, 14th May 1996, cols 219 and 220). The former Lord Chancellor has set up an advisory board to monitor the operation of the Act (Hansard, Standing Committee E, 14th May 1996, col 220): see paragraph 6 of this chapter.

3.5.3 Mediators Part III of the Act, which provides for legal aid to be available for mediation, came into force on 21st March 1997. The Legal Aid Board may enter into contracts with organisations providing mediation services only if those organisations satisfy the criteria laid down in s. 13B(7) of the Legal Aid Act 1988, as inserted by s. 27. The contract as to the conduct of the mediation must include provision requiring the mediator to have in place arrangements designed to ensure, inter alia, that the possibility of reconciliation is kept under review throughout the course of the mediation. It will be part of the remit of the mediator to inform the parties of the availability of marriage counselling in those cases where the mediator is engaged in mediation with a couple who show signs of wishing to explore the possibility of reconciliation.

3.6   Who will decide whether the parties are suitable for marriage counselling?

Marriage counselling will only be provided under s. 23 if it appears *to the marriage counsellor* to be suitable in all the circumstances (Legal Aid Act 1988, s. 13B(3), as inserted by s. 27).

4   Research into marital breakdown — causes and prevention

The Act makes provision for the Lord Chancellor to make grants in connection with research into the causes of, and ways of preventing, marital breakdown. The advisory board set up by the former Lord Chancellor, as described in paragraph 6 below, will advise on the need for, and results of, research into supporting marriage and preventing marriage breakdown.

An interdepartmental working party on family and marriage has been formed and it will consult with various organisations, 'seeking ideas as to how exactly we can intervene earlier to support family and marriage ... to elicit ideas as to exactly what we can and should do to support marriage and the family at an early and positive stage ... the working party will have to consider what more can be done to prepare young couples for marriage and to make marriage stronger — or at least to make them understand what they are taking on' (Mr Gary Streeter, Hansard, 17th June 1996, vol 279, no 117, col 546).

'The results of the consultation will inform the funding of pilot projects that have particular potential for reducing the incidence and costs of marriage breakdown.' (Mr Gary Streeter, Hansard, 17th June 1996, vol 279, no 117, col 538).

5   Conditions attached to grant-aid

It is likely that the conditions to be attached to the provision of grant-aid for marriage support services and research into marital breakdown will relate to the standards which the various services must have in place before being entitled to grant-aid, and to the systems which they have set up to enable them to monitor the success and effectiveness of their particular service. Monitoring the utility of the service provided will be the means by which each service supports its annual claim for grant-aid.

6   The Lord Chancellor's advisory board

The former Lord Chancellor has set up an advisory board to monitor the operation of the Family Law Act. It was formed to advise on the design, establishment and implementation of pilot schemes relating to the Act. It will receive and consider a report by a pilot evaluation team that will advise the Lord Chancellor on recommendations, and it will report to the Lord Chancellor on issues arising from the

Act's implementation (see Mr Jonathan Evans, Hansard, Standing Committee E, 14th May 1996, col 220).

The board is interdisciplinary and contains representatives of relevant professions and relevant academic disciplines. It has an independent chair-person. The board is required to report to the Lord Chancellor at regular intervals annually and he will publish an annual report. The board was appointed for an initial period of five years, although it was envisaged that its terms of reference might need to be reviewed earlier than that once the pilot schemes relating to the Act are completed.

Chapter Seven
Statement of Marital Breakdown

1 Form of the statement

A statement made under s. 5(1)(a) is to be known as a statement of marital breakdown, but it is generally referred to in Part II of the Act as 'a statement' (s. 6(1)).

It is intended that a statement of marital breakdown should be as neutral as possible and 'that it should not contain allegations, and so on, against the other party to the marriage, because that is not likely to be conducive to healing the relationship' (The former Lord Chancellor, Hansard, 11th January 1996, vol 568, no 24, col 310). The former Lord Chancellor explained his resistance to a system of divorce that commences with allegations of fault by the other party by saying that if:

> the allegation about the irretrievable breakdown of a marriage or the irreconcilable nature of the conduct of the parties is made at the beginning of the process ... the opportunity for steps to be taken at that stage to prevent irretrievable breakdown of the marriage has gone. You have already come to the conclusion, as an essential step for the starting of the procedure, that the marriage has already broken down. One of the most important aspects of this Bill ... is the opportunity, even at the late stage when someone is contemplating divorce, of a period ... of consideration and reflection. You cannot have such a genuine period if the parties are already committed to a situation in which it is said, 'This marriage has already irretrievably broken down'. I cannot see ... how a fault-based system can accommodate that in any realistic sense. If you are already committed to the view that your marriage has broken down there is no point in waiting a year to see whether it has or of having any procedure in place to help you find out (Hansard, 11th January 1996, vol 568, no 24, col 348).

Section 12 gives the Lord Chancellor power to make rules as to the form in which a statement of marital breakdown is to be made and as to what information must accompany it (s. 12(1)(a)).

1.1 Inquiry as to any reconciliation attempt

Rules may require the person making the statement of marital breakdown to state whether or not, since attending the information meeting as required by s. 8, he or she has made any attempt at reconciliation (s. 12(1)(b)). The former Lord Chancellor said (Hansard, 11th March 1996, vol 570, no 59, col 693):

> I believe that a requirement of this kind would be a valuable addition to the Bill as it will draw the attention of parties making a statement to the issue of reconciliation and perhaps make them question their own efforts in this regard. However, I believe very strongly that the provision should be one which requires the parties simply to state whether or not they have attempted reconciliation. It should not be assumed that attempts at reconciliation will have been appropriate in every case and there should be no punitive result in cases where parties have not attempted reconciliation. Its appropriateness depends on the circumstances of the case . . . The information meeting is intended to give parties information on the divorce process itself and on the facilities available to them if they wish to seek help in saving their marriage, and it is therefore of relevance to ask parties whether or not they have attempted reconciliation since receiving this information and before taking the serious step of making a statement of marital breakdown. . . . There is also merit in the information about reconciliation referring to the period after the information meeting because that may give a good impression of the extent to which the information meeting is successful in transmitting information to the parties.

1.2   No requirement to specify relief sought

There is no requirement when the statement of marital breakdown is made for the maker to specify at that stage whether they seek a separation order or a divorce order. The former Lord Chancellor gave the reason for this as being that 'The difficulty is knowing what effect it would have in the sense of being able to come back . . . to the other possible order. The idea is to keep the options open so far as possible' (Hansard, 29th February, vol 569, no 52, col 1693).

1.3   Where a statement is made by only one party

Where a statement of marital breakdown is made by only one party it must also state that that party (s. 6(2)):

(a)   is aware of the purpose of the period for reflection and consideration; and
(b)   wishes to make arrangements for the future.

1.4   Where a statement is made by both parties

Where a statement of marital breakdown is made by both parties it must also state that each of them (s. 6(3)):

(a)   is aware of the purpose of the period for reflection and consideration; and
(b)   wishes to make arrangements for the future.

2   Circumstances in which a statement will not be effective

A statement of marital breakdown will not be effective for the purposes of Part II of the Act if it was made at a time when:

(a)   a statement has previously been made with respect to the marriage and it is, or will become, possible:
   (i)   for an application for a divorce order; or
   (ii)   for an application for a separation order,
to be made by reference to the previous statement (s. 6(6),(7));
   (b)   such an application has been made in relation to the marriage and has not been withdrawn (s. 6(7)(b));
   (c)   a separation order is in force (s. 6(7)(c)).

3   Lodging the statement with the court

The receipt by the court of a statement of marital breakdown is to be treated as the commencement of the proceedings (s. 20(1)). For details as to the jurisdiction of the court to entertain marital proceedings, and for the definition of 'marital proceedings' see Chapter 13, paragraphs 1 and 2.

The period for reflection and consideration will start to run on the 14th day after the day on which the statement is received by the court (s. 7(3)). The period of 14 days is intended to allow time for the court to serve the statement on the other party.

A statement must be given to the court in accordance with the requirements of rules made under s. 12 (s. 6(4)), and it must also satisfy any other requirements imposed by rules made under s. 12 (s. 6(5)). For example, rules may be made requiring a party who has made a statement to provide the court with information about the arrangements that need to be made in consequence of the breakdown, and as to the time, manner and place at which such information is to be given (s. 12(1)(f),(g)). Furthermore, where a statement has been made rules may be promulgated requiring either or both of the parties:

   (a)   to prepare and produce such other documents, and
   (b)   to attend in person at such places and for such purposes,
as may be specified (s. 12(1)(h)).

4   Notifying the other party of the making of the statement

Where the statement of marital breakdown has been made by one party, rules made under s. 12(1) require the court to serve a copy of the statement on the other party (s. 7(4)(a),(b)).

4.1   Extending the period for reflection and consideration where service on the other party is delayed

If failure to comply with the rules made under s. 12 causes inordinate delay in service, the court may, on the application of the *other* party, extend the period for reflection and consideration (s. 7(4)). Any such extension of the period for reflection and consideration may be for any period not exceeding the time between:

   (a)   the beginning of the period for reflection and consideration (s. 7(5)(a)); and
   (b)   the time when service is effected (s. 7(5)(b)).

The responsibility for proving why there is good cause for extending the period is placed on the party who alleges delay in service of the statement. 'This should protect against delaying tactics and deliberate obstruction on the part of the other party' (The former Lord Chancellor, Hansard, 4th March 1996, vol 570, no 54, col 11).

4.2   Dispensing with service and alternative forms of service

Section 12(1)(e) allows the Lord Chancellor to make rules as to the circumstances in which service of the statement of marital breakdown on the other party may be dispensed with, or as to the circumstances in which service may be effected otherwise than by delivery to the party.

5   Statement made before first anniversary of the marriage

A statement of marital breakdown which is made before the first anniversary of the marriage to which it relates will not be effective for the purposes of any application for a divorce order (s. 7(6)). However, it is possible for such a statement to be used for the purposes of an application for a separation order. Although a separation order may be made before the second anniversary of the marriage, it may not be *converted* into a divorce order before the second anniversary (s. 4(1)).

6   Withdrawal of a statement

Where the parties have *jointly* given notice (in accordance with rules of court) withdrawing the statement of marital breakdown then no application may be made for a separation or divorce order by reference to that statement (s. 5(3)(a)). Where a statement has been withdrawn in accordance with s. 5(3)(a) marital proceedings come to, an end (s. 20(6)(c)).

The Act requires the parties to give *joint* notice of the withdrawal of a statement even where only one party has made it. As the former Lord Chancellor explained (Hansard, 29th February 1996, vol 569, no 52, col 1682):

The reason for that is, where the period for reflection and consideration has run for some time, the party who did not make the initial statement may well come to the conclusion that a divorce or separation is the best course of action. That may be because of matters that have arisen during that time which convince the party that the marriage has broken down. If the party who made the statement of marital breakdown is able to halt the process by withdrawing that statement independently of the other party, then the latter party will be required to make a fresh statement and go through a further period of reflection and consideration before they can apply for an order. It should be emphasised that the initial party may well be withdrawing the statement only because they have recognised some material disadvantage which they may suffer and not because the relationship has a real chance of being saved. In order for a reconciliation to be successful, both parties must be willing to attempt it. If the party who has not made the statement wishes to attempt a reconciliation, then joint notice can be made withdrawing the statement. There is no problem in that. If not, then the period for reflection and consideration already undertaken by the parties, which is likely to have been a very painful time, should not be perpetuated needlessly. Where one party can make a statement and withdraw it at will without the other party's involvement, there is a grave danger of the whole process being misused.

The former Lord Chancellor further stated (Hansard, 29th February 1996, vol 569, no 52, col 1683):

> The party who has not made the statement must be allowed to have some control over the process. It is important that we make the divorce process as non-adversarial as possible and that we stop the situation which exists at present where one party 'owns' the divorce and gets his or her divorce against the other party. This is also why, where an application for a divorce order is made by one party, the current drafting of the Bill allows for the party to a divorce who has not made the application to join in that application.

7   Lapse of a statement

7.1   Following the period for reflection and consideration

No application for a separation or divorce order may be made with reference to a particular statement of marital breakdown if a period of more than 1 year ('the specified period') (or such other further period as shall, having regard to the presumption that divorce proceedings should ordinarily be concluded within 2½ years, appear to the court to be just) has passed since the end of the period for reflection and consideration (s. 5(3)(b)).

The reason why:

> the statement does not simply lapse at the end of the period for reflection and consideration is so as to give extra time to parties for whom the period for reflection and consideration may not have proved long enough to reach decisions about future arrangements, so that they do not have to recommence the divorce process. It is important, however, that there is a set time at which the statement lapses. Allowing proceedings to drag on, with all the inevitable uncertainty, can be very harmful to children, as well as potentially to the parties. It is also important that people are aware that there is only a finite time available to them for making their arrangements. Allowing people to believe that they can apply for an extension to the lapse period if they prevaricate may encourage some people to do just that. That may be the case particularly where negotiations are acrimonious, in the sense that they may be used as a bargaining chip. (Mr Gary Streeter, Parliamentary Secretary, Lord Chancellor's Department, Hansard, 17th June 1996, vol 279, no 117, col 603)

The provisions in s. 5(3)(b) allow 'the court to extend the lapse period where it appears to the court that to do so would be just in all the circumstances ... the court would be expected to have regard to the presumption that the divorce process should ordinarily be concluded within two and a half years' (Mr Gary Streeter, Hansard, 17th June 1996, vol 279, no 117, col 603).

This is:

> an attempt to provide parties who have not applied for an extension to the period for reflection and consideration with the same overall time limit for the divorce process as those who are granted an extension to the period. The six-month extension to the period for reflection and consideration has a specific purpose. It is intended to provide additional time for parties to reconsider the step that they are taking to divorce where one party does not consent, or where they have children under 16. It is not simply an extra six months to enable parties to reach decisions on their future arrangements and it should not therefore be equated with adding on extra time to the lapse period. The Government intend to make the following provision under rules of court: where the lapse period is likely to apply and ancillary relief proceedings are still pending, parties will make an application for a divorce or separation order. The court will have power to adjourn the application. It is intended that rules of court will provide the circumstances when the court will adjourn the application. It is intended that those circumstances will be where ancillary relief proceedings have not been concluded for reasons that are beyond the control of the applicant or the other party. (Mr Gary Streeter, Hansard, 17th June, vol 279, no 117, col 604)

Presumably, the application to extend has to be made before the year elapses. However, this is not clear from the statute. It is to be assumed that rules and regulations will set out the appropriate procedure in due course.

The Act provides power for the Lord Chancellor to vary the 'specified period' by amending s. 5(3)(b) (s. 5(5)).

7.2   Suspension of lapse period

Under s. 7(7) parties are able to suspend the passing of the period of reflection and consideration by notifying the court that they wish to attempt reconciliation. Section 5(5)–(7) provides that the passing of the lapse period following the period for reflection and consideration can also be suspended for the same reason. This is intended 'to encourage attempts at reconciliation right up until the time of an application for a divorce order' (Mr Gary Streeter, Hansard, 17th June 1996, vol 279, no 117, col 603).

If the parties, before the statement 'lapses' (i.e., before 1 year has elapsed since the end of the period for reflection and consideration), *jointly* give notice to the court that they are attempting reconciliation but require additional time, then the 'specified period':

(a)   stops running on the day on which the notice is received by the court (s. 5(5)(a)); but

(b)   resumes running on the day on which *either* of the parties gives notice to the court that the attempted reconciliation has been unsuccessful (s. 5(5)(b)).

If, however, the 'specified period' is interrupted by a continuous period of more than 18 months, any application by either of the parties for a divorce order or for a separation order must be by reference to a *new* statement received by the court at any time after the end of the 18 months (s. 5(7)).

Chapter Eight
Period for Reflection and Consideration

1 Purpose of the period for reflection and consideration

Where a statement of marital breakdown has been made, a 'period for reflection and consideration' must pass *before* any application may be made for a separation or a divorce order by reference to the statement (s. 7(1)). The purpose of the period is for the parties:

(a)   to reflect on whether the marriage can be saved and to have an opportunity to effect a reconciliation (s. 7(1)(a)), and
(b)   to consider what arrangements should be made for the future (s. 7(1)(b)).

During the Second Reading of the Bill in the House of Lords the former Lord Chancellor said of the period for reflection and consideration that: 'The general view of those who were consulted by the Law Commission and the Government, following the issue of our consultation paper, was that a sufficient period of time should elapse in order to demonstrate quite clearly that the marriage had irretrievably broken down. The period should be sufficiently long to give parties a realistic timescale within which to reflect on whether the marriage could be saved but also a realistic time within which the practical questions about children, home and finances could be resolved' (Hansard, 30th November 1995, vol 567, col 702).

The irretrievable breakdown of the marriage 'is demonstrated only once the period for reflection and consideration has taken place' (The former Lord Chancellor, Hansard, 11th January 1996, vol 568, no 24, col 309). 'The point is that it is the year passing that is required. That is an absolute and objective fact. Unless the relationship has been brought together, healed or restored in that time, the Bill proposes that there should then be a basis for saying that the marriage has broken down irretrievably' (The former Lord Chancellor, Hansard, 30th November 1995, vol 567, col 310).

The former Lord Chancellor further explained the way in which the period for reflection and consideration should be used: 'Assuming that the year has now begun, the process ... is that there should be discussion between the parties, helped by a mediator, of what the future arrangements would be — all the arrangements relating to the children, property, and any other matter that may be affected by the possible dissolution of the marriage. The year is intended for that purpose. It may take a little longer. The Bill requires that, except in exceptional circumstances provided for in

Schedule 1, the arrangements should be completed before a divorce is granted'
(Hansard, 30th November 1995, vol 567, col 311).

2 Length of the period for reflection and consideration

Section 7(3) sets the period for reflection and consideration at 9 months.

In setting that period one of the factors taken into account was that 'if the divorce
process period went on too long, this would be bad for children. A lengthy period
would prolong the agony not only for the adults but also the children, which could be
damaging' (The former Lord Chancellor, Hansard, 30th November, vol 567, col 702).

2.1 Commencement of period

The period for reflection and consideration will start on the 14th day after the
statement of marital breakdown has been received by the court (s. 7(3)). The 14-day
period allows time for the court to serve the other party with the statement (s. 7(4)).
Section 12 gives the Lord Chancellor power to make rules requiring the court to carry
out service (s. 12(1)(d), and as to the circumstances in which such service may be
dispensed with or may be effected otherwise than by delivery to the other party
(s. 12(1)(e)).

The former Lord Chancellor emphasised that 'There must . . . be absolute certainty
as to the date of the period's commencement, as the divorce or separation process
depends upon the passing of a prescribed period of time in order to establish
irretrievable breakdown . . . The date on which a statement is received by the court is
a recorded fact and it is for this reason that the commencement of the period should
depend upon this date' (Hansard, 4th March 1996, vol 570, no 54, col 10).

2.2 Power to extend period where there is delay in service

Where the statement has been made by *one* party the court may, on the application
of the *other* party, extend the period for reflection and consideration where failure to
comply with the rules of service has caused inordinate delay in the service of the
statement (s. 7(4)).

For further details about such an extension see Chapter 7, paragraph 4.1.

2.3 No power to abridge period

Both the 9-month period for reflection and consideration, and the 3-month
'cooling-off' period which precedes it, are absolute periods which cannot be
abridged. In explaining the rationale for this requirement the former Lord Chancellor
said that the purpose of the period was 'to provide convincing proof that the
breakdown of the marriage is irretrievable. The period is intended to provide a
realistic time for the parties to decide whether they can be reconciled and their
marriage saved and, if not, to resolve the practical problems relating to marital
breakdown . . . I feel strongly that if one has a period required to demonstrate the
irretrievable breakdown of the marriage, in principle that period should not be
capable of abridgement. Unless and until the marriage has irretrievably broken down,
it cannot be right to grant a decree of divorce, whatever else one may do by way of

protective orders and so forth' (Hansard, 11th March 1996, vol 570, no 59, col 655–6).

Concerns were expressed during the parliamentary debates on behalf of those people trapped in violent marriages, and it was argued that in such cases there should be power to end the marriage in a shorter period than is provided by the Act. These arguments did not, however, lead to the reduction of the period for reflection and consideration. The former Lord Chancellor felt that the protective measures available in Part IV of the Act were sufficient to enable a court to deal with issues of violence effectively during the period when the separation or divorce process was in progress, and that the Children Act 1989 gave the court ample power to deal with any issues affecting the children.

3 Suspending the period for reflection and consideration — 'stopping the clock'

Where, at any time during the period for reflection and consideration, both parties wish for additional time to attempt reconciliation, then they may jointly give notice to the court to this effect (s. 7(7)).

Once formal notice has been given to the court then the period for reflection and consideration:

(a)   stops running on the day on which the notice is received by the court (s. 7(8)(b)), but

(b)   resumes running on the day on which *either* of the parties gives notice to the court that the attempted reconciliation has been unsuccessful (s. 7(8)(b)).

The whole purpose of the period for reflection and consideration is to encourage attempts at reconciliation. These provisions enable the parties to 'stop the clock' for that purpose if *both* of them wish to do so. This means that if the attempt is unsuccessful the parties do not have to restart the process again. Provided that the statement has not 'lapsed' (see s. 7(9) and Chapter 7, paragraph 7), either party can unilaterally 'start the clock' once more and continue from the point at which they suspended the process.

If the period for reflection and consideration is interrupted by a continuous period of more than 18 months, any application made by either of the parties for a divorce order or separation order must be by reference to a *new* statement received by the court at any time after the end of the 18 months (s. 7(9)).

It is important to note that the *only* way in which the clock can be stopped is by way of *formal* notice to the court. Whilst there is nothing in the Act to prevent a couple from *privately* attempting reconciliation, or to prejudice them if they do so, the clock will continue to 'tick' (The former Lord Chancellor, Hansard, 4th March 1996, vol 570, no 54, cols 19–20).

4 Lapse of the statement — the 'specified period'

The statement will normally 'lapse' 1 year after the end of the period for reflection and consideration (s. 5(3)(b)). This 1 year period is called the 'specified period'. As we have seen, the court has a discretion to extend the specified period to whatever longer period appears to the court to be just in all the circumstances. See Chapter 7, paragraph 7 for further details.

5 Extending the period for reflection and consideration

The period for reflection and consideration may be extended by one further period of 6 months in two circumstances, as set out in paragraphs 5.1 and 5.2 below.

5.1 Automatic extension where child under 16

Upon the court receiving an application for a divorce order the period for reflection and consideration will be extended automatically by one further period of 6 months when there is any child of the family under the age of 16 at the date when the application is made, *unless* the court is satisfied that delaying the making of a divorce order would be *significantly detrimental* to the welfare of any child of the family (s. 7(11), (13)).

5.1.1 No extension where there ceases to be a child Where a period for reflection and consideration has been extended under s. 7(13) and has not otherwise come to an end, it comes to an end on there ceasing to be a child of the family to whom s. 7(11) applied (s. 7(14)). For example, if there is only one child of the family who was under 16 at the date when the application for the divorce order was made, but who subsequently has his 16th birthday before the normal end of the extension, then the extended period would end on that date rather than at the end of the 6 months.

5.2 Application to extend made by one of parties

Where an application for a divorce order is made by *one* party, then the *other* party may apply for an extra period of 6 months to be added to the period for reflection and consideration (s. 7(13)). However, the party applying for the extension may only do so if:

(a)   they apply to the court within the 'prescribed period' for time for further reflection (s. 7(10)(a)); and

(b)   the requirements of s. 9 (except any imposed under s. 9(3)) are satisfied (s. 7(10)(b)).

5.2.1 The 'prescribed period' The 'prescribed period' in s. 7(10)(a) is not defined by the Act. Presumably it will be defined by rules and regulations in due course.

5.2.2 Section 9 requirements must be satisfied The party applying for the extension (assuming they have done so within the 'prescribed period') will only have their application granted if the requirements of s. 9 (except any imposed under s. 9(3)) are satisfied.

Section 9 contains provisions to ensure that the parties have settled their arrangements for the future, both in respect of financial matters and in respect of any children of the family, before a separation or divorce order is granted.

See Chapter 10 for full details of the arrangements for the future required by s. 9.

It would appear that where the conditions of s. 7(10) have been met the court *must* allow the extension of the period for reflection and consideration.

5.3 Circumstances where no extension permissible

If, at the time when the application for a divorce order is made, there is an occupation order or a non-molestation order in force in favour of the applicant, or a child of the family, made against the other party to the marriage, then s. 7(13) will not apply, and there can be no extension of the period for reflection and consideration (s. 7(12)(a)).

5.4 Effect of 6-month extension on the application for a divorce order

However, a period for reflection and consideration which is extended for 6 months under s. 7(13) is:

(a)   only extended in relation to the application for a divorce order in respect of which the application under s. 7(10) was made (s. 7(13)(b)); and

(b)   does not invalidate that application for a divorce order (s. 7(13)(a)).

6 Declaration at the end of the period for reflection and consideration

Once the period for reflection and consideration has ended, then a person applying for a separation or divorce order must comply with the conditions set out in s. 5 (see Chapter 3, paragraph 1.1). One of the requirements is that the application should be accompanied by a declaration by the party making the application that:

(a)   having reflected on the breakdown, and

(b)   having considered the requirements of Part II of the Act as to the parties' arrangements for the future,

the applicant believes that the marriage cannot be saved (s. 5(1)(d)).

Chapter Nine
Mediation

1 Introduction

The concept of mediation is the fundamental plank upon which the new system for divorce rests.

National Family Mediation has defined mediation as follows: 'Family mediation is a process in which an impartial third person assists those involved in family breakdown, and in particular separating or divorced couples, to communicate better with one another and to reach their own agreed and informed decisions about some or all of the issues relating to or arising from the separation, divorce, children, finance or property. Mediation is thus an alternative to decision-making by the courts. It is not part of the decision-making procedures of the court' (quoted by Sir Jim Lester in Standing Committee E, Hansard, 14th May 1996, col 247).

Sir Jim Lester went on to say that 'Mediation is essentially a private and informal decision-making process, and that is its strength. However, because of that it does not include the safeguards of due legal process. Therefore, it requires high standards of training and practice to secure the participation of the two parties. Experience suggests that mediation is likely to be effective only when the couples involved feel that they are committed to the process. Success is unlikely if they do not feel that commitment, or if they feel that they have not entered the process by choice, with a willingness to adhere to the results. It is not suitable for everyone' (Hansard, Standing Committee E, 14th May 1996, col 248).

These observations encapsulate the nature of mediation and the tension that exists between mediation and legal representation under the new legislation.

1.1 Mediation is not arbitration

The *Oxford English Dictionary* definition of arbitration is 'the settlement of a question at issue by one to whom the parties agree to refer their claims in order to obtain an equitable decision'. In *mediation* solutions or settlements are not imposed on the parties. The mediator does not make findings of fact. Their function is more limited. It is to assist the parties to come to a settlement themselves.

1.2 Mediation is not reconciliation

The process of reconciliation is 'to bring a person again into friendly relations with another after an estrangement' (*Oxford English Dictionary*). Mediation does not have as its prime object the aim of reconciling estranged parties. However, mediation may indirectly promote reconciliation because its process may well require the parties to address some of the issues which initially led to the breakdown of their marriage. A mediator must be aware throughout the process of mediation of the possibility of reconciliation between the couple concerned. Where there is such a possibility the mediator must ensure that the couple are given proper information about marriage counselling.

1.3 Mediation is not conciliation

Conciliation is 'to gain good will by acts which induce friendly feeling' (*Oxford English Dictionary*). Conciliation is just one of the tools used in mediation. For example, in the course of a mediation one of the parties may make a concession over a particular issue in dispute. The other party may interpret that concession as a gesture of goodwill and therefore be encouraged to make further progress in the negotiation process. However, there are many other tools which may be used in the course of mediation. A mediator may work through a wide range of strategies before finding the one which fits the nature of the parties needing assistance.

1.4 Structure of mediation organisations in the United Kingdom

Over the last 15 years various organisations have set up mediation services in different parts of the United Kingdom. Two of the main mediation bodies, the Family Mediators Association and National Family Mediation, formed the United Kingdom College of Mediators and they now operate under a joint code of practice. The College of Mediators was formally launched in the autumn of 1997, and a directory of mediation services is now available, entitled *UK College Directory and Handbook 1998/99*.

It would appear that the successful operation of the new divorce legislation will depend in part upon there being enough mediators to service its requirements. It is clear that many more mediators are necessary than are trained at present.

2 Legal aid funding for mediation

The principal provisions in relation to mediation in the Act are concerned with its funding by the Legal Aid Board. Part III of the Act (ss. 26–29), which makes provision for the availability of legal aid for mediation, came into force on 21st March 1997. The general principles of the Legal Aid Act 1988, and the references in that Act to legal advice and representation, are not affected.

Section 26 amends the Legal Aid Act 1988 by inserting a new s. 13A into that Act. It provides for legal aid to be available for mediation in family matters. 'Family matters' are defined in the new section to include those which arise under:

(a)   the Matrimonial Causes Act 1973;
(b)   the Domestic Proceedings and Magistrates' Courts Act 1978;
(c)   Parts I to IV of the Children Act 1989;
(d)   Parts II and IV of the Family Law Act 1996; or
(e)   any other enactment prescribed.

For the purposes of the Legal Aid Act 1988 various other definitions are given:

'mediator' means a person with whom the Board contracts for the provision of mediation by any person' (s. 26(2)).

'mediation' includes steps taken by a mediator in any case (s. 26(3)):

(a)   in determining whether to embark on mediation;
(b)   in preparing for mediation; and
(c)   in making any assessment under Part IIIA of the Legal Aid Act 1988 (i.e., an assessment as to whether the parties and the particular case are suitable for mediation).

The Legal Aid Board has drawn up a scheme for the recognition of individual mediators working within those organisations which have funding under the mediation pilot projects. There are management requirements and provisions for controlling the quality of the services provided. Once mediators have been recognised by the Legal Aid Board under this scheme they will be able to conduct mediation which is funded by legal aid.

2.1   Who will be eligible?

Section 27 is concerned with the provision and availability of mediation under the Legal Aid Act 1988 and it inserts a new s. 13B into that Act. Mediation is to be available to any person whose financial resources are such as, under regulations, make him eligible for mediation (Legal Aid Act 1988, s. 13B(2), as inserted by s. 27).

2.2   Who will assess which cases are suitable for mediation?

Section 13B(3) of the Legal Aid Act 1988 (as inserted by s. 27) states that a person will not be granted legal aid for mediation in relation to any dispute unless mediation appears *to the mediator* to be suitable to the dispute and the parties and all the circumstances.
    Therefore, it is the mediators themselves who will be responsible for assessing which parties and which disputes are suitable for mediation. The former Lord Chancellor said of this process of assessment: 'Of course it is very important that this is done very much in consultation with the relevant party or parties and taking into account their attitude, willingness and other circumstances. Parties may not fully understand the mediation process and will thus be unable to give a fully informed view of suitability in all the circumstances of their case' (Hansard, 4th March 1996, vol 570, no 54, col 94).

If the mediator assesses the parties or the case as unsuitable for mediation there is no 'appeal' against that decision. 'In order to have mediation, one must have a mediator who is willing to undertake it. That is where ultimately the court is the last resort because the court cannot refuse to undertake decision-making even where parties are not particularly reasonable. The answer is that one would have to try another mediator to see whether he or she would be willing to step in where his colleague had feared to tread' (The former Lord Chancellor, Hansard, 4th March 1996, vol 570, no 54, col 97).

3 Code of practice for mediation services

Section 13B(6) of the Legal Aid Act 1988 (as inserted by s. 27) provides that before the Legal Aid Board may enter into a contract for the provision of mediation, services, then the mediator must comply with a code of practice.

The code must require (Legal Aid Act 1988, s. 13B(7), as inserted by s. 27):

(a)   that parties participate in mediation only if they are willing and not influenced by a fear of violence or other harm;

(b)   that cases where either party may be influenced by the fear of violence or other harm are identified as soon as possible.

Where there are one or more children of the family, the code must also require the mediator to have arrangements designed to ensure that the parties are encouraged to consider (Legal Aid Act 1988, s. 13B(8), as inserted by s. 27):

(a)   the welfare, wishes and feelings of each child; and

(b)   whether and to what extent each child should be given the opportunity to express his or her wishes and feelings in the mediation.

See Chapter 10, paragraph 3 for detailed discussion about the arrangements to be made to safeguard the welfare of any children of the family, and for the measures instituted to ensure that they have a 'voice' in the divorce process where that is appropriate.

A contract entered into by the Legal Aid Board for the provision of mediation under Part III of the Act must also include arrangements so that (Legal Aid Act 1988, s. 13B(7), as inserted by s. 27):

(a)   the possibility of reconciliation is kept under review throughout the mediation;

(b)   each party is informed about the availability of independent legal advice.

When deciding whether or not to adopt such a code the former Lord Chancellor said 'I believe that there is a good deal of merit in having a code of practice dealing with mediation ... Such a code would be a useful way of signifying to members of the profession the subject matters that Parliament had in mind for them to address' (Hansard, 23rd January 1996, vol 568, no 30, col 1024). He added that where mediation services did not abide by the code then '... the sanction would be that the Legal Aid Board would not arrange for public money to be used in a mediation service which did not comply with the code of practice' (Hansard, 23rd January 1996, vol 568, no 30, col 1024).

Nevertheless, the former Lord Chancellor was keen to ensure that some flexibility was left to allow the mediation profession to develop, and he said: '... I feel somewhat reluctant to attempt to regulate the whole profession. I say that because it is a developing profession and, just as is the case with the legal profession, it would be quite wrong to regulate it at Government level. I do not believe that the Government should be in the position of, so to speak, dictating to the profession precisely how it should go about matters. On the other hand, where public money is being used for the purpose of purchasing particular services, it is clear that the Government need to be satisfied on behalf of the public purse that that is an appropriate position' (Hansard, 25th January 1996, vol 568, no 32, col 1190).

Section 13B(5) of the Legal Aid Act 1988 (as inserted by s. 27) provides that the Lord Chancellor may direct the Legal Aid Board to include in the contract such other provisions relating to the provisions of mediation for the purpose of legal aid as he may require.

The former Lord Chancellor explained that:

The Legal Aid Board will require mediation services with which it contracts to meet the terms of a mediation franchise specification. That specification is to be developed during the pilot study. But one option is to require that mediators and their supervisors are accredited by a relevant professional body. The board will audit compliance with the specification and non-compliance in key areas will result in suspension or termination of the contract ... I should not consider the Legal Aid Board entitled to contract with any service that did not comply with those standards. I do not believe that anyone could object to the information meetings giving information to those attending about the possible risks of attending mediation with a service that has not been accredited and approved for state funding purposes. It would be perfectly possible, for example, at the information meeting to declare which are the state accredited systems. Anyone who went to anyone else would do so at his own expense and accept the consequences. I envisage the standards set by the Legal Aid Board becoming a kite mark for quality across the profession. That would give the client the information necessary for him or her to make an appropriate judgment regarding which mediation services to use without the Government needing directly to approve the mediation services as well. (Hansard, 4th March 1996, vol 570, no 54, col 79)

4   Directions by the court with respect to mediation

After the court has received a statement of marital breakdown, it may give a direction requiring each party to attend a meeting arranged in accordance with the direction for the purpose of (s. 13(1)):

(a)   enabling an explanation to be given of the facilities available to the parties for mediation in relation to disputes between them (s. 13(1)(a)); and
(b)   providing an opportunity for each party to agree to take advantage of those facilities (s. 13(1)(b)).

The purpose behind the provisions in s. 13 is that:

> the court may realise, once the matter comes before it, that the parties have not really understood what mediation can do for them in the particular circumstances ... the court can adjourn to allow mediation to take place. I think I understand that none of us would wish the court to use some oblique pressure but, on the other hand, if the court feels that the parties, notwithstanding our efforts to inform them, do not really appreciate or have not understood the efforts that have been made or realise how mediation could help them in the circumstance of their particular case, the court should invite them to attend a meeting at which that would be clearly explained to them. In a sense it is just reinforcing the messages they have already got. (The former Lord Chancellor, Hansard, 23rd January 1996, vol 568, no 30, col 1023)

In Parliament reservations were articulated as to the parties feeling pressurised to undergo mediation, and as to whether or not mediation would be seen as truly voluntary if the parties are directed by the court to attend a meeting so that mediation can be explained to them. In response, the former Lord Chancellor said: 'I personally prefer to regard mediation as voluntary. I think the courts should be given discretion, which I am confident they will use properly, to try to ensure that where mediation is appropriate the parties will understand the benefits it holds for them' (Hansard, 23rd January 1996, vol 568, no 30, col 1023).

4.1   When may a direction be given?

A direction under s. 13 may be given *at any time*, including in the course of proceedings 'connected with' the breakdown of the marriage (s. 13(2)). The meaning of 'connected proceedings' is contained in s. 25, see Chapter 13, paragraph 4.

4.2   Who applies for the direction?

A direction under s. 13 may be given on the application of *either* of the parties or on the initiative of the court itself (s. 13(3)).

4.3   What form does the explanatory mediation meeting take?

The parties are to be required to attend the same explanatory mediation meeting *unless*:

(a)   one of them asks, or both of them ask, for separate meetings (s. 13(4)(a)); or
(b)   the court considers separate meetings to be more appropriate (s. 13(4)(b)).

These provisions reflect concern expressed during the parliamentary debates on the Act that parties should not have to attend the explanatory meeting together, particularly where there had been a history of domestic violence in the marriage. In response the former Lord Chancellor said: 'Concern was expressed ... on the possibility of intimidation where parties are required to attend together. I agree that that is something we should take all practical steps to avoid' (Hansard, 4th March 1996, vol 570, no 54, col 40).

The direction given by the court must:

(a)   specify a person chosen by the court (with that person's agreement) to arrange and conduct the meeting or meetings (s. 13(5)(a)); and
(b)   require the person specified in the direction to produce to the court, at such a time as the court may direct, a report stating (s. 13(5)(b)):
    (i)   whether the parties have complied with the direction (s. 13(5)(b)(i)); and
    (ii)   if they have, whether they have agreed to take part in any mediation (s. 13(5)(b)(ii)).

Obviously, if the parties then decide to pursue mediation, they will usually have to attend sessions with the mediator together.

5   Power of court to adjourn proceedings

Section 14 makes it clear that the court's power to adjourn *any* proceedings 'connected with' the breakdown of a marriage includes power to adjourn for the purpose of:

(a)   allowing the parties to comply with a direction under s. 13 (attending a meeting at which mediation is to be explained to them)(s. 14(1)(a)); or
(b)   enabling disputes to be resolved amicably(s. 14(1)(b)).

The meaning of 'connected proceedings' is set out in s. 25, see Chapter 13, paragraph 4.

When the court decides whether or not to allow an adjournment for either of the purposes set out in (a) and (b) above, it must have regard in particular to the need to protect the interests of any child of the family (s. 14(2)).

If the court does adjourn any proceedings connected with the breakdown of the marriage for either of those purposes, the period of the adjournment must not exceed the maximum period prescribed by rules of court (s. 14(3)). Those rules have not yet been formulated.

Unless the *only* purpose of the adjournment is to allow the parties to comply with a direction under s. 13, the court *must* order one or both of them to produce to the court a report as to (s. 14(4)):

(a)   whether they have taken part in mediation during the adjournment;
(b)   whether, as a result, any agreement has been reached between them;
(c)   the extent to which any dispute between them has been resolved as a result of any such agreement;
(d)   the need for further mediation; and
(e)   how likely it is that further mediation will be successful.

6   Mediation to be undertaken voluntarily

An important question, as already outlined, is whether mediation is to be truly voluntary or whether those who have to rely on legal aid will be forced to use mediation whilst those who are not legally aided will be free to use mediation or retain legal representation — or to have both.

Baroness Hamwee said that: 'It would be entirely wrong to introduce what might become a two tier system — proper legal advice and representation for those who can pay for it and compulsory mediation for those who do not have the funds' (Hansard, 25th January 1996, vol 568, no 32, col 1212). She expressed the hope that 'either party can withdraw the agreement to mediation at any time and then legal advice for representation kicks in' (Hansard, 25th January 1996, vol 568, no 32, col 1211). Earl Russell made the observation that '... to be truly voluntary it must be such that you can refuse to undertake it without suffering any evil consequences' (Hansard, 25th January 1996, vol 568, no 32, col 1213).

The former Lord Chancellor addressed those concerns by saying that '... where either party to the proceedings is not prepared to take part in mediation, mediation is not suitable to the dispute, the parties and all the circumstances. I cannot see that a mediator could possibly regard mediation as suitable for a dispute where either party was not prepared to take part in it' (Hansard, 25th January 1996, vol 568, no 32, col 1214).

He went on the emphasise that: 'My main point in regard to mediation is that for it to work people have to be willing to speak, to communicate. Mediation relates effectively to communication. It is difficult to mediate in a communication if neither party, or one of the parties, is not prepared to speak at all' (Hansard, 25th January 1996, vol 568, no 32, col 1214).

6.1 Mediation and legal representation

The former government committed itself to creating a 'level playing field' for parties to choose between mediation and legal representation as the appropriate method for resolving their disputes, provided that before parties decide which approach to take they have first attended a meeting with a mediator to have the mediation process properly explained to them (Mr Jonathan Evans, Hansard, Standing Committee E, 14th May 1996, col 310).

Lord Meston expressed the need for a proper choice in this way: 'People should have the ability to have recourse to law rather than to mediation. They should certainly have the ability quickly to go to court ... where there is obstructive behaviour or non-cooperation or indeed where there may be dissipation of assets to frustrate the mediation so that an injunction is necessary. Without the fall-back of recourse to law with proper legal representation, the vulnerability of the weaker party to accept a less-than-perfect mediated settlement may be very hard to resist' (Hansard, 25th January 1996, vol 568, no 32, col 1203–4).

6.2 Availability of legal aid for representation prior to mediation

Section 15(3F) of the Legal Aid Act 1988 (as inserted by s. 29) provides that a person will not be granted legal aid for legal representation for the purposes of proceedings relating to family matters, *unless* he has attended a meeting with a mediator to determine:

(a)   whether mediation appears suitable to the dispute and the parties and all the circumstances, and
(b)   in particular, whether mediation could take place without either party being influenced by fear of violence or other harm.

If mediation does appear suitable, then the mediator will help the person applying for legal representation to decide whether instead to apply for mediation (Legal Aid Act 1988, s. 15(3F)(b), as inserted by s. 29), unless the proceedings are under:

(a)   Part IV of the Family Law Act 1996: involving issues of domestic violence (Legal Aid Act 1988, s. 15(3G)(a)(i));

(b)   s. 37 of the Matrimonial Causes Act 1973: involving injunctive measures by one party to prevent the dissipation of assets by the other party (Legal Aid Act 1988, s. 15(3G)(a)(ii));

(c)   Part IV or V of the Children Act 1989: involving issues as a result of which public law orders may need to be made in relation to a child of the family (Legal Aid Act 1988, s. 15(3G)(a)(iii)); or

(d)   any other proceedings that may be prescribed (Legal Aid Act 1988, s. 15(3G)(b)); or

(e)   in such circumstances as may be prescribed (Legal Aid Act 1988, s. 15(3G)(c)).

When the Legal Aid Board are determining under s. 15(3)(a) of the Legal Aid Act 1988 whether it is *reasonable* that a person should be granted legal representation under Part III of the Family Law Act 1996 for proceedings relating to family matters it:

(a)   must have regard to whether, and to what extent, recourse to mediation would be a suitable alternative to taking the proceedings (Legal Aid Act 1988, s. 15(3H)(a), as inserted by s. 29); and

(b)   must for that purpose have regard to the outcome of the meeting with a mediator held under s. 15(3F) of the Legal Aid Act 1988, and to any assessment made by the mediator for the purposes of s. 13B(3) of the Legal Aid Act 1988 (Legal Aid Act 1988, s. 15(3H)(b), as inserted by s. 29).

It cannot be discounted that a person's refusal to undergo mediation might place a 'black mark' against their name for the purposes of an application for legal aid for legal representation. This remains a concern even though the presumption in favour of mediation which was contained in the Bill has been removed (Hansard, Standing Committee E, 14th May 1996, col 310).

The implementation of s. 29 (which came into force on 21st March 1997) has required the amendment of delegated legislation. The Civil Legal Aid (General) Amendment (No. 2) Regulations 1997 (SI 1997/1079), which came into force on 1st May 1997, amend the Civil Legal Aid (General) Regulations 1989 by inserting a new reg. 26A; this provides that the Legal Aid Act 1988, s. 15(3F), will not apply where there is no recognised mediator available to the applicant or any other party to the proceedings to hold a meeting. The Legal Aid Board has only recently 'recognised' any mediators for the purposes of the Family Law Act 1996, and so it is not yet possible to predict how the new provisions will work out in practice.

6.3   What happens if one of the parties changes their mind during the mediation process?

Baroness Hamwee queried 'the position in which one of the parties changes his or her view during the process of mediation and, having started on a course of mediation, felt that it was no longer appropriate to continue. I asked whether one could then move on, with the benefit of legal aid, into proceedings' (Hansard, 25th January 1996, vol 568, no 32, col 1215).

The former Lord Chancellor replied (Hansard, 25th January 1996, vol 568, no 32, col 1216):

It may depend somewhat on the circumstances. The tests for the grant of legal aid generally include the merits test in respect of which the Legal Aid Board would have to make a judgment. I can readily foresee circumstances ... in which difficulties arise in the mediation; for example, if it is not clear that a full disclosure has been made of all the assets. Then the mediation would have to stop and an application be made to the court in order to obtain full disclosure. In my view, it is right that in that situation legal aid would be available in appropriate circumstances for those proceedings. In situations in which the person suddenly decides that he or she has had enough and wants to stop, the circumstances might vary. The person who so decided might be the person who had legal aid. If he (or she) decided without good reason just to stop, the Legal Aid Board might wish to revoke the certificate for mediation ... What would happen then would depend on the situation in which that person was, and the application to the circumstances of the tests that presently exist under the Legal Aid Act ... The mediation is certainly not compulsory. But that is not the same as saying that unnecessary expense should be incurred by the taxpayer at the whim of unreasonable litigants. The whole underlying basis on which legal aid is granted is that the conduct of the litigation should be reasonable and that unnecessary expense would not be put on the public purse. That does not mean that mediation would be compulsory, but that the public purse might not fund it if the situation came out of an unreasonable attitude on the part of the party seeking legal aid.

Thus, the answer to Baroness Hamwee's question is unclear and will probably not be known until the Act is fully implemented and a body of experience has been built up to give an idea as to how the Act works in practice.

7 Cases not suitable for mediation

Lord Archer of Sandwell said that:

National Family Mediation points out that some situations do not admit of mediation. It says that it is possible to categorise a number of types of situation in which, from the outset, one can say that it is not appropriate. First, it says that the dispute may be incapable of being negotiated because, for example, the parties are not agreed on the facts. Someone may have to agree with one of the parties and simply adjudicate on what are the facts. Secondly, there may be irreversible imbalances of power; for example, where there is domestic violence or where a woman from a minority ethnic group may find culturally she is not in a position to be able to bargain with her husband. Thirdly, one of the parties may suffer from some mental or other impairment, with the result that he or she cannot meaningfully negotiate. Fourthly, one of the parties may feel coerced if he or she had to attend any kind of mediation process. Fifthly, there may be criminal child protection issues ... National Family Mediation emphasises that the case may not be suitable for mediation if one partner, even after agreeing to participate, demonstrates a lack of commitment by failing to keep appointments, to produce the necessary information or to abide by any agreements which have been made ... But there has been some anxiety expressed in the country that the Government are anxious to make mediation a blanket remedy to the exclusion of such other remedies as legal advice.

(See Hansard, 25th January 1996, vol 568, no 32, cols 1200–01.)

In response, the former Lord Chancellor inserted s. 15(3G) into the Legal Aid Act 1988 (s. 29). This provision states that a person does *not* have to attend a meeting with a mediator prior to being granted legal aid for legal representation if his or her case falls within one of the following categories:

(a)   Part IV of the Family Law Act 1996 (relating to cases involving domestic violence, occupation and non-molestation orders).

(b)   Section 37 of the Matrimonial Causes Act 1973 (relating to cases where injunctive orders are necessary to prevent one of the parties from dissipating family assets).

(c)   Part IV of the Children Act 1989 (relating to cases where public law orders for the protection of children).

There is also provision for the Lord Chancellor to prescribe other types of proceedings or circumstances where the requirement to attend a mediation meeting will not apply (Legal Aid Act 1988, s. 15(3G)(b),(c), as inserted by s. 29). Thus, the categories are not closed and as experience is gained as to how the Act operates in practice, other categories may be added.

8   Access to legal advice and assistance during the mediation

Parties will have access to legal advice and assistance during and after the mediation process, regardless of their eligibility for legal representation.

Mr Jonathan Evans gave an assurance to this effect in these terms: '... legal advice and assistance will be available not only in support of mediation but at its conclusion, to ensure that clients are able to seek independent legal advice on the terms of any agreement that is reached through mediation before signing it. That affords client protection against agreeing to settlements that may not be in their best interests, although I hope that once mediation has become established as a method of solving disputes and any public misunderstanding of mediation has been dispelled, it will become clear that lawyers rarely see the need to unpick an understanding that has been reached between the parties. That should not be interpreted as any sort of injunction against there being legal advice at that stage of the process. Legal advice and assistance will be available to couples who need assistance with the divorce process and advice about their legal responsibilities, as is the case now under the green form scheme' (Hansard, Standing Committee E, 14th May 1996, col 270).

He added that 'Subject to eligibility, there is nothing in the provisions to prevent mediation services being given in relation to matters concerning the child, with legal advice and support where needed, and legal aid being given for representation in

relation to property matters. Those distinctions are frequently drawn in mediation'
(Hansard, Standing Committee E, 14th May 1996, col 269).

9 Mediation and legal aid — the statutory charge

9.1 Contributions to the cost of mediation

Section 28 inserts s. 13C into the Legal Aid Act 1988 and there sets out the detail of
how mediation is to be paid for under the Act. Legally aided persons will not be
required to pay for mediation unless their financial resources make them liable to
make a contribution towards those costs. When a contribution is required from them
it will be paid to the Legal Aid Board and not to the mediator. The eligibility criteria
for legal aid will be set out in regulations in due course.

9.2 The statutory charge

Section 13C of the Legal Aid Act 1988 (as inserted by s. 28) also sets out provisions
to enable regulations to be made for the imposition of the statutory charge in relation
to any property recovered or preserved as a result of mediation.

If the statutory charge is *not* imposed in relation to property recovered or preserved
as a result of mediation, it can be argued that unjustifiable pressure to use mediation
may result (Earl Russell, Hansard, 4th March 1996, vol 570, no 54, col 101).

In reply, the former Lord Chancellor said: 'I should have thought it wise to leave
that as a discretionary power, because I want to see how the whole thing works. Apart
from anything else, mediation will apply to children's disputes where there is no
question of the statutory charge applying, because no property is recovered or
retained. There are pressures to apply the charge. Obviously the public purse might
be interested in that. On the other hand, I am anxious to see how the mediation works
in practice before deciding what should happen in relation to the statutory charge,
and how it should apply if it is decided to apply it in respect of mediation costs. Apart
from anything else, the statutory charge, if it goes on, involves a degree of cost of
enforcement, and so on. It is not a straightforward matter. Costs are involved in
relation to the statutory charge. Depending on the level of the mediation charges and
costs, we may need to be careful' (Hansard, 25th January 1996, vol 568, no 32,
col 1206).

The former Lord Chancellor went on to say: 'I have always intended that when
the statutory charge is applied through regulations to mediation in family matters
there should be some replication of the statutory disregard which applies in
matrimonial matters for advice, assistance and representation. ... The figure of
£2,500 has been in place for some time ... I should like to see the results of the pilot
study into mediation before deciding exactly how the statutory charge should apply
in that context and before any decision is taken as to the level of disregard' (Hansard,
4th March 1996, vol 570, no 54, col 102).

10 Pilot schemes

Various pilot schemes are currently being run to find out how best to implement the
Act. An advisory board has been set up to monitor the pilot schemes and to make

recommendations based on the results. An interdepartmental working party will look at all aspects of the schemes. See Chapter 6, paragraph 6 for further details.

In relation to the testing out of arrangements for mediation the former Lord Chancellor said: '... there is no question of my authorising the payment out of legal aid money to anyone who is not appropriately qualified to act as a mediator. I believe that during the course of the remarks I heard it said that the Law Society was saying that there would be a good number of lawyer mediators. I believe that it is a good profession for lawyers to follow. It has a most distinguished ancestry. There are also people other than lawyers who may have these skills. Again, it is right that they should be developed. This process is capable of being tested because mediated agreements will be the result in these situations, and the question will be how effective they are and how well they last. So all of this is capable of being tested in a very realistic way' (The former Lord Chancellor, Hansard, 4th March 1996, vol 570, no 54, col 63).

Chapter Ten
Arrangements for the Future

1 Introduction

As already discussed in Chapter 4, if an application for a divorce order or separation order is made to the court by one or both of the parties to a marriage, the court will make the order only if (s. 3(1)):

(a) the marriage has broken down irretrievably;
(b) the requirements of s. 8 about information meetings are satisfied;
(c) the requirements of s. 9 about the parties' arrangements for the future are satisfied; and
(d) the application has not been withdrawn.

It is, therefore, a fundamental procedural requirement of the Act that evidence of the parties' arrangements for the future must be produced to the court in order to satisfy the requirements of s. 9 before a divorce order can be granted, *unless* one of the exemptions in sch. 1 applies (s. 9(6),(7)). If a divorce order is made and it is subsequently found that the requirements of s. 9 have not been met, in that evidence of arrangements has not been put before the court, that order should be void (The former Lord Chancellor, Hansard, 4th March 1996, vol 570, no 54, col 23).

The former Lord Chancellor said: 'It is vital that before a divorce is granted the parties should face up to the responsibilities that have arisen in their marriage in such a way as to make all the necessary provisions for the future.... For example, it is clear that if someone is going to undertake new relationships and new responsibilities, it is important that, so far as possible, before that is done that person should know the nature of the commitments they have arising out of the earlier marriage' (Hansard, 4th March 1996, vol 570, no 54, col 24).

1.1 No need for order or agreement to have been carried into effect by time court considers arrangements for future

Section 9 is not to be read as requiring any order or agreement to have been carried into effect at the time when the court is considering whether arrangements for the future have been made by the parties (sch. 1, para. 5(1) and see further paragraphs 2.2 and 2.3 of this chapter). Furthermore, the fact that an appeal is pending against an order of the kind mentioned in s. 9(2)(a) is to be disregarded (sch. 1, para. 5(2)).

1.2   What must be produced to the court to satisfy s. 9?

In order to satisfy s. 9, the parties must product to the court one of the following (s. 9(2)):

(a)   a court order (made by consent or otherwise) dealing with their financial arrangements;

(b)   a negotiated agreement as to their financial arrangements;

(c)   a declaration by both parties that they have made their financial arrangements;

(d)   a declaration by one of the parties (to which no objection has been notified to the court by the other party) that:

(i)   he or she has no significant assets and does not intend to make an application for financial provision;

(ii)   he or she believes that the other party has no significant assets and does not intend to make an application for financial provision; and

(iii)   there are therefore no financial arrangements to be made.

1.3   Welfare of the children

In addition, the requirements of s. 11 as to the welfare of children must have been satisfied (s. 9(5)).

2   Financial arrangements

In s. 9 and sch. 1 the phrase 'financial arrangements' has the same meaning as in s. 34(2) of the Matrimonial Causes Act 1973. In s. 34(2) the definition is as follows:

'Financial arrangements' means provisions governing the rights and liabilities towards one another when living separately of the parties to a marriage (including a marriage which has been dissolved or annulled) in respect of the making or securing of payments or the disposition or use of any property, including such rights and liabilities with respect to the maintenance or education of any child, whether or not a child of the family.

2.1   Court orders

Mr Jonathan Evans (Parliamentary Secretary for the Lord Chancellor's Department) explained the reason for providing the court with power to make financial orders before the making of a divorce or separation order: 'If our policy is to ensure that people focus on the implications for their children and theirs of proceeding with a divorce, we must give courts the power to make orders relating to finance and property before the divorce or separation order is made. The execution of them is a different matter. If we could not make such order, the parties would not be able to embody agreements that they have made or have them placed in a court order during the period for reflection and consideration' (Hansard, Standing Committee E, 16th May 1996, col 363).

The object of encouraging any possible reconciliation between the parties is achieved by providing that, although the court can make financial provision orders in the period between the statement and the making of the divorce or separation order itself, those orders cannot take effect before the divorce or separation order operates, unless it falls within the criteria set out in paragraph 2.2 below.

For a discussion of the various court orders available to provide for the parties' financial arrangements, see Chapter 11. In essence, the provisions of the Matrimonial Causes Act 1973 remain as they were under the old legislation, with only minor changes to accommodate the terminology and procedure of the new Act (see s. 15, sch. 2 and sch. 8, paras 4–26). The one major change is that s. 16 of the Act provides for the division of pension rights to take place in England and Wales, and that s. 17 provides for the division of pension assets in Scotland. However, since the technical details in relation to implementing the provisions of s. 15 and s. 16 are complex, it will be some years before they come into force (see Chapter 11).

2.2   When a financial provision order may take effect

It is extremely important to note that *no* financial provision order, other than an interim order, may be made under s. 22A of the Matrimonial Causes Act 1973 (as inserted by sch. 2, para. 3) so as to *take effect before* the making of a divorce or separation order in relation to the marriage, *unless* the court is satisfied:

(a)   that the circumstances of the case are *exceptional* (Matrimonial Causes Act 1973, s. 22B(1)(a), as inserted by sch. 2, para. 3); and

(b)   that it would be *just and reasonable* for the order to be so made (Matrimonial Causes Act 1973, s. 22B(1)(b), as inserted by sch. 2, para. 3).

It was the former Lord Chancellor's intention 'to make it as clear as we can that the ordinary rule is that these orders should not take effect until the divorce itself is announced' (Hansard, 11th March 1996, vol 570, no 59, cols 716–7). Mr Jonathan Evans confirmed that the 'terminology is restrictive and it is intended to be. The provisions will operate only in exceptional circumstances' (Hansard, Standing Committee E, 16th May 1996, col 363).

The monitoring of the way in which the words 'exceptional' and 'just and reasonable' are interpreted by the courts will be one of the responsibilities placed on the advisory board (see Chapter 6, paragraph 6).

2.3   Restrictions on making financial provision orders

No financial provision order can be made while parties have 'stopped the clock' in relation to the period for reflection and consideration.

Except in the case of an interim periodical payments order, the court may not make a financial provision order under s. 22A of the Matrimonial Causes Act 1973 (as inserted by sch. 2, para. 3) at any time while the period for reflection and consideration is interrupted under s. 7(8) for the purposes of attempting reconciliation (Matrimonial Causes Act 1973, s. 22B(2), as inserted by sch. 2, para. 3).

There are other restrictions on making financial provision orders and these are fully set out in Chapter 11.

2.4   Negotiated agreements

A 'negotiated agreement' means a written agreement between the parties as to future arrangements:

(a)   which has been reached as the result of mediation or any other form of negotiation involving a third party (sch. 1, para. 7(a)); and
(b)   which satisfies such requirements as may be imposed by rules of court (sch. 1, para. 7(b)).

2.5   Declaration by both parties that they have made their financial arrangements

Where the parties make a declaration under s. 9(2)(c) then sch. 1, para. 8(1) requires that it:

(a)   must be in a prescribed form;
(b)   must, in prescribed cases, be accompanied by such documents as may be prescribed; and
(c)   must, in prescribed cases, satisfy such other requirements as may be prescribed;

However, the validity of a divorce order or separation order made by reference to such a declaration is not to be affected by any inaccuracy in the declaration (sch. 1, para. 8(2)).

2.6   Declaration by one party that he has no assets

Where the party concerned makes a declaration under s. 9(2)(d)(to which no objection has been notified to the court by the other party) that he has no assets and does not intend to apply for financial provision, that he believes the other party has no assets and does not intend to apply for financial provision, and there are therefore no financial arrangements to be made, then that declaration must comply with the requirements set out in sch. 1, para. 8(1) as set out in paragraph 2.5 above.

2.7   Child support payments

The Act 'does not oust the Child Support Agency's jurisdiction and the existence of maintenance agreements between separated parents cannot prevent either party from making voluntary application to the Child Support Agency for a child support assessment. Equally, if the parent with care, or his or her new partner, claims an income-related benefit, the Child Support Agency will seek a fair level of child maintenance from an absent parent who is able to pay, irrespective of the existence of a written agreement' (Mr Jonathan Evans, Hansard, Standing Committee E, 14th May 1996, col 206).

Section 9 'requires parties to have decided their financial arrangements before a divorce or separation order is made. That rightly encourages parties to focus on life after divorce so that the full financial impact of divorce is clear. The clause makes it clear that rights and liabilities for maintenance of children form part of the decisions about future financial arrangements' (Mr Jonathan Evans, Hansard, Standing Committee E, 14th May 1996, col 206).

3   Arrangements for the children

Before a separation or divorce order can be granted the court must be satisfied that the requirements of s. 11 as to the welfare of the children have been met (s. 9(5)). Under the old divorce legislation s. 41 of the Matrimonial Causes Act 1989 imposed a duty on the court in decree proceedings to consider whether there were any children of the family and, if so, to consider whether it should exercise any of its powers under the Children Act 1989; if the court considered that it may need to exercise those powers, and exceptional circumstances made that action desirable, the court was able to stay the grant of a decree absolute of divorce or nullity or a decree of judicial separation.

Under the new legislation, s. 11 imposes upon the court not only the main duties which are already set out in s. 41 of the Matrimonial Causes Act 1973, but also new provisions which place additional duties on the court when it makes a decision as to whether or not it should exercise any of its powers under the Children Act 1989 with respect to any child of the family. However, s. 41 of the Matrimonial Causes Act 1973 remains in force.

In any proceedings for a separation or divorce order the court must consider whether there are any children to whom s. 11 applies, and, where there are such children, whether it should exercise any of its powers under the Children Act 1989 with respect to any of them (s. 11(1)).

During the parliamentary debates much emphasis was placed on the need to reduce the conflict experienced by children during the breakdown of marriage. The former Lord Chancellor quoted an extract from *The Exeter Family Study* (page 54):

... parental conflict has proved to have by far the closest association with any difficulties experienced by children. The general conclusion to be drawn from a review of this literature is that high levels of conflict ... are closely associated with poorer outcomes for children. Some studies have shown that measurable behavioural difficulties can be identified in high conflict families before the breakdown of the marriage, and may even largely explain any later effects of family disruption.

(See Hansard, 23rd January 1996, vol 568, no 30, col 1012.)

This theme runs through all of the provisions in the Act which relate to the welfare of children of the parties involved in the separation and divorce process.

Mr Elfyn Llwyd explained that s. 11 'sets out the principle that parents who are divorcing should have regard to the interests and views of their children. It enshrines in the Bill a right for children in such circumstances to be consulted about important arrangements that their parents seek to make for their future, which is of vital interest and great importance to children. The views and opinions that children hold should be taken into account when important decisions are made about their lives. ... Indeed, if parents fail to agree arrangements for children and the issue goes to court, the court must consider the children's ascertainable views. It is extremely important that the voice of the child is heard' (Hansard, 17th June 1996, vol 279, no 117, cols 587–8).

Mr Gary Streeter pointed out that s. 11 'also extends the list of factors currently in section 41 of the Matrimonial Causes Act 1973 that a court should take into account when deciding whether to exercise its powers under the Children Act. These now include: requirements to regard children's welfare as paramount; that the court should have regard to the wishes and feelings of the child concerned; the principle that, in addition to the child's welfare being best served by having regular contact with those with parental responsibility, there should also be regular contact with other members of the family; the requirement for the court to have particular regard to any risk to the child that may be caused by the actual of proposed arrangements for the child's future' (Hansard, 17th June 1996, vol 279, no 117, col 593).

3.1   To which children will s. 11 apply?

Section 11 applies to (s. 11(5)):

(a)   any child of the family who is under 16 at the date when the court considers the case; and
(b)   any child of the family who has reached 16 and in relation to whom the court directs that s. 11 should apply.

3.2   In what circumstances will the court postpone the divorce or separation order as a result of s. 11?

Where, in any case to which s. 11 applies, it appears to the court that (s. 11(2)):

(a)   the circumstances of the case require it, or are likely to require it, to exercise any of its powers under the Children Act 1989 with respect to any such child;
(b)   that it is not in a position to exercise that power without giving further consideration to the case; and
(c)   there are exceptional circumstances which make it desirable in the interests of the child that the court should give a direction under this section,

the court may direct that the order of separation or divorce is not to be made until the court orders otherwise.

3.3   What factors must the court consider?

3.3.1   Welfare of the child is paramount   In deciding whether the circumstances of the case are such as to require it, or likely to require it, to exercise any of its powers under the Children Act 1989 the court must treat the welfare of the child as paramount (s. 11(3)).

3.3.2   Other factors   In making that decision, the court must have particular regard, on the evidence before it, to (s. 11(4)):

(a)   the wishes and feelings of the child considered in the light of his age and understanding and the circumstances in which those wishes were expressed;
(b)   the conduct of the parties in relation to the upbringing of the child;

(c)   the general principle that, in the absence of evidence to the contrary, the welfare of the child will be best served by:

    (i)   his having regular contact with those who have parental responsibility for him and with other members of his family; and

    (ii)   the maintenance of as good a continuing relationship with his parents as is possible; and

(d)   any risk to the child attributable to:

    (i)   where the person with whom the child will reside is living or proposes to live;

    (ii)   any person with whom that person is living or with whom he proposes to live; or

    (iii)   any other arrangements for his care and upbringing.

3.4   *What powers under the Children Act 1989 may the court exercise?*

In practice, the powers under the Children Act 1989 which the court may exercise are:

(a)   to make an order under s. 8, either of its own motion or under s. 10;

(b)   to make a family assistance order under s. 16;

(c)   to make a direction for investigation by the local authority under s. 37(1);

(d)   to request the preparation of a court welfare officers' report under s. 7(1).

3.5   *Separate representation of children*

Section 64 allows the Lord Chancellor to make regulations to provide for the separate representation of children in proceedings in England and Wales which relate to any matter in respect of which a question has arisen, or may arise, under:

(a)   Part II of the Family Law Act 1996 (proceedings for separation and divorce);

(b)   Part IV of the Family Law Act 1996 (domestic violence, occupation orders and non-molestation orders);

(c)   the Matrimonial Causes Act 1973; or

(d)   the Domestic Proceedings and Magistrates' Courts Act 1978.

However, the regulations may provide for separate representation for children only in specified circumstances (s. 64(2)).

Mr Gary Streeter said 'The Government believe that the voice of the child should be heard in proceedings regarding his or her welfare. There are already a number of ways in which that is provided for. The voice of the child can be heard through the report of a welfare officer under the Children Act 1989 and through the offices of the Official Solicitor in private law proceedings in the High Court and county court, and, under section 10(8) of the Children Act 1989, a child may bring his or her own application, be represented and apply for legal aid for such representation' (Hansard, 17th June 1996, vol 279, no 117, col 585).

4   Schedule 1 exceptions

If the court is satisfied, on an application made by one of the parties after the end of the period for reflection and consideration, that the circumstances of the case fall within one of the four categories listed in sch. 1, paras 1–4, then it may make a divorce or separation order even though the requirements of s. 9(2) have *not* been satisfied (s. 9(7)). Thus, sch. 1 supplements the provisions of s. 9 (s. 9(6)).

4.1 Delay, obstruction, inability to obtain information

The circumstances referred to in s. 9(7)(a) and set out in sch. 1, para. 1 ('the first exemption') are that:

    (a)   the requirements of s. 11 (in relation to the welfare of children) have been satisfied;

    (b)   the applicant has, during the period for reflection and consideration, taken such steps as are reasonably practical to try to reach agreement about the parties' financial arrangements; and

    (c)   the applicant has applied to the court for financial relief and has complied with all court requirements but:

        (i)   the other party has delayed in complying with court requirements or has otherwise been obstructive; or

        (ii)   for reasons which are beyond the control of the parties, the court has been prevented from obtaining the information it requires to determine the financial position of the parties.

The former Lord Chancellor explained that 'There are circumstances — for example, not responding to correspondence from the applicant's solicitors or refusing to instruct his or her solicitor so that matters may progress — where one party is being obstructive to the applicant without necessarily being obstructive of the court's process. I believe that the court, which will have before it all the papers relevant to the case, should be entitled to make its own judgment, taking into account all the circumstances of the case, as to whether behaviour has been obstructive or not' (Hansard, 11th March 1996, vol 570, no 59, col 715).

He also said that: 'The object is to try to ensure that that party does not without proper reason drag out the process of having the arrangements made. The idea behind the exemption is therefore reasonably clear. Any form of obstruction, which the court regards as simply obstruction, could be taken into account' (Hansard, 11th March 1996, vol 570, no 59, col 715).

4.2 Ill health, disability, injury

The circumstances referred to in s. 9(7)(b) and set out in sch. 1, para. 2 ('the second exemption') are that:

    (a)   the requirements of s. 11 (welfare of children) have been satisfied;

    (b)   the applicant has, during the period for reflection and consideration, taken such steps as are reasonably practicable to try to reach agreement about the parties' financial arrangements;

    (c)   because of:

        (i)   the ill health or disability of the applicant, the other party or a child of the family (whether physical or mental); or

(ii)   an injury suffered by the applicant, the other party or a child of the family,

the applicant has not been able to reach agreement with the other party about those arrangements and is unlikely to be able to do so in the foreseeable future; and

(d)   a delay in making the order applied for under s. 3 (i.e., a divorce or separation order):

(i)   would be significantly detrimental to the welfare of any child of the family; or

(ii)   would be seriously prejudicial to the applicant.

4.3   Inability to contact the other party

The circumstances referred to in s. 9(7)(c) and set out in sch. 1, para. 3 ('the third exemption') are that:

(a)   the requirements of s. 11 have been satisfied;

(b)   the applicant has found it impossible to contact the other party; and

(c)   as a result, it has been impossible for the applicant to reach agreement with the other party about their financial arrangements.

4.4   Domestic violence

The circumstances referred to in s. 9(7)(d) and set out in sch. 1, para. 4 ('the fourth exemption') are that:

(a)   the requirements of s. 11 have been satisfied;

(b)   an occupation order or a non-molestation order is in force in favour of the applicant or a child of the family, made against the other party;

(c)   the applicant has, during the period for reflection and consideration, taken such steps as are reasonably practicable to try to reach agreement about the parties' financial arrangements;

(d)   the applicant has not been able to reach agreement with the other party about those arrangements and is unlikely to be able to do so in the foreseeable future; and

(e)   a delay in making the order applied for under s. 3 (i.e., a divorce or separation order):

(i)   would be significantly detrimental to the welfare of any child of the family; or

(ii)   would be seriously prejudicial to the applicant.

5   Directions in respect of marriages mentioned in the Marriage Act 1949

If the parties:

(a)   were married to each other in accordance with usages of a kind mentioned in s. 26(1) of the Marriage Act 1949 (marriages which may be solemnised on authority of superintendent registrar's certificate), and

(b)   are required to cooperate if the marriage is to be dissolved in accordance with those usages, the court may, on the application of either party, direct that there must also be produced to the court a *declaration* by *both* parties that they have taken such steps as are required to dissolve the marriage in accordance with those usages (s. 9(3)).

A direction under s. 9(3):

(a)   may only be given if the court is satisfied that in all the circumstances of the case it is just and reasonable to give it (s. 9(3)(a)); and

(b)   may be revoked at any time (s. 9(3)(b)).

This provision was introduced to tackle problems which are, for example, common to both Moslem and Jewish law. Lord Meston explained that 'First, the observant cannot remarry without a religious divorce; a secular divorce is not enough in the eyes of their particular faiths. Secondly, in both cases it is only the husband who can initiate the procedure and therefore, by that very fact, the wife is at some disadvantage. The result in practice is that the husband's willingness to initiate the procedure becomes a bargaining counter in the financial proceedings' (Hansard, 23rd January 1996, vol 568, no 30, col 1004).

Chapter Eleven
Financial Provision

1 Introduction

In the Law Commission's 1990 Report (Law Com No 192) and in the subsequent White Paper 'Looking to the Future: Mediation and the Ground for Divorce', few proposals were made in connection with orders for financial provision and property adjustment save a determined attempt to move away from the somewhat archaic terminology of 'ancillary relief' to more readily understood wording.

Speaking at the Second Reading, the former Lord Chancellor stated 'The intention is that the current law relating to financial provision on divorce should be amended by Schedule 2 only to the extent that is necessary as a result of changes in the Bill to the law relating to divorce and judicial separation and, no more' (Hansard, 30th January 1996, vol 568, no 34, col 1416).

Therefore, the principal source of law on financial provision and property adjustment remains Part II of the Matrimonial Causes Act 1973, as amended, most recently by s. 166 of the Pensions Act 1995 and schs 2 and 8 to the 1996 Act. Schedule 8 makes a number of minor amendments, the most important of which have been noted.

Section 15 of the 1996 Act confirms that sch. 2 amends the 1973 Act and provides:

> (2) The main object of Schedule 2 is:
> (a) to provide that, in the case of divorce or separation, an order about financial provision may be made under that Act before a divorce or separation order is made; but
> (b) to retain (with minor changes) the position under that Act where marriages are annulled.

Throughout this chapter the provisions referred to also apply in nullity proceedings unless otherwise stated. Chapter 15, paragraph 9 specifically deals with financial provision and property adjustment orders in nullity proceedings.

At various stages of the passage of the Bill, the former Lord Chancellor acknowledged the need for a thorough review of this area of law. Arguably what has been done in the 1996 Act is no more than to modify the present arrangements so that they are consistent with the new regime for obtaining divorce and separation orders.

However, the Act contains three important developments:

(a)   it introduces interim lump sum orders (see paragraph 2.4 of this chapter);
(b)   it permits a lump sum order or property adjustment order to be made in variation proceedings so that a clean break may be achieved (see paragraph 6.5.2 of this chapter); and
(c)   it establishes the principle of pension splitting or pension sharing (see paragraphs 7.4 and 7.5 of this chapter).

2   Financial provision and property adjustment orders

2.1   The orders

Schedule 2 of the Family Law Act 1996 amends Part II of the Matrimonial Causes Act 1973. Section 21 of the 1973 Act is substituted by sch. 2, para. 2(1) of the Act and principally contains relevant definitions.

2.1.2   Financial provision order   For the purposes of the Act this is:

(a)   an order that a party must make in favour of another person such periodical payments, for such term, as may be specified (a 'periodical payments order');
(b)   an order that a party must, to the satisfaction of the court, secure in favour of another person such periodical payments, for such term, as may be specified (a 'secured periodical payments order');
(c)   an order that a party must make a payment in favour of another person of such lump sum or sums as may be specified (an 'order for the payment of a lump sum').

(1973 Act, s. 21(1).)

2.1.3   Property adjustment order   By s. 21(2) of the 1973 Act this is defined as follows:

(a)   an order that a party must transfer such of his or her property as may be specified in favour of the other party or a child of the family;
(b)   an order that a settlement of such property of a party as may be specified must be made, to the satisfaction of the court, for the benefit of the other party and of the children of the family, or either or any of them;
(c)   an order varying, for the benefit of the parties and of the children of the family, or either or any of them, any marriage settlement;
(d)   an order extinguishing or reducing the interest of either of the parties under any marriage settlement.

2.1.3   Property   The term 'property' relates to any property to which the party is entitled either in possession or in reversion (1973 Act, s. 21(4)) and presumably continues to include real and personal property.

2.1.4   Marriage settlement   This means an ante-nuptial or post-nuptial settlement made in respect of the parties (including one made by will or codicil).

It is important to note the following:

(a)   the reference in s. 21(1) of the 1973 Act to 'another person' means in effect either the other party to the marriage or, if the order is to be made in favour of a child of the family, the child in question or such person as may be specified, for the benefit of the child: s. 21(3);

(b)   where a property adjustment order involves the settlement of property as in s. 21(2)(b), the court preserves a degree of scrutiny in the requirement that such a settlement must be to the satisfaction of the court;

(c)   the court has power to make orders requiring the settlement of property or varying, extinguishing or reducing an interest in a marriage settlement even though there are no children of the family: s. 21(5).

2.2   Timing of the orders

Schedule 2, para. 3 of the Act introduces a new section, s. 22A, to be inserted before s. 23 of the 1973 Act.

Section 22A(1) of the 1973 Act provides:

(1)   On an application made under this section, the court may at the appropriate time make one or more financial provision orders in favour of —
   (a)   a party to the marriage to which the application relates; or
   (b)   any of the children of the family.

'At the appropriate time' is defined in s. 22A(2) of the 1973 Act 'as any time' —

(a)   after a statement of marital breakdown has been received by the court and before any application for a divorce order or for a separation order is made to the court by reference to that statement;

(b)   when an application for a divorce order or separation order has been made under s. 3 of the 1996 Act and has not been withdrawn;

(c)   when an application for a divorce order has been made under s. 4 of the 1996 Act and has not been withdrawn;

(d)   after a divorce order has been made;

(e)   when a separation order is in force.

2.3   Limits on the powers of the court

Whilst the court is able to make (a) a combined order against the parties on one occasion, (b) separate orders on different occasions, (c) different orders in favour of different children and (d) different orders from time to time in favour of the same child, it may not make more than one periodical payments order or more than one lump sum order in favour of the same party whether in the course of the proceedings or by reference to a divorce or separation order: 1973 Act, s. 22A(3).

2.4   Interim orders

Section 22A(4) of the 1973 Act provides:

If it would not otherwise be in a position to make a financial provision order in favour of a party or child of the family, the court may make an interim periodical payments order, an interim order for the payment of a lump sum or a series of such orders, in favour of that party or child.

In its 1990 Report (Law Com No 192), the Law Commission recommended that the court continue to have power to make an interim periodical payments order. Although the Law Commission had proposed that a final order for periodical payments might be made during the period for reflection and consideration, thus making irrelevant maintenance pending suit, the need for an interim order arises when the court is not in a position to make the final order (Law Com No 192, para. 6.1, p. 49). The Act therefore repeals s. 22 of the Matrimonial Causes Act 1973 which permitted the court to make orders for maintenance pending suit. Where a final periodical payments order cannot be made at an early stage, the court will instead make an interim order.

However, neither that Report, nor the White Paper 'Looking to the Future: Mediation and the Ground for Divorce' recommended that the court should have power to make interim lump sum orders.

Nevertheless, at the Committee stage of the Bill in the House of Lords, Lord Meston tabled an amendment to enable the court to make an interim lump sum order at an interlocutory stage, recognising that if litigation or negotiations became protracted, parties may need more than an interim periodical payments order (Hansard, 30th January 1996, vol 568, no 34, col 1416).

At that stage, the former Lord Chancellor agreed to consider the proposed amendment and to seek advice from his Ancillary Relief Advisory Group (Hansard, 30th January 1996, vol 568, no 34, col 1419).

At the Report stage the former Lord Chancellor indicated that he accepted the need for interim lump sum orders and the provision to give effect to this was incorporated in the Bill (Hansard, 4th March 1996, vol 570, no 54, col 129).

This is an important development. Although s. 22A of the 1973 Act does not indicate the purpose to which interim lump sums may be put, Lord Meston indicated some of the needs which might be met by an interim lump sum order, namely, capital to fund lawyers or expert witnesses, to purchase a house, put down a deposit or to fund unexpected needs. He also acknowledged that it would be necessary to exercise the power with caution in case it distorted the ability of the court to deal fairly with matters at the final disposal of the case (Hansard, 30th January 1996, vol 568, no 34, col 1416).

These concerns are reflected in the wording of s. 25(5) of the 1973 Act (introduced by sch. 8, para. 9(6)) which sets out the matters to be taken into account by the court in deciding whether to make an interim order of any type (see paragraph 3 of this chapter).

2.5 Lump sum orders

There are some provisions in s. 22A of the 1973 Act which apply specifically to lump sum orders. First, the court may provide for the payment of the lump sum by instalments and require the payment of the instalments to be secured to the satisfaction of the court: s. 22A(5)(a) and (b).

Secondly, where the court orders the payment of the lump sum (not the interim lump sum) to be by instalments or directs that payment of the lump sum or part of it be deferred, the court may on or *at any time* after the making of the order make an order for the amount deferred, or the instalments, to carry interest. Not surprisingly, this is known as 'the order for interest' and the court may require the payment of interest from the date of the lump sum order until the date when payment is made: s. 22A(7) and (8).

Speaking on this provision at the Report Stage, the former Lord Chancellor indicated that it was important that the court should have complete discretion as to what rate of interest should be payable. The individual circumstances of the case would dictate whether a penal rate of interest is required (Hansard, 4th March 1996, vol 570, no 54, col 130).

2.6   Property adjustment orders

Schedule 2, para. 5 of the Act inserts a new 23A into the 1973 Act. This section deals with some specific matters relating to property adjustment orders (see paragraph 2.1.3 above) in divorce or separation proceedings.

Section 23A(1) of the 1973 Act provides that 'at the appropriate time' (see paragraph 2.2 above) the court may make one or more property adjustment orders.

However, if the court makes more than one property adjustment order in favour of the same party, whether in the course of proceedings or by reference to a divorce or separation order, each order must fall within a different paragraph of s. 21(2): s. 23A(2).

So that there may be a sense of finality about the proceedings for a property adjustment order, the court is required, so far as is practicable, to make on one occasion all such provision as can be made by way of a property adjustment order as it thinks fit: s. 23A(3).

3   Factors to be considered in dealing with applications for financial provision and property adjustment orders

3.1   Introduction

The court continues to have a very wide discretion as to the nature and terms of the orders to be made on an application for financial provision.

Section 25 of the Matrimonial Causes Act 1973 directs the court to take account of all the circumstances of the case. In addition, it requires the court to take account of a number of specific matters when considering how to exercise its powers for the benefit of a party to the marriage, a child of the family or a child of the family who is not the natural child of the party against whom the order is to be made: s. 25(2), (3) and (4).

The well-known provisions of s. 25 remain essentially intact despite attempts by Baroness Young at both the Report Stage and at Third Reading on 11th March 1996 to replace the section with provisions based on Scottish law, clarifying the division of the assets. The Lord Chancellor's response was that such provisions were inappropriate in a Bill of this kind but he acknowledged the need for a thorough review of this area of law.

Since then the Ancillary Relief Advisory Group chaired by the Rt Hon. Lord Justice Thorpe has considered the issue. It concluded that the introduction of a statutory presumption of equal division of assets was inappropriate and that the current criteria for dividing assets should be codified. In September 1998 the Lord Chancellor's Department responded by announcing that it was no longer considering a presumption of equal division of assets in divorce.

3.2 The general duty

This is set out in s. 25(1) as follows:

It shall be the duty of the court in deciding whether to exercise its powers under any of sections 22A to 24A above and, if so, in what manner, to have regard to all the circumstances of the case, first consideration being given to the welfare while a minor of any child of the family who has not attained the age of eighteen

(as amended by the 1996 Act, sch. 8, para. 9(2)).

3.3 Specific matters to consider on an application for provision for a spouse

These are set out in s. 25(2) of the 1973 Act (as amended by the 1996 Act, sch. 8, para. 9(3)) as follows:

(2)   As regards the exercise of the powers of the court under section 22A or 23 above to make a financial provision order in favour of a party to a marriage or the exercise of its powers under section 23A, 24 or 24A above ... the court shall in particular have regard to the following matters:
(a)   the income, earning capacity, property and other financial resources which each of the parties to the marriage has or is likely to have in the foreseeable future, including in the case of earning capacity any increase to that capacity which it would in the opinion of the court be reasonable to expect a party to the marriage to take steps to acquire;
(b)   the financial needs, obligations and responsibilities which each of the parties to the marriage has or is likely to have in the foreseeable future;
(c)   the standard of living enjoyed by the family before the breakdown of the marriage;
(d)   the age of each party to the marriage and the duration of the marriage;
(e)   any physical or mental disability of either of the parties to the marriage;
(f)   the contributions which each of the parties has made or is likely in the foreseeable future to make to the welfare of the family including any contribution by looking after the home or caring for the family;
(g)   the conduct of each of the parties whatever the nature of the conduct and whether it occurred during the marriage or after the separation of the parties or (as the case may be) dissolution or annulment of the marriage if that conduct is such that it would in the opinion of the court be inequitable to disregard it;
(h)   the value to each of the parties to the marriage of any benefit which, by reason of the dissolution or annulment of the marriage, that party will lose the chance of acquiring.

Section 25B, inserted into the 1973 Act by s. 166 of the Pensions Act 1996, which come into force on 1st August 1996, provides as follows:

> (1) the matters to which the court is required to have regard under section 25(2) above include —
> (a) in the case of paragraph (a), any benefits under a pension scheme which a party to the marriage has or is likely to have; and
> (b) in the case of paragraph (h), any benefits under a pension scheme which, by reason of dissolution or annulment of the marriage, a party to the marriage will lose the chance of acquiring, and accordingly, in relation to benefits under a pension scheme, s. 25(2)(a) above shall have effect as if 'in the foreseeable future' were omitted.

See paragraph 7 of this chapter for a full discussion of division of pension assets.

The amended provisions are significant because:

(a) they refer to the forms of financial provision, now available (see paragraph 2 above) following amendments to the 1973 Act; and

(b) they arguably give the issue of conduct, always a vexed question, greater prominence by the emphasis on '*whatever* the nature of the conduct' although the court retains a discretion to determine the extent to which such conduct is taken into account and the effect, if any, on the outcome of the application.

The issue of the relevance of conduct throughout the divorce process but particularly in relation to financial and property matters was raised on numerous occasions during the passage of the Bill.

Initially, the former Lord Chancellor expressed satisfaction with the present arrangements. He had sought advice from his Ancillary Relief Group and stated 'The Group considered that the current provision worked well — it was reviewed in 1984, which led to the current provision and there was no call for change. I accept that advice. Ancillary relief proceedings are not the appropriate means of identifying in detail the cause of marital breakdown. I am satisfied that it is right that conduct should be taken into account to the extent that it is necessary to reach a proper distribution of the property between the parties and that the present test on which this is done is the appropriate one' (Hansard, 4th March 1996, vol 570, no 54, col 131).

Nevertheless, concern continued to be expressed that courts were reluctant to take into account even the most serious forms of conduct (for example, assisting a husband in his suicide attempt with a view to gaining as many of his assets as possible: *Kyte* v *Kyte* [1987] 3 All ER 1041).

In response, the Bill was subsequently amended, Mr Jonathan Evans explaining the position of the government:

> ... there is a perception that conduct is not, in practice, taken into account by the courts. Anecdotal evidence suggests that if conduct it taken into account, only conduct of a financial nature is considered. I said on Second Reading that I would arrange for those issues to be examined and I have studied a number of cases which relate to the role of conduct. Some of the perceptions about conduct not being taken into account are not substantiated by case law ... The Lord Chancellor's Ancillary

Relief Advisory Group believes that conduct is fully considered; it did not think that the role of conduct needed reform.

Nevertheless, Mr Evans tabled amendment ... 'to emphasise that conduct of the parties of whatever nature, should it be inequitable for the court to disregard it, has to be taken into account and that it is not only conduct in the course of ancillary relief proceedings that is to be considered.' (Standing Committee E, 16th May 1996, col 370.)

It remains to be seen of course how this shift in emphasis will affect the outcome of applications for financial provision. The former Lord Chancellor suggested that there was no change in the status quo. In dealing with Commons Amendments on 27th June 1996, he stated that 'The role of conduct in ancillary relief proceedings has not changed and there is therefore no question, as has been suggested in some quarters, of conduct being introduced through the back door' (Weekly Hansard, 27th June 1996, no 1672, col 1113).

3.4   Specific matters to consider on an application for financial provision for a child

Section 25(3) of the 1973 Act (as amended by sch. 8, para. 9(4)) directs the court to have regard in particular to the following matters in these circumstances:

(a)   the financial needs of the child;

(b)   the income earning capacity (if any), property and other financial resources of the child;

(c)   any physical or mental disability of the child;

(d)   the manner in which he was being and in which the parties to the marriage expected him to be educated or trained;

(e)   the considerations mentioned in relation to the parties to the marriage in s. 25(2)(a)–(c) and (e).

Furthermore, where the application relates to a child of the family who is not the child of the party against whom the order is sought, the court must also have regard under s. 25(4) of the 1973 Act:

(a)   to whether the party assumed any responsibility for the child's maintenance and, if so, to the extent to which, and the basis upon which, that party assumed such responsibility and to the length of time for which that party discharged such responsibility;

(b)   to whether in assuming and discharging such responsibility that party did so knowing that the child was not his or her own;

(c)   to the liability of any other person to maintain the child.

3.5   Matters to be considered: interim orders

Section 25(5) of the 1973 Act, as inserted by sch. 8, para. 9(6) of the Act, emphasises that when the court is dealing with an application for an interim order the court is not required to carry out its duty to consider the matters in s. 25 in such a way that it would cause an inappropriate delay having regard:

(a) to any immediate need for an interim order;

(b) to the matters in relation to which it is practicable for the court to inquire before making an interim order; and

(c) to the ability of the court to have regard to any matter and to make appropriate adjustments when subsequently making a financial provision order which is not interim.

3.6 'Clean break' approach

By virtue of the Matrimonial Family Proceedings Act 1984, a new s. 25A was added to the 1973 Act.

Section 25A(1) (as amended by 1996 Act, sch. 8, para. 10(2) and (3)) provides:—

> If the court decides to exercise any of its powers under any of sections 22A to 24A above in favour of a party to a marriage (other than its power to make an interim periodical payments order or an interim order for the payment of a lump sum), it shall be the duty of the court to consider whether it would be appropriate so to exercise those powers that the financial obligations of each party towards the other will be terminated as soon after the grant of the divorce order or decree of nullity as the court considers just and reasonable.

The aim of the provision is to achieve wherever possible a settlement of the parties' claims on a 'once and for all basis' thus enabling the parties to put the past behind them and begin a new life, not overshadowed by the relationship that has broken down.

Section 25A(2) deals with the situation where the court makes a periodical payments order in favour of one of the parties. It requires the court to consider whether the order should be for a fixed period to terminate after the recipient should have had sufficient time to adjust without undue hardship to the ending of the financial provision.

The provisions set out below apply where the court would have power to make a financial provision order in favour of a party to a marriage (s. 25A(3)) but considers that it would be inappropriate to do so.

Section 25A(3), as substituted by sch. 8, para. 10(4) of the 1996 Act, permits the court to direct that one party may not at any time apply to the court for the making of any periodical payments or secured periodical payments order against the other party.

Where such a direction is given by the court in exercising its powers under s. 22A before the making of a divorce order, the court is required to provide for the direction not to take effect until the divorce order is made: s. 25A(3A)(a) and (b), inserted by sch. 8, para. 10(4).

Furthermore, if an application has already been made to the court, the court may dismiss the application: s. 25A(3). The court will give the direction or dismiss the application where it considers that no continuing obligation should be imposed on the other party to the marriage: s. 25A(3)(b).

Section 25A(3) of the 1973 Act therefore enables the court to impose a clean break arrangement on the parties *of its own motion* in the absence of an application for financial provision.

4 Relationship between making orders for financial provision and their coming into effect

4.1 Timing of orders

As has already been noted in paragraph 2 of this chapter, orders for financial provision and/or property adjustment may be made 'at the appropriate time' (as defined in s. 22A(2)).

In effect, the earliest date on which an order may be made is after the statement of marital breakdown has been received by the court, but it is equally possible for an order to be made after a divorce order or whilst a separation order is in force: s. 22A(2) (but see paragraph 4.4 below).

However, because of the provisions of s. 9 of the Family Law Act 1996 as to the parties' arrangements for the future (see Chapter 10), it is likely that the order will have been made before the divorce or separation order is made.

The requirement to put in place financial arrangements during the period for reflection and consideration was criticised during the passage of the Bill on the grounds that the parties would inevitably be engaged in two conflicting activities at the same time.

Speaking at the Committee stage, Edward Leigh quoted from correspondence he had received from Peter Duckworth and Ruth Deech respectively as follows:

Indeed what is proposed is a radical alteration from the present law, whereby you cannot obtain substantive orders for ancillary relief before decree nisi to a situation where all the relevant financial orders not only can but must be made before the divorce even if in general terms they will not take effect until afterwards. Translated into practical terms, it is my view that these proposals will eliminate any realistic prospect of reconciliation within the 12-month period, for the simple reason that parties will be so preoccupied with sorting out their children and property they will have no time to think. (Hansard, 24th April 1996, vol 276, no 1722, col 504)

As ancillary relief is already a vengeful process, the pressure to settle in twelve months will make it worse in every respect. (Hansard, 24th April 1996, vol 276, no 1722, col 505)

Nevertheless, the need in the majority of cases for financial arrangements to be made *before* the divorce or separation order is made has been a fundamental tenet of the legislation confirmed by the former Lord Chancellor at the Second Reading (Hansard, 30th November 1995, vol 567, col 703) as follows:

A very important requirement in the Bill is the requirement that parties decide all arrangements relating to their children, finance and home before a separation or divorce order can be made. This is an important and significant change from the Law Commission's recommendation. In making this change the Government have been influenced by those who responded to their consultation paper who were of the view that parties who marry should discharge their obligations undertaken when they contracted their earlier marriage, and also their responsibilities which they undertook when they became parents before they become free to remarry. The

Bill provides for certain narrow exceptions to the requirement that all arrangements should be decided before divorce in order to protect vulnerable parties, such as those who are sick, disabled or being prevented from making arrangements by vindictive and obstructive spouses, and also to protect the children of such parties.

4.2 Coming into effect of orders

Sections 22B(1) and 23B(1) of the Matrimonial Causes Act 1973, as inserted by sch. 2, paras 3 and 5 of the 1996 Act, provide that with the exception of an interim order, no financial provision order or property adjustment order may be made so as to take effect before the making of a divorce or separation order.

4.3 Coming into effect — exceptions to the rule

The court has power to direct that the order is to take effect *before* the divorce or separation order if it is satisfied (a) that the circumstances of the case are exceptional and (b) that it would be just and reasonable for the order to be so made: 1973 Act, s. 22B(1)(a) and (b) and s. 23B(1)(a) and (b).

In explaining the need for the above provision, the former Lord Chancellor indicated that his Ancillary Relief Advisory Group had identified situations where it would be just and reasonable for the order to take effect at an earlier date. These included where the husband and wife are living in the same house with children, there are insufficient funds to enable one spouse to seek alternative accommodation and the application for financial provision is contested (Hansard, 4th March 1996, vol 570, no 54, col 127).

The requirement to show that the circumstances are 'exceptional' was introduced by the former Lord Chancellor at Third Reading to answer concerns that if the order came into effect too soon it would destroy any prospect of reconciliation (Hansard, 11th March 1996, vol 570, no 54, col 716).

In practice, however, it is likely that there will be instances of parties who meet the criteria laid down by the Ancillary Relief Advisory Group and whose needs during the period for reflection and consideration may not be met by a combination of interim orders and orders under Part IV of the Act.

4.4 Restrictions on orders

Sections 22B(2) and (3) and 23B(2) and (3) of the 1973 Act set out circumstances where an order for financial provision (*other than an interim order*) or property adjustment may not be made. These are as follows:

(a)   while the period for reflection and consideration is interrupted under s. 7(8) of the 1996 Act (that is, where the parties 'stop the clock' to attempt a reconciliation — see Chapter 8, paragraph 3); or

(b)   where a statement of marital breakdown has been received by the court but the provisions of s. 5(3) or s. 7(9) of the 1996 Act apply (i.e., the parties have jointly given notice to withdraw the statement or a period of 1 year has passed since the end of the period for reflection and consideration (s. 5(3)) or the period for reflection and consideration is interrupted by a continuous period of more than 18 months during which the parties have 'stopped the clock' (s. 7(9)).

Furthermore, by virtue of ss. 22B(4) and 23B(4) of the 1973 Act no financial provision or property adjustment order may be made after a divorce order has been made or while a separation order is in force except:

(a)   in response to an application made *before* the divorce order or separation order was made; or

(b)   on a subsequent application with leave of the court.

5   Duration of orders

5.1   Duration of orders in favour of a party to a marriage

Subject to s. 25A(2) and s. 31(7) of the 1973 Act (see paragraphs 3 and 6 of this chapter) an order for periodical payments or secured periodical payments made in favour of a party to the marriage may last for whatever period the court thinks fit with the following limitations:

5.1.1   Commencement of the term   Section 28(1)(a) of the 1973 Act (as substituted by the 1996 Act, sch. 2, para. 7(1)) provides:

a term specified in the order which is to begin before the making of the order shall begin no earlier:

(i)   where the order is made by virtue of section 22A(2)(a) or (b) above, unless sub-paragraph (ii) below applies, than the beginning of the day on which the statement of marital breakdown in question was received by the court;

(ii)   where the order is made by virtue of section 22A(2)(b) above and the application for the divorce order was made following cancellation of an order preventing divorce under section 10 of the 1996 Act, than the date of the making of that application;

(iii)   where the order is made by virtue of section 22A(2)(c) above, than the date of the making of the application for the divorce order; or

(iv)   in any other case, than the date of the making of the application of which the order is made

This allows the court, if it thinks fit, to back-date its order for unsecured or secured periodical payments. What that date will be depends upon the circumstances in which the order is made.

The general principle, confirmed in s. 28(1)(a)(iv), is that the earliest date to which an order may be back-dated is the date of the making of the application for the order in question.

5.1.2   End of the term   Section 28(1)(b) (as substituted by the 1996 Act, sch. 2, para. 7(1)) provides:

a term specified in a periodical payments order or secured periodical payments order shall be so defined as not to extend beyond:

(i)   in the case of a periodical payments order, the death of the party by whom the payments are to be made; or (ii)　in either case, the death of the party in whose favour the order was made or the remarriage of that party following the making of a divorce order or decree of nullity;

At the Report stage it was proposed that a periodical payments order should automatically come to an end when the party in whose favour it had been made began to cohabit with another person as if they were married. The former Lord Chancellor rejected the proposal for two reasons:

(a)　a cohabitant has no legal duty to maintain the other party; and

(b)　there would be considerable evidential difficulties in determining whether such cohabitation was taking place (Hansard, 4th March 1996, vol 570, no 54, col 131).

Where the court makes an order under s. 22A or s. 23 of the 1973 Act which is of limited duration, it may direct that the party in whose favour the order is made shall not be entitled to apply under s. 31 for an extension to the term of the order (s. 28(1A), as amended by the 1996 Act, sch. 8, para. 14(1) and (2)). Where such a direction is incorporated into an order made at any time before the making of a divorce order, it shall provide for the direction not to take effect until a divorce order is made: s. 28(1B), inserted by the 1996 Act, sch. 8, para. 14(3).

5.2　Duration of orders in favour of a child of the family

Where the court retains jurisdiction to make a periodical payments order or secured periodical payments order in favour of a child of the family, s. 29 of the 1973 Act governs the position on duration of such orders. In essence, an order normally comes to an end once the child attains his 17th birthday unless the child is still receiving an education or training at that age, in which case the order may remain in force until the child's 18th birthday: s. 29(2)(a) and (b).

Although it is exceptional, the order may continue after the child's 18th birthday if he is receiving an education or training or there are special circumstances: s. 29(3).

Schedule 2, para. 7(2) of the 1996 Act inserts subs. (1A) into s. 29 of the 1973 Act which confirms that a periodical payments order of either type for the benefit of a child shall be for such term as the court thinks fit. Section 29(1B), also inserted, deals with the back-dating of orders. The provisions are identical to those relating to a party to a marriage (see paragraph 5.1 above).

Whilst the remarriage of either party will not affect orders in favour of a child, the death of the paying party will bring the periodical payments order to an end unless it is secured: s. 29(4).

6　Variation of orders: Matrimonial Causes Act 1973, s. 31

6.1　Introduction

The law on variation of orders is set out in s. 31 of the 1973 Act.

The 1996 Act makes two major amendments to the section (see paragraphs 6.5.2 and 6.7 below) together with a number of consequential amendments set out in sch. 8

which deal in particular with the variation of an order made during the period for reflection and consideration.

6.2   Scope of s. 31 — orders that may be varied

By virtue of s. 31(2) of the 1973 Act, the following orders may be varied:

(a)   any interim order for maintenance;

(b)   any periodical payments order (unless the order was for a fixed term and a direction has been made prohibiting an application to the court for an extension of the term) (see paragraph 5 above);

(c)   any secured periodical payments order;

(d)   an order for the payment of a lump sum in a case in which the payment is to be by instalments

(e)   any deferred order made by virtue of s. 21(1)(c) (lump sums) which includes provision made by virtue of —

(i)   s. 25B(4), or

(ii)   s. 25C

(provision in respect of pension rights);

(f)   any other order for the payment of a lump sum, if it is made at a time when no divorce order has been made, and no separation order is in force, in relation to the marriage;

(g)   any order under s. 23A of a kind referred to in s. 21(b)(c) or (d) (i.e., a settlement of property order or order varying a marriage settlement) which is made on or after the making of a separtion order;

(h)   any order under s. 23A which is made at a time when no divorce order has been made and no separation order is in force, in relation to the marriage;

(i)   any order made under s. 24A(1) for the sale of property (as amended by the 1996 Act, sch. 8, para. 16(2)).

6.3   Orders that may not be varied

There is no power to vary the amount of a lump sum order once a divorce order has been made or separation order is in force. The most that the court may do is to adjust the arrangements for paying the lump sum if it is to be paid by instalments.

There is no power to vary a transfer of property order under s. 21(2)(a) of the 1973 Act nor any power to vary an order for settlement of property or modify the terms of a marriage settlement when such orders are made on or after the making of a divorce order.

These provisions therefore remain unchanged despite the recommendations of the Law Commission in its 1990 Report that 'the court should have power to vary property settlement orders, including variation of marriage settlement orders, which were made in contemplation of, at, or after the making of a separation or divorce order, or any time thereafter' (Law Com No 192, para. 6.4, p. 49). The Law Commission also recognised the need for the parties to know where they stand and therefore went on to recommend that the power to vary should only arise when the original order contains a clause permitting a later application to vary: (Law Com No 192, para. 6.5, p. 50).

The former Lord Chancellor resisted attempts to implement the above recommendations or to give courts a general power to vary property adjustment orders, confirming that this matter would be included in the major review of this area of law. He acknowledged that at present the courts have to use their limited powers to set aside orders as in *Barder* v *Barder* [1988] AC 20 (Hansard, 4th March 1996, vol 570, no 54, col 130).

6.4 Limits on power to vary an order made during the period for reflection and consideration

Section 31(4A) and (4B) of the 1973 Act (as inserted by the 1996 Act, sch. 8, para. 16(4)) governs the situation where an application is made to vary an order for payment of a lump sum or an order under s. 23A made at a time when no divorce order has been made and no separation order is in force.

6.4.1 Timing of the application to vary   The power to vary the order may be exercised (a) only on an application made before the order has taken effect and (b) only if, at the time when the application is made, no divorce or separation order has been made since the original order was granted.

Once the application to vary is made to the court the original order will not take effect until the application has been dealt with: s. 31(4A)(b).

6.4.2 Scope of the court's powers   Whilst the court may vary the terms of the order, it is not permitted to vary a financial provision order made under s. 22A of the 1973 Act, other than an interim order, or a property adjustment order made under s. 23A of the 1973 Act in such a way that the order then takes effect before the making of the divorce or separation order unless the court is satisfied that the circumstances of the case are exceptional and that it would be just and reasonable for the variation to be so made: s. 31(4B) (see paragraph 4.3 of this chapter).

6.5 What can the court do on a variation application?

6.5.1 General position   On a variation application the court has power to vary or discharge the order or suspend the provisions temporarily or revive any provision so suspended: 1973 Act, s. 31(1). The most common forms of variation application are by the recipient of maintenance seeking to have the order increased or by the payer seeking to have the order reduced.

Arrears of maintenance may be remitted by virtue of s. 31(2A).

As a general rule the court has no power to make a property adjustment order on an application for variation of either type of periodical payments order. Further, no lump sum can be ordered on an application for variation of either type of periodical payments order in favour of a spouse, although a lump sum order can be made in an application relating to provision for a child: s. 31(5).

6.5.2 Powers of the court where a 'clean break' order is made on a variation application   A 'clean break' order may arise where either (a) the court discharges the existing order under s. 31(1) of the 1973 Act; or (b) in fulfilling the requirement to consider whether the order should in future be of limited duration, the court directs that the order be made or secured only for such further period as will be sufficient to enable the recipient of the provision to adjust without undue hardship to the termination of the payments: s. 31(7).

In either of the above cases, the court now has power under s. 31(7B) of the 1973 Act (as inserted by the 1996 Act, sch. 8, para. 16(7)) to make supplemental provision consisting of any of:

(a) an order for the payment of a lump sum in favour of a party to the marriage;

(b) one or more property adjustment orders in favour of a party to the marriage;

(c) a direction that the party in whose favour the original order discharged or varied was made is not entitled to make any further application for —

(i) a periodical payments or secured periodical payments order, or

(ii) an extension of the period to which the original order is limited by any variation made by the court.

Thus, the court may in appropriate circumstances, make a 'compensating' property adjustment order or lump sum order where it imposes a clean break arrangement of some kind. However, if the court makes more than one property adjustment order in favour of the same party, each order must be different from the one previously made: s. 31(7E).

These provisions implement recommendations made by the Law Commission in its 1990 Report (Law Com No 192, para. 6.9 and 6.10, pp. 50 and 51) and will avoid 'difficulties such as those manifested in *S* v *S* ([1987] 1 FLR 71) where a court was unable directly to order the husband to pay a sufficient lump sum to compensate the wife for loss of future periodical payments ... such an arrangement can be brought about by the agreement between the parties, but if the payer will not agree the court cannot order it' (Law Com No 192, para. 6.9, p. 50).

Further, s. 31(7B) enables the court to ensure that its order is 'watertight' by directing that the recipient of maintenance will not be entitled to make any further application for an order or extension of the term.

Where a lump sum order is made in these circumstances, the court may order payment by instalments and the instalments may be secured: s. 31(7C).

Payment of the lump sum may be deferred and where there is a delay in payment or payment by instalments the court may, on or at any time after making the order require interest to be paid: s. 31(7D).

6.6   Factors to be taken into account in variation proceedings

In exercising its powers to vary under s. 31 of the 1973 Act, the court is directed by s. 31(7) to have regard to all the circumstances of the case, first consideration being given to the welfare whilst a minor of any child of the family under 18. The circumstances include any change in any of the matters to which the court was required to have regard when making the original order.

6.7   Powers of the court on a variation application where the divorce does not proceed

Schedule 2, para. 8 of the 1996 Act introduces a new s. 31A into the 1973 Act to deal with the situation where parties to a marriage become reconciled following the making of certain types of order for financial provision but before the divorce order is made or, for other reasons, the divorce does not proceed.

Under s. 31A of the 1973 Act, on the *joint* application of the parties, the court may vary or discharge the following orders:

(a)   an order for the payment of a lump sum under s. 22A of the 1973 Act in favour of a party;

(b)   a lump sum order in favour of a child of the family but where the payment has not yet been made; or

(c)   a property adjustment order under s. 23A of the 1973 Act.

Where the parties have become reconciled (as opposed to the case where the divorce simply does not proceed), the court may make a number of additional orders. It may order the repayment of an amount equal to the whole or any part of the lump sum: s. 31A(2). Similarly, if a property adjustment order has been made and has already taken effect (this will be very rare in practice), the court may order the person to whom the property was transferred to transfer the whole or part of that property (or property appearing to the court to represent that property) in favour of a party to the marriage or a child of the family. Likewise, the court may vary any settlement to which the original order related: s. 31A(3)(a) and (b).

If the court varies or discharges the order in these circumstances, it may make such supplemental provision (including a further property adjustment order or order for the payment of a lump sum) as it thinks appropriate: s. 31A(4).

The court is not permitted to make an order under s. 31(3) or (4) unless it appears to the court that the order will not prejudice the interests of:

(a)   any child of the family; or

(b)   any person who has acquired any right or interest in the property and is not a party to the marriage or child of the family: s. 31A(7).

No specific guidance is offered to the courts as to how these powers should be exercised except that, as indicated above, the parties must have become reconciled. It does not appear that the reconciliation must have lasted for a prescribed period of time.

These provisions are essential given the need to balance the requirement to make financial arrangements before the divorce against the encouragement of the parties to attempt a reconciliation throughout the period for reflection and consideration.

The section provides a mechanism for dealing with the future of orders which may have been made prematurely and implements recommendations made by the Law Commission (Law Com No 192, para. 5.54).

7   Division of pension assets

7.1   Prior to the Pensions Act 1995

After the family home, pension rights are likely to be the most valuable asset which the parties to a marriage have. Nevertheless, under the original provisions of the Matrimonial Causes Act 1973, the court had no specific power to split or 'earmark' pensions in proceedings for orders for ancillary relief nor did the court have power to order one party to the marriage to purchase a pension for the benefit of the other.

Despite this, the court was required to take account, in looking at the factors listed in s. 25(2) of the value of any benefits (for example, a pension) which by reason of dissolution or annulment of the marriage that party will lose the chance of acquiring: 1973 Act, s. 25(2)(h).

If the court is prepared to recognise this loss (in particular in relation to the middle-aged, non-working applicant) it may require the other party to pay a compensating lump sum or to transfer the matrimonial home outright to the vulnerable party.

It has been recognised that on occasions the property transferred or purchased with the lump sum provided will contain an in-built pension fund. In *B* v *B* [1989] 1 FLR 119, Anthony Lincoln J awarded the wife £225,000 for a home and held that further pension protection was unnecessary on the grounds that in 15 years' time she would no longer need a four-bedroomed house and could make provision for herself out of the proceeds of sale.

Furthermore, the court may make a deferred periodical payments or lump sum order, the order becoming effective on the date on which the pension is paid. In all of the above instances, the pension rights remain untouched and are retained by the scheme member.

If the divorce petition was based on 5 years' separation, the respondent could defend the divorce on the ground that he or she would suffer grave financial or other hardship if decree were to be granted and it would in all the circumstances be wrong to dissolve the marriage: s. 5(1) of the 1973 Act. Even where a prima facie case of grave financial hardship was established, a decree of divorce would be granted if the petitioner could make specific arrangements to alleviate the hardship: *Le Marchant* v *Le Marchant* [1977] 3 All ER 610 and *K* v *K* (*Financial Relief: Widow's Pension*) [1997] 1 FLR 35.

An interesting development, albeit of limited scope, in this area was the case of *Brooks* v *Brooks* [1995] 3 WLR 141. The House of Lords confirmed that a pension scheme which enabled a husband to nominate benefits in favour of his wife constituted a 'post-nuptial settlement' which was capable of being varied under s. 24(1)(c) of the 1973 Act to give the former wife an interest in the pension fund.

7.2   Pensions Act 1995

Section 166 of the Pensions Act 1995 inserts new sections, ss. 25B, 25C and 25D into the Matrimonial Causes Act 1973.

By s. 25B(1) the court is specifically required to have regard to (a) any benefits under a pension scheme which a party to the marriage has or is likely to have and (b) to any benefits under a pension scheme which, by reason of dissolution or annulment of the marriage, a party will lose the chance of acquiring. Thus the court's duty to give full consideration to pension rights is reinforced.

The amendments also remove the reference to 'foreseeable future' as far as benefits under a pension scheme are concerned. This will enable the court to take into account any pension benefits which a party to the marriage has accrued irrespective of the length of time before the pension becomes payable.

A pension scheme is defined in s. 25D(4) as meaning an occupational pension or personal pension scheme.

The new s. 25B(2)(a) and (b) requires the court to consider whether to make an order in respect of the pension benefits and, if so, the terms of the order.

If the court decides to exercise its powers, it may order that once any payment under the scheme becomes due to the party with pension rights (often described as 'the yielding party'), the trustees or managers of the scheme in question will be required to make a payment for the benefit of the other party (commonly referred to as 'the receiving party'): s. 25B(4).

Although the Pensions Act 1995 offers no guidance to the court as to the circumstances in which such an order may be made, nor as to the principles to be applied in quantifying the payment, s. 25B(5) does limit the amount to be paid to the receiving party by stating that it shall not exceed the amount of the payment which is due at that time to the yielding party.

Section 25B(7) provides that the yielding party may be ordered to commute the whole or any part of his pension if he has the right to do so.

In addition, s. 25C enables the court to order trustees or managers of a pension scheme who have power to determine to whom a lump sum should be paid when it becomes due, to exercise that power in favour of the receiving party: s. 25C(2)(a). Even where the trustees or managers have no discretion, an order in similar terms may be made: s. 25C(2)(c).

Finally, where the yielding party has power to nominate a beneficiary of a lump sum, the court may require that party to nominate the receiving party as the beneficiary: s. 25C(2)(b).

Again, and in line with other lump sum orders available, no specific guidance is given to the court as to the principles to be applied in apportioning the lump sum. However, speaking at the Second Reading of the Family Law Bill, Mr Roger Freeman, for the former government, confirmed that 'the courts will not be constrained to a 50:50 allocation: they will have the flexibility to order whatever allocation or none, as seems appropriate' (Hansard, 25th March 1996, vol 274, no 76, col 750).

The section also provides that once such an order is made, copies will be served on the yielding party, as the scheme member, and on the trustees or managers of the scheme. Once the scheme matures, the trustees or managers will have the responsibility of paying the income and/or lump sum to the receiving party. The administration costs of the process will be borne by the yielding and receiving parties: s. 25D(2)(d).

Section s. 25D deals with a number of administrative matters to be dealt with by regulations, including the question of transfer of pension benefits from one scheme to another and the need for the trustees or managers of the new scheme to be notified of an order made under this section in order to be bound by its terms.

For a recent case explaining the court's powers under these provisions, see *T* v *T* *(Financial Relief: Pensions)* [1998] 1 FLR 1072, where Singer, J., *inter alia*, rejected the arguments of counsel for the applicant wife to the effect that the court was required to compensate the wife for her actual or potential lost pension benefits. The judge refused to make an earmarking order in respect of the income or lump sum derived from the husband's pension but did earmark a portion of the death in service benefits available under the husband's pension scheme.

7.3   Coming into force of s. 166, Pensions Act 1995

The Pensions Act 1995 (Commencement) (No 5) Order 1996 (SI 1996 No 1675) provides for the coming into force of s. 166 of the Pensions Act 1995.

The provisions of s. 166 were brought into force on 1st August 1996 except as follows:

(a)   s. 25D(2)–(4) of the 1973 Act (empowering the Lord Chancellor to make regulations) came into force on 27th June 1996;

(b)   periodical payments made by a pension scheme to a receiving party may not be ordered so as to commence before 6th April 1997; and

(c)   ss. 25B and 25C of the 1973 Act (dealing with periodical payments and lump sums, respectively) do not apply to proceedings commenced by petition before 1st July 1996.

7.4   The pensions debate — 'earmarking' versus pension splitting (or 'pension sharing')

The provisions set out above enable a court to 'earmark' or attach a pension scheme so as to provide financial support in some form for the receiving party who has not remarried in the meantime, once the yielding party becomes entitled to the benefits of the pension scheme.

It is designed to meet the needs of the receiving party at a time when that party might otherwise have to resort to state benefits.

It is an important and, arguably, long overdue development but there is an influential body of opinion which takes the view that a court should have the power to order that pensions be split at the time of the divorce proceedings, thus enabling each party to make pension arrangements independently of the other. This was advocated by the Pensions Management Institute in its May 1993 Report 'Pensions and Divorce', summarised at [1993] Fam Law 380.

Two specific advantages are seen in pension splitting:

(a)   it is not affected by the premature death of the yielding party before the pension scheme becomes payable. This would bring the earmarking arrangement to an end.

(b)   it is more consistent with the clean break philosophy.

During the passage of the Family Law Bill, an amendment was tabled to introduce pension splitting arrangements.

At the Report stage in the House of Lords, Baroness Hollis of Heigham sought to establish the principle that courts and couples should have the option of splitting pensions on divorce.

She explained the need for this as follows:

Pensions are often the largest single asset in a marriage, especially if the couple have been married a long time. The pension usually belongs to the husband . . . The husband has earned the pension, but so has his wife in supporting him, bringing up their children, perhaps working in a part-time job and perhaps helping to care for their mutual parents. She, in middle age, faces divorce. If the husband and wife cannot share the pension, if it is ring-fenced and cannot be touched, how can you have a fair financial settlement at divorce? If there is not a fair financial settlement, then it is likely to be the loyal wife and mother who suffers as she faces an old age without a pension of her own and without a share of her husband's pension.

(Hansard, 29th February 1996, vol 569, no 52, col 1610.)

In supporting the amendment, Lord Meston stated 'In the Pensions Act (1995) we have earmarking which is very much half a loaf. It has serious consequences for the clean break principle in divorce. The great advantage of pension splitting is that it will facilitate the clean break which is especially important to avoid hostility and animosity in divorce cases' (Hansard, 29th February 1996, vol 569, no 52, col 1624).

The government resisted the introduction of pension splitting, Lord Mackay of Ardbrecknish identifying numerous problems associated with the introduction of such an arrangement which included the question of the status of the non-employed former spouse within the pension scheme, the complexity of splitting SERPS and Guaranteed Minimum Pensions and the tax advantages which would accrue to divorcing couples and might be resented by those who remained married (Hansard, 29th February 1996, vol 569, no 52, cols 1630, 1631 and 1632).

He concluded by stating 'This is an important and far-reaching issue. It deserves proper attention and proper legislation encompassing not just divorce law, but also pensions law and tax law and probably trust law, inheritance and intestacy law. That is why I propose to your Lordships a Green Paper with proper consultation' (Hansard, 29th February 1996, vol 569, no 52, col 1632).

The Green Paper was published in late July 1996 (see paragraph 7.7 below).

Despite the concerns of the government, the amendment was carried and was accepted, Mr Roger Freeman indicating the position of the government at the Second Reading as follows: 'The Government accept, however, that pension splitting is right in principle' (Hansard, vol 274, no 76, col 750). A new clause was introduced at the Remaining Stages of 17th June 1996 to deal with pension splitting and became s. 16 of the 1996 Act.

7.5 Pension splitting

Section 16 of the Family Law Act 1996 amends s. 25B and s. 25D of the Matrimonial Causes Act 1973.

The amendments establish the concept of pension splitting. The court is now required to consider, in particular, where the court determines to make such an order (in relation to the pension) whether the order should provide for the accrued rights of the party with pension rights to be divided between that party and the other party in such a way as to reduce the pension rights of the party with those rights and to create pension rights for the other party: s. 25B(2)(c), inserted by s. 16(2) of the 1996 Act. Such an order is to be known as 'a pensions adjustment order': s. 25B(8), inserted by s. 16(3) of the 1996 Act.

Careful reading of the above provision reveals that it establishes the principle of pension splitting, but *does not* give the courts the powers that are necessary to give effect to it. When asked what was the point in leaving in the Bill a declaration of no legal effect (Mr Tony Marlow (Hansard, 17th June 1996, vol 279, no 117, col 555)),

Mr Oliver Heald, the Parliamentary Under-Secretary of State for Social Security, explained 'the Government's proposal was for a Green Paper to examine all the issues in detail so that we would be able, after proper consultation, to put in place the regulations to give effect to the principle that is outlined ... The Government's approach was to accept the principle, to have the clause in the Bill but to go about the business of the consultations and preparations that are needed to make pension splitting a reality' (Hansard, 17th June 1996, vol 279, no 117, col 556).

The effect of s. 25B(8) (as inserted by s. 16(3) of the 1996 Act) is that if a pensions adjustment order is made, it shall be done in a prescribed manner with benefits payable on prescribed conditions except that the court shall *not* have the power:

(a)   to require the trustees or managers to provide benefits under their own scheme if they are able and willing to create the rights for the other party by making a transfer payment to another scheme and the trustees and managers of that other scheme are able and willing to accept such a payments and to create those rights; or

(b)   to require the trustees or managers of the scheme to make a transfer to another scheme —

(i)   if the scheme is an unfunded scheme (unless the trustees or managers are able and willing to make such a transfer payment); or

(ii)   in prescribed circumstances.

An unfunded scheme is one where there is no tangible fund and where the contributions of present employees are funding the pensions of existing pension recipients.

7.6   Arrangements for the future and division of pension assets

Chapter 10 described the arrangements for the future and their importance in obtaining a divorce or separation order.

It should be noted that s. 9(8) of the Family Law Act 1996 provides that if the parties' arrangements for the future include a division of pension assets, any declaration under s. 9(2) must be a statutory declaration.

7.7   The Green Paper

As promised, the government issued a Consultation Paper (Cm 3345) entitled 'The Treatment of Pensions on Divorce'. The Paper establishes a number of principles and then poses a series of questions for consideration.

The principle of pension splitting is basically established, but it is proposed that:

(a)   such an arrangement should only occur when a marriage is terminated (para. 3.3);

(b)   pension splitting should not apply retrospectively to divorce settlements already reached (para. 3.5);

(c)   pensions should not be treated differently from any other asset and it is not appropriate that only the pension accruing over the period of the marriage should be available for pension splitting (paras 3.6, 3.7 and 3.8);

(d)   pension splitting should not extend to pension assets which have not already accrued at the time of the divorce (para. 3.9);

(e)   courts should use their best endeavours to offset pension assets against other assets particularly when pension assets are relatively small (para. 3.22);

(f)   in the interests of the clean break philosophy, it should not be possible to vary a pension splitting order at any future date (para. 5.8); and

(g)   pension splitting should apply to all pension schemes except overseas arrangements and the basic state pension since on divorce a divorced person can already improve his or her basic retirement entitlement by substituting the former spouse's national insurance record for his or her own up to the date of termination of the marriage (paras 3.11 and 3.19).

The Green Paper makes proposals as to the method to be adopted for valuing pensions, recognising that a capital value must be placed on pension rights which have accrued to date (paras 4.1 and 4.2).

With private pensions, it is proposed to use the cash equivalent transfer value approach (CETV) since there is no practical alternative. For the state earnings-related pension (SERPS), the DSS will provide a notional capitalised valuation of rights built up to date for the purpose of the divorce proceedings (paras 4.4 and 4.19).

Pension splitting options are considered. The court should decide in principle whether the pension should be split. The trustees or managers of a private pension scheme would have the discretion to decide whether to offer scheme membership, external transfer or a choice of either to a former spouse (paras 5.3 and 5.5).

If the court has power to order the splitting of SERPS rights, the Paper recognises that these rights must be retained within the state scheme (para. 5.16).

The status of the former spouse in the pension scheme is discussed. After examining various options, the Paper concludes that it would be desirable for the former spouse to be in a new category of membership with rights including the right to information, to access to the internal disputes procedure and to the Pensions Ombudsman and to transfer out of the scheme (paras 6.10 and 6.11).

Consideration is also given to the question of whether it would be necessary to continue the earmarking or attachment arrangements if pension splitting was introduced. It is acknowledged that time will tell how much use is made of the arrangements — abolition would achieve simplicity but would give the courts less flexibility.

7.8   The White Paper

In February 1997 the government issued a White Paper (CM 3564) entitled 'Pension Rights on Divorce'. The Paper again proposed the introduction of pension splitting (now more commonly described as 'pension sharing'). Significant primary legislation will be required to achieve this.

The Department of Social Security issued a press release on 5th June 1997 announcing the intention to produce a draft Bill for consultation during the 1998 session. The draft legislation was duly published in June 1998 and comments were invited.

The main purpose of the Bill is to introduce the option of pension sharing on divorce or on the granting of a decree of nullity.

Pension sharing will not be compulsory and it is anticipated that loss of a pension may be compensated for from other assets or indeed by an earmarking arrangement, as presently available.

Pension sharing will not apply to the State Basic Pension.

It is anticipated that the provisions will not come into effect until April 2000 at the earliest because of the preparatory work necessary to ensure that these fundamental changes work effectively.

8 Relationship between financial provision orders and the Child Support Acts 1991 and 1995

8.1 Introduction

The Child Support Act 1991, as amended by Child Support Act 1995, came into force in April 1993. It established a new regime for determining the level of maintenance to be provided by an 'absent' parent for the benefit of his or her 'qualifying child'.

8.2 The new regime

Briefly, the 1991 Act imposes a duty on each parent of a qualifying child to be responsible for maintaining that child: s. 1(1).

A child is a 'qualifying child' if:

(a)   one or both parents is, in relation to him, an absent parent; or
(b)   both of his parents are, in relation to him, absent parents: s. 3(1).

The child must, normally be below the age of 16 years and may be a child adopted by the absent parent.

An 'absent parent' for the purpose of the 1991 Act is defined by s. 3(2) as:

(a)   that parent is not living in the same household with the child; and
(b)   the child has his home with a person who is, in relation to him, a person with care.

The 1991 Act states that 'an absent parent shall be taken to have met his responsibility to maintain any qualifying child of his by making periodical payments of maintenance ... as may be determined in accordance with the provisions of this Act': s. 1(2).

8.3 The Child Support Agency

The Child Support Agency was established to trace the absent parent in appropriate cases and to carry out a maintenance assessment to determine the parent's liability to maintain the child.

The consequence of the implementation of the 1991 Act is that maintenance is now dealt with for a qualifying child either by a maintenance assessment being carried out by the Child Support Agency or by the parents entering into a written maintenance agreement which may then be incorporated into the preamble of a court order.

8.4 Jurisdiction of the court

The effect of s. 8(3) of the 1991 Act is to limit the power of the court to make a periodical payments order to the case of a non-qualifying child who is nevertheless 'a child of the family' (as defined in s. 52(1) of the 1973 Act) — for example, a stepchild.

However, the court continues to retain the power to make an interim lump sum order, a lump sum order or a property adjustment order in favour of *any* child of the family (see paragraph 2 of this chapter).

8.5 Effect of the 1996 Act on child support

As has already been, noted, the Family Law Act 1996 requires the parties to demonstrate to the court that arrangements for the future (including settlement of financial and property matters) have been made as a precondition to obtaining a divorce or separation order: s. 9 and s. 3(1)(c).

It was, therefore, clear that during the process leading to the making of the arrangements (whether by mediation or court proceedings) regard must be had to the provisions of the child support legislation since those provisions will have an impact on the other arrangements as to finance and property arrived at between the parties.

This was confirmed by Mr Jonathan Evans, the former Parliamentary Secretary, Lord Chancellor's Department, who stated '... the Bill does not oust the CSA's jurisdiction'. He then went on to explain 'how those who deal with mediation deal with those issues in relation to the CSA. When couples use mediation to sort out financial and property matters and arrangements for children, the mediators ensure that full note is taken of the actual or likely CSA calculation. All couples are informed of the possible impact of the CSA formula on their arrangements. It is stressed that the balance of assets and financial responsibilities must take account of the actual or possible future effect of the CSA' (Standing Committee E, 14th May 1996, col 206).

Given the emphasis in the Act on reflection and consideration during which period the parties are not obliged to live apart and the encouragement to be given to attempt a reconciliation, it is anticipated that fewer couples will be living in separate households at the time of mediation. Hence, the impact of the child support legislation on the parties' *future* arrangements is likely to be particularly relevant.

9 Financial provision orders and the statutory charge

9.1 The statutory charge and proceedings

Section 16(6) of the Legal Aid Act 1988 establishes the principle that where an assisted person recovers or preserves property (including capital) in the proceedings and a deficiency is suffered by the Legal Aid Board in funding the proceedings then 'there shall be a first charge for the benefit of the Board on any property'.

The need to advise clients at the outset of proceedings of the implications of s. 16 is well known to practitioners. Clients will also be warned that the statutory charge applies where property is recovered or preserved 'under any compromise or settlement arrived at to avoid the proceedings or bring them to an end': s. 16(7).

The harsh operation of the provisions is mitigated to a limited extent as follows:

(a)   the first £2,500 of property recovered or preserved is exempt from the charge; and

(b)   the enforcement of the charge may be postponed where property is recovered or preserved which is to be used to provide accommodation for the assisted person and/or his dependants (Civil Legal Aid (General) Regulations 1989, regs 94 and 95, as amended). Simple interest of course accrues until the charge is redeemed.

9.2   The statutory charge and mediation

By virtue of s. 13C of the Legal Aid Act 1988 (as inserted by s. 28 of the 1996 Act), it is clear that regulations may be made for the imposition of the statutory charge to property recovered or preserved as a result of mediation (see Chapter 9, paragraph 2).

10   Financial provision and property adjustment orders — procedural amendments

The procedure for applications for ancillary relief is contained in Family Proceedings Rules 1991, as amended.

Along with the pilot schemes planned for information meetings and the like, the Lord Chancellor's Department introduced a pilot scheme on 1st October 1996 to test proposals to amend the present procedure. Certain nominated county courts tested and assessed the proposed new procedure: others acted as a control.

The principal impetus for the change was the concern expressed at the extent to which litigation costs run out of control in individual cases as litigants conduct a war of attrition which not uncommonly leads them to incur costs that in total exceed the value of the assets in dispute.

Initially, the new procedure was embodied in *Practice Direction (Ancillary Relief Procedure: Pilot Scheme)* [1996] 2 FLR 368, with draft rules annexed. This has now been replaced by the Family Proceedings (Amendment No. 2) Rules 1997 (SI 1997 No. 1056) which came into force on 21st April 1997.

The procedure is fully described in *A Practical Approach to Family Law*, Black, Bridge and Bond (5th edn), Blackstone Press Limited.

11   Changes to grounds for financial provision orders

Under the provisions of s. 1 of the Domestic Proceedings and Magistrates' Courts Act 1978, a party to a marriage may apply to the magistrates' court for an unsecured periodical payments order and/or a lump sum order of up to £1,000 on one or more of the following grounds, namely, that the other party has:

(a)   failed to provide reasonable maintenance for the applicant; or

(b)   failed to provide, or to make a proper contribution towards, the reasonable maintenance for the child of the family; or

(c)   behaved in such a way that the applicant cannot reasonably be expected to live with the respondent; or

(d)   deserted the applicant.

Section 18 of the 1996 Act amends s. 1 of the 1978 Act by omitting paragraphs (c) and (d).

This implements the recommendation of the Law Commission in its 1990 Report. The Commission felt that it was 'undesirable that cases which might later proceed to the divorce courts should have started off by one of the parties alleging fault ... when the divorce court comes to deal with children and financial matters during the period for consideration and reflection, it is unlikely that a husband would forget that his wife has already made a number of allegations in court about his behaviour. This could undermine the effectiveness of any attempts at conciliation or mediation.'(Law Com No 192, p. 25).

Further, s. 18(2) of the 1996 Act amends s. 7(1) of the 1978 Act. Section 7 enables the court to formalise an adhoc maintenance arrangement and direct the making of unsecured periodical payments where the parties have lived apart for a continuous period exceeding 3 months, neither party having deserted the other. The amendment removes 'neither party having deserted the other'. Again, this is in line with recommendations of the Law Commission which felt that 'Section 7 ... should, no longer be limited to cases where neither party ... has deserted the other but cover all types of separation' (Law Com No 192, p. 25). In practice, little use is made of any of the provisions of the 1978 Act since the coming into force of the Child Support Act 1991.

Chapter Twelve
The Hardship Bar

1 Introduction

The provisions governing the circumstances in which an order preventing divorce might be made are set out in s. 10 of the Act ('the hardship bar'). Those provisions are intended to apply to all divorces. Under the old legislation, the hardship bar applied only to divorces based on the ground of 5 years' separation.

Under the old legislation the bar was used in a few cases, for example, 'where there was a loss of a pension which was considered a grave financial hardship. It was also used in practice as affecting the course of negotiations. Some would call it a bargaining factor ... the noble Lord, Lord Mishcon ... spoke of the existence of the bar as something that could influence parties even though they had not got to the stage of invoking the bar in connection with the settlement arrangements between the parties' (The former Lord Chancellor, Hansard, 4th March 1996, vol 570, no 54, cols 29–30).

Under the old legislation the hardship bar had come to be seen as something of a 'dead letter' as a result of the rarity with which it was invoked. Many involved in the divorce debates have indicated that the new hardship bar contained in the Act should be a meaningful provision.

The new hardship bar applies to 'substantial' hardship experienced as a result of the dissolution of the marriage, rather than to the more restrictive 'grave' hardship test applied under the old legislation and (as before) it covers not just financial hardship, but other hardships as well.

2 Who can apply for an order preventing divorce?

An application for an order preventing divorce can be made only by a *party to the marriage*, even if the application asserts that the dissolution will result in hardship to the children. (The former Lord Chancellor, Hansard, 4th March 1996, vol 570, no 54, cols 25–6).

3 When can the court make an order preventing divorce?

If one of the parties to a marriage has applied for a divorce order, the court may, on the application of the other party, order that the marriage is not to be dissolved (s. 10(1)).

4 What conditions need to be satisfied before the court makes an order preventing divorce?

An order preventing divorce may be made only if the court is satisfied (s. 10(2)):

(a) that the dissolution of the marriage would result in substantial financial or other hardship to the other party or to a child of the family; and

(b) that it would be wrong, in all the circumstances (including the conduct of the parties and the interests of any child of the family), for the marriage to be dissolved.

4.1 Meaning of 'substantial'

The word 'substantial' replaces the word 'grave' which was used in the old hardship bar. The former Lord Chancellor said that he had used the word ''substantial' to indicate to a lay person that he or she would have to be able to identify something on which the court could find as occasioning hardship. The reason that this is a more ample provision than the previous one is that the word 'grave' indicates a higher standard of hardship' (Hansard, 4th March 1996, vol 570, no 54, col 30).

4.2 Meaning of 'hardship'

The word 'hardship' refers to objective hardship. The former Lord Chancellor gave the example of 'a child who had a particular disability. The family home in which he lived was adapted in order that the disability could be catered for. When the husband and wife split up, they could not afford to keep that home. As very often happens, the total available to the family was less than was available for the house. Therefore, they had to sell the house as a consequence of the break-up of the marriage. It would take some time to adapt another house for the purposes of the child's disability. This is an example of an objective type of hardship to a child of the marriage occasioned by the granting of a divorce at a particular time. Therefore, under this amendment, the divorce may well be postponed until new arrangements have been made, if it is possible at all to make them' (Hansard, 4th March 1996, vol 570, no 54, cols 30–31).

The hardship to which the provision refers must be hardship occasioned by the *order* dissolving the marriage, rather than from the marriage breakdown. 'It is then left to the courts to decide whether there is hardship in any particular case and whether or not an order should be made in the light of the circumstances referred to in the later part of the clause' (The former Lord Chancellor, Hansard, 4th March 1996, vol 570, no 54, col 32).

It is likely that cases relating to 'hardship' under the Matrimonial Causes Act 1973 will continue to be referred to when interpreting s. 10 of the 1996 Act. The usual case of financial hardship is where the dissolution of the marriage will result in one of the parties losing a pension (see, for example, *Le Marchant* v *Le Marchant* [1977] 1 WLR 559). There are other types of hardship apart from financial hardship, for example where the dissolution of the marriage will result in the divorced person being regarded as a social outcast in their own community (see *Banik* v *Banik* [1973] 1 WLR 960).

'Hardship' as defined in the Act specifically includes the loss of a chance to obtain a future benefit (as well as the loss of an existing benefit) (s. 10(6)). This would include, as mentioned above, the loss of a chance to benefit from a spouse's pension rights in the future. Although ss. 16 and 17 of the Act provide for the division of pension assets on divorce it will take some years for them to be fully implemented and, in any event, there will be some types of pension assets which might not be capable of division under the Act. Therefore, s. 10(6) covers any possible cases which might fall into this category.

Once the hardship criterion has been established, the court then proceeds to take into account the other factors mentioned in s. 10(2)(b), namely, 'that it would be wrong in all the circumstances (including the conduct of the parties and the interests of any child of the family), for the marriage to be dissolved'.

5   Application to cancel an order preventing divorce

If one or both of the parties apply for the cancellation of an order preventing divorce, then the court *must* cancel the order *unless* it is still satisfied:

   (a)   that the dissolution of the marriage would result in substantial financial or other hardship to the party in whose favour the order was made or to a child of the family (s. 10(3)(a)); and

   (b)   that it would be wrong, in all the circumstances (including the conduct of the parties and the interests of any child of the family), for the marriage to be dissolved (s. 10(3)(b)).

If an order preventing a divorce is cancelled, the court may make a divorce order in respect of the marriage *only* if an application is made under s. 3 or s. 4(3) (application to convert a separation order into a divorce order) *after* the cancellation (s. 10(4)).

An order preventing divorce may include conditions which must be satisfied before an application for cancellation may be made under s. 10(3) (s. 10(5)).

Chapter Thirteen
Jurisdiction, Definitions and Transitional Arrangements

1 General jurisdiction

Section 19 of the Act governs the jurisdiction of the court to entertain:

(a) 'marital proceedings'; and
(b) any other jurisdiction conferred on the court under Part II of the Family Law Act 1996 or any other statute, *in consequence of* the making of a statement of marital breakdown.

1.1 Conditions for exercise of jurisdiction

Section 19(2) states that the court can only exercise jurisdiction if:

(a) at least one of the parties was domiciled in England and Wales on the statement date (i.e., the date when the statement was received by the court: s. 19(7));
(b) at least one of the parties was habitually resident in England and Wales throughout the period of 1 year ending with the statement date; or
(c) nullity proceedings are pending in relation to the marriage when the marital proceedings commence.

1.2 Continuing jurisdiction

Where a separation order is in force, or where an order preventing divorce has been cancelled, the court continues to have jurisdiction to hear an application made in relation to such orders and may exercise any other jurisdiction which is conferred on it in consequence of such an application (s. 19(3) and (4)).

2 Definition of 'marital proceedings'

2.1 Meaning of 'marital proceedings'

'Marital proceedings' are those proceedings which are commenced when a statement of marital breakdown is received by the court (s. 20(1), (2)). They include the following:

(a)   separation proceedings — if an application for a separation order has been made under s. 3 by reference to the statement and not withdrawn (s. 20(3)(a));
(b)   divorce proceedings — if an application for a divorce order has been made under s. 3 by reference to the statement and not withdrawn (s. 20(3)(b)).

Marital proceedings are to be treated as being *both* divorce proceedings and separation proceedings at any time when no application by reference to the statement, either for a divorce order or for a separation order, is outstanding (s. 20(4)).

Where an application is made for the *conversion* of a separation order into a divorce order under s. 4(3) of the Act, then those proceedings are also marital proceedings and divorce proceedings (s. 20(5)).

2.2   Commencement of marital proceedings

'Marital proceedings' are commenced when a statement of marital breakdown is received by the court (s. 20(1), (2)).

2.3   Ending of marital proceedings

Marital proceedings come to an end (s. 20(6)):

(a)   on the making of a separation order;
(b)   on the making of a divorce order;
(c)   on the withdrawal of the statement by a notice in s. 5(3)(b) (i.e., where a period of more than one year — the 'specified period' — has passed since the end of the period of reflection and consideration, see Chapter 7, paragraph 7);
(d)   at the end of the 'specified period' mentioned in s. 5(3)(b), if no application for a separation or divorce order by reference to the statement is outstanding;
(e)   on the withdrawal of all applications for a separation or a divorce order which are outstanding at the end of the period mentioned in s. 5(3)(b). (Note that it is possible for there to be both an application for a separation order and an application for a divorce order before the court at the same time. This provision means that marital proceedings will only end if all applications that have been made under s. 3 are withdrawn)(s. 20(6)(e));
(f)   on the withdrawal of an application under s. 4(3) to convert a separation order into a divorce order.

3   Stay of proceedings

Schedule 3 to the Family Law Act 1996 amends sch. 1 to the Domicile and Matrimonial Proceedings Act 1973, which relates to orders to stay proceedings where there are proceedings in other jurisdictions (s. 19(5)). The court may exercise its jurisdiction under the 1996 Act, subject to any order for a stay under sch. 1 to the Domicile and Matrimonial Proceedings Act 1973 (s. 19(6)).

4   'Connected proceedings'

Section 25 of the Family Law Act 1996 defines those proceedings which are 'connected' with the breakdown of marriage. The intention behind this definition is to facilitate the giving of directions in respect of mediation under s. 13, since 'in circumstances in which there are connected proceedings, if one is proceeding on the basis of mediation, it may be desirable that the connected proceedings should be held up to some extent while mediation is undertaken' (Mr Jonathan Evans, Hansard, Standing Committee E, 14th May 1996, col 280).

For the purposes of Part II of the Act, proceedings are 'connected' with the breakdown of the marriage if they are (s. 25(2)):

(a)   proceedings under Parts I to V of the Children Act 1989 with respect to a child of the family; or

(b)   proceedings resulting from an application:

(i)   for, or for the cancellation of, an order preventing divorce in relation to the marriage;

(ii)   by either party to the marriage for an order under Part IV of the Family Law Act 1996;

(iii)   for the exercise, in relation to a party to the marriage or child of the family, of any of the court's powers under Part II of the Matrimonial Causes Act 1973;

(iv)   made otherwise to the court with respect to, or in connection with, any proceedings connected with the breakdown of the marriage.

And, at the time of the proceedings (s. 25(1)):

(a)   a statement has been received by the court with respect to the marriage and it is, or may become, possible for an application for a divorce order or separation order to be made by reference to that statement;

(b)   such an application in relation to the marriage has been made and not withdrawn; or

(c)   a divorce order has been made, or a separation order is in force, in relation to the marriage.

5   Transitional arrangements

Schedule 9, para. 1 sets out the transitional arrangements for those parties who have been living apart immediately before the beginning of the transitional period. The 'transitional period' means the period of 2 years beginning with the day on which s. 3 is brought into force (sch. 9, para. 1(3)).

The Lord Chancellor may by order provide for the application of Part II of the Act to marital proceedings which:

(a)   are begun during the transitional period, and

(b)   relate to parties to a marriage who immediately before the beginning of that period were living apart,

subject to such modifications (which may include omissions) as may be prescribed (sch. 9, para. 1(1)).

The Lord Chancellor may, in particular, make provision as to the evidence which a party who claims to have been living apart from the other party immediately before the beginning of the transitional period must produce to the court (sch. 9, para. 1(2)).

It would appear to the authors that these provisions mean that parties who can prove that they have been living apart for some time just prior to the implementation of the Act, with the intention of petitioning for divorce under the old legislation, may not have to start right at the beginning of the new separation and divorce process when the Act does come into force. However, it is necessary to wait and see what orders are made under this provision in due course.

6 Interpretation

Section 24 sets out the interpretation given to various phrases used in the Act.

Chapter Fourteen
Intestacy

1 Introduction[1]

Intestacy arises where an individual dies without having made a valid will or having made a valid will it nevertheless does not effectively dispose of any of his property. It is also possible for there to be a partial intestacy in circumstances where the deceased made a valid will which only effectively disposes of part of his estate.

The rules governing the administration of the deceased's estate in these circumstances are laid down in the Administration of Estates Act 1925 and the Law Reform (Succession) Act 1995 and, so far as they relate to a surviving spouse, are set out briefly below. The provisions are unaffected by the Family Law Act 1996 except that s. 21 of that Act now regulates the position in the event of one party dying intestate whilst a separation order remains in force.

2 Administration of Estates Act 1925, as amended by the Trusts of Land and Appointment of Trustees Act 1996

2.1 Section 33 and a trust of land

The effect of s. 33 of the 1925 Act, as amended, is to impose a statutory trust of land in respect of both the real and personal property of the estate in respect of which the deceased died intestate.

The administrators of the estate have a power to postpone the sale of both types of asset and, in any event, personal chattels must not be sold unless this is necessary to pay debts or meet expenses, for example, funeral and testamentary expenses.

Where there is a partial intestacy, pecuniary legacies will be paid out of such proceeds of sale: any balance remaining after the discharge of these liabilities is described as 'the residue'.

3 Rules of entitlement on intestacy

3.1 The surviving spouse

For these purposes, the surviving spouse must survive the intestate by 28 days, beginning with the date of death in order to inherit: Law Reform (Succession) Act 1995, s. 1.

---

[1] The authors are indebted to Helen Brown and Robert Evans for assistance in the preparation of this chapter.

3.2   Entitlement where the intestate is survived by a spouse and issue

In these circumstances, the surviving spouse will be entitled to personal chattels absolutely. These are defined in s. 55 of the 1925 Act and include furniture, jewellery and ornaments but specifically exclude chattels used by the deceased for business purposes, money and securities for money.

Furthermore, the surviving spouse has an absolute entitlement to £125,000 free of tax and costs. This is known as 'the statutory legacy' and interest accrues on this legacy at the rate of 6% per annum from the date of death until the legacy is paid.

As far as the residuary estate is concerned, the surviving spouse is entitled to a life interest in one-half of the estate. In practical terms, this means that one-half of the remaining estate will be invested to provide an income for the survivor who will, however, have no entitlement to the capital.

The remainder of the estate passes to the issue on statutory trusts which are regulated by s. 47(i) of the 1925 Act and provide in essence that the estate is to be divided equally amongst the intestate's children who acquire a vested interest by either (a) attaining the age of 18 years or (b) marrying below that age.

Should such a child die before the intestate but leave issue, those issue share the child's entitlement provided that they fulfil in due course the conditions to acquire a vested interest.

3.3   Entitlement where the intestate is survived by a spouse and his parents or brothers and sisters of the whole blood or their issue but the intestate leaves no issue

In these circumstances, the surviving spouse is entitled to personal chattels and a statutory legacy of £200,000, interest at the rate of 6% per annum from the date of death to the date of payment and one-half of the residue absolutely.

The remainder of the estate passes to the parents, equally if more than one. If neither parent survives, then the residuary estate passes to the brothers and sisters of the whole blood, equally if more than one, or their issue on statutory trusts.

3.4   Entitlement where the intestate is survived by a spouse and no issue, parents or brothers and sisters of the whole blood or their issue.

In these circumstances, the surviving spouse is entitled to the whole of the estate absolutely.

3.5   Elections available to a surviving spouse

The surviving spouse is permitted to make a number of elections. These include the redemption of a life interest (under s. 47A of the 1925 Act) so that a capital sum is received in place of income and taking the matrimonial home as part of his absolute entitlement (assuming, of course, that the doctrine of automatic survivorship does not apply in any event).

There are a number of conditions to be fulfilled for each type of election but the principal one, common to both forms of election, is that written notice must be given to the administrators within 12 months of the grant of letters of administration.

4   Meaning of the term 'spouse'

The rules as to entitlement on intestacy, as set out above, refer to a 'surviving spouse' and hence entitlement depends upon the existence of a valid marriage between the intestate and survivor at the date of death.

5   Effect of a divorce order

Should a divorce order have been made terminating the marriage, the surviving former spouse will not be automatically entitled to any part of the estate under the intestacy provisions. Instead, a claim may be made under s. 1(1) of the Inheritance (Provision for Family and Dependants) Act 1975 for reasonable financial provision provided that the claimant has not remarried.

'Reasonable financial provision' is defined under s. 1(2)(a) as 'such financial provision as it would be reasonable in all the circumstances of the case for a husband or wife to receive, whether or not that provision is required for his or her maintenance'. A claim would fail, of course, if the ancillary relief order made in the divorce proceedings had specifically dismissed the right to make an application under the 1975 Act.

6   Effect of a separation order

Provisions relating to proceedings for a decree of judicial separation under s. 17 of the Matrimonial Causes Act 1973 are repealed in sch. 10 to the Family Law Act 1996 and replaced by a separation order which is available in the same circumstances as a divorce order: s. 3(1) of the 1996 Act.

The provisions relating to the effects of a decree of judicial separation in s. 18 of the 1973 Act are likewise repealed but the effect of the party to the marriage dying intestate where a separation order is in force is dealt with in s. 21 of the 1996 Act.

Section 21 provides that where

(a)   a separation order is in force, and
(b)   while the parties to the marriage remain separated, one of them dies intestate as respects any real or personal property,

that property devolves as if the other had died before the intestacy occurred.

A separation order may be brought to an end by a joint application of the parties to the court to cancel the order: s. 2(3)(b) of the 1996 Act.

Speaking at the Report stage of the Bill, Lord Simon of Glaisdale expressed concern about the effect of the separation order on an intestacy arguing that the provision discriminates against a spouse who has a conscientious objection to divorce. He stated 'It is discriminatory in favour of divorce and against separation, where there is always a chance of reconstituting the marriage' (Hansard, 4th March 1996, vol 570, no 54, cols 50 and 51).

In reply, the then Lord Chancellor explained that the provision was in the Bill only because, for reasons of convenience, a number of provisions had been repealed (notably s. 18 of the Matrimonial Causes Act 1973) to which the measure corresponded. He went on to state '. . . on the whole, experience seems to be that when parties become separated, the husband, for example, does not intend or wish for his separated wife, if the separation has lasted until death, to benefit from his estate' (Hansard, 4th March 1996, vol 570, no 54, col 53).

He also justified the retention of the existing position by reminding the House of Lords that this has been the law since 1970 (Matrimonial Proceedings and Property Act 1970, s. 40(1)) and that he had consulted with his Ancillary Relief Advisory Group whose view was 'that we should stick with the existing law' (Hansard, 4th March 1996, vol 570, no 54, col 53).

It is important to remember that, in any event, such a surviving spouse may well have preserved an entitlement to a widow's pension and will be able to apply for provision under the Inheritance (Provision for Family and Dependants) Act 1975.

Chapter Fifteen
Nullity

1 Introduction

A decree of nullity may be granted where a marriage is void or voidable. A void marriage is void *ab initio* and treated as never having taken place because of some fundamental flaw in the capacity of the parties or the process of marriage itself. By contrast, a voidable marriage is valid and subsisting until steps are taken to set it aside. Decrees of nullity are comparatively rare. In 1996, 669 decrees absolute of nullity were granted (Annual Abstract of Statistics, No. 134, The Stationery Office).

2 Review of the law of nullity

The law of nullity was reviewed by the Law Commission in 1970 (Law Com No 33). The importance of the availability of the decree of nullity where a marriage is void was incontrovertible but criticisms had been levelled 'against the anomalous nature of the voidable marriage' (Bromley and Lowe, *Family Law*, 8th edn, Butterworths, 1992). The Law Commission examined whether the concept should be abolished, but recommended its retention principally because certain Christian denominations and their members draw a clear distinction between annulment and the dissolution of marriage and would be offended if the distinction were blurred. However, certain reforms were advocated and these were implemented in the Nullity of Marriage Act 1971. The Act was subsequently repealed and the provisions re-enacted in the Matrimonial Causes Act 1973.

The law of nullity was not subject to the same comprehensive review as that of divorce when the Law Commission produced its Consultative Document 'Facing the Future: A Discussion Paper on the Ground for Divorce', the Law Commission stating that 'we decided ... to review whether the substantive law of divorce was working satisfactorily ...'.

In the Law Commission's subsequent Report no specific recommendations were made in relation to nullity because the principal object of the Report was to make proposals to reform the law of divorce. At most, there was a tacit recognition of the need to retain the present provisions.

Nullity received little attention in the Lord Chancellor's Department's Consultation Paper, consultees simply being asked whether wilful refusal by the respondent to consummate the marriage should cease to be a ground on which a marriage could be declared voidable — some respondents to the Law Commission's Report having expressed the view that this ground should be removed since it was inconsistent with the removal from divorce law of the need to allege fault.

In the subsequent White Paper, the government indicated that it did not propose to make any change in the law of nullity and hence the Family Law Act 1996 makes little reference to nullity except in relation to the timing of the decree absolute and to financial provision (see paragraphs 5, 9 and 10 of this chapter) the Lord Chancellor confirming at Report Stage 'The Bill does not amend the law of nullity' (Hansard, 4th March 1996, vol 570, no 54, col 132).

3   The present law — Matrimonial Causes Act 1973

As already stated, a decree of nullity may be obtained where the marriage in question is void or voidable. Sections 11 and 12 of the Matrimonial Causes Act 1973 set out the grounds on which a marriage is void or voidable and relate to marriages contracted on or after 31st July 1971.

These sections, along with s. 13 of the 1973 Act which contains a number of bars to relief preventing a decree of nullity being granted where a marriage is voidable, are unchanged by the Family Law Act 1996.

3.1   Void marriages

Strictly speaking, where a marriage is void, there is no need for the parties involved to obtain a decree of nullity but there are two advantages in doing so:

(a)   the status of the parties is clarified, thus avoiding complications which could arise if one party wished to remarry;

(b)   a decree of nullity is necessary if one party wishes to obtain financial provision or property adjustment orders (see paragraphs 9 and 10 of this chapter).

The grounds for a void marriage are set out in s. 11 of the 1973 Act and are as follows:

(a)   That it is not a valid marriage under the provisions of the Marriage Acts 1949 to 1983, i.e., where:

(i)   the parties are within the prohibited degrees of relationship (which can be relationship by blood or by marriage), for example, where they are father and daughter, brother and sister, son and step-mother; or

(ii)   either party is under the age of 16; or

(iii)   the parties have intermarried in disregard of certain requirements as to the formation of marriage, for example, where they marry according to the rites of the Church of England in a place which is not a church or other building in which banns may be published or without observing the requirements as to banns, licences, etc., both being aware of the irregularity at the time of the marriage.

(b)   That at the time of the marriage either of the parties was already lawfully married.

(c)   That the parties are not respectively male and female.

(d)   In the case of polygamous marriage entered into outside England and Wales, that either party was at the time of the marriage domiciled in England and Wales.

3.2   Voidable marriages

Because a voidable marriage is valid and subsisting until steps are taken to set it aside, a decree of nullity is essential to bring such a marriage to an end.

The exhaustive list of grounds for a voidable marriage is set out in s. 12 of the 1973 Act as follows:

(a)   That it has not been consummated owing to the incapacity of either party to consummate it.

(b)   That it has not been consummated owing to the wilful refusal of the respondent to consummate it.

(c)   That either party to the marriage did not validly consent to it whether in consequence of duress, mistake, unsoundness of mind or otherwise.

(d)   That at the time of the marriage either party, though capable of giving a valid consent, was suffering (whether continuously or intermittently) from mental disorder within the meaning of the Mental Health Act 1983 of such a kind or to such an extent as to be unfitted for marriage.

(e)   That at the time of the marriage the respondent was suffering from venereal disease in a communicable form.

(f)   That at the time of the marriage the respondent was pregnant by someone other than the petitioner.

3.3   Bars to relief where a marriage is voidable

Section 13 of the Matrimonial Causes Act 1973 sets out the bars which may apply where a marriage is voidable. In such circumstances, a decree of nullity will be refused but it is always open to one of the parties to apply for a divorce or separation order in due course.

3.3.1   Absolute bar applicable to all voidable marriages   The court shall not grant a nullity decree on the grounds that the marriage is voidable if the respondent satisfies the court:

(a)   that the petitioner, knowing that he could have the marriage annulled, so conducted himself in relation to the respondent as to lead the respondent reasonably to believe that he would not seek to do so; *and*

(b)   that it would be unjust to the respondent to grant the decree (s. 13(1)).

3.3.2   Bars applicable only to certain voidable marriages.

(1)   Time bar   Where the proceedings for a decree of nullity are based on the grounds set out in s. 12(c), (d), (e) or (f) of the 1973 Act, that is, lack of consent, mental disorder, venereal disease or pregnancy by someone other than the petitioner, a decree will be refused unless the proceedings are instituted within a period of 3 years from the date of the marriage: s. 13(2) of the 1973 Act.

There is a limited exception to this rule by virtue of an amendment made by s. 2 Matrimonial and Family Proceedings Act 1984 whereby a judge may grant leave to institute proceedings on any of these grounds after the expiration of the 3 year period if:

(a)   he is satisfied that the petitioner has at some time during the 3-year period suffered from a mental disorder within the meaning of the Mental Health Act 1983; *and*

(b)   he considers that in all the circumstances of the case it would be just to grant leave for the institution of proceedings (see s. 13(2) and (4) of the 1973 Act).

(2)   Knowledge of the petitioner   The court shall not grant a decree on the grounds set out in s. 12(e) and (f) of the 1973 Act (venereal disease and pregnancy) unless it is satisfied that at the time of the marriage the petitioner was ignorant of the fact alleged (s. 13(3) of the 1973 Act). This is an absolute bar.

4   Procedure for a decree of nullity

Because the Family Law Act 1996 does not amend the law relating to nullity, it is anticipated that the existing procedure will continue to apply and that the petition will be heard in open court, with the original provisions of s. 41 of the Matrimonial Causes Act 1973 (relating to arrangements for the children of the family) unaffected by the provisions of s. 11 of the Family Law Act 1996. The key provisions relating to information meetings and mediation will not therefore apply.

5   Timing of the decree absolute of nullity

The decree of nullity is granted in two stages: nisi and absolute. Schedule 8, para. 6 of the 1996 Act replaces s. 15 of the 1973 Act with a newly worded provision as follows:

Every decree of nullity of marriage shall in the first instance be a decree nisi and shall not be made absolute before the end of six weeks from its grant unless:
(a)   the High Court by general order from time to time fixes a shorter period; or
(b)   in any particular case, the court in which the proceedings are for the time being pending from time to time by special order fixes a shorter period than the period otherwise applicable for the time being by virtue of this section.

In essence, this confirms the present position, namely that a minimum period of 6 weeks must elapse between the decree nisi and absolute unless the High Court or court dealing with a particular case fixes a shorter period of time. Speaking on this matter at the Report stage, the Lord Chancellor stated 'This brings the legislation in line with current practice as the period has actually been fixed at six weeks since 1972' (Hansard, 4th March 1996, vol 570, no 54, col 140).

Section 15B(2) of the 1973 Act, as inserted, goes on to provide that where a decree of nullity has been granted and no application for it to be made absolute has been made by the party to whom it was granted then, at any time after the expiration of 3 months from the earliest date on which the petitioner could have made such an application, the party against whom the decree was granted may make an application to the court for the decree absolute.

6 Intervention by Queen's Proctor

The possibility of intervention by Queen's Proctor, albeit rarely invoked, is retained in s. 15A(1)(a) and (b), as introduced into the 1973 Act by sch. 8, para. 6. Intervention may occur at the direction of the court or by any person giving information to the Queen's Proctor during the proceedings or before the decree nisi is made absolute.

7 Intervention by a third party

In addition to the possibility of intervention by Queen's Proctor above, s. 15B(1) of the 1973 Act permits any person in circumstances where a decree of nullity has been granted but not made absolute to show cause why the decree should, not be made absolute by reason of material facts not having been brought before the court.

In such a case, the court may:

(a)   make the decree absolute; or
(b)   rescind the decree; or
(c)   require further inquiry; or
(d)   otherwise deal with the case as it thinks fit.

8 Effect of the decree of nullity

8.1 Void marriages

The decree of nullity is necessarily declaratory only in these circumstances. Nevertheless, by virtue of the Legitimacy Act 1976, children of a void marriage are treated as being legitimate if at the time of conception or insemination (or the celebration of the marriage if this is later) both or either of the parties reasonably believed that the marriage was valid and the father was domiciled in England and Wales at the time of the birth or if he died before the birth, was so domiciled immediately before his death.

8.2 Voidable marriages

A decree of nullity operates to annul the marriage only from the date of the decree absolute. The marriage is treated as having existed up to that time: s. 16 of the Matrimonial Causes Act 1973 and hence children of the union are automatically legitimate. Remarriage may take place after decree absolute. Neither party may claim on the intestacy of the other.

9 Financial provision and property adjustment orders

9.1 Schedule 2 and nullity proceedings

In Chapter 11 the nature of financial provision and property adjustment orders as set out in sch. 2 the Family Law Act 1996 was explained. Section 15(2) of the 1996

Act states that the main object of sch. 2 is to provide that, in the case of divorce or separation, an order about financial provision may be made (but not normally come into force) under the 1973 Act *before* a divorce order or separation order is made (s. 15(2)(a)) but to retain (with minor changes) the position under the 1973 Act where marriages are annulled: s. 15(2)(b).

Schedule 8, para. 4 of the 1996 Act amends s. 23 of the Matrimonial Causes Act 1973 by substituting new wording in respect of financial provision orders in nullity proceedings, the effect of which is to bring the form of financial provision available in such proceedings in line with that available in the divorce or separation process. (The Lord Chancellor, Hansard, 4th March 1996, vol 570, no 54, col 132.)

Furthermore, sch. 2, para. 6 of the 1996 Act amends s. 24 of the 1973 Act by substituting new wording in respect of property adjustment orders in nullity proceedings. Again, this is to ensure that there is no distinction between the form of property adjustment order available in the divorce or separation process and that available in nullity proceedings.

9.2   Financial provision orders — the general principles

Section 23(1) of the 1973 Act provides that, on or after granting a decree of nullity of marriage (whether before or after the decree is made absolute), the court may, on an application made under the section, make one or more financial provision orders in favour of —

(a)   either party to the marriage; or
(b)   any child of the family.

As with financial provision orders in the divorce or separation process, s. 23(9)(a) confirms that the powers of the court may be exercised differently in favour of different children.

9.3   Financial provision orders and dismissal of proceedings

Section 23(3) of the 1973 Act, as inserted, provides that where any such proceedings are dismissed, the court may (either immediately or within a reasonable period after the dismissal) make any one or more financial provision orders in favour of each child of the family.

From time to time, further financial provision orders of that or any other kind may be made in favour of a child: s. 23(9)(c).

9.4   Financial provision orders — interim orders

Section 23(2) of the 1973 Act provides as follows:

Before granting a decree in any proceedings for nullity of marriage, the court may make against either or each of the parties to the marriage —

(a)   an interim periodical payments order, an interim order for the payment of a lump sum, or a series of such orders, in favour of the other party;

(b)   an interim periodical payments order, an interim order for the payment of a lump sum, a series of such orders or any one or more other financial provision orders in favour of each child of the family.

The effect of this subsection is to permit the court to make orders before granting a decree of nullity and replaces the court's power to make orders for maintenance pending suit. It is another example of the way in which the amending provisions of the 1996 Act seek to achieve consistency in the form of financial provision orders available.

The value of an interim lump sum order in particular has been highlighted in Chapter 11 above, but it should be noted that initially the former Lord Chancellor resisted the proposal that orders of this kind should be available in nullity proceedings. Speaking at the Report Stage, the Lord Chancellor explained his position by stating that 'The Bill does not amend the law of nullity. For this reason, Schedule 2 ... makes only minor modifications to the law relating to financial provision on nullity. I am accordingly unable ... to confer a statutory power on the court to make interim lump sum orders on nullity ... I will, however, take the need for a statutory power to make interim orders on nullity fully into account when I am reviewing the whole of the substantive law relating to financial provision on divorce and nullity in the future' (Hansard, 4th March 1996, vol 570, no 54, col 132).

Concern was expressed in the same debate that 'nullity proceedings are somehow discriminated against in connection with interim lump sum orders' (Lord Meston, Hansard, 4th March 1996, vol 570, no 54, col 135).

However, when the Bill was being considered in Standing Committee 16th May 1996, the government accepted an amendment to the Bill tabled by Mr Elfyn Llwyd to enable interim lump sum orders to be made in nullity proceedings.

In considering the Common Amendments on 27th June 1996, the Lord Chancellor welcomed this development stating that 'The Government had it in mind to give the court similar powers in relation to nullity in this House but were concerned not to come forward with amendments on nullity which would risk being beyond the scope of the Bill. I was delighted to see that the amendments were made in the other place and that they did not go beyond the scope of the Bill' (Hansard, 27th July 1996, vol 573, no 1672, col 1113).

9.5   Financial provision orders — the lump sum orders

9.5.1   Purpose of the lump sum order   Section 23(4) and (5) of the Matrimonial Causes Act 1973, as substituted, acknowledges that a lump sum order may be made by the court for the benefit of the other party to the marriage or a child of the family 'for the purpose of enabling that other party to meet any liabilities or expenses reasonably incurred by him or her in maintaining himself or herself or any child of the family before making an application under this section in his or her favour'.

This provision largely reproduces s. 2(2) of the Domestic Proceedings and Magistrates' Courts Act 1978 and is a recognition that a lump sum order is extremely versatile and is not simply available to purchase one party's interest in assets accumulated during the marriage.

9.5.2   Payment by instalment and interest   The court may order the lump sum to be paid by instalments which may be secured: s. 23(6) of the 1973 Act.

As with orders made in the divorce or separation process, the court may on or at any time after the making of the main order, make an order for interest to be paid where the payment of the lump sum is deferred or to be by instalments.

9.6   Financial provision orders — the coming into effect of the order

Section 23(10) of the 1973 Act provides that where an order is made under s. 23(1) in favour of a party to the marriage on or after the granting of the decree of nullity of marriage, neither the order, nor any settlement made in pursuance of the order takes effect *unless* the decree has been made absolute.

This preserves the present position. It means that it will not be possible in nullity proceedings to apply to the court to have the main orders brought into effect at an earlier date and is in contrast with the position in relation to orders in the divorce or separation process as laid down in s. 22B (see Chapter 11).

10   Property adjustment orders

The provisions of s. 24 of the Matrimonial Causes Act 1973 have been substituted by sch. 2, para. 6 of the 1996 Act.

10.1   Powers of the court

Section 24(1) and (2) provides as follows:

(1)   On or after granting a decree of nullity of marriage (whether before or after the decree is made absolute), the court may, on an application made under this section, make one or more property adjustment orders in relation to the marriage.

(2)   The court shall exercise its powers under this section, so far as is practicable, by making on one occasion all such provision as can be made by way of one or more property adjustment orders in relation to the marriage as it thinks fit.

Section 24(3) goes on to state:

(3)   Subsection (2) above does not affect section 31 or 31A below.

(See Chapter 11, paragraph 6.)

10.2   Coming into effect of the order

Such orders are to take effect on the grant of the decree absolute — there is no provision for earlier implementation of the order: s. 24(4) of the 1973 Act.

11   Use of conveyancing counsel

Under the provisions of s. 30 of the Matrimonial Causes Act 1973, the court may direct, when making a secured periodical payments or a property adjustment order, that the matter be referred to conveyancing counsel for him to settle a proper instrument to be executed by all parties. This power is retained in ss. 23(11) and 24(5), as substituted by the 1996 Act.

Chapter Sixteen
Venue and Transfer

1 The statutory framework

The rules governing venue and transfer are set out in the Family Law Act 1996 (Part IV) (Allocation of Proceedings) Order 1997 (SI 1997 No. 1896 (L.32)).

2 Which court?

2.1 Basic rule

Proceedings may be issued in either the family proceedings court or in the county court (Article 4(1)). *However*, the county court must be a divorce county court, *or* a family hearing centre *or* a care centre (see Article 2).

Note the Lambeth, Shoreditch and Woolwich County Courts and the Principal Registry of the Family Division may also hear applications under Part IV of the Act.

2.2 Exceptions

If the applicant is under 18 or needs the leave of the court to make the application (because he is under 16) then the application must be made in the High Court (Article 4(2)).

If family proceedings (see Chapter 21) are pending in a county court or a family proceedings court, Article 4(3) permits a Part IV application to be made in those proceedings.

2.3 Restriction on jurisdiction of family proceedings court

Section 59 of the Act provides that a magistrates' court shall not be competent to entertain any application, or make any order, involving any disputed question as to a party's entitlement to occupy any property by virtue of a beneficial estate or interest or contract, or by virtue of any enactment giving him the right to remain in occupation, unless it is unnecessary to determine the question in order to deal with the application or to make the order.

It is also worth noting that by the same section magistrates may decline jurisdiction if they consider that the case can be more conveniently dealt with by another court.

2.4 Transfer of tenancies

An application for a transfer of tenancy order (see Chapter 26) cannot be made in the family proceedings court.

3 Transfer

3.1 Transfer from one family proceedings court to another

A family proceedings court *must* transfer proceedings to another family proceedings court where —

(a) it considers that it would be *appropriate* for those proceedings to be heard together with other family proceedings which are pending in the receiving court; and
(b) the receiving court, by its justices clerk, consents to the transfer (Article 7).

3.2 Transfer from family proceedings court to county court

A family proceedings court *may* transfer proceedings to a county court where it considers that —

(a) it would be *appropriate* for those proceedings to be heard together with other family proceedings which are pending in that court; or
(b) the proceedings involve —
   (i) a conflict with the law of another jurisdiction,
   (ii) some novel and difficult point of law,
   (iii) some question of general public interest; or
(c) the proceedings are exceptionally complex (Article 8(1)).

Proceedings *must* be transferred where —

(a) a child under the age of 18 is the respondent to the application or wishes to become a party to the proceedings; or
(b) a party to the proceedings is a person who, by reason of mental disorder within the meaning of the Mental Health Act 1983, is incapable of managing and administering his property and affairs (Article 8(2)).

3.3 Transfer from family proceedings court to High Court

By Article 9, a family proceedings court *may* transfer proceedings to the High Court where it considers that it would be *appropriate* for those proceedings to be heard together with other family proceedings which are pending in that court.

3.4 Transfer from one county court to another

A county court *may* transfer proceedings to another county court where —

(a) it considers that it would be *appropriate* for those proceedings to be heard together with other family proceedings which are pending in that court;

(b)   the proceedings involve the determination of a disputed question as to a party's entitlement to occupy property and the property in question is situated in the district of another county court; or

(c)   it seems necessary or expedient so to do (Article 10).

3.5   Transfer from county court to family proceedings court

A county court *may* transfer proceedings to a family proceedings court where —

(a)   it considers that it would be *appropriate* for those proceedings to be heard together with other family proceedings which are pending in that court; or

(b)   it considers that the criterion —

(i)   as set out in paragraph 3.2(a) above no longer applies because the proceedings with which the transferred proceedings were to be heard have been determined,

(ii)   as set out in paragraph 3.2(b) or (c) above does not apply (Article 11).

3.6   Transfer from county court to High Court

Article 12 permits a county court to transfer proceedings to the High Court where it considers that the proceedings are *appropriate* for determination in the High Court.

3.7   Transfer from High Court to family proceedings court

Article 13 permits the High Court to transfer proceedings to a family proceedings court where it considers that it would be *appropriate* for those proceedings to be heard together with other family proceedings which are pending in that court.

3.8   Transfer from High Court to county court

The High Court *may* transfer proceedings to a county court where it considers that —

(a)   it would be *appropriate* for those proceedings to be heard together with other family proceedings which are pending in that court;

(b)   the proceedings are *appropriate* for determination in a county court; or

(c)   it is *appropriate* for an application made by a child under the age of 18 to be heard in a county court (Article 14).

3.9   Disposal following arrest

Article 15 provides that where a person is brought before —

(a)   a relevant judicial authority in accordance with s. 47(7)(a); or

(b)   a court by virtue of a warrant issued under s. 47(9);

and the matter is not disposed of forthwith, the matter *may* be transferred to be disposed of by the relevant judicial authority or court which issued the warrant or, as the case may be, which attached the power of arrest under s. 47(2) or (3), if different.

4   Note

Proceedings will not be invalid merely because they are commenced or transferred in contravention of a provision of the Order (Article 18).

All the above powers of transfer may be exercised by the court either on application or of its own motion.

Chapter Seventeen
Associated Persons and Relevant Child

1 Introduction

As will be seen later (Chapter 21), in determining whether a client will be able to obtain a non-molestation order under the Famiy Law Act 1996 the first matter to be ascertained is whether the applicant and respondent are 'associated' within the meaning of the Act, or, where the person sought to be protected is a child, whether the child is a 'relevant' child. The concept of 'associated persons' is also used in applications for s. 33 occupation orders.

2 Associated persons

The list of 'associated persons' appears in s. 62(4) and (5) of the Act. The list is a long one and embraces categories of persons who prior to the new legislation could not obtain injunctive relief unless they were able to rely upon behaviour which was capable of amounting to a tort or threatened tort, and so bring a civil action to which injunctive relief might attach.

2.1 Definition

Persons are 'associated' with each other if:

    (a)   They are married (s. 62(3)(a)).
    (b)   They have been married (s. 62(3)(a)).
    (c)   They are cohabitants (i.e., a man and a woman who, although not married to each other, are living together as husband and wife) (ss. 62(1)(a) and 62(3)(b)).
    (d)   They are former cohabitants (i.e., a man and woman who have lived together as husband and wife (s. 62(3)(b)).[1]
    (e)   They live in the same household (s. 62(3)(c)).
    (f)   They have lived in the same household (s. 62(3)(c)).
    (g)   They are relatives (s. 62(3)(d)). 'Relative' is defined by s. 63, the interpretation section, of the Act to include the following:

---

[1] *Unless* they have subsequently married each other (s. 62(1)(b)), in which case, although no longer former cohabitants they will still be 'associated' by virtue of s. 62(3)(a).

father
mother
stepfather
stepmother
son
daughter
stepson
stepdaughter
grandmother
grandfather
grandson
granddaughter

of a person *or* of that person's spouse or former spouse; and

brother
sister
uncle
aunt
niece
nephew

(whether of the full blood or of the half blood or by affinity)[2] of a person *or* of that person's spouse or former spouse.

It should be noted that cohabitants and former cohabitants are treated as though they were married to each other for the purpose of the above definition.

(h)   They have agreed to marry one another (whether or not that agreement has been terminated) (s. 62(3)(c)).

(i)   They are parents of the same child (s. 62(3)(f)).

(j)   They have or have had parental responsibility for the same child (s. 62(3)(f)) (unless one of those persons is a body corporate — s. 62(6)). The most obvious example of a body corporate in this context would be a local authority which would of course acquire parental responsibility for a child upon the making of a care order: Children Act 1989, s. 33(3)(a)).

(k)   They are parties to the same family proceedings (other than proceedings under the Act) (s. 62(3)(g)). The exception to this is where one of the parties is a body corporate, e.g., a local authority (s. 62(6)).

2.1.1   Exclusions from (e) and (f) above   In relation to persons who live together or who have lived together in the same household (categories (e) and (f) above), the Law Commission (Law Com No 207, May 1992) was of the view that it was inappropriate for the new jurisdiction to be enlisted to resolve disputes between tenant and landlord or those in similar relationships, or to deal with issues such as sexual harassment at work. It was thought that the remedies provided under property or employment law were more suitable. Accordingly, even if people are living

---

[2] 'Affinity' means relationship by marriage.

together (or have lived together) in the same household they will *not* be included in the categories of 'associated persons' if one is merely the other's employee, tenant, lodger or boarder (s. 62(3)(c)).

2.1.2 Homosexual couples   It should also be noted that categories (e) and (f) listed above do not require that the persons be of different gender, nor that they live (or have lived) together *as man and wife*. The Law Commission was urged to consider extending the range of persons to be protected by new legislation. Faced with the choice between a modest extension of the categories on the one hand, and the removal of every restriction so as to throw the jurisdiction open to all on the other, it chose a middle path in recommending a widening of the range of applicants to include anyone who is associated with the respondent by virtue of a family relationship or something closely akin to such a relationship. In this context the Commission stated that 'We have in mind instances such as two people who have lived together as close friends or in a homosexual relationship' (Law Com No 207, para. 3.20).

So, a non-molestation order can be obtained by a member of a homosexual couple who are living (or who have lived) in the same household.

2.1.3 Associated persons in adoption   In recognition of the fact that strong feelings (and hence the need for injunctive relief) may arise in connection with adoption proceedings, the Act provides that a child who is adopted or who has been freed for adoption, the relatives of such a child and the child's new adoptive carers shall be 'associated persons' for the purposes of the Act. So, the following are 'associated persons' by virtue of s. 62(5) of the Act:

- the natural parent of an adopted child and the child
- the natural parent of a child who has been freed for adoption and the child
- the 'natural grandparent' (i.e., the parent of a natural parent) of an adopted child and the child
- the natural grandparent of a child who has been freed for adoption and the child
- the natural parent of an adopted child and the adoptive parent of that child
- the natural parent of an adopted child and any person who has applied for an adoption order in respect of the child
- the natural parent of a child who has been freed for adoption and any person who has applied for an adoption order in respect of the child
- the natural parent of an adopted child and any person with whom the child has been placed for adoption at any time
- the natural parent of any child who has been freed for adoption and any person with whom the child has been placed at any time for adoption
- the natural grandparent of an adopted child and the adoptive parent of that child
- the natural grandparent of an adopted child and any person who has applied for an adoption order in respect of the child
- the natural grandparent of a child who has been freed for adoption and any person who has applied for an adoption order in respect of the child
- the natural grandparent of an adopted child and any person with whom the child has been placed for adoption at any time
- the natural grandparent of any child who has been freed for adoption and any person with whom the child has been placed at any time for adoption.

3   Relevant child

By s. 62(2) of the Act a 'relevant child' in relation to any proceedings under the Act means:

(a)   any child who is living with either party to the proceedings;
(b)   any child who might reasonably be expected to live with either party to the proceedings;
(c)   any child in relation to whom an order under the Adoption Act 1976 is in question in the proceedings;
(d)   any child in relation to whom an order under the Children Act 1989 is in question in the proceedings;
(e)   any other child whose interests the court considers relevant.

Chapter Eighteen
Matrimonial Home Rights

1 Introduction

The Matrimonial Homes Act 1967 was intended to protect those spouses who were not owners of the matrimonial home and thus had no security of tenure. It did so by creating 'rights of occupation', meaning that if a non-owning spouse was in occupation of the matrimonial home, she had a right not to be evicted or excluded from it by her husband save by court order. If she was not in occupation, she had a right with the leave of the court to enter into the home. Further, by making the statutory rights of occupation a charge on the interest of the property owning spouse, an element of protection against third parties was provided. Subsequently, the Matrimonial Proceedings and Property Act 1970 and the Matrimonial Homes and Property Act 1981 brought further refinement of the scheme to protect the non-property owning spouse, with the Matrimonial Homes Act 1983 (hereinafter MHA) describing itself as a statute 'to consolidate certain enactments relating to the rights of a husband or wife to occupy a dwelling-house that has been a matrimonial home'.

2 Modifications to existing statutory rights

The Family Law Act 1996 largely reproduces the MHA provisions, but it also resolves a problem identified by the Law Commission (Law Com No 207, May 1992, para. 4.4), namely that the MHA gave no power to make orders in respect of a property which the parties intended to be their home but in which they never actually lived together. The example given was of a couple selling their existing home and living in temporary, rented accommodation while renovating a new home, bought in the sole name of the husband. If the relationship broke down at that point, the wife had no MHA rights and the court no jurisdiction to regulate the occupation of the home. It was, therefore, recommended that the court should have power to make orders in respect of any dwelling-house which is, *or was intended to be*, the joint home of the parties.

Otherwise, modifications to the MHA scheme are minimal. The statutory rights are re-named 'matrimonial home rights' and changes of terminology are made to ensure consistency with a number of statutes conferring security of tenure, e.g., the Rent (Agriculture) Act 1976, the Rent Act 1977 and the Housing Acts.

3   Matrimonial home rights

Where one spouse is entitled to occupy a dwelling-house[1] by virtue of a beneficial estate or interest or contract, or by virtue of any enactment giving him the right to remain in occupation, and the other spouse is not so entitled, s. 30 of the 1996 Act gives the non-entitled spouse matrimonial home rights. Those rights are defined by s. 30(2) as:

(a)   if in occupation, a right not to be evicted or excluded from the dwelling-house or any part of it by the other spouse except with the leave of the court, given by order under s. 33;

(b)   if not in occupation, a right with the leave of the court to enter into and occupy the dwelling-house.

If a spouse has an equitable, rather than a legal, interest in the home, s. 30(9) provides that she has the same matrimonial home rights as a spouse with no interest whatsoever in it.

4   Effects of matrimonial home rights

4.1   Payments in respect of the dwelling-house

A spouse who has matrimonial home rights may pay rent, meet mortgage repayments and pay other household outgoings and her payments will have the same effect as if made by her husband (s. 30(3)). For example, if the husband fails to pay the rent, the wife can pay on his behalf and the landlords are bound to accept her payment. It matters not that the payments are made pursuant to an order ancillary to an occupation order (see Chapter 19). Mortgagees may treat mortgage repayments by the wife as payments by her husband, but the fact that they do so does not preclude her from claiming a beneficial interest in the matrimonial home based on her repayments (s. 30(5)). If she discharges mortgage repayments, she is entitled under s. 55(2) to be made a party to proceedings brought by the mortgagees, if:

(a)   she has applied to the court before the action is finally disposed of; and

(b)   the court sees *no special reason against* her being joined; and

(c)   the court is satisfied that she may be expected to take such action in respect of her husband's liability as might affect the outcome of proceedings (e.g., clearing mortgage arrears.)

(s. 55(3)).

4.2   Security of tenure

Occupation by the spouse with matrimonial home rights is, by virtue of s. 30(4), treated as occupation by the other spouse for the purposes of the Rent (Agriculture)

---

[1] Defined by s. 63(1) as including any building, or part of a building which is occupied as a dwelling; any caravan, houseboat or structure which is occupied as a dwelling and any yard, garden, garage or out-house belonging to the dwelling-house and occupied with it.

Act 1976, the Rent Act 1977 and the Housing Acts. This provision may help the wife to stave off possession proceedings, but it must be remembered that her matrimonial home rights are against her husband, rather than his landlord. If an application is to be made for the transfer of a tenancy, see Chapter 26.

5 'Matrimonial home'

Section 30(7) provides that s. 30 of the Act does not apply to a dwelling-house which:

(a)   has at no time been; and
(b)   was at no time intended by the spouses to be their matrimonial home.

6 Duration of matrimonial home rights

Under s. 30(8) of the Act, in line with the provisions of the MHA, rights continue only so long as:

(a)   the marriage subsists (unless the rights are extended by court order); and
(b)   the other spouse is entitled to occupy the dwelling-house (unless the rights are, by s. 31, a charge on the dwelling-house).

7 Extension of matrimonial home rights

An order may be made under s. 33(5) extending the rights beyond the death of the other spouse or the termination of the marriage. Note that such an order can only be made during the subsistence of the marriage.

8 Protection against third parties

Matrimonial home rights are a registrable charge, thus protecting the wife against subsequent purchasers and chargees. Where the title to the legal estate is registered, a notice under the Act is entered on the register (s. 31(10)). In the case of unregistered land, a Class F land charge should be registered. If a wife is entitled to a charge in respect of two or more dwelling-houses, only one can be registered at any one time (sch. 4, para. 2). By virtue of s. 56(2), where a mortgagee of land which consists of or substantially consists of a dwelling-house brings an action for the enforcement of his security and there is registered either a Class F land charge or a notice under the Act, notice of the action must be served by the mortgagee on the person on whose behalf the land charge is registered or the notice entered.

9 Conveyancing and miscellaneous

Schedule 4 to the Act deals with conveyancing and other provisions supplementary to ss. 30 and 31. In summary:

(a)   a contract for the sale of a house affected by a registered charge must include a term requiring cancellation of the registration before completion;

(b)   cancellation of registration is effected by satisfying the Chief Land Registrar, in the prescribed manner, of death, termination of marriage or order of the court;

(c)   a wife may agree in writing to release all or part of her matrimonial home rights;

(d)   a wife may agree in writing that any other charge on her husband's estate shall rank in priority to her own charge.

Chapter Nineteen
Occupation Orders

1 Introduction

It has long been recognised by judges, practitioners and some lay people that a great deal of confusion surrounded the various orders which the courts may make in relation to the occupation of, or exclusion from, a family home on the breakdown of a relationship. The Family Law Act 1996 attempts to simplify matters by granting courts the power to make a single order in relation to the home (referred to in the Act as the 'dwelling-house'). The order is known as an 'occupation order'. The terms which may be included in the order, and the criteria to be applied by the courts in deciding whether or not to grant the order, will depend on the status or classification of the applicant and of the respondent according to their property rights entitlements.

2 Background

The Law Commission (Law Com No 207) recognised that potential applicants for occupation orders fell into two main categories: those who were entitled to occupy the home by virtue of a legal or beneficial interest or a contractual or statutory right (including rights of occupation granted by the Matrimonial Homes Act 1983) ('entitled applicants') and those who were not ('non-entitled applicants'). The Commission favoured drawing a distinction between the two categories of applicants chiefly on the basis that the serious impact of an occupation order on the property rights of a respondent is easier to justify in the case of an entitled applicant than where the applicant has no such entitlement. It recommended that non-entitled applicants should be able to apply for orders against only former spouses, cohabitants or former cohabitants. That recommendation, as we see below, has been followed.

3 The scheme

Application can be made under five different sections of Part IV of the Act for an occupation order. To decide which section is applicable in a particular case you must determine the status of not only the applicant but also the respondent. The scheme of the Act favours married couples and property owners by offering them a greater level of protection. The basic format is as follows:

(a)   If the applicant is ENTITLED (see paragraph 4.1 below) — whether or not the respondent is also entitled — apply under s. 33

(b)   If the applicant is NOT ENTITLED — *but the respondent is entitled* — and

   (i)   the parties are *former spouses*, apply under s. 35; or

   (ii)   the parties are *cohabitants* or *former cohabitants*, apply under s. 36.

(c)   If *neither* the applicant *nor* the respondent is *entitled* and

   (i)   the parties are *spouses* or *former spouses*, apply under s. 37; or

   (ii)   the parties are *cohabitants* or *former cohabitants*, apply under s. 38.

4   Entitled applicant (applications under s. 33)

4.1   'Entitled applicant'

Under s. 33(1)(a)(i) and (ii) an applicant is an entitled applicant if she is entitled to occupy a dwelling-house by virtue of:

- a beneficial estate or interest, or
- a contract, or
- any enactment giving her the right to remain in occupation, or
- matrimonial home rights in relation to the dwelling-house

(See Chapter 18 on these rights.)

4.2   Conditions

The court has jurisdiction to grant an occupation order under s. 33 provided that the dwelling-house either:

(a)   *is* the home of the applicant and of another person with whom she is associated,[1] or

(b)   *has been* the home of the applicant and of another person with whom she is associated, or

(c)   was at any time *intended* by the applicant and a person with whom she is associated to be their home.

4.3   What a s. 33 order may contain

A s. 33 order may contain *any* of the following provisions:

(a)   enforcing the applicant's entitlement to remain in occupation as against the respondent;

(b)   requiring the respondent to permit the applicant to enter and remain in the dwelling-house;

---

[1] See Chapter 17 on 'Associated persons'. Note that s. 62(3)(e) includes within the list of associated persons a couple who have agreed to marry whether or not the agreement has been terminated. If the agreement has been terminated, an application under s. 33 cannot be made more than 3 years after the day on which it was terminated.

(c) requiring the respondent to permit the applicant to enter and remain in part of the dwelling-house;

(d) regulating the occupation of the dwelling-house by either or both parties

(e) prohibiting, suspending or restricting the exercise by the respondent of his right (whether by virtue of a beneficial estate or interest, contract or enactment) to occupy the dwelling-house;

(f) restricting or terminating the respondent's matrimonial home rights;

(g) requiring the respondent to leave the dwelling-house;

(h) requiring the respondent to leave part of the the dwelling-house;

(i) excluding the respondent from a defined area in which the dwelling-house is included (s. 33(3)).

Because orders containing any of the above provisions effectively *regulate* the occupation of the home, the Law Commission helpfully refers to them as *regulatory* orders, as opposed to *declaratory* orders which declare or extend existing rights and *grant* rights.

4.4 The test for regulatory orders

Section 33(6) of the Act provides that in deciding whether or not to make any of the above regulatory orders under s. 33(3), the court shall have regard to all the circumstances including:

(a) the respective housing needs and housing resources of the parties and of any relevant child;

(b) the respective financial resources of the parties;

(c) the likely effect of any order, or of any decision by the court not to exercise its powers under s. 33(3), on the health, safety or well-being of the parties and of any relevant child;

(d) the conduct of the parties in relation to each other and otherwise.

In accordance with s. 33(7) the court *must* make an order if it appears that the applicant or any relevant child is likely to suffer *significant*[2] *harm* attributable to conduct of the respondent if an order is *not* made, *unless* it appears that:

(a) the respondent or any relevant child is likely to suffer significant harm if the order is made; and

(b) the harm likely to be suffered by the respondent or the child in that event is *as great as*, or *greater than*, the harm attributable to conduct of the respondent which is likely to be suffered by the applicant or child if the order is not made.

4.5 The test explained

In cases where the question of significant harm does not arise the court has *power* to make an order taking into account the four factors considered above (i.e., housing

---

[2] It is not thought likely that the word 'significant' will cause any difficulty in relation to the Act. In *Humberside County Council* v *B* [1993] 1 FLR 257, Booth J took the view that the dictionary definition of significant as 'considerable, noteworthy or important' was apt and helpful.

needs and housing resources, financial resources, health, safety or well-being and conduct). However, in cases where there is a likelihood of significant harm, the power becomes a *duty* (the section says 'shall', so it is mandatory) and the court must make an order after balancing the degree of harm likely to be suffered by both parties and by any children concerned. If both parties are able to establish significant harm, but neither is able to show *greater* harm, then the court still has the *power* to make an appropriate order, but is not under a *duty* to do so.

It is very likely that in cases where it can be established that there is a risk of significant harm to a child, the child's interests will become in effect the paramount consideration since it is that factor which will have imposed a duty on the court to make an order.

4.6 'Harm' etc. defined

'Harm' is defined in s. 63 of the Act. In relation to a person who is aged 18 or more, harm means 'ill-treatment or the impairment of health' and in relation to a child it means 'ill-treatment or the impairment of health or impairment of development'.

'Ill-treatment' includes forms of ill-treatment which are not physical. In the case of a child, the phrase includes sexual abuse.

'Health' includes physical and mental health.

'Development' means physical, intellectual, emotional, social or behavioural development.

4.7 Duration

There was often confusion and misunderstanding about the time limits governing ouster and exclusion orders. The Act represents a new start. Section 33(10) provides that orders under s. 33 (i.e., in the case of *entitled* applicants) may be for a specified period, until the occurrence of a specified event or until further order.

4.8 Declaratory orders

The Law Commission recommended that the court should have power to make an occupation order with a variety of terms, not only regulatory (as above) but also declaratory. In the case of a s. 33 application, s. 33(4) of the Act provides that an occupation order may *declare* that the applicant is *entitled to occupy a dwelling-house* by virtue of a beneficial estate or interest or contract or by virtue of an enactment giving her the right to remain in occupation, or declare that the applicant *has* matrimonial home rights. This power to make declaratory orders is unlikely to be frequently invoked as an entitled applicant already has, by definition, the right to occupy the dwelling-house and has no need for those rights to be declared by the court. However, one circumstance which may cause the court to use this power is where there is an initial dispute between the parties about whether the applicant is in fact an entitled applicant.

5   Non-entitled applicant and entitled respondent (applications under ss. 35 and 36)

5.1 Introduction

If a person is not entitled to occupy a dwelling-house by virtue of:

- a beneficial estate or interest
- a contract
- any enactment giving him the right to remain in occupation
- matrimonial home rights in relation to the dwelling-house (see Chapter 18)

she will still be entitled to apply for an occupation order, but only against a spouse, former spouse, cohabitant or former cohabitant (see Chapter 17 for the definition of these categories).

Where the applicant is non-entitled but the respondent is an entitled respondent (i.e., entitled to occupy the dwelling-house by virtue of a beneficial estate or interest, or contract or by virtue of any enactment) the application should be made under s. 35 of the Act if the parties are former spouses, or under s. 36 if they are cohabitants or former cohabitants. As will be seen below (paragraph 6) where neither the applicant nor the respondent is entitled to occupy the dwelling-house, then the application for an occupation order must be made under s. 37 in the case of spouses or under s. 38 in the case of cohabitants or former cohabitants.

5.2 Occupation rights

If the court grants an occupation order under s. 35 or 36 (see paragraph 5.3 below as to criteria to be applied), the order *must* include in the case of an applicant who is already in occupation of the dwelling-house a provision giving the applicant the right not to be evicted or excluded from the dwelling-house or any part of it by the respondent for the period specified in the order together with a provision prohibiting the respondent from evicting the applicant during that period (ss. 35(3) and 36(3)).

And in the case of an applicant who is not in occupation the occupation order *must* contain a provision giving the applicant the right to enter into and occupy the dwelling-house for the period specified in the order and requiring the respondent to permit the exercise of that right (ss. 35(4) and 36(4)).

The court's power to confer these rights in an appropriate case is necessary because the applicant under s. 35 or 36 is by definition 'non-entitled'. The Law Commission described the rights as 'occupation rights' and we adopt their shorthand in what follows.

5.3 The test for occupation rights orders

Sections 35(6) and 36(6) set out the criteria to which the court is to have regard in exercising its power to give to non-entitled applicants occupation rights under s. 35(3) or (4), and s. 36(3) or (4). The criteria differ according to whether the non-entitled applicant is a former spouse on the one hand, or a cohabitant/former cohabitant on the other.

5.3.1 If parties are former spouses (s. 35) When the parties are former spouses, in deciding whether or not to make an occupation order containing occupation rights under s. 35(3) or (4) of the Act, the court must have regard under s. 35(6) to all the circumstances including:

(a) the respective housing needs and housing resources of the parties and of any relevant child;

(b)   the respective financial resources of the parties;

(c)   the likely effect of any order, or of any decision by the court not to exercise its powers under s. 35(3) or (4), on the health, safety or well-being of the parties and of any relevant child;

(d)   the conduct of the parties in relation to each other and otherwise;

and

(e)   the length of time that has elapsed since the parties ceased to live together;

(f)   the length of time that has elapsed since the marriage was dissolved or annulled;

(g)   the existence of any pending proceedings between the parties for property adjustment orders under the Matrimonial Causes Act 1973, s. 24, or for an order for financial relief against parents under the Children Act 1989, sch. 1, para. 1(2)(d) or (e) or proceedings relating to the legal or beneficial ownership of the dwelling-house.

5.3.2   If parties are cohabitants or former cohabitants (s. 36)   When the parties are cohabitants or former cohabitants, in deciding whether or not to make an occupation order containing occupation rights under s. 36(3) or (4) of the Act, the court must have regard under s. 36(6) to all the circumstances including:

(a)   the respective housing needs and housing resources of the parties and of any relevant child;

(b)   the respective financial resources of the parties;

(c)   the likely effect of any order, or of any decision by the court not to exercise its powers under s. 36(3) or (4), on the health, safety or well-being of the parties and of any relevant child;

(d)   the conduct of the parties in relation to each other and otherwise;

(e)   the nature of the relationship — note that in this respect the court is specifically required by s. 41(2) to have regard to the fact that the parties have not given each other 'the commitment involved in marriage';

(f)   the length of time they have lived together as man and wife;

(g)   whether there are or have been any children who are children of both parties or for whom the parties have or have had parental responsibility;

(h)   the length of time that has elapsed since the parties ceased to live together;

(i)   the existence of any pending proceedings for an order for financial relief against parents under Children Act 1989, sch. 1, para. 1(2)(d) or (e) or proceedings relating to the legal or beneficial ownership of the dwelling-house.

5.4   Regulatory orders

As we have seen above in paragraph 5.2, if the court decides to make an order under s. 35 or s. 36 of the Act it *must* include a provision dealing with occupation rights. In addition the court *may* grant an order containing any of the following provisions (ss. 35(5) and 36(5)):

(a)   regulating the occupation of the dwelling-house by either or both parties;

(b) prohibiting, suspending or restricting the exercise by the respondent of his right (whether by virtue of a beneficial estate or interest, contract or enactment) to occupy the dwelling-house;

(c) requiring the respondent to leave the dwelling-house;

(d) requiring the respondent to leave part of the dwelling-house;

(e) excluding the respondent from a defined area in which the dwelling-house is included.

5.5 The test for regulatory orders

5.5.1 If parties are former spouses (s. 35)

When the parties are former spouses, in deciding whether or not to make a regulatory order under s. 35(5) the court must have regard under s. 35(6) and (7) to all the circumstances including:

(a) the respective housing needs and housing resources of the parties and of any relevant child;

(b) the respective financial resources of the parties;

(c) the likely effect of any order, or of any decision by the court not to exercise its powers under s. 35(3) or (4), on the health, safety or well-being of the parties and of any relevant child;

(d) the conduct of the parties in relation to each other and otherwise;

(e) the length of time that has elapsed since the parties ceased to live together.

But again, as with regulatory orders granted under s. 33(3) to entitled applicants, the court *must* make an order if it appears likely that that the applicant or any relevant child will suffer significant harm attributable to conduct of the respondent if an order is not made, *unless* the harm caused to the respondent or to any relevant child will be as great as or greater than the harm attributable to conduct of the respondent which is likely to be suffered by the applicant or any relevant child if the order is not made (s. 35(8)).

5.5.2 If parties are cohabitants or former cohabitants (s. 36)

When the parties are cohabitants or former cohabitants, in deciding whether to make a regulatory order under s. 36 the court must have regard to all the circumstances including:

(a) the respective housing needs and housing resources of the parties and of any relevant child;

(b) the respective financial resources of the parties;

(c) the likely effect of any order, or of any decision by the court not to exercise its powers under s. 36(3) or (4), on the health, safety or well-being of the parties and of any relevant child;

(d) the conduct of the parties in relation to each other and otherwise.

In addition the court must have regard to the following questions:

- whether the applicant or any relevant child is likely to suffer significant harm attributable to conduct of the respondent if the regulatory provision is not included in the order and

- whether the harm likely to be suffered by the respondent or child if the provision is included is as great as or greater than the harm attributable to conduct of the respondent which is likely to be suffered by the applicant or child if the provision is not included.

(See s. 36(6)–(8)).

5.6   Death of either party

Orders under ss. 35 and 36 of the Act cannot be made after the death of either party, nor can they continue to have effect after the death of either party (ss. 35(9) and 36(9)).

5.7   Duration

Orders under ss. 35 and 36 are limited in the first instance to a specified period, not exceeding 6 months. A s. 35 (i.e., former spouse) order may be extended on more than one occasion for a further period not exceeding 6 months, but a s. 36 (i.e., cohabitants or former cohabitants) order may only be so extended on one occasion (ss. 35(10) and 36(10)).

6   Non-entitled applicant and non-entitled respondent (applications under ss. 37 and 38)

6.1   Introduction

Where neither the applicant nor the respondent is entitled (by virtue of a beneficial estate or interest, or contract or by virtue of any enactment) to occupy the dwelling house, then the application for an occupation order must be made under s. 37 if the parties are spouses or former spouses, or under s. 38 in the case of cohabitants or former cohabitants. Such applicants will be comparatively rare since in most cases at least one of the parties will be entitled to occupy or remain in occupation of the dwelling-house. The Law Commission identified two such categories, namely squatters and bare licencees. Such people were able to obtain orders under the Domestic Violence and Matrimonial Proceedings Act 1976 and it was not considered appropriate that they should be excluded from the protection afforded by the new legislation.

6.2   Regulatory orders only are obtainable

The court may make an order under s. 37 or s. 38 of the Act:

(a)   requiring the respondent to permit the applicant to enter and remain in the dwelling-house;

(b)   requiring the respondent to permit the applicant to enter and remain in part of the dwelling-house;

(c)   regulating the occupation of the dwelling-house by either or both parties;

(d)   requiring the respondent to leave the dwelling-house;

(e)   requiring the respondent to leave part of the dwelling-house;
(f)   excluding the respondent from a defined area in which the dwelling-house is included.

6.3   The test for the orders

6.3.1   If parties are spouses or former spouses (s. 37)   When the parties are spouses or former spouses, in deciding whether to make an order the court shall have regard to all the circumstances including:

(a)   the respective housing needs and housing resources of the parties and of any relevant child;
(b)   the respective financial resources of the parties;
(c)   the likely effect of any order, or of any decision by the court not to exercise its powers under s. 37(3), on the health, safety or well-being of the parties and of any relevant child;
(d)   the conduct of the parties in relation to each other and otherwise.

As with regulatory orders granted under s. 33(3) to entitled applicants, the court *must* make an order if it appears likely that the applicant or any relevant child will suffer significant harm attributable to conduct of the respondent if an order is not made, *unless* the harm caused to the respondent or to any relevant child will be as great as or greater than the harm attributable to conduct of the respondent which is likely to be suffered by the applicant or any relevant child if the order is not made (s. 37(4)).

6.3.2   If parties are cohabitants or former cohabitants (s. 38)   When the parties are cohabitants or former cohabitants, in deciding whether to make an order the court shall have regard to all the circumstances including:

(a)   the respective housing needs and housing resources of the parties and of any relevant child;
(b)   the respective financial resources of the parties;
(c)   the likely effect of any order, or of any decision by the court not to exercise its powers under s. 38(3), on the health, safety or well-being of the parties and of any relevant child;
(d)   the conduct of the parties in relation to each other and otherwise.

In addition the court must have regard to the following questions:

●   whether the applicant or any relevant child is likely to suffer significant harm attributable to conduct of the respondent if the regulatory provision is not included in the order; and
●   whether the harm likely to be suffered by the respondent or child if the provision is included is as great as or greater than the harm attributable to conduct of the respondent which is likely to be suffered by the applicant or child if the provision is not included.

6.4 Duration

Orders under ss. 37 and 38 are limited in the first instance to a specified period, not exceeding 6 months. A s. 37 (i.e., spouse or former spouse) order may be extended on more than one occasion for a further period not exceeding 6 months, but a s. 38 (i.e., cohabitants or former cohabitants) order may only be so extended on one occasion (ss. 37(5) and 38(6)).

7 Third parties as representatives

Section 60 allows rules of court to be made authorising a prescribed person ('a representative') to act on behalf of victims of domestic violence. The rules will set out the conditions to be satisfied before a representative may apply on behalf of another and the considerations which will be taken into account by the court in exercising its powers when a representative is acting. This may seem a curious inclusion when a proposal by the Law Commission that the police should have the power to pursue civil remedies on behalf of an aggrieved party was rejected on the advice of the Home Affairs Select Committee in its Report on Domestic Violence (March 1993, HMSO), on the grounds that it would involve a novel extension of police powers from a criminal function to a civil function.

Chapter Twenty
Orders Ancillary to Occupation Orders

1 Introduction

An application to court for an occupation order will generally be made at a time of crisis. At such times financial matters are often an added anxiety to distraught clients. The suggestion made in Working Paper No 113, 'Domestic Violence and Occupation of the Family Home', prior to the Law Commission, that the court ought to have the power to make orders ancillary to the grant of occupation orders relating to the discharge of rent, mortgage instalments and other outgoings[1] received particularly warm support from practitioners.

2 The court's powers

2.1 The basic provision

Section 40(1)(a) of the Act provides that the court *may* on making an order under ss. 33, 35 or 36 (but not under ss. 37 or 38) — or at any time thereafter — impose on either party obligations as to:

- the repair and maintenance of the dwelling-house
- the discharge of rent
- the discharge of mortgage payments
- the discharge of other outgoings, affecting the dwelling-house.

It is anticipated that this power will be particularly useful when an occupation order continues for some time or while the outcome of proceedings under the Matrimonial Causes Act 1973 is awaited.

2.2 Payment of rent to ousted, entitled respondent

The Law Commission also suggested that the court should have power to order an occupying party to make payments to the other for that occupation. Under the old law only a non-entitled spouse could be ordered to make such payments, but the

---

[1] The court had this ancillary jurisdiction only under Part III of the Matrimonial Homes Act 1983, the whole of which is repealed by the 1995 Act.

Commission saw no reason in principle why *any* person who is occupying property which another is prima facie entitled to occupy, whether solely or jointly, should not, in an appropriate case, be ordered to compensate the other person. Section 40 provides, therefore, that the court may order a party occupying the dwelling-house (whether the applicant is an entitled applicant or not) to make periodical payments to the other party in respect of the accommodation, where the other party would (but for the order) be entitled to occupy the dwelling-house by virtue of a beneficial estate or interest or contract or by virtue of any enactment. It should be noted that such an order cannot be made against a non-entitled respondent.

2.3 Furniture and contents

The court may grant to either party possession or use of furniture or other contents of the dwelling-house and order either party to take reasonable care of any furniture or other contents and/or to take reasonable steps to keep the dwelling-house and any furniture or other contents secure[2] (s. 40 (1)(c)–(e)).

2.4 The test

In deciding whether, and, if so, how to exercise its powers the court must have regard under s. 40(2) to all the circumstances of the case including:

(a) the financial needs and financial resources of the parties; and

(b) the financial obligations which they have or are likely to have in the foreseeable future to each other and to any relevant child.

2.5 Duration

An order under s. 40 ceases to have effect when the occupation order to which it relates comes to an end (s. 40(3)).

---

[2] The obligation to take reasonable care of furniture and to keep the house, furniture and contents secure goes beyond the proposals contained in the draft Bill which appears in Appendix A of the Law Commission's Report.

Chapter Twenty-One
Non-Molestation Orders

1 Introduction

This remedy is one which a person may seek against another person with whom she is associated, either for her own sake or for the sake of a child. A child under 16 may also apply for such an order but only with the court's leave (see Chapter 23).

A non-molestation order is an order prohibiting a person (referred to in the Act as 'the respondent') from molesting another person who is *associated* with the respondent or who is a *relevant child* (s. 42(1)(a) and (b)). The order is defined in such a way that it is unnecessary, in a suitable case, to obtain separate orders to protect an adult and a child.

In determining, therefore, whether a client will be able to obtain a non-molestation order under the Act the first matter to be ascertained is whether the applicant and respondent are 'associated persons'[1] within the meaning of the Act (see Chapter 17) or, where the person sought to be protected is a child, whether that child is a 'relevant' child.

2 When an order may be made

Section 42(2) allows the court to make a non-molestation order in the following circumstances:

(a) if an application has been made by a person who is associated with the respondent:
　　(i) in other family proceedings;
　　(ii) in the absence of any other family proceedings (i.e., a 'free standing' application); or
(b) without an application being made:
　　(i) in any family proceedings to which the respondent is already a party;
　　(ii) if the court considers that the order should be made for the benefit of any other party to the proceedings or any relevant child.

---

[1] A note of caution: although persons who have agreed to marry are associated persons (s. 62(1)(e)), they are not permitted to apply for a non-molestation order if more than 3 years have elapsed since the engagement was broken off unless the application is made in the course of other family proceedings (s. 42(4)).

The latter provision, similar to the power conferred on the court by s. 10 of the Children Act 1989 to make any s. 8 order of its own motion in any family proceedings, is a particularly welcome innovation in the realm of care proceedings. It enables a court to make a non-molestation order in the course of care proceedings (since these are brought under Part IV of the Children Act 1989 and, therefore, fall within the definition of 'family proceedings' — see below) of its own motion.

3 Family proceedings

Family proceedings are defined in s. 63 of the Act as any proceedings under:

(a) the inherent jurisdiction of the High Court in relation to children;
(b) Part II and Part IV of the Family Law Act 1996;
(c) the Matrimonial Causes Act 1973;
(d) the Adoption Act 1976;
(e) the Domestic Proceedings and Magistrates' Courts Act 1978;
(f) Part III of the Matrimonial and Family Proceedings Act 1984;
(g) Parts I, II and IV of the Children Act 1989;
(h) s. 30 of the Human Fertilisation and Embryology Act 1990.

By the operation of s. 42(3) of the Act the court may specifically make a non-molestation order in proceedings in which the court has made an emergency protection order which includes an exclusion requirement under s. 44 of the Children Act 1989 (see Chapter 27). That specific inclusion in the definition of 'family proceedings' is necessary because proceedings under s. 44 of the Children Act 1989 (for an emergency protection order) are not proceedings under Parts I, II or IV of the Children Act 1989, s. 44 being contained in Part V of the Children Act 1989.

4 The test

Whether or not a non-molestation order is made lies within the discretion of the court. In exercising its discretion the court is enjoined to have regard to all the circumstances including the need to secure the health, safety and well-being of the applicant, the other party to the proceedings or the relevant child (s. 42 (5)(a) and (b)).

If the court is considering making an order of its own motion the same considerations apply in relation to the beneficiary of the order.

This test places less emphasis than the previous law on the violence or threatened violence of the respondent. The Law Commission took the view that the problem with singling out violence was that 'the response of the court would be dictated by the nature of the defendant's behaviour, rather than the effect upon the applicant or child concerned' (Law Com No 207, para. 3.6).

5 Molestation

The Commission found no evidence that under the old law problems had been caused by lack of a statutory definition and recommended that there should be no such definition and so nowhere in the Act is 'molestation' defined. The courts will continue, therefore, to be guided by the old case law which establishes that the term includes, but is wider than, violence (see *Davis* v *Johnson* [1979] AC 264 per Viscount Dilhorne: 'Violence is a form of molestation, but molestation may take place without the threat or use of violence and still be serious and inimical to mental or physical health.').

Any form of serious pestering or harassment is included in the concept of molestation (*Vaughan* v *Vaughan* [1973] 1 WLR 1159: respondent calling at applicant's house in the early hours of the morning and late at night, and following her to her place of work when he was aware that she was frightened of him).

In *Horner* v *Horner* [1982] 2 All ER 495 it was held that sending the applicant threatening letters and intercepting her on her way home amounted to molestation. Similarly, in *Johnston* v *Walton* [1990] 1 FLR 350, sending partially nude photographs of the applicant to a national newspaper for publication with intent to cause her distress was held to merit injunctive relief as conduct amounting to molestation, thus making it plain that direct contact is unnecessary.

In *C* v *C (Non-molestation order: Jurisdiction), The Times*, 16th December 1997, it was held by Sir Stephen Brown P that the word 'molestation' implied some quite deliberate conduct which was aimed at a high degree of harassment of the other party sufficient to call for the intervention of the court. Applying that test, the husband's application seeking to prevent his former wife from giving further information to newspaper reporters which would perpetuate the publication of articles which were offensive to him, was dismissed. The President observed that the conduct complained of came nowhere near molestation as envisaged by s. 42 of the Act.

Under the old law a common form of a 'non-mol' order was in the form of a restraint from 'assaulting molesting or otherwise interfering'. Where appropriate, after general words of restraint, more precise phrasing could be included to restrain specific kinds of behaviour of which complaint was being made. This dual, flexible approach is preserved by s. 42(6) of the Act which provides that: 'A non-molestation order may be expressed so as to refer to molestation in general, to particular acts of molestation, or to both.'

So, the court may impose a general injunction on a respondent such as 'not to molest the applicant, whether by actual or threatened violence or by harassing or pestering her', followed by a more specific restraint such as forbidding the respondent from interfering with the applicant's motor vehicle. (See the precedents reproduced in the Appendix.)

6 Duration

The Law Commission took the view that fixed time limits were inevitably arbitrary and capable of restricting the courts' ability to react flexibly to family problems, and in particular it was concerned that orders should be capable of enduring beyond the end of a relationship. It therefore recommended that the courts should be able to make non-molestation orders for any specified period or until further order. That recommendation has been embodied in s. 42(7) of the Act which provides that: 'A non-molestation order may be made for a specified period or until further order.'

Finally, a non-molestation order made in the course of family proceedings ceases if those proceedings are withdrawn or dismissed (s. 42(8)).

7 Third parties as representatives

Section 60 allows rules of court to be made authorising a prescribed person ('a representative') to act on behalf of victims of domestic violence. The rules will set out the conditions to be satisfied before a representative may apply on behalf of another and the considerations which will be taken into account by the court in exercising its powers when a representative is acting.

Chapter Twenty-Two
Ex Parte Orders and Undertakings

1 Introduction

The Law Commission was very conscious of the dangers inherent in the grant of ex parte orders, such as the risk of injustice being done to a respondent where the applicant's side of the story only is heard or the possibility of a misconceived or malicious application. These drawbacks have led the courts to emphasis the draconian nature of ex parte orders. There is ample authority to the effect that an order which requires a respondent to vacate the matrimonial home should seldom, if ever, be granted (see e.g., *G v G (Ouster: Ex Parte Application* [1990] 1 FLR 395; *Shipp v Shipp* [1988] 1 FLR 345).

Nevertheless, the Commission accepted the proposition that there are bound to be occasions and circumstances when ex parte orders are both desirable and necessary. Section 45 of the Act, therefore, preserves the power of the court to grant both occupation and non-molestation orders ex parte. It is very likely, however, that the extreme caution which characterised the treatment of ex parte applications under the old law (particularly in the case of ouster or exclusion orders) will be observed by the courts in the exercise of its ex parte jurisdiction under the new Act.

2 The test

The overriding principle is that the court should only exercise its discretion to make an order ex parte where it is *just and convenient* to do so (s. 45(1)).

In determining whether to grant an order ex parte the court must have regard to all the circumstances including:

(a)   any risk of significant harm to the applicant or a relevant child, attributable to conduct of the respondent if the order is not made immediately (s. 45(2)(a));[1]

(b)   whether it is likely that the applicant will be deterred or prevented from pursuing the application if an order is not made immediately (s. 45 (2)(b));

(c)   whether there is reason to believe that the respondent is aware of the proceedings, but is deliberately evading service and that the applicant or a relevant child will be seriously prejudiced by the delay involved in effecting service of the

---

[1] The link between the risk of significant harm and the respondent's conduct did not appear in the Family Homes and Domestic Violence Bill.

proceedings (where the court is a magistrates' court) or (in any other case) in effecting substituted service (s. 45 (2)(c)).

3 Safeguards

Although not included in the Commission's draft Bill, s. 45(3) provides that where the court does make an ex parte order (whether a non-molestation or occupation order), it must give the respondent an opportunity to make representations as soon as just and convenient at a ' full hearing', defined by s. 45(5) as 'a hearing of which notice has been given to all the parties in accordance with rules of court'.

4 Undertakings

From a practitioner's perspective undertakings are extremely useful. They can save time and, importantly, save face in that a client is able to walk away from the application without findings of fact against him. Most people take the view that an undertaking is a satisfactory way of resolving an application. It is unsurprising, therefore, that s. 46 enables the court to accept an undertaking from any party (it will usually be the respondent) where it has power to make an occupation order or a non-molestation order (s. 46(1)).

As under the old law,[2] no power of arrest can be attached to an undertaking (s. 46(2)).

4.1 More powers of arrest — fewer undertakings

By s. 46(3) the court is prevented from accepting an undertaking in a case where apart from this section it would have attached a power of arrest to the order. In other words, if the court takes the view that the grounds are made out for attaching a power of arrest to a non-molestation or occupation order, it may not in those circumstances accept an undertaking instead of making an order. This provision will result in fewer undertakings because s. 47 of the Act imposes on the court (see Chapter 25) an *obligation* to attach a power of arrest in all cases where it appears to the court that the respondent has used or *threatened* violence against the applicant or a relevant child *unless* it is satisfied that in all the circumstances of the case the applicant or child will be adequately protected without one (s. 47(2)). The result will be more powers of arrest, hence fewer undertakings.

4.2 Enforceability

As before, an undertaking given to the court is enforceable as if it were an order of the court (s. 46(4)).

---

[2] See *McConnell* v *McConnell* (1980) Fam Law 214, and *Carpenter* v *Carpenter* [1988] 1 FLR 121.

Chapter Twenty-Three
The Child as Applicant

1 Introduction

Since 1991 children have had the opportunity to play a full role in family proceedings which are likely to determine their future. The Family Proceedings Rules 1991 (SI 1991 No 1247) initially introduced a procedure whereby, in public law proceedings, the solicitor acting on behalf of the guardian ad litem is required to act on the instructions of the minor if her instructions are in conflict with those of the guardian (rr. 4.11 and 4.12). Subsequent amendments to the Rules produced r. 9.2A. This rule permits minors in private law proceedings to appear without a guardian ad litem or next friend either with the leave of the court or if represented by a solicitor who considers that the minor is of sufficient understanding to give instructions. Where the minor has been represented by a guardian or next friend, she may apply to court for leave to continue the proceedings without such assistance. Leave will be granted if the court is satisfied that the child has sufficient understanding to participate in the proceedings (Children Act 1989, s. 10(8) and 1991 Rules, r. 9.2A(6)). The 'sufficient understanding' test is used in the Act, although the difficulties it has created in practice have led at least one judge (a member of the Family Proceedings Rules Committee) to believe that no child should enter proceedings without a guardian or next friend unless the court is satisfied, applying the welfare test, that such a direction is appropriate in the particular circumstances of the case (see Thorpe, J (as he then was), 'Independent Representation for Minors' [1994] Fam Law 20).

2 The new provisions

A child under the age of 16 may not apply for an occupation order or a non-molestation order without the leave of the court (s. 43(1)). Leave will be granted only if the court is satisfied that the child has *sufficient understanding* to make the proposed application (s. 43(2)).

3 'Sufficient understanding'

The issue of the sufficiency of a child's understanding was considered by the House of Lords in *Gillick* v *West Norfolk & Wisbech Area Health Authority and Another* [1986] AC 112, [1986] 1 FLR 224. It was held that the parental right to decide whether or not medical treatment could be given to a child under 16 terminated if and when the child achieved a sufficient understanding and intelligence to enable her to understand fully what was proposed. Lord Scarman used the phrase: 'the attainment by a child of an age of sufficient discretion to enable him or her to exercise a wise choice in his or her own interests' (at p. 188A).

The 'Gillick competent' test was approved by the Court of Appeal in *Re S (A Minor) (Independent Representation)* [1993] 2 FLR 437 as the appropriate test under the Children Act 1989 and related Rules. It was held that except in a straightforward matter, or in the case of an older child, the court would be unlikely to grant leave to a minor to take part in proceedings without a next friend or guardian unless the child proposed to be legally represented. In that event, the real issue would be whether the child had sufficient understanding to give coherent instructions. Sir Thomas Bingham MR said (at p. 444G–H):

> Different children have differing levels of understanding at the same age. And understanding is not an absolute. It has to be assessed relatively to the issues in the proceedings. Where any sound judgment calls for insight and imagination which only maturity and experience can bring, both the court and the solicitor will be slow to conclude that the child's understanding is sufficient.

In *Re CT (A Minor) (Wardship: Representation)* [1993] 2 FLR 278 the Court of Appeal made it plain that by virtue of r. 9.2A(10) the court, rather than a solicitor, has the ultimate right to decide whether a child who comes before it as a party without a next friend or guardian ad litem has the necessary ability, having regard to his understanding, to instruct his solicitor. Waite LJ expressed his hope and expectation that instances where a challenge is directed to a solicitor's view of his minor client's ability to instruct him will be rare, and that cases where the court felt bound to question such ability of its own motion would be rarer still. He said (at p. 289D):

> If and when such instances do arise, I would expect them to be resolved by a swift, pragmatic enquiry conducted in a manner which involved the minimum delay and the least possible distress to the child concerned. It would be very unsatisfactory if such issues themselves became a subject of detailed medical or other professional investigation.

More recently, when considering an application by a 14-year-old girl for leave to apply for a s. 8 order, Stuart-White J held in *Re C (Residence: Child's Application for Leave)* [1995] 1 FLR 927 that:

- the principles in s. 10(9) of the Children Act 1989 which normally apply to applications for leave to apply for s. 8 orders do not apply to applications by children
- in dealing with such applications, the best interests of the child are important, although not paramount
- such applications should be approached cautiously, because once a child is a party to proceedings between warring parents, the child will be exposed to hearing evidence of the parents which it might be better for the child not to hear

- the court could consider matters in addition to the issue of whether the child had sufficient understanding to make the proposed application, in particular the likelihood of success of the application.

4 Separate representation of children

The Lord Chancellor is empowered by s. 64(1) to make regulations providing for the separate representation of children in proceedings under Parts II and IV of the Act.

5 Practice

Article 4(2) of the Family Law Act 1996 (Part IV) (Allocation of Proceedings) Order 1997 requires an application to be commenced in the High Court if:

(a) the application is brought under Part IV by an applicant who is under 18; or
(b) the application is for the grant of leave under s. 43 (leave of the court required for applications by children under 16).

Chapter Twenty-Four
Variation and Discharge of Orders

1 General

Either the respondent or the applicant may apply to court to vary or discharge an occupation or non-molestation order (s. 49(1)).

2 Court's own motion

Where a court has made a non-molestation order of its own motion under s. 42(2)(b) (see Chapter 21), the court itself may vary or discharge the order, even though no separate application has been made to do so (s. 49(2)).

3 Power of arrest

The court may of its own motion vary or discharge a power of arrest attached to a non-molestation or occupation order made ex parte (s. 49(4)).

Chapter Twenty-Five
Enforcement

1 Introduction

The Domestic Violence and Matrimonial Proceedings Act (DVMPA) 1976 permitted the High Court and county courts to attach a power of arrest to an injunction containing an exclusion order or restraining one party from using violence. The Domestic Proceedings and Magistrates' Court Act (DPMCA) 1978 allowed magistrates to attach powers of arrest in broadly similar circumstances. The Law Commission pointed out that powers of arrest have tended to be attached to a minority of injunctions: figures for 1989 (the last year for which figures were available) show that out of a total of 20,419 injunctions granted under the DVMPA, powers of arrest were attached in only 5, 870 cases.[1] The Law Commission recommended that where there has been actual or threatened violence, the court should be required to attach a power of arrest to any specified provisions of an order in favour of any eligible applicant unless in all the circumstances the applicant or child would be adequately protected without such a power.[2] A further example of the unsatisfactory nature of the old legislation was that the High Court and county courts did not share the powers of magistrates to issue arrest warrants or to remand a person arrested pursuant to a power of arrest (in custody, on bail or for medical reports) pending proceedings being taken for breach of an order. The Act extends the powers of the High Court and county courts to bring them in line with those already enjoyed by magistrates' courts.

2 Powers of arrest

Where:

    (a)   the court makes an occupation order or a non-molestation order; *and*
    (b)   it appears to the court that the respondent has used or *threatened* violence against the applicant or a relevant child,

the court *must* attach power of arrest to one or more provisions of the order *unless* it is satisfied that in all the circumstances the applicant or child will be adequately protected without one (s. 47(1) and (2)).

---

[1] Law Com No 207, May 1992, para. 5.11.
[2] Law Com No 207, para. 5.13.

This represents a significant extension of the court's powers to attach a power of arrest to orders, since under the old law the judge had to be satisfied, first, that the respondent had caused actual bodily harm to the applicant or any child concerned and, secondly, that the respondent was likely to do so again.[3]

3 Ex parte orders

If an order is made ex parte, the court has a discretion to attach to one or more of its provisions a power of arrest if it appears to the court that:

(a)   the respondent has used or *threatened* violence against the applicant or a relevant child; *and*

(b)   there is a risk of *significant harm*[4] to the applicant or child, attributable to the conduct of the respondent, if the power of arrest is not attached *immediately* (s. 47(3)).

If the court does attach a power of arrest to an order made ex parte, the power of arrest may be ordered to have effect for a shorter time than other provisions of the order. Any period specified may be extended by the court (on one or more occasions) on an application to vary or discharge the relevant order (s. 47(4) and (5)).

4 Arrest without warrant

If a power of arrest is attached to provisions of an order, s. 47(6) permits a constable to arrest without warrant a person whom he has reasonable cause of suspecting to be in breach of any such provision. Similar powers exist in the case of breach of an exclusion requirement of an interim care order or an emergency protection order (sch. 6, paras 1(8) and 3(8)).

5 Warrants for arrest

Where an order has been made but no power of arrest has been attached, or one has been attached only to certain provisions of the order, a mechanism now exists whereby an applicant who considers that the respondent has failed to comply with the order may apply to 'the relevant judicial authority' for a warrant for the arrest of the respondent (s. 47(8)).

5.1   The relevant judicial authority

The relevant judicial authority is defined by s. 63 as:

(a)   where the order was made by the High Court, a judge of that court;

(b)   where the order was made by a county court, a judge or district judge of that or any other county court;

(c)   where the order was made by a magistrates' court, any magistrates' court.

5.2   The test

---

[3] Section 2, DVMPA 1976.

[4] See Chapter 19, paras 4.5 and 4.6 for explanation of 'significant' and for definition of 'harm'.

A warrant will be issued only if the application is substantiated on oath *and* the court has reasonable grounds for believing that the respondent has failed to comply with the order (s. 47(9)).

6 The courts' powers following arrest

When a respondent is arrested pursuant to a power of arrest, he must be brought before the relevant judicial authority within 24 hours of the time of his arrest.[5] If the matter is not disposed of forthwith, the court may remand him. The same applies where a person is brought before the court by virtue of a warrant.

Schedule 5 of the Act gives the High Court and county courts powers to remand corresponding to those which apply in magistrates' courts under ss. 128 and 129 of the Magistrates' Courts Act 1980. In county courts, the powers may be exercised by a judge or a district judge. The powers are as follows.

6.1 Remand in custody or on bail

Where a court has power to remand a person under s. 47 it may:

(a)   remand him in *custody*; or
(b)   remand him on *bail*, either:
    (i)   by taking a recognisance[6] from him (with or without sureties), such recognisance to be 'conditioned' in accordance with para. 2(3), *or*
    (ii)   by fixing the amount of the recognisances with a view to their being taken subsequently (and in the meantime committing the person to custody) (sch. 5, para. 2(1)).

The court may direct that the recognisance be *conditioned* for the appearance of the remanded person:

(a)   before that court at the end of the period of remand; *or*
(b)   at every time and place to which the hearing may from time to time be adjourned (sch. 5, para. 2(3)).

If bail is granted, the court may require the remanded person to comply with 'such requirements' as appear to the court to be necessary to ensure that he does not interfere with witnesses or otherwise obstruct the course of justice (s. 47(12)).

6.2 The period of remand

A period of remand may not exceed *8 clear days* unless:

(a)   the person is remanded on bail and both he and the other party agree to a longer period;

---

[5] In reckoning the 24 hours, no account is taken of Christmas Day, Good Friday or Sundays: s. 47(7).
[6] A recognisance is an obligation or bond acknowledged before a court, its object being to secure the performance of some act by the person agreeing to be bound.

(b) a case is adjourned under s. 48(1) for a medical examination and report to be made, when the court may remand for the period of adjournment (but see the limitations in s. 48, below) (sch. 5, para. 2(5)).

6.3 Further remand

If the court is satisfied that a remanded person is unable, because of illness or accident, to appear at the relevant time, he may be remanded in his absence (and the 8 days time limit does not apply) (sch. 5, para. 3(1)). Otherwise, a person may be remanded in his absence by the court's enlarging his recognisance and those of any sureties to a later date (sch. 5, para. 3(2)).

For the avoidance of doubt, para. 2(2) of sch. 5 specifically provides that a person brought before the court after remand may be further remanded.

7 Remand for medical examination

Where the court has reason to consider that a medical report will be required, it may remand a person to enable a medical examination and report to be made. A remand must not exceed 4 weeks at a time or 3 weeks if the remand is in custody (s. 48(2) and (3)).

Section 48(4) gives to the civil courts powers similar to those of the Crown Court to make an order under s. 35 of the Mental Health Act 1983, remanding for a report on mental condition where there is reason to suspect that the person arrested is suffering from mental illness or severe mental impairment.

8 Extension of magistrates' courts' powers

Section 50 gives magistrates' courts the power, already available to the High Court and county courts, to suspend execution of a committal order. It must be satisfied that there has been breach of a 'relevant requirement' defined as an occupation order, or non-molestation order or an exclusion requirement[7] included in an interim care order or an emergency protection order. Section 50 allows magistrates to direct that the execution of the order of committal should be suspended for such a period or on such terms and conditions as they may specify.

The powers of magistrates' courts are further extended by s. 51. This entitles them to make a hospital order or guardianship order under s. 37 of the Mental Health Act 1983, or an interim hospital order under s. 38 of that Act in the case of a person suffering from mental illness or severe mental impairment who could otherwise be committed to custody for breach of an order.

9 Procedure

The rules governing the enforcement of Part IV orders appear in new r. 3.9A of the Family Proceedings Rules 1991 (inserted by the Family Proceedings (Amendment No. 3) Rules 1997) and new rr. 20 and 21 of the Family Proceedings Courts (Matrimonial Proceedings) Rules 1991 (inserted by the Family Proceedings Court

---

[7] For 'exclusion requirement', see Chapter 27.

(Matrimonial Proceedings etc.) (Amendment) Rules 1997). In what follows, the references are, first, to the Family Proceedings Rules 1991 and, secondly, to the Family Proceedings Court (Matrimonial Proceedings etc.) Rules 1991.

9.1   Powers of arrest

Where the court attaches a power of arrest to one or more of the provisions of a Part IV order, it must set out those provisions (*and only those provisions*) in Form FL406 (r. 3.9A(1)(a); r. 20(1)(a)). The form will be found in sch. 2 to the Family Proceedings (Amendment No. 3) Rules 1997 and in sch. 1 to the Family Proceedings Court (Matrimonial Proceedings etc.) (Amendment) Rules 1997.

A copy of Form FL406 must be delivered to the officer for the time being in charge of any police station for the applicant's address, or of such other police station as the court may specify. With the form must be delivered a statement showing that the respondent has been served with the order or informed of its terms (whether by being present when the order was made, or by telephone or otherwise): r. 3.9A(1)(b); r. 20(1)(b).

If the relevant provisions of the order are varied or discharged, the proper officer (in the county court) or the justices' clerk (in the family proceedings court) must:

(a)   immediately inform the police officer to whom the copy form was delivered (and, if the applicant's address has changed, the officer for the time being in charge of the police station for the new address); and

(b)   deliver a copy of the order to any police officer so informed who received a copy of the form (r. 3.9A; r. 20(2)).

9.2   Warrant of arrest

An application for the issue of a warrant of arrest must be made in Form FL407. The warrant itself must be issued in Form FL408. Again, the forms will be found in sch. 2 to the Family Proceedings (Amendment No. 3) Rules 1997 and in sch. 1 to the Family Proceedings Court (Matrimonial Proceedings etc.) (Amendment) Rules 1997. In the magistrates' court, the warrant must be delivered by the justices' clerk to the officer for the time being in charge of any police station for the respondent's address or of such other police station as the court may specify (r. 20(3)).

9.3   Powers of the court on respondent's arrest

The court before whom a person is brought following his arrest may:

(a)   determine whether the fact and the circumstances which led to the arrest amounted to disobedience of the order; or

(b)   adjourn the proceedings.

If the court does adjourn, the arrested person may be released and thereafter dealt with within 14 days of the date on which he was arrested. However, he must be given not less than 2 days' notice of the adjourned hearing (r. 3.9A(4)(a) and (b); r. 20(4)(a) and (b)).

Note: nothing in the rules governing the county court prevents the issue of a notice under CCR Ord. 29, r. 1(4) if the arrested person is not dealt with within the 14-day period.

9.4 Committal

9.4.1 High Court and county court The existing rules relating to the court's power to suspend the execution of a committal order (RSC Ord. 52, r. 7); applications to the High Court for leave to enforce by committal (RSC Ord. 52, r. 2); committal for breach of order (CCR Ord. 29, r. 1); undertakings (CCR Ord. 29, r. 1A); and the discharge of a person in custody (CCR Ord. 29, r. 3) all apply, with the necessary modifications, to the enforcement of Part IV orders (r. 3.9A(5)).

9.4.2 The family proceedings court For the first time, the family proceedings court has the power to deal with committal proceedings. The relevant rules appear in paras. (6) to (13) of r. 20. In most respects, they reflect the familiar contents of CCR Ord. 29.

(a) Service In general, an order will not be enforced by committal unless:

(a) a copy of the order in Form FL404 has been served personally on the respondent; and
(b) where the order requires the respondent to do an act, the order has been so served before the expiry of the time within which he was to do the act, and was accompanied by a copy of an order made between the date of the order and the date of service, fixing that time (r. 20(6)).

(b) Penal notice When the order is drawn up, the justices' clerk must:

(a) where the order made is (or includes) a non-molestation order; and
(b) where the order made is an occupation order and the court so directs,

issue a copy of the order indorsed with or incorporating a notice as to the consequences of disobedience (r. 20(7)).

(c) Notice to show cause If the respondent fails to obey an order, at the request of the applicant the justices' clerk will issue a notice in Form FL418 warning the respondent that an application will be made for him to be committed. Subject to para. (12), the notice must be served personally on the respondent (r. 20(8)).

(d) The request for issue of notice to show cause Rule 20(9) requires the request for issue of the notice to be treated as a complaint. The request must:

(a) identify the provisions of the order or undertaking which it is alleged have been disobeyed or broken;
(b) list the ways in which it is alleged that the order or undertaking has been disobeyed or broken; and
(c) be supported by a statement which is signed and declared to be true and which states the grounds on which the application is made.

Unless service is dispensed with under para. (12), a copy of the statement must be served with the notice.

(e)   Committal order   If a committal order is made (it will be in Form FL419), it must include provision for the issue of a warrant of committal in Form FL420. Unless the court otherwise orders:

(a)   a copy of the order must be served personally on the person to be committed either before or at the time of the execution of the warrant; or

(b)   the order for the issue of the warrant may be served on the person to be committed at any time within 36 hours after the execution of the warrant (r. 20(10)).

(f)   Dispensing with personal service   Rule 20(11) allows an order requiring a person to abstain from doing an act to be enforced by committal order notwithstanding that it has not been served personally if the court is satisfied that, pending such service, the respondent had notice of the order either:

(a)   by being present when the order was made; or

(b)   by being notified of the terms of the order (whether by telephone or otherwise).

Rule 20(12) permits the court to dispense with service of a copy of the order under para. (6) or a notice under para. (8) if the court thinks it just to do so. Where service of a notice to show cause is dispensed with under para. (12), the court may of its own motion fix a date and time when the person to be committed is to be brought before the court (r. 20(13)).

(g)   Undertakings   Paragraphs (6) to (10), (12) and (13) apply to the enforcement of undertakings with the necessary modifications, and as if for para. (6) there was substituted a requirement for a copy of Form FL422 recording the undertaking to be delivered by the justices' clerk to the party giving the undertaking by handing him a copy before he leaves the court building, or by posting a copy to him at his place of residence (where the same is known) or through his solicitor. If delivery cannot be effected in this way, the clerk will deliver a copy of Form FL422 to the party for whose benefit the undertaking was given and that party must serve it personally as soon as is practicable (r. 20(14)).

(h)   Purging contempt   Provision for a contemnor to apply to the court for his discharge appears in r. 20(15).

(i)   Suspended committal orders   Rule 20(16) allows the court to suspend the execution of a committal order for such period or on such terms as it may specify. The order must be served on the respondent personally by the applicant, unless the court otherwise directs (r. 20(17)).

9.5   Adjourned consideration of penalty

All courts are empowered to adjourn consideration of the penalty to be imposed for contempts found proved. Such consideration may be restored if the respondent does not comply with any conditions specified by the court (r. 3.9A(6); r. 20(18)).

9.6   Bail

Applications for bail made by a person arrested under a power of arrest or a warrant of arrest may be made orally or in writing. Where made in writing, the application must contain:

(a)   the applicant's full name;

(b)   the address of the place where the applicant is detained at the time of making the application;

(c)   the address at which the applicant would reside if bail were granted;

(d)   the amount of the recognisance in which he would agree to be bound; and

(e)   the grounds on which the application is made and, where a previous application has been refused, full details of any change in circumstances which has occurred since that refusal r. 3.10(2); (r. 21(2)).

Forms are prescribed for the recognisance of the applicant (Form FL410) and that of a surety (Form FL411).

Chapter Twenty-Six
Transfer of Tenancies

1 Introduction

The Matrimonial Homes Act 1983 allowed the court 'on decree ... or at any time thereafter' to transfer certain tenancies between spouses or former spouses. No power, however, existed to transfer tenancies in the case of cohabitees. The Law Commission drew attention to the difficulties in cases such as *Ainsbury* v *Millington* [1986] 1 All ER 73, [1986] 1 FLR 331 where deadlock arose as a result of neither joint tenant being prepared to agree to the transfer to the other or to determine the tenancy so that it could be regranted to one alone. It reached the firm conclusion that the Matrimonial Homes Act power to transfer tenancies should be extended to cohabitants, whether they are joint tenants or not.

As to the issue of whether it would be appropriate to have statutory guidelines governing the exercise of this extended power, the Law Commission pointed out that in cases under s. 30 of the Law of Property Act 1925, the court has regard to the underlying basis of the trust. That was considered by the Commission to be an equally important factor to be taken into account by the court on an application for a transfer. The Law Commission also recommended that when the court makes an order for the transfer of a tenancy it should have the power to direct the payment of compensation by the transferee to the transferor. A compensation order was seen as a way of compensating a tenant for the loss of his tenancy, not a means of providing cohabitants with maintenance or capital payments. The Commission concluded that the power to order a compensation payment would be valuable, although the probability was that such a payment would be appropriate only in a very small number of cases. (Law Com No 207, para. 6.11).

2 The relevant tenancies

By virtue of sch. 7, para. 1 of the Family Law Act 1996 the tenancies to which the Act applies are:

- a protected or statutory tenancy within the meaning of the Rent Act 1977
- a statutory tenancy within the meaning of the Rent (Agriculture) Act 1976
- a secure tenancy within the meaning of s. 79 of the Housing Act 1985
- an assured tenancy or assured agricultural occupancy within the meaning of Part 1 of the Housing Act 1988.

3   When can the court make an order?

3.1   Spouses

Where one spouse is entitled (either in his own right or jointly with the other spouse) to occupy a dwelling-house by virtue of a relevant tenancy, the court may, sch. 7, para. 2, permits the court to make an order on granting:

- a decree of divorce
- a decree of nullity
- a decree of judicial separation

'... or at any time thereafter'.

3.2   Cohabitants

Where one cohabitant is entitled (either in his own right or jointly with the other cohabitant) to occupy a dwelling-house by virtue of a relevant tenancy and the cohabitants cease to live together as husband and wife, sch. 7, para. 3 permits the court to make an order at any time *after they cease so to live together.*

4   The dwelling-house

Under sch. 7, para. 4 the court can only make an order if the dwelling-house is or was:

(a)   in the case of spouses, a matrimonial home;
(b)   in the case of cohabitants, a home in which they lived together as husband and wife.

5   The criteria

In deciding whether to make an order, the court must have regard to all the circumstances of the case, including:

(a)   the circumstances in which the tenancy was granted to either or both spouses or cohabitants or the circumstances in which either or both became a tenant;
(b)   the matters set out in s. 33(6)(a)–(c) of the Act (see Chapter 19);
(c)   where only one cohabitant is a tenant, the further matters set out in s. 36(6)(e)–(h) of the Act (see Chapter 19);
(d)   the suitability of the parties as tenants.

(See sch. 7, para. 5.)

6   Part II orders

6.1   Protected, secure or assured tenancy or assured agricultural occupancy

Schedule 7, para. 7 provides that the court may by order direct that from a specified date the estate or interest of one spouse or cohabitant be transferred to and vested in the other spouse or cohabitant. The transfer is effected by virtue of the order itself. Any liabilities or obligations contained in the lease which fall due after the transfer are unenforceable against the transferor.

6.2 Statutory tenancies: Rent Act 1977 and Rent (Agriculture) Act 1976

The court may by order direct that from a specified date one spouse or cohabitant shall cease to be entitled to occupy the dwelling-house and the other spouse or cohabitant shall be *deemed* to be the tenant (sch. 7, paras 8 and 9).

7 Supplementary provisions

7.1 Compensation

On making a Part II order the court may direct that the transferee make a payment to the transferor. It must have regard under sch. 7, para. 10(4) to all the circumstances of the case, including:

(a) the financial loss which would otherwise be suffered by the transferor as a result of the order;

(b) the financial needs and financial resources of the parties;

(c) the financial obligations which the parties have, or are likely to have in the foreseeable future, including financial obligations to each other and to any relevant child.

7.2 Directions

By sch. 7, para. 10(2) payment of a sum may be:

- deferred (wholly or partially) until a specified date or the occurrence of a specified event
- by instalments

No direction under para. 10(2) may be given unless it appears to the court that *immediate* payment of the sum will cause the transferee financial hardship which would be greater than the financial hardship caused to the transferor if the direction were given. For example, if the court concludes that Ms X should pay £2,500 to her former cohabitant to compensate him for his loss of the tenancy, it must consider whether immediate payment of the sum would cause Ms X financial hardship which would be greater than the financial hardship caused to Mr Y if the compensation payment was to be deferred or made by instalments.

At any time before the sum is paid in full, the court may exercise its powers under sch. 7, para. 10(2) or vary any direction already given.

7.3 Liabilities and obligations in respect of the dwelling-house

Where a Part II order is made, the court may direct under sch. 7, para. 11 that both spouses or cohabitants shall be jointly and severally liable for obligations in respect of the dwelling-house (whether or not arising under the tenancy) which:

(a) are due to be discharged by one only of them at the date of the order; or

(b) will become due in the period up to the date of the transfer.

The court may direct either party to indemnify the other against expenses arising in connection with the discharge of any obligation.

8 Miscellaneous

Note the following:

(a) The date on which any Part II orders take effect cannot be earlier than the date of decree absolute (sch. 7, para. 12).

(b) Remarriage bars a former spouse from applying for a Part II order (sch. 7, para. 13(1)).

(c) Rules of court give landlords an opportunity to be heard on any application. (Rule 3.8(12) of the Family Proceedings Rules 1991 as amended by the Family Proceedings (Amendment No. 3) Rules 1997 provides for the application to be served on the other cohabitant or spouse on the landlord).

(d) Rules of court will also specify a period from the grant of decree after which no application may be made for an order without the leave of the court which granted the decree (sch. 7, para. 14(2)).

(e) Schedule 7 does not affect the operation of ss. 30 and 31 of the Act (i.e., the other spouse's matrimonial home rights, see Chapter 18 (sch. 7, para. 15(1)).

(f) Part II orders are in addition to the court's powers under ss. 33, 35 and 36 of the Act, see Chapter 19 (sch. 7, para. 15(2)).

(g) Rules 2.62(4) to (6) and r. 2.63 (investigation and requests for future information) of the FPR 1991 (as amended) apply, as does r. 3.6(7) to (9) (Married Women's Property Act 1882), with the necessary modifications.

Chapter Twenty-Seven
Protection of Children: Exclusion Requirements

1 Introduction

The Law Commission's Working Paper No 113, Appendix A raised the issue of ouster orders for the protection of children. The proposed power to oust an abuser or suspected abuser from the home rather than removing the child received much support in principle on consultation but there was no support for its use as a long-term alternative to a care order. The Law Commission considered that if it is in the child's long-term interests for an ouster order to be continued instead of a care order being made, it would be more appropriate for the non-abusing parent to apply for a private law remedy against the abuser. It was, therefore, recommended that the Children Act 1989 should be amended to give the court power to make a short-term, emergency ouster order for the protection of children. The power is intended to be a supplement to an emergency protection order or an interim care order, rather than an alternative. Instead of using the word 'ouster', the Act has created an *exclusion requirement*.

2 Amendments to the Children Act 1989

The new provisions of the Children Act 1989 (ss. 38A, 38B, 39(3A) and (3B), 44A, 44B and 45(8A) and (8B)) appear in sch. 6 to the Family Law Act 1996, taking effect by virtue of s. 52. In this chapter, *all* references hereinafter are references to the Children Act 1989.

3 Interim care orders

Section 38 of the Children Act 1989 permits the court to make an interim care order ('ICO') where care proceedings are adjourned or the court exercises its jurisdiction under s. 37(1) to direct a local authority to undertake an investigation of a child's circumstances. Before making such an order, the court must be satisfied that there are reasonable grounds for believing that circumstances with respect to a child are as mentioned in s. 31(2). Those circumstances are that:

  (a) the child concerned is suffering, or likely to suffer, significant harm (s. 31(2)(a)); and
  (b) the harm, or likelihood of harm, is attributable to:

(i)   the care given to the child, or likely to be given to him if the order were not made, not being what it would be reasonable to expect a parent to give to him (s. 31(2)(b)(i)), or

(ii)   the child's being beyond parental control (s. 31(2)(b)(ii)).

4   Exclusion requirement conditions: interim care order

Where:

(a)   the court makes an ICO based on s. 31(2)(a) and (b)(i) (see above),[1] and

(b)   the conditions set out in s. 38A(2) are satisfied,

the court may include an exclusion requirement in the ICO (s. 38A(1)).

4.1   Section 38A(2) conditions

The s. 38A(2) conditions are that:

(a)   there is reasonable cause to believe that if a person ('the relevant person') is excluded from a dwelling-house in which the child lives, the child will cease to suffer, or cease to be likely to suffer, significant harm; and

(b)   another person living in the dwelling-house (whether or not a parent of the child)

(i)   is able and willing to give the child the care which it would be reasonable to expect a parent to give him, and

(ii)   consents to the inclusion of the exclusion requirement.

5   Exclusion requirement

By s. 38A(3) an exclusion requirement can:

(a)   require the relevant person to *leave* the dwelling-house in which he is living with a child;

(b)   *prohibit* the relevant person from entering a dwelling-house in which the child lives;

(c)   *exclude* the relevant person from a defined area in which a dwelling-house in which the child lives is situated.

6   Powers of arrest

Section 38A(2) and (5) allows the court to attach a power of arrest to an exclusion requirement It may have effect for a shorter period than the exclusion requirement itself (s. 38A(2) and (6)).

---

[1] But not s. 31(2)(b)(ii), and so the power is not available where the ICO is being made because the child is *beyond parental control*.

7 Undertakings

Wherever the court has power to include an exclusion requirement in an ICO, it may accept an undertaking from the relevant person. The undertaking is enforceable as if it were an order of the court (s. 38B(1) and (3)).

8 Duration

An exclusion requirement may take effect for a shorter period than the other provisions of the ICO (s. 38A(4)).

It *automatically* ceases to have effect if the local authority removes the child from the home to other accommodation for a continuous period of more than 24 hours, as will an undertaking (ss. 38A(10) and 38B(3)(b)).

9 Extension, variation and discharge

The duration of both an exclusion requirement and a power of arrest may be extended by the court on one or more occasions on an application to vary or discharge the ICO (s. 38A(7)).

A person who is not entitled to apply for the ICO to be discharged, but is a person to whom an exclusion requirement applies, may apply to vary or discharge the ICO but only in so far as it imposes the exclusion requirement or a power of arrest (ss. 39(3A) and (3B)).

10 Emergency protection order

Section 44 of the Children Act 1989 empowers the court to make an emergency protection order ('EPO') if, but only if, it is satisfied that there is reasonable cause to believe that the child is likely to suffer significant harm if:

(a)   he is not removed to accommodation provided by or on behalf of the applicant; or
(b)   he does not remain in the place in which he is then being accommodated.

(See s. 44(1)(a)(i) and (ii).)

A local authority may apply for an EPO if inquiries are being made with respect to the child under s. 47(1)(b),[2] those inquiries are being frustrated by access to the child being unreasonably refused and the authority has reasonable cause to believe that access to the child is required as a matter of urgency (s. 44(1)(b)).

The NSPCC may apply for an EPO in similar circumstances.

11 Exclusion requirement conditions: emergency protection order

The court may include an exclusion requirement in an EPO where the conditions set out in s. 44A(2) are satisfied.

---

[2] Where a local authority have reasonable cause to suspect that a child who lives, or is found, in their area is suffering, or is likely to suffer, significant harm, the authority are obliged to make such inquiries as they consider necessary to enable them to decide whether they should take any action to safeguard or promote the child's welfare.

11.1   Section 44A(2) conditions

The s. 44A(2) conditions are that :

(a)   there is reasonable cause to believe that, if a person ('the relevant person') is excluded from a dwelling-house in which the child lives, then
    (i)   in the case of an order based on s. 44(1)(a), the child will not be likely to suffer significant harm, even though the child is not removed or, as the case may be, does not remain, or
    (ii)   in the case of an order based on s. 44(1)(b) or (c), the inquiries will cease to be frustrated and
(b)   another person living in the dwelling-house (whether or not a parent of the child)
    (i)   is able and willing to give the child the care which it would be reasonable to expect a parent to give him and
    (ii)   consents to the inclusion of the exclusion requirement.

Otherwise, ss. 44A, 44B and 45(8A) and (8B) contain provisions identical (mutatis mutandis) to those set out above in respect of exclusion requirements included in an ICO.

12   Procedure

The Family Proceedings (Amendment No. 3) Rules 1997 insert a new r. 4.24A into the Family Proceedings Rules 1991. The rule applies where the court includes an exclusion requirement in an ICO or an EPO. New Forms C11 (supplement for an application for an EPO), C23 (Emergency Protection Order) and C33 (Interim Care Order) appear in sch. 1 to the 1997 Rules.

12.1   The applicant's obligations

Rule 4.24A(2) requires the applicant to:

(a)   prepare a separate statement of the evidence in support of the application;
(b)   serve that statement personally on the relevant person with a copy of the order containing the exclusion requirement (and of any power of arrest); and
(c)   inform the relevant person of his right to apply to discharge or vary the exclusion requirement.

12.2   Power of arrest

Where a power of arrest is attached to an exclusion requirement, the applicant must deliver to the officer for the time being in charge of the police station for the area in which the dwelling-house in which the child lives is situated (unless the court specifies another police station):

(a)   a copy of the order; and

(b)   a statement showing that the relevant person has been served with the order or informed of its terms (whether by being present when the order was made, or by telephone or otherwise) (r. 4.24A(3)).

Rules 3.9(5), 3.9A (except paras (1) and (3)) and 3.10 apply, with the necessary modifications, to the service, variation, discharge and enforcement of any exclusion requirement to which a power of arrest is attached as they apply to an order made on an application under Part IV of the Family Law Act (as to which provisions, see Chapter 25).

12.3   Variation or discharge

Any application by the relevant person for variation or discharge of an exclusion requirement must, by virtue of r. 4.24A(5), be served on all parties to the proceedings.

12.4   Obligations on the cessation of an exclusion requirement

Where an exclusion order ceases to have effect, whether as a result of the removal of the child, the discharge of the ICO or EPO or otherwise, the applicant must inform the relevant person, the parties to the proceedings, any police officer to whom a copy of the order was delivered and, where necessary, the court (r. 4.24A(6)).

12.5   Notification of consent

The 1997 Rules also amend r. 4.24 of the 1991 Rules, which rule sets out the procedure for signifying consent in specified cases. New r. 4.24(1) requires any written consent given for the purposes of ss. 38A(2) or 44A(2) to include a statement that the person giving consent:

(a)   is able and willing to give to the child the care which it would be reasonable to expect a parent to give to him; and
(b)   understands that the giving of consent could lead to the exclusion of the relevant person from the dwelling-house in which the child lives.

Chapter Twenty-Eight
Procedure

1 Introduction

Applications under Part IV of the Act may be made in the High Court, county court, or in the family proceedings court, subject to the restrictions already considered in Chapter 16. Where the application is made in either the High Court or in the county court, the procedure is governed by the Family Proceedings (Amendment No. 3) Rules 1997 (SI 1997 No. 1893 (L29)) which substantially amend the Family Proceedings Rules 1991. However, where the application is made in the family proceedings court, the relevant procedure appears in the Family Proceedings Courts (Matrimonial Proceedings etc.) (Amendment) Rules 1997 (SI 1997 No. 1894 (L30)) which substantially amend the Family Proceedings Courts (Matrimonial Proceedings etc.) Rules 1991. Set out below is the procedure to be followed in each case. In the section dealing with the High Court/county court procedure, reference to 'the Rules' is a reference to the Family Proceedings Rules 1991 as amended. In the section dealing with procedure in the family proceedings courts, reference to 'the rules' is a reference to the Family Proceedings Courts (Matrimonial Proceedings etc.) (Amendment) Rules 1991.

2 High Court and county court procedure

2.1 The application

Applications for an occupation order or a non-molestation order must be made in Form FL401, to be found in Appendix 1 to the Rules. Form FL401 has been drafted so that it may be used to apply for either a non-molestation order, or an occupation order or both (r. 3.8(1)). (For examples of completed FL401s, see the Precedents at the end of this book.)

An application to vary, extend or discharge a Part IV order must be made in Form FL403 (r. 3.9(8)).

2.2 The child as applicant

An application by a child under 16 is treated, in the first instance, as an application to the High Court for leave (r. 3.8(2)).

2.3   The supporting statement

Rule 3.8(4) provides that an application must be supported by a statement which is signed by the applicant and sworn to be true. (For an example of such statements, see the Precedents section.)

2.4   Contents of statement

When drafting the supporting statement the statutory criteria for making the order sought should always be borne in mind. It will be helpful for the court to have the written evidence presented under discrete subheadings which reflect the specific considerations which the court has to take into account, thereby assisting the judge to carry out the balancing exercise. Accordingly, after dealing with the background, a sub-paragraph entitled 'housing needs and housing resources' might be included, followed by one dealing with 'financial resources', then 'health, safety, well-being etc.' and, lastly, 'conduct'. Where the issue of significant harm arises, it will be helpful to set out in a separate paragraph what is alleged to constitute the significant harm likely to be caused to the applicant and/or any relevant child. If you are acting for the respondent in a case where the applicant has alleged significant harm to herself and/or any relevant child, it would be as well to have a separate heading in your statement dealing with the comparative harm to both sides so that the court is assisted in comparing the hardship likely to be caused by making the order with the hardship likely to be caused by refusing it.

2.5   Ex parte applications

Where an application is made ex parte, the statement must contain the reasons why notice was not given (r. 3.8(5)).

2.6   Service

The respondent must be served with the following documents:

- Form FL401
- notice of hearing in Form FL402
- the sworn statement in support.

Service must be *personal* and *not less than two days before the hearing date* (r. 3.8(6)). However, by r. 3.8(7) the court may abridge the two-day period.

   The court will, if asked to do so, serve the application where the applicant is acting in person.

2.6.1   Mortgagees and landlords   A copy of an application for an occupation order must be served by the applicant by first class post on the mortgagee or, as the case may be, the landlord of the dwelling-house, with a notice in Form FL416 informing him of his right to make representations in writing or at any hearing (r. 3.8(11)).

   If the application is for the transfer of a tenancy, notice of the application must be served by the applicant on the other cohabitant or other spouse and on the landlord. Any person so served shall be entitled to be heard on the application (r. 3.8(12)).

2.7 Statement of service

At or before the hearing of the proceedings a statement of service must be filed in Form FL415.

2.8 The hearing

Unsurprisingly, the Rules provide for applications to be heard in chambers unless the court otherwise directs (r. 3.9(1)). The order will be issued in Form FL404. (For an example of a typical order see the Precedents section.) The court may direct that a further hearing be held to consider representations made by a mortgagee or a landlord (r. 3.9(7)).

2.9 The order

Where an order is made ex parte, a copy of the order, the application and the sworn statement must be served on the respondent personally (r. 3.9(2)). After an inter partes hearing, the order must be served personally on the respondent (r. 3.9(4)). Again, where the applicant is acting in person, the court will effect service if requested (r. 3.9(5)).

A copy of an occupation order must be served by first class post on the mortgagee or, as the case may be, the landlord (r. 3.9(3)).

2.10 Miscellaneous

Rules 2.62(4)–(6) and 2.63, providing respectively for the investigation of, and request for further information within, ancillary relief proceedings, now apply, with the necessary modifications, to an application for an occupation order and to an application for the transfer of a tenancy (r. 3.8(13)).

3 Procedure in the family proceedings court

3.1 The application

Applications for an occupation order or a non-molestation order in the family proceedings court must be made in Form FL401, to be found in sch. 1 to the Rules (r. 3A(1)). Form FL401 has been drafted so that it may be used to apply for either a non-molestation order, or an occupation order or both. (For an example of a completed FL401, see the Precedents section at the end of this book.)

An application to vary, extend or discharge a Part IV order must be made in Form FL403 (r. 12B).

3.2 The supporting statement

Rule 3A(3) provides that an application must be supported by a statement which is signed by the applicant and is declared to be true or, with the leave of the court, by oral evidence.

3.3 Contents of statement

The practice recommended at paragraph 2.4 above should be adopted when drafting statements.

3.4   Ex parte applications

In the family proceedings court an application may be made ex parte with the leave of the justices' clerk or of the court. The application should be filed at the time when the application is made, or as directed by the justices' clerk. The evidence in support of such an application must state the reasons why notice was not given (r. 3A(4)).

3.5   Service

The respondent must be served with the following documents:

- Form FL401
- notice of hearing in Form FL402
- any sworn statement in support.

Service must be *personal* and *not less than two business days prior to the date on which the application will be heard* (r. 3A(5)).

Where the applicant is acting in person, service of the application may, with the leave of the justice's clerk, be effected in accordance with r. 4 (r. 3A(7)).

3.5.1   Mortgagees and landlords
A copy of an application for an occupation order must be served by first class post on the mortgagee or, as the case may be, on the landlord of the dwelling-house, with a notice in Form FL416 informing him of his right to make representations in writing or at any hearing (r. 3A(10)).

3.6   Statement of service

After service of the application, a statement of service in Form FL415 must be filed (r. 3A(11)).

3.7   The hearing

The order will be issued in Form FL404 (r. 12A(1)). (For an example of a typical order see the Precedents section.) Practitioners will find the *pro forma* order drafted by District Judge Gordon Ashton ([1998] Fam Law 4) of great assistance. The court may direct that a further hearing be held to consider representations made by a mortgagee or a landlord (r. 12A(7)).

3.8   The order

Where an order is made ex parte, a copy of the order, the application and the supporting statement must be served on the respondent personally (r. 12A(2)). After an inter partes hearing, the order must be served personally on the respondent (r. 12A(5)). Again, where the applicant is acting in person, service of an inter partes order may, with the leave of the justices' clerk, be effected in accordance with r. 4 (r. 12A(6)).

A copy of an occupation order must be served by first class post on the mortgagee or, as the case may be, the landlord (r. 12A(4)).

3.9 Miscellaneous

In the family proceedings court, where an application has been served in accordance with r. 4(1) and, after an order has been made, it appears to the court that the application did not come to the knowledge of the respondent in due time, the court may set aside the order and give directions for a rehearing (r. 24).

Chapter Twenty-Nine
Appeals

The only specific appeal provision in the Act deals with appeals from the magistrates' courts. However, the Family Proceedings Rules 1991 already make provision for appeals against orders or decisions of district judges in family proceedings and proceedings under Part IV of the Act are now included within the definition of family proceedings by virtue of s. 63 of the Act.

1 The general rule

From the magistrates' court an appeal lies to the High Court against:

(a) the *making* by the magistrates of any order under Part IV of the Act;
(b) any *refusal* by the magistrates to make an order under Part IV of the Act

(see s. 61(1)).

2 No appeal

You *cannot* appeal against a decision by a magistrates' court to decline jurisdiction because it considers that the case can be more conveniently dealt with by another court (s. 61(1)).

3 What the High Court can do

The appellate court can make any order it deems necessary (including incidental or consequential orders) to give effect to its determination of the appeal and can direct that the case be re-heard by the magistrates' court (s. 61(2), (3)).

4 Enforcement

For the purposes of enforcement, variation, revival or discharge of orders, any High Court order made on appeal (except one directing that the case be re-heard by a magistrates' court) shall be treated as if it were a magistrates' court order (s. 61(4)).

5 Procedure

Appeals from Part IV orders are governed by new r. 8.1A of the Family Proceedings Rules (inserted by r. 7 of the Family Proceedings (Amendment No. 3) Rules 1997). The effect of new r. 8.1A is to apply to such appeals r. 4.22 and rr. 8.1 and 8.2 of the Family Proceedings Rules 1991, with necessary modifications. Accordingly, in what follows a rule referred to by number means the rule so numbered in the Family Proceedings Rules 1991. The procedure described below applies to appeals both from the magistrates' courts to the High Court and from the district judge to the judge.

5.1 What the appellant must do

5.1.1 Documents The appellant must file and serve the following documents:

(a) notice of the appeal in writing, setting out the grounds upon which he relies;
(b) a certified copy of the summons or application and of the order appealed against, and of any order staying its execution;
(c) a copy of any notes of the evidence;
(d) a copy of any reasons given for the decision (r. 4.22(2)(a)–(d), as applied by r. 8.1A(1)(a)).

Note that where an appeal lies to the High Court, the appellant must file the above documents in the registry of the High Court which is *nearest* to the magistrates' court from which the appeal is brought (r. 8.1A(3)).

5.1.2 Persons to be served The appellant must file and serve the above documents on the parties to the proceedings in the court below, and on any guardian ad litem (r. 4.22(2)) and on the justices' clerk of the magistrates' court from which the appeal is brought (r. 8.1A(2)).

5.1.3 Time limits The notice of appeal must be filed and served *within 14 days* after the determination against which the appeal is brought *or*, with the leave of the court, within such other time as the court or judge may direct (r. 4.22(3)).

All other documents must be filed and served *as soon as is practicable* after service of the notice of appeal (r. 4.22(4)).

5.2 What the respondent must do

Within 14 days of receipt of the notice of appeal the respondent must file and serve on all other parties to the appeal a notice in writing setting out his grounds if he intends to argue in the appeal that the decision of the court below should be varied or affirmed on grounds other than those relied on by the court below, or if he intends to argue by way of cross-appeal that the decision of the court below was wrong in whole or in part (r. 4.22(5)).

5.3 Powers of the district judge

If the appeal is from the magistrates' court to the High Court, an application to withdraw the appeal, or to have it dismissed with the consent of all the parties or to amend the grounds of the appeal, may be heard by the district judge (r. 4.22(7)).

Moreover, a district judge may dismiss any appeal for want of prosecution and may deal with any question of costs arising out of the dismissal or withdrawal of an appeal (r. 8.1A(5)).

5.4   The hearing

The appeal will be heard in chambers unless otherwise directed (r. 8.1(5)). It does not operate as a stay of proceedings unless the court so orders (r. 8.1(6)). If the appeal is to the High Court it must be heard by a single judge of the High Court, unless the President otherwise directs (r. 4.22(8)).

5.5   Extension of time

An application to extend the time for appealing must be supported by a certificate (together with a copy) by the appellant's solicitor setting out the reasons for the delay and the relevant dates (r. 8.2(4)(e)).

5.6   The approach of the appeal court

The court is not bound to allow the appeal on the ground merely of misdirection or improper reception or rejection of evidence unless, in the opinion of the court, substantial wrong or miscarriage of justice has been occasioned thereby (r. 8.2(6)).

5.7   Final orders

Rule 8.1A(6) provides that any order or decision granting or varying an order (or refusing to do so) in proceedings for a s. 33(4) occupation order, an occupation order containing any s. 33(3) provisions where the applicant or the respondent has matrimonial home rights or a transfer of tenancy shall be treated as a final order for the purposes of CCR Ord. 37, r. 6. On an appeal from such an order, the judge may exercise his own discretion in substitution for that of the district judge. The provisions of CCR Ord. 37, r. 6 will apply.

6   Appeals against hospital orders and guardianship orders

Where appeals are brought against such orders the justices' clerk is obliged to send a copy of any written evidence considered by the magistrates' court to the registry of the High Court in which the documents relating to the appeal are filed (r. 8.1A(4)).

Chapter Thirty
Transitional Provisions

1 Pending applications for orders relating to occupation and molestation

By para. 8(2) of sch. 9 to the Family Law Act 1996, any application for an order or injunction under:

- the Domestic Violence and Matrimonial Proceedings Act 1976
- s. 1 or 9 of the Matrimonial Homes Act 1983
- the Domestic Proceedings and Magistrates' Courts Act 1978[1]

which is pending immediately before the commencement of the repeal of any of those enactments will not be affected by any provision of the Act. That presumably means that the court would treat any such application as if the statute under which it was being made was still in existence and make such orders as would have been made under the old legislation.

2 Pending applications under sch. 1 to the Matrimonial Homes Act 1983[2]

Nothing in the Act will affect any application for an order under sch. 1 to the Matrimonial Homes Act 1983 which is pending immediately before the commencement of the repeal of that Schedule (sch. 9, para. 9).

3 Existing orders

3.1 General rule

Any beneficiary of an existing order[3] under the Domestic Violence and Matrimonial Proceedings Act 1976, or under ss. 1 or 9 of the Matrimonial Homes Act 1983, or under the Domestic Proceedings and Magistrates' Courts Act 1978 can rest assured

---

[1] The Domestic Violence and Matrimonial Proceedings Act 1976 is repealed in its entirety by the Act, as is the Matrimonial Homes Act 1983 (although significant parts of the latter are re-enacted) together with ss. 16–18, s. 28(2) and para. 53 of sch. 2 of the Domestic Proceedings Magistrates' Courts Act 1978.
[2] This Schedule deals with the transfer of certain tenancies on divorce etc.
[3] An 'existing order' means an order which is in force immediately before the commencement of the repeal of the Act under which it was granted or was made or granted after the repeal but in proceedings brought *before* the repeal (sch. 9, para. 10(1)(a) and (b)).

that nothing in the Act (but see the two exceptions below) will prevent such an order remaining in force or affect the enforcement of such an order (sch. 9, para. 10(2)(a) and (b)).

3.2 Exceptions

There are two qualifications to the general rule stated above. First, on an application to extend, vary or discharge an existing order the court may, if it thinks it *just and reasonable* to do so, treat the application as an application for an order under the Act (sch. 9, para. 10(3)).

Secondly, if an order is made under the Act between parties with respect to whom an existing order is in force, the subsequent order discharges the existing order (sch. 9, para. 10(4)).

4 Matrimonial home rights

Any reference in any enactment, instrument or document, to rights of occupation under the Matrimonial Homes Act 1983 shall be construed (so far as is required to continue the effect of the instrument or document) as referring to matrimonial home rights under the Act (sch. 9, para. 11(1)).

Any reference in the Act or any enactment, instrument or document, to matrimonial home rights under the Act, shall be construed as including, in relation to times, circumstances and purposes before the commencement of ss. 30–32 of the Act, a reference to rights of occupation under the Matrimonial Homes Act 1983 (sch. 9, para. 11(2)).

4.1 Registration

Any reference, wherever appearing, to registration under s. 2(8) of the Matrimonial Homes Act 1983 shall be construed as being or including a reference to registration under s. 5(6) of the Act (sch. 9, para. 12(1)).

In accordance with sch. 9, para. 12(2) any references in the Act or anywhere else to registration under s. 31(10) of the Act shall be construed as including a reference to registration :

- under s. 2(7) of the Matrimonial Homes Act 1967, or
- under s. 2(8) of the Matrimonial Homes Act 1983, and
- by caution under s. 2(7) of the Matrimonial Homes Act 1967

Note that in ss. 30 and 31 of, and sch. 4 to, the Act, any reference to orders made under s. 33 shall be consrued as including a reference to an order made under s. 1 of the Matrimonial Homes Act 1983.

4.2 Cautions

Any caution lodged before 14th February 1981 is not affected by the Act.

Appendix
Notes to the Precedents

1.   The notes for guidance which form part of Form FL401 are lengthy. The form is therefore reproduced in full only in Precedent 1.

2.   The format of Form FL404 (the order) is also lengthy. Precedent 3 is an example of the complete form. Thereafter, we have gratefully adopted the suggestions of District Judge Gordon Ashton in his excellent article, 'Family Law Act Injunctions: Preparing the Orders' [1998] Fam Law 4, which contains an invaluable *pro forma*.

No 1: APPLICATION AGAINST FORMER FLATMATE FOR A NON-MOLESTATION ORDER

Application for:	To be completed by the Court
a Non-Molestation order	Date issued
~~an Occupation Order~~	
Family Law Act 1996 (Part IV)	Case number

The Court   Barchester County Court

Please read the accompanying notes as you complete this form.

1   About you (the applicant)

State your title (Mr, Mrs etc.), full name,
address, telephone number and date of birth
(if under 18):

Ms Jane Saward
17 Bryan Close
Denham, Barchester 01265 353242

State your solicitor's name, address,
reference, telephone, FAX and DX numbers:

Lowe and Craftee [Ref AB] 2 Litigation Close,
Denham, Barchester 01265 724190
DX Denham 4190

2   About the respondent

State the respondent's name, address and date
of birth (if known):

Alistair Diamond
14 Kingdom Way
Denham, Barcheste   (DOB: 5/1/1972)

3   The Order(s) for which you are applying

This application is for:

☑ a non-molestation order

☐ an occupation order

☐ Tick this box if you wish the Court to hear
your application without notice being given
to the respondent. The reasons relied on for an
application being heard without notice must
be stated in the statement in support.

4   Your relationship to the respondent (the person to be served with this application)

Your relationship to the respondent is:

Please tick only one of the following.

1 ☐ Married

2 ☐ Were married

3 ☐ Cohabiting

4 ☐ Were cohabiting

5 ☑ Both of you live or have lived in the same household

6 ☐ Relative
       State how related:

7 ☐ Agreed to marry.
       Give the date the agreement was made. If the agreement has ended, state when.

8 ☐ Both of you are parents of or have parental responsibility for a child

9 ☐ One of you is a parent of a child and the other has parental responsibility for that child

10 ☐ One of you is the natural parent or
grandparent of a child adopted or
freed for adoption, and the other is:

(i)   the adoptive parent
or (ii)   a person who has applied for
an adoption order for the
child
or (iii) a person with whom the
child has been placed for
adoption
or (iv)   the child who has been
adopted or freed for
adoption.
State whether (i), (ii), (iii) or (iv):

11 ☐ Both of you are parties to the same
family proceedings (see also Section
11 below).

5   Application for a non-molestation order

If you wish to apply for a non-molestation
order, state briefly in this section the order
you want.

*I want the respondent to stop pestering
me, telephoning me and leaving notes, etc,
on my car.*

Give full details in support of your
application in your supporting evidence

6   Application for an occupation order

If you do not wish to apply for an occupation
order, please go to section 9 of this form.

(A)   State the address of the dwelling-house to
which your application relates:

(B)   State whether it is occupied by you or the
respondent now or in the past, or whether it
was intended to be occupied by you or the
respondent:

(C)   State whether you are entitled to occupy the
      dwelling-house
           ☐   Yes   ☐   No

(D)   State whether the Respondent is entitled to
      occupy the dwelling-house

      ☐   Yes   ☐   No

      If yes, explain why:

**On the basis of your answer to (C) and (D)
above, tick one of the boxes 1 to 5 below to
show the category into which you fit**

1 ☐ a spouse who has matrimonial home
       rights in the dwelling-house, or a
       person who is entitled to occupy it by
       virtue of a beneficial estate or interest
       or contract or by virtue of any
       enactment giving him or her the right
       to remain in occupation.

       If you tick box 1, state whether there
       is a dispute or pending proceedings
       between you and the respondent
       about your right to occupy the
       dwelling-house.

2 ☐ a former spouse with no existing right
       to occupy, where the respondent
       spouse is entitled.

3 ☐ a cohabitant or former cohabitant
       with no existing right to occupy,
       where the respondent cohabitant or
       former cohabitant is so entitled.

4 ☐ a spouse or former spouse who is not
       entitled to occupy, where the
       respondent spouse or former spouse
       is also not entitled.

5 ☐ a cohabitant or former cohabitant
       who is not entitled to occupy, where
       the respondent cohabitant or former
       cohabitant is also not entitled.

Matrimonial Home Rights

If you do have matrimonial home rights
please:

State whether the title to the land is registered
or unregistered (if known):

If registered, state the Land Registry title
number (if known):

**If you wish to apply for an occupation
order, state briefly here the order you
want.** Give full details in support of your
application in your supporting evidence.

7   **Application for additional order(s) about
       the dwelling-house**

If you want to apply for any of the orders
listed in the notes to this section, state what
order you would like the court to make:

8   **Mortgage and rent**

Is the dwelling-house subject to a mortgage?
☐   Yes   ☐   No

If yes, please provide the name and address of
the mortgagee:

Is the dwelling-house rented?
☐   Yes   ☐   No

If yes, please provide the name and address of
the landlord:

9   At the Court

Will you need an interpreter at court?

☐   Yes   ☑   No

If 'Yes', specify the language:

If you need an interpreter because you do not
speak English, you are responsible for
providing your own.

If you need an interpreter or other facilities
because of a disability, please contact the
court to ask what help is available.

10   Other information

State the name and date of birth of any child
living with or staying with, or likely to live
with or stay with, you or the respondent: **Not applicable**

State the name of any other person living in
the same household as you and the
respondent, and say why they live there: **Not applicable**

11   Other Proceedings and Orders

If there are any other current family
proceedings or orders in force involving you
and the respondent, state the type of
proceedings or orders, the court and the case
number. This includes any application for an
occupation order or non-molestation order
against you by the respondent.   **Not applicable**

**This application is to be served upon the
respondent**

Signed	Date
Jane Saward	19/10/97

Application for a non-molestation order or occupation order

Notes for Guidance

Section 1
If you do not wish your address to be made known to the respondent, leave the space on the form blank and complete Confidential Address Form C8. The court can give you this form.

If you are under 18, someone over 18 must help you make this application. That person, who might be one of your parents, is called a 'next friend'.

If you are under 16 you need permission to make this application. You must apply to the High Court for permission, using this form. If the High Court gives you permission to make this application, it will then either hear the application itself or transfer it to a county court.

Section 3
An urgent order made by the court before notice of the application is served on the respondent is called an ex-parte order. In deciding whether to make an ex-parte order the court will consider all the circumstances of the case including:

- *any risk of significant harm to the applicant or a relevant child, attributable to conduct of the respondent, if the order is not made immediately*

- *whether it is likely that the applicant will be deterred or prevented from pursuing the application if an order is not made immediately*

- *whether there is reason to believe that the respondent is aware of the proceedings but is deliberately evading service and that the applicant or a relevant child will be seriously prejudiced by the delay involved.*

If the court makes an ex-parte order, it must give the respondent an opportunity to make representations about the order as soon as just and convenient at a full hearing.

'Harm' in relation to a person who has reached the age of 18 means ill-treatment or the impairment of health and in relation to a child means ill-treatment or the impairement of health and development. 'Ill-treatment', includes forms of ill-treatment which are not physical and, in relation to a child, includes sexual abuse. The court will require evidence of any harm which you allege in support of your application. This evidence should be included in the statement accompanying this application.

Section 4
For you to be able to apply for an order you must be related to the respondent in one of the ways listed in this section of the form. If you are not related in one of these ways you should seek legal advice.

Cohabitants *are a man and a woman who, although not married to each other, are living or have lived together as husband and wife. People who have cohabited, but have then married, will not fall within this category, but will fall within the category of married people.*

Those who live or have lived in the same household do not include people who share the same household because one of them is the other's employee, tenant, lodger or boarder.

You will only be able to apply as a relative of the respondent if you are:

(A) the father, mother, stepfather, stepmother, son, daughter, stepson, stepdaughter, grandmother, grandfather, grandson or granddaughter of the respondent or of the respondent's spouse or former spouse.

(B) the brother, sister, uncle, aunt, niece or nephew (whether of the full blood or of the half blood or by marriage) of the respondent or of the respondent's spouse or former spouse.

This includes, in relation to a person who is living or has lived with another person as husband and wife, and person who would fall within (A) or (B) if the parties were married to each other (for example your cohabitee's father or brother).

Agreements to marry: *You will fall within this category only if you make this application within three years of the termination of the agreement. The court will require the following evidence of the agreement:*

 evidence in writing
or *the gift of an engagement ring in contemplation of marriage*
or *evidence that a ceremony has been entered into in the presence of one or more other persons assembled for the purpose of witnessing it.*

Parents and parental responsibility: *You will fall within this category if*

both you and the respondent are either the parents of a child or have parental responsibility for that child

or if one of you is the parent and the other has parental responsibility.

Under the Children Act 1989, parental responsibility is held automatically by a child's mother, and by the child's father if he and the mother were married to each other at the time of the child's birth or have married subsequently. Where this is not the case parental responsibility can be acquired by the father in accordance with the provisions of the Children Act 1989.

Section 5
A non-molestation order can forbid the respondent to molest you or a relevant child. Molestation can include, for example, violence, threats, pestering and other forms of harassment. The court can forbid particular acts of the respondent, molestation in general, or both.

Section 6
If you wish to apply for an occupation order but you are uncertain about your answer to any of the questions in this part of the application form, you should seek legal advice.

(A) A dwelling-house includes any building or part of a building which is occupied as a dwelling; any caravan, houseboat or structure which is occupied as a dwelling; and any yard, garden, garage or outhouse belonging to it and occupied with it.

Section 6 (continued)

(C) & (D) The following questions give examples to help you to decide if you or the respondent, or both of you, are entitled to occupy the dwelling-house:

(a)   Are you the sole legal owner of the dwelling-house?

(b)   Are you and the respondent joint legal owners of the dwelling-house?

(c)   Is the respondent the sole legal owner of the dwelling-house?

(d)   Do you rent the dwelling-house as sole tenant?

(e)   Do you and the repondent rent the dwelling-house as joint tenants?

(f)   Does the respondent rent the dwelling-house as sole tenant?

If you answer

- **Yes** *to (a) (b), (d) or (e) you are likely to be entitled to occupy the dwelling-house*

- **Yes** *to (c) or (f) you may not be entitled (unless, for example, you are a spouse and have matrimonial home rights — see the notes under 'Matrimonial Home Rights' below)*

- **Yes** *to (b), (c), (e) or (f), the respondent is likely to be entitled to occupy the dwelling-house*

- **Yes** *to (a) or (d) the respondent may not be entitled (unless, for example, he is a spouse and has matrimonial home rights).*

Box 1 *For example, if you are sole owner, joint owner, or if you rent the property. If you are not a spouse, former spouse, cohabitant or former cohabitant of the respondent, you will only be able to apply for an occupation order if you fall within this category.*

If you answer **Yes** *to this question, it will not be possible for a magistrates' court to deal with the application, unless the court decides that it is unnecessary for it to decide this question in order to deal with the application or make an order. If the court decides that it cannot deal with the application, it will transfer the application to a County Court.*

Box 2 *For example, if the respondent was married to you and is sole owner or rents the property.*

Box 3 *For example, if the respondent is or was cohabiting with you and is sole owner or rents the property.*

Matrimonial Home Rights
Where one spouse is entitled to occupy the dwelling-house by virtue of a beneficial estate or interest or contract or by virtue of any enactment giving him or her the right to remain in occupation, and the other spouse is not so entitled, the spouse who is not entitled has matrimonial home rights. These are a right, if the spouse is in occupation, not to be evicted or excluded from the dwelling-house except with the leave of the court and, if the spouse is not in occupation, the right with the leave of the court to enter into and occupy the dwelling-house.

Matrimonial home rights do not exist if the dwelling-house has never been, and was never intended to be, the matrimonial home of the two spouses. If the marriage has come to an end, matrimonial home rights will also have ceased, unless a court order has been made during the marriage for the rights to continue after the end of the marriage.

Occupation Orders *The possible orders are:*

If you have ticked box 1 above, *an order under section 33 of the Act may:*

- *enforce the applicant's entitlement to remain in occupation as against the respondent*

- *require the respondent to permit the applicant to enter and remain in the dwelling-house or part of it*

- *regulate the occupation of the dwelling-house by either or both parties*

- *if the respondent is also entitled to occupy, the order may prohibit, suspend or restrict the exercise by him, of that right*

- *restrict or terminate any matrimonial home rights of the respondent*

- *require the respondent to leave the dwelling-house or part of it*

- *exclude the respondent from a defined area around the dwelling-house*

- *declare that the applicant is entitled to occupy the dwelling-house or has matrimonial home rights in it*

- *provide that matrimonial home rights of the applicant are not brought to an end by the death of the other spouse or termination of the marriage.*

If you have ticked box 2 or box 3 above, *an order under section 35 or 36 of the Act may:*

- *give the applicant the right not to be evicted or excluded from the dwelling-house or any part of it by the respondent for a specified period*

- *prohibit the respondent from evicting or excluding the applicant during that period*

- *give the applicant the right to enter and occupy the dwelling-house for a specified period*

- *require the respondent to permit the exercise of that right*

- *regulate the occupation of the dwelling-house by either or both of the parties*

- *prohibit, suspend or restrict the exercise by the respondent of his right to occupy*

- *require the respondent to leave the dwelling-house or part of it*

- *exclude the respondent from a defined area around the dwelling-house.*

If you have ticked box 4 or box 5 above, *an order under section 37 or 38 of the Act may:*

Section 6 (continued)

- *require the respondent to permit the applicant to enter and remain in the dwelling-house or part of it*

- *regulate the occupation of the dwelling-house by either or both of the parties*

- *require the respondent to leave the dwelling-house or part of it*

- *exclude the respondent from a defined area around the dwelling-house.*

You should provide any evidence which you have on the following matters in your evidence in support of this application. If necessary, further statements may be submitted after the application has been issued.

If you have ticked box 1, 4 or 5 above, the court will need any available evidence of the following:

- *the housing needs and resources of you, the respondent and any relevant child*

- *the financial resources of you and the respondent*

- *the likely effect of any order, or of any decision not to make an order, on the health, safety and well-being of you, the respondent and any relevant child*

- *the conduct of you and the respondent in relation to each other and otherwise.*

If you have ticked box 2 above, the court will need any available evidence of:

- *the housing needs and resources of you, the respondent and any relevant child*

- *the financial resources of you and the respondent*

- *the likely effect of any order, or of any decision not to make an order, on the health, safety and well-being of you, the respondent and any relevant child*

- *the conduct of you and the respondent in relation to each other and otherwise*

- *the length of time that has elapsed since you and the respondent ceased to live together*

- *the length of time that has elapsed since the marriage was dissolved or annulled*

- *the existence of any pending proceedings between you and the respondent:*

  under section 23A of the Matrimonial Causes Act 1973 (property adjustment orders in connection with divorce proceedings etc.)
- *or under Schedule 1 para. 1(2)(d) or (e) of the Children Act 1989 (orders for financial relief against parents)*
- *or relating to the legal or beneficial ownership of the dwelling-house.*

If you have ticked box 3 above, the court will need any available evidence of:

- *the housing needs and resources of you, the respondent and any relevant child*

- *the financial resources of you and the respondent*

- *the likely effect of any order, or of any decision not to make an order, on the health, safety and well-being of you, the respondent and any relevant child*

- *the conduct of you and the respondent in relation to each other and otherwise*
- *the nature of you and the respondent's relationship*
- *the length of time during which you have lived together as husband and wife*
- *whether you and the respondent have had any children, or have both had parental responsibility for any children*
- *the length of time which has elapsed since you and the respondent ceased to live together*
- *the existence of any pending proceedings between you and the respondent under Schedule 1 para. 1(2)(d) or (e) of the Children Act 1989 or relating to the legal or beneficial ownership of the dwelling-house.*

Section 7
Under section 40 of the Act the court may make the following additional orders when making an occupation order:

- *impose on either party obligations as to the repair and maintenance of the dwelling-house*
- *impose on either party obligations as to the payment of rent, mortgage or other outgoings affecting it*
- *order a party occupying the dwelling-house to make periodical payments to the other party in respect of the accommodation, if the other party would (but for the order) be entitled to occupy it*
- *grant either party possessions or use of furniture or other contents*
- *order either party to take reasonable care of any furniture or other contents*
- *order either party to take reasonable steps to keep the dwelling-house and any furniture or other contents secure.*

Section 8
If the dwelling-house is rented or subject to a mortgage, the landlord or mortgagee must be served with notice of the proceedings in Form FL416. He or she will then be able to make representations to the court regarding the rent or mortgage.

Section 10
A person living in the same household may, for example, be a member of the family or a tenant or employee of you or the respondent.

No 2: SWORN STATEMENT/AFFIDAVIT IN SUPPORT OF APPLICATION AGAINST FORMER FLATMATE FOR NON-MOLESTATION ORDER

IN THE BARCHESTER COUNTY COURT   No of Matter:
IN THE MATTER OF AN APPLICATION UNDER
THE FAMILY LAW ACT 1996

> Filed on behalf of the Applicant.
> Deponent: Applicant; No 1
> Date sworn: 19th October 1997
> Date filed: 19th October 1997

BETWEEN:

JANE SAWARD

Applicant

– and –

ALISTAIR DIAMOND

Respondent

AFFIDAVIT OF THE APPLICANT

I, JANE SAWARD, postgraduate student, of 17 Bryan Close, Denham in Barchester, MAKE OATH and say as follows:

1. I am the Applicant herein and I make this affidavit in support of my application under section 42 of the Family Law Act 1996 for an order in the terms of my application to restrain the Respondent from molesting me. I am now the sole tenant of the above address, which is a two-bedroomed flat which I rent from a private landlord.

2. The Respondent and I were both undergraduate students at Barchester University and we shared the above-mentioned flat for the last year of our degree course. There was never any sexual relationship between us[1]; we were just students living in the same household. The Respondent approached me at the end of the second year of our degree course and asked whether I would consider sharing

---

[1] This application is possible under the new Act whereas it would have created difficulties under the old law. The applicant and respondent have never lived together as man and wife, as the affidavit makes clear, and so the court would not have had jurisdiction under the Domestic Violence and Matrimonial Proceedings Act 1976. Now, however, the fact the applicant and respondent have lived in the same household gives the court jurisdiction to make a s. 42 non-molestation order. Jane and Alistair are 'associated persons' by virtue of s. 62(3)(c) of the Act.

accommodation with him during our final year. We had always got on reasonably well and I agreed to do so. We found the flat during the summer vacation and we moved into it together in October 1995 as joint tenants. We shared the rent and some of the bills. We usually bought food separately, however.

3. In about March 1997 the Respondent began to behave very strangely. He became involved with a religious cult called the Barchester Living Angels. One of the tenets of that cult is that the world will end in the next 3 years. He started to neglect his studies and to spend more and more time spreading the message of the cult. He tried to involve me in what he used to refer to as his 'life's work', but I made it clear that I was not interested at all. At first he seemed to accept my attitude. During May 1997 he left the flat for about 3 weeks to go on retreat with the cult in Stonehenge. When he returned, his behaviour took a turn for the worse. He began to leave notes around the flat to the effect that unless I joined the cult I would perish in the apocalypse to come. By July he had ceased to take part in university life and in August he left the flat stating that he intended to preach the message of the cult full-time. I was frankly very relieved to see him go. I have secured a further year's tenancy of the flat.

4. Since his departure, however, the Respondent has pestered me day and night to join the cult. He sends garishly coloured envelopes to my address containing letters urging me to join him before it's too late, as he puts it. He telephones me at all hours of the day and night begging me to repent my sins and follow the teachings of the Barchester Angels. He has even turned up at the university to try to persuade me. Almost every day he leaves me notes on the windscreen of my car. I am, frankly, at the end of my tether. Recently, the Respondent has taken to telling me on the telephone that I would be better off dead than risking my soul by not joining the cult. I am fearful of what the Respondent might do to me in this state of mind[2]. I am under particular pressure from my postgraduate course, the workload of which is extremely onerous. I have been prescribed tranquillisers by my GP because of the stress caused by the Respondent's behaviour towards me[3].

5. The facts stated in this affidavit are within my own knowledge.

6. In all the circumstances I respectfully ask this Honourable Court to grant to me the relief I seek in my Notice of Application.

SWORN at the Barchester County Court
at 12 Promenade Way,
Barchester
this 19th October 1997   Before me ....

An officer of the Court appointed by the
Judge to take affidavits

---

[2] Under s. 42(5) in deciding whether to exercise its powers under the section, and if so, in what manner the court is enjoined to have regard to all the circumstances including the need to secure the health, safety and well being of the applicant.

[3] See footnote 2.

No 3: NON-MOLESTATION ORDER AGAINST FORMER FLATMATE

IN THE BARCHESTER COUNTY COURT

Case Number:

| [Order] | [Direction]
Family Law Act 1996 | Sheet *1* of *7* |

BETWEEN:

JANE SAWARD

Applicant

– and –

ALISTAIR DIAMOND

Respondent

Upon hearing counsel for the Applicant and for the Respondent
AND upon reading the Applicant's statement sworn on 19th October 1997

| Ordered by | [Mr] [Mrs] Justice
~~[His]~~ [Her] Honour Judge Kirby
[Deputy] [District Judge [of the Family Division]
Justice[s] of the Peace
[Assistant] Recorder
Clerk of the Court |

on   1st December 1997

FL404 Order or Direction

Orders under Family Law Act 1996 Part IV

(General heading followed by Notice A or Notice B and numbered options as appropriate)

Notice A — order includes non-molestation order — penal notice mandatory

Important Notice to the Respondent ALISTAIR DIAMOND

This order gives you instructions which you must follow. You should read it all carefully. If you do not understand anything in this order you should go to a solicitor, Legal Advice Centre or Citizens Advice Bureau. You have a right to ask the court to change or cancel the order but you must obey it unless the court does change or cancel it.

You must obey the instructions contained in this order. If you do not, you will be guilty of contempt of court, and you may be sent to prison.

~~*Notice B — order does not include non-molestation order — *penal notice*~~ *discretionary*

Important Notice to the Respondent [name]

This order gives you instructions which you must follow. You should read it all carefully. If you do not understand anything in this order you should go to a solicitor, Legal Advice Centre or Citizens Advice Bureau. You have a right to ask the court to change or cancel the order but you must obey it unless the court does change or cancel it.

You must obey the instructions contained in this order. *[If you do not, you will ~~be guilty of contempt of court, and you may be sent to prison.]~~

Occupation orders under s. 33 of the Family Law Act 1996

1.   The court declares that the applicant [name] is entitled to occupy [*address of home or intended home*] as [*his/her*] home. **OR**

2.   The court declares that the applicant [name] has matrimonial home rights in [*address of home or intended home*]. **AND/OR**

3.   The court declares that the applicant [name]'s matrimonial home rights shall not end when the respondent [name] dies or their marriage is dissolved and shall continue until ... or further order.

It is ordered that:

4.   The respondent [name] shall allow the applicant [name] to occupy [*address of home or intended home*] **OR**

5.   The respondent [name] shall allow the applicant [name] to occupy part of [*address of home or intended home*]: [*specify part*]

6.   The respondent [name] shall not obstruct, harass or interfere with the applicant [name]'s peaceful occupation of [*address of home or intended home*]

7.   The respondent [name] shall not occupy [*address of home or intended home*] **OR**

8.   The respondent [name] shall not occupy [*address of home or intended home*] from [*specify date*] until [*specify date*] **OR**

9.   The respondent [name] shall not occupy [*specify part of address of home or intended home*] **AND/OR**

10.   The respondent [name] shall not occupy [*address or part of address*] between [*specify dates or times*]

11.   The respondent [name] shall leave [*address or part of address*] [forthwith] [within —— [*hours/days*] of service on [*him/her*] or this order.] **AND/OR**

12.   Having left [*address or part of address*], the respondent [name] shall not return to, enter or attempt to enter [or go within [*specify distance*] of] it.

Occupation orders under ss. 35 & 36 of the Family Law Act 1996

It is ordered that:

13. The applicant [name] has the right to occupy [*address of home or intended home*] and the respondent [name] shall allow the applicant [name] to do so. **OR**

14. The respondent [name] shall not evict or exclude the applicant [name] from [*address of home or intended home*] or any part of it namely [*specify part*]. **AND/OR**

15. The respondent [name] shall not occupy [*address of home or intended home*]. **OR**

16. The respondent [name] shall not occupy [*address of home or intended home*] from [*specify date*] until [*specify date*] **OR**

17. The respondent [name] shall not occupy [*specify part of address of home or intended home*] **OR**

18. The respondent [name] shall leave [*address or part of address*] [forthwith] [within —— [*hours/days*] of service on [*him/her*] of this order.] **AND/OR**

19. Having left [*address or part of address*] the respondent [name] shall not return to, enter or attempt to enter [or go within [*specify distance*] of] it.

Occupation orders under ss. 37 & 38 of the Family Law Act 1996

It is ordered that:

20. The respondent [name] shall allow the applicant [name] to occupy [*address of home or intended home*] or part of it namely: [*specify*]. **AND/OR**

21. [One or both of the provisions in paragraphs 6 & 10 above may be inserted] **AND/OR**

22. The respondent [name] shall leave [*address or part of address*] [forthwith] [within —— [*hours/days*] of service on [*him/her*] of this order.] **AND/OR**

23. Having left [*address or part of address*], the respondent [name] may not return to, enter or attempt to enter [or go within [*specify distance*] of] it.

Additional provisions which may be included in occupation orders made under ss. 33, 35 or 36 of the Family Law Act 1996

It is ordered that:

24. The [*applicant [name]*] [*respondent [name]*] shall maintain and repair [*address of home or intended home*] **AND/OR**

25. The [*applicant [name]*] [*respondent [name]*] shall pay the rent for [*address of home or intended home*] **OR**

26. The [*applicant [name]*] [*respondent [name]*] shall pay the mortgage payments on [*address of home or intended home*] **OR**

27. The [*applicant [name]*] [*respondent [name]*] shall pay the following for [*address of home or intended home*]: [specify outgoings as bullet points].

28. The [*party in occupation*] shall pay to the [*other party*] £   each [*week, month, etc*] for [*address of home etc*].

29. The [*party in occupation*] shall keep and use the [*furniture*] [*contents*] [*specify if necessary*] of [*address of home or intended home*] and the [*applicant [name]*] [*respondent [name]*] shall return to the [*party in occupation*] the [*furniture*] [*contents*] [*specify if necessary*] [*no later than [date/time]*].

30. The [*party in occupation*] shall take reasonable care of the [*furniture*] [*contents*] [*specify if necessary*] of [*address of home or intended home*].

31. The [*party in occupation*] shall take all reasonable steps to keep secure [*address of home or intended home*] and the furniture or other contents [*specify if necessary*].

Duration

Occupation orders under s. 33 of the Family Law Act 1996
32.   This order shall last until [*specify event or date*]. **OR**

33.   This order shall last until a further order is made.

Occupation orders under ss. 35 & 37 of the Family Law Act 1996
34.   This order shall last until [*state date which must not be more than 6 months from the date of this order*].

35.   The occupation order made on [*state date*] is extended until [*state date which must not be more than 6 months from the date of this extension*].

Occupation orders under ss. 36 & 38 Family Law Act 1996
36.   This order shall last until [*state date which must not be more than 6 months from the date of this order*].

37.   The occupation order made on [*state date*] is extended until [*state date which must not be more than 6 months from the date of this extension*] and must end on that date.

Non-molestation orders

It is ordered that:
38.   The respondent ALISTAIR DIAMOND is forbidden to use or threaten violence against the applicant JANE SAWARD **AND**

39.   The respondent ALISTAIR DIAMOND is forbidden to intimidate, harass or pester JANE SAWARD the applicant **AND**

40.   The respondent ALISTAIR DIAMOND is forbidden to communicate with the applicant JANE SAWARD.

These orders will last until 30th November 1998.

41.   No order as to costs save legal aid taxation of both parties' costs.

No 4: APPLICATION BY WIFE AGAINST HUSBAND FOR A NON-MOLESTATION ORDER MADE EX PARTE

Application for:	To be completed by the Court
a Non-Molestation Order	Date issued
~~an Occupation Order~~	
Family Law Act 1996 (Part IV)	Case number
The Court Barchester County Court	

Please read the accompanying notes as you complete this form.

1   **About you (the applicant)**

State your title (Mr, Mrs etc.), full name, address, telephone number and date of birth (if under 18):

Mrs Jane Grey, 18 Marsh Avenue, Basset, Barchester, 01263 356243

State your solicitor's name, address, reference, telephone, FAX and DX numbers:

Black and White [ref DB], 4 Cathedral Avenue, Denham, Barchester, 01265 742183, DX Denham 41

2   **About the respondent**

State the respondent's name, address and date of birth (if known):

David Grey. 18 Marsh Avenue, Basset, Barcheste (DOB: 5/1/1962)

3   **The Order(s) for which you are applying**

This application is for:

☑   a non-molestation order

☐   an occupation order

☑   Tick this box if you wish the Court to hear your application without notice being given to the respondent. The reasons relied on for an application being heard without notice must be stated in the statement in support.

4   **Your relationship to the respondent (the person to be served with this application)**

Your relationship to the respondent is:

Please tick only one of the following

1 ☑ Married

2 ☐ Were married

3 ☐ Cohabiting

4 ☐ Were cohabiting

5 ☐ Both of you live or have lived in the same household

6 ☐ Relative
        State how related:

7 ☐ Agreed to marry.
        Give the date the agreement was made. If the agreement has ended, state when.

8 ☐ Both of you are parents of or have parental responsibility for a child

9 ☐ One of you is a parent of a child and the other has parental responsibility for that child

10 ☐ One of you is the natural parent or grandparent of a child adopted or freed for adoption, and the other is:

    (i)   the adoptive parent

or (ii)   a person who has applied for an adoption order for the child

or (iii)   a person with whom the child has been placed for adoption

or (iv)   the child who has been adopted or freed for adoption.

State whether (i), (ii), (iii) or (iv):

11 ☐ Both of you are parties to the same family proceedings (see also Section 11 below).

5   Application for a non-molestation order

If you wish to apply for a non-molestation order, state briefly in this section the order you want.

I want the respondent to stop assaulting me and threatening me with violence.

Give full details in support of your application in your supporting evidence

6   Application for an occupation order

If you do not wish to apply for an occupation order, please go to section 9 of this form.

(A)   State the address of the dwelling-house to which your application relates:

(B)   State whether it is occupied by you or the respondent now or in the past, or whether it was intended to be occupied by you or the respondent:

(C)   State whether you are entitled to occupy the
      dwelling-house
              ☐   Yes   ☐   No

(D)   State whether the respondent is entitled to the
      occupy dwelling-house
              ☐   Yes   ☐   No

      If yes, explain why:

      **On the basis of your answer to (C) and (D)
      above, tick one of the boxes 1 to 5 below to
      show the category into which you fit:**

      1   ☐   a spouse who has matrimonial home
              rights in the dwelling-house, or a
              person who is entitled to occupy it by
              virtue of a beneficial estate or interest
              or contract or by virtue of any
              enactment giving him or her the right
              to remain in occupation.

              If you tick box 1, state whether there
              is a dispute or pending proceedings
              between you and the respondent
              about your right to occupy the
              dwelling-house.

      2   ☐   a former spouse with no existing right
              to occupy, where the respondent
              spouse is entitled.

      3   ☐   a cohabitant or former cohabitant
              with no existing right to occupy,
              where the respondent cohabitant or
              former cohabitant is so entitled.

      4   ☐   a spouse or former spouse who is not
              entitled to occupy, where the
              respondent spouse or former spouse
              is also not entitled.

      5   ☐   a cohabitant or former cohabitant
              who is not entitled to occupy, where
              the respondent cohabitant or former
              cohabitant is also not entitled.

Matrimonial Home Rights

If you do have matrimonial home rights
please:

State whether the title to the land is registered
or unregistered (if known):

If registered, state the Land Registry title
number (if known):

**If you wish to apply for an occupation
order, state briefly here the order you
want.** Give full details in support of your
application in your supporting evidence.

7   **Application for additional order(s) about
the dwelling-house**

If you want to apply for any of the orders
listed in the notes to this section, state what
order you would like the court to make:

8   **Mortgage and rent**

Is the dwelling-house subject to a mortgage?
  ☐   Yes   ☐   No

If yes, please provide the name and address of
the mortgagee:

Is the dwelling-house rented?
  ☐   Yes   ☐   No

If yes, please provide the name and address of
the landlord:

9   At the Court

Will you need an interpreter at court?
☐   Yes   ☑ No

If 'Yes', specify the language:

If you need an interpreter because you do not
speak English, you are responsible for
providing your own.

If you need an interpreter or other facilities
because of a disability, please contact the
Court to ask what help is available.

10   Other information

State the name and date of birth of any child
living with or staying with, or likely to live
with or stay with you or the respondent:

Andrew Grey (DOB: 19/7/90)
Peter Grey (DOB: 1/11/91)

State the name of any other person living in
the same household as you and the
respondent, and say why they live there: **Not applicable**

11   Other Proceedings and Orders

If there are any other current family
proceedings or orders in force involving you
and the respondent, state the type of
proceedings or orders, the court and the case
number. This includes any application for an
occupation order or non-molestation order
against you by the respondent.   **Not applicable**

~~This application is to be served upon the~~
~~respondent~~

Signed	Date
Jane Grey	*7/12/97*

No 5: SWORN STATEMENT/AFFIDAVIT IN SUPPORT OF AN EX-PARTE APPLICATION BY WIFE AGAINST HUSBAND FOR A NON-MOLESTATION ORDER

IN THE BARCHESTER COUNTY COURT   No of Matter:
IN THE MATTER OF AN APPLICATION UNDER
THE FAMILY LAW ACT 1996

> Affidavit No 1
> Deponent: Jane Grey
> Date sworn: 7.12.97
> Date filed: ....

BETWEEN:

JANE CECILIA GREY

Applicant

– and –

DAVID GREY

Respondent

AFFIDAVIT OF THE APPLICANT

I, JANE CECILIA GREY of 18 Marsh Avenue, Barset in Barchester, a housewife, MAKE OATH and say as follows:

1. I am the Applicant herein and I make this affidavit in support of my application for a non-molestation order against the Respondent and for a power of arrest to be attached thereto.[1]

2. The Respondent and I married[2] on the 30th July 1989. There are two children of the family: Andrew, who was born on 19th July 1990 and is therefore aged 7, and Peter, who was born on 1st November 1991 and is 6. We have lived at 18

---

[1] On an inter partes application the court is obliged to attach a power of arrest if the conditions set out in s. 47(2) are satisfied. In the case of an ex parte order, the court may attach a power of arrest to one or more provisions of the order if it appears to the court (a) that the respondent has used or threatened violence against the applicant or a relevant child, and (b) that there is a risk of significant harm to the applicant or child attributable to conduct of the respondent if the power of arrest is not attached immediately: s. 47(3).
[2] Jurisdiction to make a non-molestation order under s. 42 is derived in this case from the fact that the parties are married to each other. By virtue of s. 62(3)(a) they are 'associated persons'. Under s. 42(5) in deciding whether to exercise its powers under the section, and if so, in what manner the court is enjoined to have regard to all the circumstances including the need to secure the health, safety and well being of the applicant.

Marsh Avenue, since January 1992. It is a 3-bedroomed house which the Respondent and I are buying with the assistance of a mortgage in the sum of £75,000.

3. The Respondent has been very unhappy since we moved to our current home. He resents the fact that we have a large mortgage and are therefore unable to afford luxuries such as going out with our friends or having holidays.

4. The Respondent's conduct has gradually deteriorated over this year. He has cut down my housekeeping allowance by £75 a month since January 1997 so that he can go out drinking with workmates at least twice a week. When he comes home after these drinking sessions he is verbally abusive to me and very critical of my appearance, the state of the house and the way in which I look after the children. He usually abuses me from the time of his return home (at about midnight) until about 2 am, when he tends to fall into a drunken sleep.

5. In early October 1997 I consulted a solicitor about the Respondent's behaviour as I wanted advice about divorce proceedings. On 13th October 1997, when I told the Respondent what I had done, he went berserk. He picked up every item on the dining table and threw it against the wall. He then got hold of my arms and twisted them behind my back, so I could not move. The Respondent told me that if I discussed our marriage with a stranger again he would punish me severely. He punched me 3 times in the face, shouting that this was a warning of what I would get if I dared to seek further legal advice.

6. I was so scared by the Respondent's conduct on the 13th October that I decided I would not pursue divorce proceedings. The Respondent has, however, continued to act violently. On 3 occasions he has thrown his dinner at me and on both 20th and 23rd October he came home after an evening out drinking and punched me about the body several times.

7. On 5th November the Respondent came home at about 1.30 am. He had clearly been drinking heavily. I was in bed when he returned. The Respondent came upstairs, pulled me out of bed and pushed me on to the bedroom floor. He kicked me several times. He then punched me twice in the face, causing me to sustain a broken nose and two black eyes. He told me that I could expect to be hurt regularly by way of punishment for the fact that I had chosen to consult solicitors. Following his assault upon me, the Respondent fell asleep on the sofa in the living room. I collected the two children of the family from their bedrooms and we left the matrimonial home at about 4.30 am. We are staying temporarily with my mother and father.

8. I make my application for a non-molestation order ex parte:[3]

---

[3] Section 45 provides that the court may where it considers that it is just and convenient to do so, make an order even though the respondent has not been given notice of the proceedings. In determining whether to do so the court must have regard to all the circumstances including any risk of significant harm to the applicant or a relevant child attributable to conduct of the respondent if the order is not made immediately, whether it is likely that the applicant will be deterred or prevented from pursuing the application if an order is not made immediately and whether there is reason to believe that the respondent is aware of proceedings but is deliberately evading service and that the applicant or child will be seriously prejudiced by the delay involved in effecting alternative service.

(a) because I fear that I will suffer significant harm if I return to the matrimonial home without the protection of an order; and

(b) if the order is not made immediately, and the Respondent becomes aware that I have consulted solicitors again, his behaviour towards me will be so aggressive that I do not believe I will feel able to make the application inter partes.

9. In all the circumstances, I invite the Court to grant an order in the terms of my application.

Sworn by JANE CECILIA GREY

At

This 7th day of December 1997

Before me

Solicitor

No 6: EX PARTE NON-MOLESTATION ORDER AGAINST HUSBAND

IN THE BARCHESTER COUNTY COURT   No. of Matter:

   BETWEEN:

JANE CECILIA GREY

Applicant

– and –

DAVID GREY

Respondent

8th December 1997   District Judge Fuller

Ex parte: Yes

Applicant represented by counsel   Present: Yes

Statement read: Jane Grey, 7.12.97

NOTICE

Notice A:

Important Notice to David Grey

This order gives you instructions which you must follow. You should read it all carefully. If you do not understand anything in this order you should go to a solicitor, Legal Advice Centre or Citizens Advice Bureau.
You have a right to ask the court to change or cancel the order but you must obey it unless the court does change or cancel it.
You must obey the instructions contained in this order. If you do not, you will be guilty of contempt of court, and you may be sent to prison.

ARREST   A power of arrest applies to paragraphs 1 and 2 hereof until 12th December 1997 at 4 p.m.

IT IS ORDERED THAT:
1.   The Respondent is forbidden to use or threaten violence against the Applicant;
2.   The Respondent is forbidden to intimidate, harass or pester the Applicant;
UNTIL 12th December 1997 at 4 p.m.
3.   Costs reserved, certificate for counsel;
4.   The application will be further considered on 12th December 1997 at 10.30 a.m.

No 7: APPLICATION AGAINST HOMOSEXUAL PARTNER FOR A NON-MOLESTATION ORDER

Application for:	To be completed by the Court
a Non-Molestation Order	Date issued
~~an Occupation Order~~	
Family Law Act 1996 (Part IV)	Case number
The Court Clerkenwell County Court	

Please read the accompanying notes as you complete this form.

1   About you (the applicant)

State your title (Mr, Mrs etc.), full name,
address, telephone number and date of birth
(if under 18):

Ms Jamie Mason, 14 Paddington Villas,
Essex Road, London N1. 0171-359 5111

State your solicitor's name, address,
reference, telephone, FAX and DX numbers:

Maiden and Co. [ref SB], 2 Henry Road,
London N5. 0171-359 0102. DX Kings Cross 5194

2   About the respondent

State the respondent's name, address and date
of birth (if known):

Jill Baker, 14 Paddington Villas, Essex Road,
London N1. (DOB: 2/3/1963)

3   The Order(s) for which you are applying

This application is for:

☑   a non-molestation order

☐   an occupation order

☐   Tick this box if you wish the Court to hear
your application without notice being given
to the respondent. The reasons relied on for an
application being heard without notice must
be stated in the statement in support.

4   Your relationship to the respondent (the person to be served with this application)

Your relationship to the respondent is:

Please tick only one of the following.

1 ☐ Married

2 ☐ Were married

3 ☐ Cohabiting

4 ☐ Were cohabiting

5 ☑ Both of you live or have lived in the same household

6 ☐ Relative
       State how related:

7 ☐ Agreed to marry.
       Give the date the agreement was
       made. If the agreement has ended,
       state when.

8 ☐ Both of you are parents of or have
       parental responsibility for a child

9 ☐ One of you is a parent of a child and
       the other has parental responsibility
       for that child

10 ☐ One of you is the natural parent or grandparent of a child adopted or freed for adoption, and the other is:

(i)   the adoptive parent

or (ii)   a person who has applied for an adoption order for the child

or (iii)   a person with whom the child has been placed for adoption

or (iv)   the child who has been adopted or freed for adoption.

State whether (i), (ii), (iii) or (iv):

11 ☐ Both of you are parties to the same family proceedings (see also Section 11 below).

5   Application for a non-molestation order

If you wish to apply for a non-molestation order, state briefly in this section the order you want.

I want the respondent to stop assaulting me and threatening me with violence.

Give full details in support of your application in your supporting evidence

6   Application for an occupation order

If you do not wish to apply for an occupation order, please go to section 9 of this form.

(A)   State the address of the dwelling-house to which your application relates:

(B)   State whether it is occupied by you or the respondent now or in the past, or whether it was intended to be occupied by you or the respondent:

(C)   State whether you are entitled to occupy the
      dwelling-house
                □   Yes   □   No

(D)   State whether the respondent is entitled to
      occupy the dwelling-house
                □   Yes   □   No

      If yes, explain why:

      **On the basis of your answer to (C) and (D)
      above, tick one of the boxes 1 to 5 below to
      show the category into which you fit:**

      1 □   a spouse who has matrimonial home
             rights in the dwelling-house, or a
             person who is entitled to occupy it by
             virtue of a beneficial estate or interest
             or contract or by virtue of any
             enactment giving him or her the right
             to remain in occupation.

             If you tick box 1, state whether there
             is a dispute or pending proceedings
             between you and the respondent
             about your right to occupy the
             dwelling-house.

      2 □   a former spouse with no existing right
             to occupy, where the respondent
             spouse is entitled.

      3 □   a cohabitant or former cohabitant
             with no existing right to occupy,
             where the respondent cohabitant or
             former cohabitant is so entitled.

      4 □   a spouse or former spouse who is not
             entitled to occupy, where the
             respondent spouse or former spouse
             is also not entitled.

      5 □   a cohabitant or former cohabitant
             who is not entitled to occupy, where
             the respondent cohabitant or former
             cohabitant is also not entitled.

Matrimonial Home Rights

If you do have matrimonial home rights please:

State whether the title to the land is registered or unregistered (if known):

If registered, state the Land Registry title number (if known):

If you wish to apply for an occupation order, state briefly here the order you want. Give full details in support of your application in your supporting evidence.

7   **Application for additional order(s) about the dwelling-house**

If you want to apply for any of the orders listed in the notes to this section, state what order you would like the court to make:

8   **Mortgage and rent**

Is the dwelling-house subject to a mortgage?
☐   Yes   ☐   No

If yes, please provide the name and address of the mortgagee:

Is the dwelling-house rented?
☐   Yes   ☐   No

If yes, please provide the name and address of the landlord:

---

9   At the Court

Will you need an interpreter at court?
☐   Yes   ☑   No

If 'Yes', specify the language:

If you need an interpreter because you do not
speak English, you are responsible for
providing your own.

If you need an interpreter or other facilities
because of a disability, please contact the
Court to ask what help is available.

10   Other information

State the name and date of birth of any child
living with or staying with, or likely to live
with or stay with you or the respondent:

State the name of any other person living in
the same household as you and the
respondent, and say why they live there: **Not applicable**

11   Other Proceedings and Orders

If there are any other current family
proceedings or orders in force involving you
and the respondent, state the type of
proceedings or orders, the court and the case
number. This includes any application for an
occupation order or non-molestation order
against you by the respondent.   **Not applicable**

**This application is to be served upon the
respondent**

Signed   Date

J. Mayson   19/11/97

No 8: AFFIDAVIT IN SUPPORT OF APPLICATION AGAINST A HOMOSEXUAL PARTNER FOR NON-MOLESTATION ORDER

IN THE CLERKENWELL COUNTY COURT   No of Matter:
IN THE MATTER OF AN APPLICATION UNDER
THE FAMILY LAW ACT 1996

> Filed on behalf of the Applicant.
> Deponent: Applicant; No 1
> Date sworn: 19th November 1997
> Date filed: 19th November 1997

BETWEEN:

JANIE MASON

Applicant

– and –

JILL BAKER

Respondent

AFFIDAVIT OF THE APPLICANT

I, JANIE MASON, hairdresser, of 14 Paddington Villas, Essex Road, London N1 MAKE OATH and say as follows:

1. I am the Applicant herein and I make this affidavit in support of my application under section 42 of the Family Law Act 1996 for a non-molestation order against the Respondent in the terms of my application.

2. The Respondent and I live together at the above address. It is a one-bedroomed flat privately rented in our joint names. We have lived together for about seven years since Jill left her husband, after he discovered that she and I were having a relationship[1]. We were very happy together until about 2 months ago when Jill

---

[1] This application is possible under the new Act whereas it would have created difficulties under the old law. Although the parties are living together in a sexual relationship they have never lived together as man and wife and so the court would not have had jurisdiction under the Domestic Violence and Matrimonial Proceedings Act 1976. Now, however, the fact that the applicant and respondent live in the same household gives the court jurisdiction to make a s. 42 non-molestation order. Janie and Jill are 'associated persons' by virtue of s. 62(3)(c) of the Act.

began to behave very strangely. She has been under a great deal of pressure recently because her ex-husband (they are now divorced) has now met someone else and he and his new partner have been trying to prevent Jill from seeing her two children, a son aged 9 and a daughter aged 12. Jill desperately loves her children and she has been very distressed by her ex-husband's conduct.

3. About 7 weeks ago I returned home from work. The Respondent was already at the flat and she had a tumbler of whiskey in her hand. It was obvious to me that she had been drinking heavily. As soon as I came through the door she rounded upon me, accusing me of being in contact with her ex-husband and telling lies about her. I told her not to be so silly and tried to reassure her that I would help in her fight to see her children. There has never been any trouble of such a kind between us before. Jill refused to be reassured and then stormed out of the flat.

4. The following day the Respondent apologised to me. We both went off to work as usual and in the evening I returned home. As soon as I came through the door it was obvious to me that the Respondent had once again been drinking heavily. On this occasion the Respondent was very abusive towards me and accused me once again of helping her ex-husband. I tried to ignore her and went into the kitchen to prepare dinner. As I left the room I noticed that the Respondent filled the glass she was holding from the whiskey decanter. She then followed me into the kitchen and picked up a knife from the table. It had a 12 inch blade and I knew it to be extremely sharp. I begged her to put the knife down, but she refused to do so. Her eyes were glazed and she was crying and shouting at the same time. Suddenly she lunged at me with the knife. I managed to dodge out of her way and fled into the living room and then out of the flat. I stayed the night with my mother.

5. The following day the Respondent telephoned me at the salon where I work and said how sorry she was about her behaviour towards me and asked me to come back to the flat. In fact I had no choice but to return because my mother's flat is a warden-controlled flat in a local authority sheltered housing complex and it would have been impossible for me to stay there for more than one night. Upon my return after work to the flat the Respondent was once again very apologetic. The evening passed without any incident, but I was extremely concerned about the Respondent's mental state. She alternately raged against her ex-husband and would then burst into tears.

6. On Thursday the 10th November the Respondent once again returned to our flat in a drunken state and began to abuse me. She did not use any weapon on this occasion but she ranted and raved about her ex-husband and how I was helping him. I feel very worried for my safety.[2] I have nowhere else to stay and I respectfully ask the protection of this Honourable Court against the Respondent. I am unwilling to report this matter to the police because I do not want the

---

[2] Under s. 42(5) in deciding whether to exercise its powers under the section, and if so, in what manner the court is enjoined to have regard to all the circumstances including the need to secure the health, safety and well-being of the applicant.

sanction of the criminal law to be visited on Jill. I just want to be protected from her.

7. The facts stated in this affidavit are within my own knowledge.

6. In all the circumstances I respectfully ask this Honourable Court to grant to me the relief I seek in my Notice of Application.

SWORN at the Clerkenwell County Court
at Duncan Terrace, London N1
this 19th November 1997   Before me ....

An officer of the Court appointed by the Judge to take affidavits

No 9: NON-MOLESTATION ORDER AGAINST HOMOSEXUAL PARTNER

<u>IN THE CLERKENWELL COUNTY COURT</u>   <u>No:</u>

<u>BETWEEN:</u>

JANIE MASON

Applicant

– and –

JILL BAKER

Respondent

29th November 1997   Her Honour Judge Barclay

Ex parte: No

Applicant: represented by solicitor   Present: Yes

Respondent: represented by counsel   Present: Yes

Statements read: of Applicant, sworn 19th November 1997

NOTICE

Notice A:

Important Notice to Jill Baker

This order gives you instructions which you must follow. You should read it all
carefully. If you do not understand anything in this order you should go to a solicitor,
Legal Advice Centre or Citizens Advice Bureau.
You have a right to ask the court to change or cancel the order but you must obey it
unless the court does change or cancel it.
You must obey the instructions contained in this order. If you do not, you will be
guilty of contempt of court, and you may be sent to prison.

IT IS ORDERED THAT:
1.   The Respondent is forbidden to use or threaten violence against the Applicant;
UNTIL 28th May 1998
2.   The Respondent do pay the Applicant's taxed costs;
3.   Legal aid taxation of the Applicant's costs;
4.   Certificate for counsel.

No 10: APPLICATION BY A MOTHER FOR A NON-MOLESTATION ORDER AGAINST A VIOLENT SON

Application for:	To be completed by the Court
a Non-Molestation Order	Date issued
~~an Occupation Order~~	
Family Law Act 1996 (Part IV)	Case number

The court   Barchester County Court

Please read the accompanying notes as you complete this form.

1   About you (the applicant)

State your title (Mr, Mrs etc.), full name,
address, telephone number and date of birth
(if under 18):

*Mrs Harriet Amanda Wilkes, 32 Sandy Lane,
Barset, Barchester. 01265 405131*

State your solicitor's name, address,
reference, telephone, FAX and DX numbers:

*Lowe and Craftee [ref CB], 2 Litigation Close,
Denham, Barchester. 01265 724190*

                                    DX Denham 4190

2   About the respondent

State the respondent's name, address and date
of birth (if known):

*Andrew David Wilkes, 32 Sandy Lane,
Barset, Barchester. (DOB: 19/7/1960)*

3   The Order(s) for which you are applying

This application is for:

☑   a non-molestation order

☐   an occupation order

☐   Tick this box if you wish the Court to hear
your application without notice being given
to the respondent. The reasons relied on for an
application being heard without notice must
be stated in the statement in support.

4   Your relationship to the respondent (the person to be served with this application)

Your relationship to the respondent is:

Please tick only one of the following:

1 ☐ Married

2 ☐ Were married

3 ☐ Cohabiting

4 ☐ Were cohabiting

5 ☐ Both of you live or have lived in the
       same household

6 ☑ Relative
       State how related:
       The respondent is my son.

7 ☐ Agreed to marry.
       Give the date the agreement was
       made. If the agreement has ended,
       state when.

8 ☐ Both of you are parents of or have
       parental responsibility for a child

9 ☐ One of you is a parent of a child and
       the other has parental responsibility
       for that child

10 ☐ One of you is the natural parent or grandparent of a child adopted or freed for adoption, and the other is:

(i) the adoptive parent

or (ii) a person who has applied for an adoption order for the child

or (iii) a person with whom the child has been placed for adoption

or (iv) the child who has been adopted or freed for adoption.

State whether (i), (ii), (iii) or (iv):

11 ☐ Both of you are parties to the same family proceedings (see also Section 11 below).

5 Application for a non-molestation order

If you wish to apply for a non-molestation order, state briefly in this section the order you want.

I want the respondent to stop threatening me, using violence against me & demanding/taking money from me.

Give full details in support of your application in your supporting evidence

6 Application for an occupation order

If you do not wish to apply for an occupation order, please go to section 9 of this form.

(A) State the address of the dwelling-house to which your application relates:

(B) State whether it is occupied by you or the respondent now or in the past, or whether it was intended to be occupied by you or the respondent:

(C)   State whether you are entitled to occupy the
      dwelling-house
              ☐   Yes   ☐   No

(D)   State whether the respondent is entitled to the
      dwelling-house
              ☐   Yes   ☐   No

      If yes, explain why:

**On the basis of your answer to (C) and (D)
above, tick one of the boxes 1 to 5 below to
show the category into which you fit:**

   1 ☐   a spouse who has matrimonial home
           rights in the dwelling-house, or a
           person who is entitled to occupy it by
           virtue of a beneficial estate or interest
           or contract or by virtue of any
           enactment giving him or her the right
           to remain in occupation.

           If you tick box 1, state whether there
           is a dispute or pending proceedings
           between you and the respondent
           about your right to occupy the
           dwelling-house.

   2 ☐   a former spouse with no existing right
           to occupy, where the respondent
           spouse is entitled.

   3 ☐   a cohabitant or former cohabitant
           with no existing right to occupy,
           where the respondent cohabitant or
           former cohabitant is so entitled.

   4 ☐   a spouse or former spouse who is not
           entitled to occupy, where the
           respondent spouse or former spouse
           is also not entitled.

   5 ☐   a cohabitant or former cohabitant
           who is not entitled to occupy, where
           the respondent cohabitant or former
           cohabitant is also not entitled.

Matrimonial Home Rights

If you do have matrimonial home rights please:

State whether the title to the land is registered or unregistered (if known):

If registered, state the Land Registry title number (if known):

If you wish to apply for an occupation order, state briefly here the order you want. Give full details in support of your application in your supporting evidence.

7   **Application for additional order(s) about the dwelling-house**

If you want to apply for any of the orders listed in the notes to this section, state what order you would like the court to make:

8   **Mortgage and rent**

Is the dwelling-house subject to a mortgage?
☐   Yes   ☐   No

If yes, please provide the name and address of the mortgagee:

Is the dwelling-house rented?
☐   Yes   ☐   No

If yes, please provide the name and address of the landlord:

9   At the Court

Will you need an interpreter at court?
☐   Yes   ☑   No

If 'Yes', specify the language:

If you need an interpreter because you do not speak English, you are responsible for providing your own.

If you need an interpreter or other facilities because of a disability, please contact the Court to ask what help is available.

10   Other information

State the name and date of birth of any child living with or staying with, or likely to live with or stay with, you or the respondent: **Not applicable**

State the name of any other person living in the same household as you and the respondent, and say why they live there: **Not applicable**

11   Other Proceedings and Orders

If there are any other current family proceedings or orders in force involving you and the respondent, state the type of proceedings or orders, the court and the case number. This includes any application for an occupation order or non-molestation order against you by the respondent.   **Not applicable**

This application is to be served upon the respondent

Signed   Date

H . Wilkes   7/12/97

No 11: SWORN STATEMENT/AFFIDAVIT IN SUPPORT OF APPLICATION BY A MOTHER FOR A NON-MOLESTATION ORDER AGAINST A VIOLENT SON

IN THE BARCHESTER COUNTY COURT   No of Matter:
IN THE MATTER OF AN APPLICATION UNDER
THE FAMILY LAW ACT 1996

> Affidavit No: 1
> Deponent: H. Wilkes
> Date sworn: 7.12.97
> Date filed: ....

BETWEEN:

HARRIET AMANDA WILKES

Applicant

– and –

ANDREW DAVID WILKES

Respondent

AFFIDAVIT OF THE APPLICANT

I, HARRIET AMANDA WILKES of 32, Sandy Lane, Barset in Barchester, a housewife, MAKE OATH and say as follows:

1. I am the Applicant herein and I make this affidavit in support of my application for a non-molestation order[1] against the Respondent. The Respondent is my son[2]. He was born on 19th July 1960 and is, therefore, aged 37 years.

2. My home is a two-bedroomed flat which I have rented from the local authority since 1980. The Respondent moved in to live with me about 6 months ago when his marriage broke down.

---

[1] Under s. 42(5) in deciding whether to exercise its powers under the section, and if so, in what manner the court is enjoined to have regard to all the circumstances including the need to secure the health, safety and well-being of the applicant.

[2] This application is possible under the new Act whereas it might have created difficulties under the old law since the applicant would have had to rely on a civil action for assault. The applicant and respondent are 'associated persons' by virtue of s. 62(3)(d) because they are relatives. Moreover, in this example the applicant and respondent live in the same household and are therefore associated persons by virtue of s. 62(3)(c) of the Act.

3. Over the past 6 months, the Respondent has become increasingly violent to me. He constantly asks me for money and when I try to refuse, he threatens me with physical violence until I give him at least £5. This happens once or twice a week.

4. Last week on Thursday 1st December I refused to give him any money, pointing out as I always do that my pension is not intended to support two people. He draws income support in his own right, but makes no contribution towards bills or the cost of the food that I provide for him. When I refused to give him any money, the Respondent pushed me out of the way and helped himself to £5 from my purse.

5. I am 76 years old and I am not in good health. I was very shaken up when the Respondent pushed me last week. I have been very frightened by the Respondent's behaviour. If he is willing to behave himself, I would not mind if he continued to live in my flat. I do, however, seek the protection of this Court by a non-molestation order preventing the Respondent from assaulting or molesting me.

Sworn by HARRIET AMANDA WILKES

At

This 7th day of December 1997

Before me

Solicitor

No 12: NON-MOLESTATION ORDER AGAINST A VIOLENT SON

IN THE BARCHESTER COUNTY COURT   No. of matter:

BETWEEN:

HARRIET AMANDA WILKES

<u>Applicant</u>

– and –

ANDREW DAVID WILKES

<u>Respondent</u>

15th December 1997   District Judge Townsend

Ex parte: No

Applicant: represented by solicitor   Present: Yes

Respondent: no representation   Present: Yes

Statements: of Applicant, sworn 7th December 1997

NOTICE

Notice A:

Important Notice to Andrew David Wilkes

This order gives you instructions which you must follow. You should read it all carefully. If you do not understand anything in this order you should go to a solicitor, Legal Advice Centre or Citizens Advice Bureau.
You have a right to ask the court to change or cancel the order but you must obey it unless the court does change or cancel it.
You must obey the instructions contained in this order. If you do not, you will be guilty of contempt of court, and you may be sent to prison.

ARREST: A power of arrest applies to paragraphs 1, 2 and 3 until 14th December 1998

IT IS ORDERED THAT:
1.   The Respondent is forbidden to use or threaten violence against the Applicant;
2.   The Respondent is forbidden to intimidate, harass or pester the Applicant;
3.   The Respondent is forbidden to ask the Applicant for money or to take money from her;
UNTIL 14th December 1998
4.   No order as to costs save for legal aid taxation of the Applicant's costs. Certificate for counsel.

No 13: APPLICATION BY WIFE AGAINST HUSBAND (JOINT OWNERS) FOR A NON-MOLESTATION ORDER, AN OCCUPATION ORDER REQUIRING HIM TO LEAVE AND AN ANCILLARY ORDER RE MORTGAGE PAYMENTS

Application for:	To be completed by the Court
a Non-Molestation Order	Date issued
an Occupation Order	
Family Law Act 1996 (Part IV)	Case number
The Court	

Please read the accompanying notes as you complete this form.

1   **About you (the applicant)**

State your title (Mr, Mrs etc.), full name, address, telephone number and date of birth (if under 18):

Deborah King, 15 Nayford Road, London E5 8RD. 0181-801 6111

State your solicitor's name, address, reference, telephone, FAX and DX numbers:

Davies and Jones, 56 High Street, Shoreditch, London. 0171-272 9328

2   **About the respondent**   *DX 262*

State the respondent's name, address and date of birth (if known):

Joe King, 15 Nayford Road, London E5 8RD. (DOB: 19/7/1960)

3   **The Order(s) for which you are applying**

This application is for:

☑   a non-molestation order

☑   an occupation order

☐   Tick this box if you wish the Court to hear your application without notice being given to the respondent. The reasons relied on for an application being heard without notice must be stated in the statement in support.

4 Your relationship to the respondent (the person to be served with this application)

Your relationship to the respondent is:

Please tick only one of the following.

1 ☑ Married

2 ☐ Were married

3 ☐ Cohabiting

4 ☐ Were cohabiting

5 ☐ Both of you live or have lived in the same household

6 ☐ Relative
State how related:

7 ☐ Agreed to marry.
Give the date the agreement was made. If the agreement has ended, state when.

8 ☐ Both of you are parents of or have parental responsibility for a child

9 ☐ One of you is a parent of a child and the other has parental responsibility for that child

10 ☐ One of you is the natural parent or grandparent of a child adopted or freed for adoption, and the other is:

         (i)   the adoptive parent

 or (ii)   a person who has applied for an adoption order for the child

 or (iii)   a person with whom the child has been placed for adoption

 or (iv)   the child who has been adopted or freed for adoption.

State whether (i), (ii), (iii) or (iv):

11 ☐ Both of you are parties to the same family proceedings (see also Section 11 below).

5   Application for a non-molestation order

If you wish to apply for a non-molestation order, state briefly in this section the order you want.

An order preventing the respondent from threatening me and from using violence against me.

Give full details in support of your application in your supporting evidence

6   Application for an occupation order

If you do not wish to apply for an occupation order, please go to section 9 of this form.

(A)   State the address of the dwelling-house to which your application relates:

15 Nayford Road, London E5 8RD.

(B)   State whether it is occupied by you or the respondent now or in the past, or whether it was intended to be occupied by you or the respondent:

It is occupied by both of us.

(C)   State whether you are entitled to occupy the
      dwelling-house
              ☑ Yes   ☐ No

      If yes, explain why:
      I am a joint legal and beneficial owner.

(D)   State whether the respondent is entitled to
      occupy the dwelling-house
              ☑ Yes   ☐ No

      If yes, explain why:
      The respondent is a joint legal and beneficial owner.

**On the basis of your answer to (C) and (D)
above, tick one of the boxes 1 to 5 below to
show the category into which you fit:**

1 ☑ a spouse who has matrimonial home
       rights in the dwelling-house, or a
       person who is entitled to occupy it by
       virtue of a beneficial estate or interest
       or contract or by virtue of any
       enactment giving him or her the right
       to remain in occupation.

       If you tick box 1, state whether there
       is a dispute or pending proceedings
       between you and the respondent
       about your right to occupy the
       dwelling-house.

2 ☐ a former spouse with no existing right
       to occupy, where the respondent
       spouse is entitled.

3 ☐ a cohabitant or former cohabitant
       with no existing right to occupy,
       where the respondent cohabitant or
       former cohabitant is so entitled.

4 ☐ a spouse or former spouse who is not
       entitled to occupy, where the
       respondent spouse or former spouse
       is also not entitled.

5 ☐ a cohabitant or former cohabitant
       who is not entitled to occupy, where
       the respondent cohabitant or former
       cohabitant is also not entitled.

Matrimonial Home Rights

If you do have matrimonial home rights
please:

State whether the title to the land is registered
or unregistered (if known):

If registered, state the Land Registry title
number (if known):

**If you wish to apply for an occupation
order, state briefly here the order you
want.** Give full details in support of your
application in your supporting evidence.

*I seek an order requiring the respondent
to leave the matrimonial home.*

7   **Application for additional order(s) about
the dwelling-house**

If you want to apply for any of the orders
listed in the notes to this section, state what
order you would like the court to make:

*I seek an order requiring the respondent
to discharge the monthly mortgage
instalments.*

8   **Mortgage and rent**

Is the dwelling-house subject to a mortgage?
               ☑ Yes   ☐ No

If yes, please provide the name and address of
the mortgagee:

Bank of Wales, 15 High Street, Cardiff

Is the dwelling-house rented?
               ☐ Yes   ☑ No

If yes, please provide the name and address of
the landlord:

9   At the Court

Will you need an interpreter at court?
☐   Yes   ☑   No

If 'Yes', specify the language:

If you need an interpreter because you do not
speak English, you are responsible for
providing your own.

If you need an interpreter or other facilities
because of a disability, please contact the
Court to ask what help is available.

10   Other information

State the name and date of birth of any child
living with or staying with, or likely to live
with or stay with you or the respondent:

David King (DOB : 15/12/1985)
Julie King (DOB : 3/3/1987)

State the name of any other person living in
the same household as you and the
respondent, and say why they live there:

11   Other proceedings and orders

If there are any other current family
proceedings or orders in force involving you
and the respondent, state the type of
proceedings or orders, the court and the case
number. This includes any application for an
occupation order or non-molestation order
against you by the respondent.   **Not applicable**

**This application is to be served upon the
respondent**

Signed	Date
Deborah King	*21/11/97*

No 14: AFFIDAVIT IN SUPPORT OF AN APPLICATION BY WIFE AGAINST HUSBAND (JOINT OWNERS) FOR A NON-MOLESTATION ORDER, AN OCCUPATION ORDER REQUIRING HIM TO LEAVE AND AN ANCILLARY ORDER RE MORTGAGE PAYMENTS

IN THE SHOREDITCH COUNTY COURT   No of Matter:
IN THE MATTER OF AN APPLICATION UNDER
THE FAMILY LAW ACT 1996

> Filed on behalf of the Applicant.
> Deponent: Applicant; No 1
> Date sworn: 21st November 1997
> Date filed: 21st November 1997

BETWEEN:

DEBORAH KING

Applicant

– and –

JOE KING

Respondent

AFFIDAVIT OF THE APPLICANT[1]

I, DEBORAH KING, housewife, of 15 Nayford Road, London E5 MAKE OATH and say as follows:

1. I am the Applicant herein and I make this affidavit in support of my application under the Family Law Act 1996 for an order in the terms of my application to restrain the Respondent from molesting me[2] and for an order that the Respondent be required to leave the former matrimonial home at the above address.

---

[1] As will be seen this affidavit is in support of an application by a wife for a non-molestation order against her husband and for an order that he be excluded from the matrimonial home. They are 'associated persons' by virtue of s. 62(3)(a) of the Act. They are, moreover, joint owners of the property in which they live and so the wife's application for an occupation order is made under s. 33 of the Act, she being a person entitled to occupy a dwelling-house by virtue of a beneficial estate or interest (i.e., an 'entitled applicant'; see Chapter 19, paragraph 4).

[2] Under s. 42(5) in deciding whether to exercise its powers under the section, and if so, in what manner the court is enjoined to have regard to all the circumstances including the need to secure the health, safety and well being of the applicant, and of any relevant child.

2. The Respondent and I were married on the 5th January 1980. We have two children, namely David King who was born on the 15th December 1985 and Julie King who was born on the 3rd March 1987.

3. Housing Needs and Housing Resources[3]

    The house in which we live is a three-bedroomed terraced house which is in our joint names. It is subject to a mortgage of approximately £60,000. We bought the property about 5 years ago. It is worth about £90,000. I have no other accommodation available to me. The Respondent on the other hand does have somewhere else to stay, namely, with his mistress as explained below.

4. Financial Resources[4]

    I have no income save for child benefit of about £75 per month. The Respondent is employed as a British Telecom engineer and takes home approximately £1,300 per month.

5. Conduct[5]

    My marriage was happy until approximately 3 years ago when the Respondent began to drink excessively. I tried to discuss the problem with him, but his reaction was to tell me that it was nothing to do with me. I became increasingly concerned because his drunken behaviour began to upset the children. David in particular would become very frightened when the Respondent shouted at me and he would ask me, 'Why does Daddy fall over so much?'.

6. Approximately 6 months ago I started to suspect that the Respondent was seeing another woman because there were several occasions when the telephone rang and when I picked up the receiver and spoke the number the telephone would go dead. The Respondent began to stay out later and later and when he returned, sometimes in the early hours of the morning, he was abusive and argumentative to the extent that the children would wake up and Julie would often cry and need to be comforted by me.[6] Last week I confronted the Respondent about the telephone calls and he confessed to me that he was seeing someone else. He told me that she was a divorcee living in Highgate, and that she owned her own flat.

---

[3] The applicant is seeking an order under s. 33(3)(f), namely an order requiring the respondent to leave the dwelling-house. In deciding whether to exercise its powers under the subsection and if so in what manner, the court is enjoined to have regard to all the circumstances, including the housing needs and housing resources of the parties and of any relevant child, the financial resources of the parties, the likely effect of any order, or of any decision by the court not to exercise its powers under subs. (3) on the health, safety or well-being of the parties and of any relevant child, and the conduct of the parties in relation to each other and otherwise (s. 33(6)).

[4] See footnote 3.

[5] See footnote 3.

[6] This is relevant to consideration of the the the health, safety or well being of any relevant child.

7.   On the 17th September 1997 at about 2.00 pm, the Respondent came back from
     the public house where he had been since about 11.30 am. I had cooked a
     Sunday roast for the family. As soon as he came through the door I realised that
     the Respondent was the worse for drink. His speech was slurred and his eyes
     were glazed. I said nothing, but served the meal. Suddenly the Respondent
     exploded with rage, shouted something about the meal being cold and threw his
     plate against the wall. The children began to cry and when I went to clear up
     the mess the Respondent pushed me over and tried to kick me. By now the
     children were screaming. I went into the kitchen and the Respondent followed
     me and put his hands around my throat. I was terrified. At that moment David
     came into the kitchen and told the Respondent to leave me alone. A general
     struggle took place between myself and the Respondent as a result of which I
     was struck in the face several times. I still have the red marks where the blows
     landed. I managed to call the police who arrived within minutes. They arrested
     the Respondent and took him down to the police station where they kept him
     for several hours until he was sober. When he returned to the matrimonial home
     the Respondent was very subdued and apologised for what had happened. I told
     him that I intended to divorce him and he said that he didn't blame me.

8.   Since then there have been no further incidents of violence but I am very afraid
     of what the Respondent might do should he drink to excess once again. I can
     see no future in the marriage and I intend to file for divorce as soon as possible.
     In the meantime I want the Respondent to be excluded from the former
     matrimonial home. I believe that his presence is causing a great deal of tension
     in the home which is causing significant harm to the children. They have cried
     a lot since the incident on the 17th September and the teachers at the school
     both children attend have told me that the children have become aggressive and
     badly behaved[7]. Fortunately the Respondent has somewhere else to stay,
     namely with his mistress in Highgate.

9.   If the court does not make an order, the children and I will continue to be in an
     intolerable situation. I am not prepared to see the children suffer further.

10. Ancillary Orders[8]

     As explained, I have no income apart from child benefit. I would not be in a
     position to pay the mortgage without the Respondent's assistance. In the
     circumstances I respectfully ask that this Honourable Court orders the
     Respondent to pay the mortgage payments in respect of the matrimonial home
     and to meet the bills for the utilities. The total outgoings come to about £950.

---

[7] This evidence, if accepted by the court, should ensure that an order is made since it will persuade the
court that if the order is not made it is likely that the children will suffer significant harm attributable to
conduct of the respondent (s. 33(7)). Of course it will be open to the respondent to adduce evidence that
there is a likelihood that he or the children will suffer significant harm if the order is made and that harm
is as great or greater than the harm likely to be suffered by the applicant or the child if the order is not
made (see s. 33(7) (a) and (b)).
[8] See Chapter 20.

In the past the Respondent has paid me housekeeping of £250 per week out of which I discharged all the bills including the mortgage.

11. In all the circumstances I ask that this Honourable Court grants me the relief sought in my Notice of Application.

SWORN at the Shoreditch County Court

at

this 21st November 1997   Before me...

An officer of the Court appointed by the Judge to take affidavits

No 15: ORDER AGAINST JOINT OWNER HUSBAND: NON-MOLESTATION ORDER, OCCUPATION ORDER AND ANCILLARY ORDER RE MORTGAGE PAYMENTS

IN THE SHOREDITCH COUNTY COURT   Case No:

BETWEEN:

DEBORAH KING

Applicant

– and –

JOE KING

Respondent

8th December 1997   District Judge Kirby

Ex parte: No

Applicant: represented by counsel   Present: Yes

Respondent: represented by counsel   Present: Yes

Statements of Applicant, sworn 21st November 1997 and of

Respondent, sworn on 7th December 1997

Evidence: taken from Applicant and Respondent

NOTICE

Notice A:

Important Notice to Joe King

This order gives you instructions which you must follow. You should read it all carefully. If you do not understand anything in this order you should go to a solicitor, Legal Advice Centre or Citizens Advice Bureau.
You have a right to ask the court to change or cancel the order but you must obey it unless the court does change or cancel it.

You must obey the instructions contained in this order. If you do not, you will be guilty of contempt of court, and you may be sent to prison.

ARREST: A power of arrest applies to paragraphs 1, 2 and 4 hereof until 7th June 1998

IT IS ORDERED THAT:
1.   The Respondent shall leave 15, Nayford Road, London E5 forthwith and
2.   Having left 15, Nayford Road the Respondent shall not return to, enter or attempt to enter or go within 25 yards of the property;
3.   The Respondent shall pay the mortgage repayments to the Bank of Wales in respect of the Bank's mortgage on 15, Nayford Road;
These orders shall last until 7th June 1998
4.   The Respondent is forbidden to use or threaten violence against the Applicant.
This order shall last until 7th June 1988
5.   Legal aid taxation of both parties' costs. Certificate for counsel.

**No 16: APPLICATION BY AN ENTITLED COHABITANT FOR
A NON-MOLESTATION ORDER AND AN OCCUPATION ORDER
REGULATING THE OCCUPATION OF THE DWELLING-HOUSE
AGAINST AN ENTITLED RESPONDENT**

Application for:	To be completed by the Court
a Non-Molestation Order	Date issued
an Occupation Order	
Family Law Act 1996 (Part IV)	Case number

The Court   Barchester County Court

Please read the accompanying notes as you complete this form.

1   About you (the applicant)

State your title (Mr, Mrs etc.), full name,
address, telephone number and date of birth
(if under 18):

Joan Smith, 20 Mulberry Avenue,
Basset, Barchester

State your solicitor's name, address,
reference, telephone, FAX and DX numbers:

Lowe and Crabtree [Ref CB], 2 Litigation Close,
Denham, Barchester. 01265 724190.

2   About the respondent   DX Denham 4190

State the respondent's name, address and date
of birth (if known):

Raymond Jones, 20 Mulberry Avenue,
Basset, Barchester.

3   The Order(s) for which you are applying

This application is for:

☑   a non-molestation order

☑   an occupation order

☐   Tick this box if you wish the Court to hear
your application without notice being given
to the respondent. The reasons relied on for an
application being heard without notice must
be stated in the statement in support.

4 Your relationship to the respondent (the person to be served with this application)

Your relationship to the respondent is:

Please tick only one of the following.

1 ☐ Married

2 ☐ Were married

3 ☐ Cohabiting

4 ☑ Were cohabiting

5 ☐ Both of you live or have lived in the same household

6 ☐ Relative
State how related:

7 ☐ Agreed to marry.
Give the date the agreement was made. If the agreement has ended, state when.

8 ☐ Both of you are parents of or have parental responsibility for a child

9 ☐ One of you is a parent of a child and the other has parental responsibility for that child

10 ☐ One of you is the natural parent or
grandparent of a child adopted or
freed for adoption, and the other is:

    (i)   the adoptive parent
or (ii)   a person who has applied for
           an adoption order for the
           child
or (iii)   a person with whom the
           child has been placed for
           adoption
or (iv)   the child who has been
           adopted or freed for
           adoption.
State whether (i), (ii), (iii) or (iv):

11 ☐ Both of you are parties to the same
family proceedings (see also Section
11 below).

5   Application for a non-molestation order

If you wish to apply for a non-molestation
order, state briefly in this section the order
you want.

Give full details in support of your
application in your supporting evidence

*An order forbidding the respondent from
using violence against me.*

6   Application for an occupation order

If you do not wish to apply for an occupation
order, please go to section 9 of this form.

(A)   State the address of the dwelling-house to
which your application relates:

*20 Mulberry Avenue, Barset,
Barchester.*

(B)   State whether it is occupied by you or the
respondent now or in the past, or whether it
was intended to be occupied by you or the
respondent:

It is occupied by us both.

(C) State whether you are entitled to occupy the
     dwelling-house
          ☑ Yes   ☐   No

     If yes, explain why:
     *I am, with the respondent, a party to a
     local authority tenancy of the property.*

(D) State whether the respondent is entitled to
     occupy the dwelling-house
          ☑ Yes   ☐   No

     If yes, explain why:
     See above.

     **On the basis of your answer to (C) and (D)
     above, tick one of the boxes 1 to 5 below to
     show the category into which you fit:**

     1 ☑ a spouse who has matrimonial home
           rights in the dwelling-house, or a
           person who is entitled to occupy it by
           virtue of a beneficial estate or interest
           or contract or by virtue of any
           enactment giving him or her the right
           to remain in occupation.

           If you tick box 1, state whether there
           is a dispute or pending proceedings
           between you and the respondent
           about your right to occupy the
           dwelling-house.

     *I have issued proceedings for a
     transfer of tenancy.*

     2 ☐ a former spouse with no existing right
           to occupy, where the respondent
           spouse is entitled.

     3 ☐ a cohabitant or former cohabitant
           with no existing right to occupy,
           where the respondent cohabitant or
           former cohabitant is so entitled.

     4 ☐ a spouse or former spouse who is not
           entitled to occupy, where the
           respondent spouse or former spouse
           is also not entitled.

     5 ☐ a cohabitant or former cohabitant
           who is not entitled to occupy, where
           the respondent cohabitant or former
           cohabitant is also not entitled.

Matrimonial Home Rights

If you do have matrimonial home rights please:

State whether the title to the land is registered or unregistered (if known):

If registered, state the Land Registry title number (if known):

If you wish to apply for an occupation order, state briefly here the order you want. Give full details in support of your application in your supporting evidence.

Until the hearing of my application for a tenancy transfer, I seek an order that the respondent does not occupy the home between 5.00pm and 8.30am each day.

7   **Application for additional order(s) about the dwelling-house**

If you want to apply for any of the orders listed in the notes to this section, state what order you would like the court to make:

8   **Mortgage and rent**

Is the dwelling-house subject to a mortgage?
☐ Yes   ☐ No

If yes, please provide the name and address of the mortgagee:

Is the dwelling-house rented?
☑ Yes   ☐ No

If yes, please provide the name and address of the landlord:

*Basset County Council
Shire Hall
Basset*

9   At the Court

Will you need an interpreter at court?

☐   Yes   ☑   No

If 'Yes', specify the language:

If you need an interpreter because you do not
speak English, you are responsible for
providing your own.

If you need an interpreter or other facilities
because of a disability, please contact the
Court to ask what help is available.

10   Other information

State the name and date of birth of any child
living with or staying with, or likely to live
with or stay with you or the respondent: *N/A*

State the name of any other person living in
the same household as you and the
respondent, and say why they live there: *N/A*

11   Other Proceedings and Orders

If there are any other current family
proceedings or orders in force involving you
and the respondent, state the type of
proceedings or orders, the court and the case
number. This includes any application for an
occupation order or non-molestation order
against you by the respondent.   **Not applicable**

**This application is to be served upon the
respondent**

*My application for a tenancy transfer was
issued on 1st October 1997 in this Court,
Title No: 97/0039.*

Signed   *Joan Smith*   Date   *7/12/97*

No 17: SWORN STATEMENT/AFFIDAVIT IN SUPPORT OF APPLICATION BY AN ENTITLED COHABITANT FOR A NON-MOLESTATION ORDER AND AN OCCUPATION ORDER REGULATING THE OCCUPATION OF THE DWELLING-HOUSE AGAINST AN ENTITLED RESPONDENT

IN THE BARCHESTER COUNTY COURT   No of Matter:
IN THE MATTER OF AN APPLICATION UNDER
THE FAMILY LAW ACT 1996

> Affidavit No 1
> Deponent: J. Smith
> Date sworn: 7.11.97
> Date filed: ....

BETWEEN:

JOAN SMITH

Applicant

– and –

RAYMOND JONES

Respondent

AFFIDAVIT OF THE APPLICANT

I, JOAN SMITH, of 20 Mulberry Avenue, Barset in Barchester, a part-time care assistant, MAKE OATH and say as follows:

1.   I am the Applicant herein and I make this affidavit in support of my application for a non-molestation order[1] and an occupation order[2] regulating the occupation by the Respondent of our home.

2.   The Respondent and I started to live together as man and wife in 1992. We have lived at the above address since 1st January 1994. We occupy our two-bedroomed flat by virtue of a tenancy agreement made between the local authority and the Respondent and me on the 1st January 1994.[3]

3.   My relationship with the Respondent broke down in about September 1997. We agreed that we should live separate lives, but we have failed to agree on the fate of our joint tenancy. Accordingly, I have issued an application for a transfer of the tenancy into my sole name.

---

[1] Under s. 42(5) in deciding whether to exercise its powers under the section, and if so, in what manner the court is enjoined to have regard to all the circumstances including the need to secure the health, safety and well-being of the applicant.

[2] The applicant is a joint tenant of the dwelling-house and being, therefore, an entitled applicant makes her application for an occupation order under s. 33 of the Act.

[3] The applicant and the respondent are, therefore, 'associated persons' by virtue of s. 62(3)(b) of the Act, i.e., they are cohabitants. They also qualify because they live in the same household: s. 62(3)(c).

4. <u>Housing Needs and Housing Resources</u>[4]

Neither the respondent nor I have any alternative accommodation available to us.

5. <u>Financial Resources</u>[5]

I earn £120 per week net as a care assistant. The Respondent is a lorry driver and to the best of my knowledge he earns in excess of £1,000 per month.

6. <u>Conduct</u>[6]

Since the Respondent has become aware of my intended application, he has behaved towards me in a childish and spiteful fashion. For example, he removes my washing up from the kitchen and dumps it in the lounge. Whenever he walks past me in the flat, he barges into me, knocking me against walls or doors as he does so.

7. The Respondent works might shifts and is therefore away from the flat between 6 pm and 8 am every night. I leave the home for work at about 8.30 am and return thereto at about 5 pm.

8. My application for a tenancy transfer is due to be heard in 12 weeks' time, on 1st February 1998. I am fearful for my safety if I have to live with the Respondent in the circumstances I have described and without the protection of a court order. So far, I have suffered bruising to my arms and legs when the Respondent has pushed into me. I very much fear that if an order regulating his conduct is not made, I may suffer far more serious injury.

9. Given our respective working hours, and in the light of the Respondent's behaviour towards me, I respectfully invite the court to make an order pending the determination of my application for a transfer of the tenancy:

    (1) forbidding the Respondent from assaulting or molesting me, and

    (2) regulating the occupation of the flat by the Respondent by providing that he should only be entitled to be present in the flat between 8.30 am and 5.00 pm every day.

Sworn by JOAN SMITH etc.

---

[4] The applicant is seeking an order under s. 33(3)(f), namely an order requiring the respondent to leave the dwelling-house. In deciding whether to exrecise its powers under the subsection and if so in what manner, the court is enjoined to have regard to all the circumstances including, the housing needs and housing resources of the parties and of any relevant child, the financial resources of the parties, the likely effect of any order, or of any decision by the court not to exercise its powers under subs. (3) on the health, safety or well-being of the parties and of any relevant child, and the conduct of the parties in relation to each other and otherwise (s. 33(6)).

[5] See footnote 4.

[6] See footnote 4.

No 18: ORDER AGAINST ENTITLED RESPONDENT: NON-MOLESTATION ORDER AND OCCUPATION ORDER REGULATING THE OCCUPATION OF THE HOME

IN THE BARCHESTER COUNTY COURT   No. of matter:

BETWEEN:

JOAN SMITH

Applicant

– and –

RAYMOND JONES

Respondent

1st December 1997   Before District Judge Kirby

Ex parte: No

Applicant: represented by counsel   Present: Yes

Respondent: represented by counsel   Present: Yes

Statements: Applicant of 7th November 1997, Respondent of 15th November 1997

Evidence: Applicant and Respondent

NOTICE

Notice A:

Important Notice to Raymond Jones

This order gives you instructions which you must follow. You should read it all carefully. If you do not understand anything in this order you should go to a solicitor, Legal Advice Centre or Citizens Advice Bureau.

You have a right to ask the court to change or cancel the order but you must obey it unless the court does change or cancel it.

You must obey the instructions contained in this order. If you do not, you will be guilty of contempt of court, and you may be sent to prison.

IT IS ORDERED THAT:

1.   The Respondent shall not occupy the home at 20, Mulberry Avenue, Barset between 5 p.m. and 9 a.m. each day;

This Order shall last until the determination of the Applicant's application for a transfer of the tenancy in respect of the said home or 1st March 1998, whichever is the earlier;

2.   The Respondent is forbidden to use or threaten violence against the Applicant;

3.   The Respondent do pay the Applicant's costs, to be taxed if not agreed;

4.   Legal aid taxation of the Applicant's costs. Certificate for counsel.

No 19: APPLICATION BY A NON-ENTITLED COHABITANT FOR NON-MOLESTATION ORDER, OCCUPATION ORDER AND AN ANCILLARY ORDER AGAINST ENTITLED RESPONDENT

Application for:	**To be completed by the Court**
a Non-Molestation Order	Date issued
an Occupation Order	
Family Law Act 1996 (Part IV)	Case number
The Court Clerkenwell County Court	

Please read the accompanying notes as you complete this form.

1   About you (the applicant)

State your title (Mr, Mrs etc.), full name,
address, telephone number and date of birth
(if under 18):

*Ms Susan White, 15 De Vere Mansions,
Richmond Avenue, London N5.
0171- 806 5111*

State your solicitor's name, address,
reference, telephone, FAX and DX numbers:

*Jones and Cox, 12 Richmond Avenue,
London N5 (Ref BL). 0171-806 5113.
Fax 0171- 806 5114.*

2   About the respondent

State the respondent's name, address and date
of birth (if known):

*Stan Brown, 15 De Vere Mansions
Richmond Avenue, London N5.
(DOB: 19/7/1960)*

3   The Order(s) for which you are applying

This application is for:

☑   a non-molestation order

☑   an occupation order

☐   Tick this box if you wish the Court to hear
your application without notice being given
to the respondent. The reasons relied on for an
application being heard without notice must
be stated in the statement in support.

4   **Your relationship to the respondent (the person to be served with this application)**

Your relationship to the respondent is:

Please tick only one of the following.

1 ☐ Married

2 ☐ Were married

3 ☐ Cohabiting

4 ☑ Were cohabiting

5 ☐ Both of you live or have lived in the same household

6 ☐ Relative
State how related:

7 ☐ Agreed to marry.
Give the date the agreement was made. If the agreement has ended, state when.

8 ☐ Both of you are parents of or have parental responsibility for a child

9 ☐ One of you is a parent of a child and the other has parental responsibility for that child

10 ☐ One of you is the natural parent or
grandparent of a child adopted or
freed for adoption, and the other is:

   (i)   the adoptive parent
or (ii)   a person who has applied for
           an adoption order for the
           child
or (iii)   a person with whom the
           child has been placed for
           adoption
or (iv)   the child who has been
           adopted or freed for
           adoption.
State whether (i), (ii), (iii) or (iv):

11 ☐ Both of you are parties to the same
family proceedings (see also Section
11 below).

5 Application for a non-molestation order

If you wish to apply for a non-molestation
order, state briefly in this section the order
you want. Give full details in support of your
application in your supporting evidence

*An order forbidding the respondent to
use or threaten violence against me.*

6 Application for an occupation order

If you do not wish to apply for an occupation
order, please go to section 9 of this form.

(A) State the address of the dwelling-house to
which your application relates:

*15 De Vere Mansions, Richmond
Avenue, London N5.*

(B) State whether it is occupied by you or the
respondent now or in the past, or whether it
was intended to be occupied by you or the
respondent:

We both occupy it.

(C)   State whether you are entitled to occupy the
       dwelling-house
              ☐   Yes   ☑   No

(D)   State whether the respondent is entitled to
       occupy the dwelling-house
              ☑   Yes   ☐   No

If yes, explain why:

The local authority tenancy is in his name only.

**On the basis of your answer to (C) and (D)
above, tick one of the boxes 1 to 5 below to
show the category into which you fit:**

1   ☐   a spouse who has matrimonial home
        rights in the dwelling-house, or a
        person who is entitled to occupy it by
        virtue of a beneficial estate or interest
        or contract or by virtue of any
        enactment giving him or her the right
        to remain in occupation.

        If you tick box 1, state whether there
        is a dispute or pending proceedings
        between you and the respondent
        about your right to occupy the
        dwelling-house.

2   ☐   a former spouse with no existing right
        to occupy, where the respondent
        spouse is entitled.

3   ☑   a cohabitant or former cohabitant
        with no existing right to occupy,
        where the respondent cohabitant or
        former cohabitant is so entitled.

4   ☐   a spouse or former spouse who is not
        entitled to occupy, where the
        respondent spouse or former spouse
        is also not entitled.

5   ☐   a cohabitant or former cohabitant
        who is not entitled to occupy, where
        the respondent cohabitant or former
        cohabitant is also not entitled.

Matrimonial Home Rights

If you do have matrimonial home rights
please:

State whether the title to the land is registered
or unregistered (if known):

If registered, state the Land Registry title
number (if known):

**If you wish to apply for an occupation
order, state briefly here the order you
want.** Give full details in support of your
application in your supporting evidence.

*An order requiring the respondent to vacate
the home for a period of 3 months.*

7   **Application for additional order(s) about
       the dwelling-house**

If you want to apply for any of the orders
listed in the notes to this section, state what
order you would like the Court to make:

*I would like the respondent to pay
two-thirds of the rent.*

8   **Mortgage and rent**

Is the dwelling-house subject to a mortgage?
                    ☐ Yes   ☐ No

If yes, please provide the name and address of
the mortgagee:

Is the dwelling-house rented?
                    ☑ Yes   ☐ No

If yes, please provide the name and address of
the landlord:

*London Borough of Enford, Town Hall,
London N5.*

9   At the Court

Will you need an interpreter at court?
☐   Yes   ☑   No

If 'Yes', specify the language:

If you need an interpreter because you do not
speak English, you are responsible for
providing your own.

If you need an interpreter or other facilities
because of a disability, please contact the
Court to ask what help is available.

10   Other information

State the name and date of birth of any child
living with or staying with, or likely to live
with or stay with, you or the respondent: *N/A*

State the name of any other person living in
the same household as you and the
respondent, and say why they live there: *N/A*

11   Other Proceedings and Orders

If there are any other current family
proceedings or orders in force involving you
and the respondent, state the type of
proceedings or orders, the court and the case
number. This includes any application for an
occupation order or non-molestation order
against you by the respondent.

**This application is to be served upon the
respondent**

Signed   Date

Susan White   *19/11/97*

No 20: SWORN STATEMENT/AFFIDAVIT IN SUPPORT OF APPLICATION BY A NON-ENTITLED COHABITANT FOR NON-MOLESTATION ORDER, OCCUPATION ORDER AND AN ANCILLARY ORDER AGAINST AN ENTITLED RESPONDENT

IN THE CLERKENWELL COUNTY COURT   No of Matter:
IN THE MATTER OF AN APPLICATION UNDER
THE FAMILY LAW ACT 1996

> Filed on behalf of the Applicant.
> Deponent: Applicant; No 1
> Date sworn: 19th November 1997
> Date filed: 19th November 1997

BETWEEN:

SUSAN WHITE

Applicant

– and –

STAN BROWN

Respondent

AFFIDAVIT OF THE APPLICANT

I, SUSAN WHITE, housewife, of 15 De Vere Mansions, Richmond Avenue, London N5, MAKE OATH and say as follows:

1. I am the Applicant herein and I make this affidavit in support of my application under sections 42 and 36[1] of the Family Law Act 1996 for a non-molestation order and an occupation order against the Respondent in the terms of my application and for an order ancillary to the occupation order under section 40.

2. The Respondent and I have lived together as man and wife[2] for 10 years at the above address. It is a local authority flat in his sole name. When I first met the Respondent he was the tenant of the flat. Two years after we met, the

---

[1] The applicant is seeking an order under s. 36(5)(b), namely an order suspending the exercise by the respondent of his right to occupy the dwelling-house. Any order under s. 35 (former spouses) or s. 36 must of course contain declaratory provisions namely in the case of an applicant who is in occupation, a right not to be evicted or excluded from the house or any part of it by the respondent and prohibiting the respondent from evicting or excluding the applicant. In the case of an applicant who is not in occupation, an order must give the applicant the right to enter into and occupy the house and require the respondent to permit the applicant to exercise that right (s. 35(3) and (4), s. 36(3) and (4)).

[2] As we shall see below, the nature of the parties' relationship is one of the factors which the court must consider when deciding whether to make a declaratory order. Do not forget s. 41 which obliges the court when considering 'the nature of the relationship' between cohabitants and former cohabitants to have regard to the fact that they have not 'given each other the commitment involved in marriage'.

Respondent promised me that he would make sure that I was put on the tenancy as well in case anything happened to him, but he has never done that. I am particularly annoyed that the Respondent has not kept his promise because I was on the council waiting list in an adjoining borough and 2 years ago I was offered a flat by that borough. I declined the offer because as far as I was aware my accommodation was secure. The Respondent also hinted several times that we would get married in due course.

3.   Housing Needs and Housing Resources[3]

I have no other accommodation available to me. The Respondent's parents however own a large semi-detached house in Barnet where the Respondent would be able to stay.

4.   Financial Resources

The Respondent is employed as a warehouse foreman. He earns about £250 per week. I am working only part-time at the moment because of a back injury. I am a librarian and take home less than £120 per week. The weekly rent on the flat is £70.

5.   Conduct

About 3 weeks ago the Respondent and I went to an all-night 'rave'. During the course of the night we were both offered drugs. I declined the offer, but the Respondent, despite my trying to dissuade him from doing so, decided to accept. I believe that the Respondent took a mixture of drugs including Ecstasy and LSD. I stayed with the Respondent during the party in an attempt to make sure that he kept out of trouble.

6.   The following day the Respondent was extremely depressed which I assumed was a reaction to the drugs he had taken. Over the succeeding days his depression became worse and his behaviour has become more and more bizarre. He has become paranoid and apt to fly off the handle. I have tried to persuade him to see a doctor but he has refused to do so.

---

[3] In deciding whether to make a *declaratory* order the court must have regard to all the circumstances including the housing needs and housing resources of the parties and of any relevant child, the financial resources of the parties, the likely effect of any order, or any decision by the court not to exercise its powers on the health, safety or well-being of the parties and of any relevant child, and the conduct of the parties in relation to each other and otherwise, the nature of the parties' relationship, the length of time they have lived together as husband and wife, whether there are or have been any children who are children of both parties, or for whom both parties have or have had parental responsibility, the length of time that has elapsed since the parties ceased to live together and the existence of any pending proceedings between the parties. In deciding whether to make a *regulatory* order the court must have regard to all the circumstances including the first four criteria mentioned above and the following two questions: (a) whether the applicant or any relevant child is likely to suffer significant harm attributable to conduct of the respondent if the regulatory order is not made, and (b) whether the harm likely to be suffered by the respondent or child if the regulatory order is made is as great as or greater than the harm attributable to conduct of the respondent which is likely to be suffered by the applicant or child if the regulatory order is not made (s. 36(7) and (8)).

7. Two nights ago the Respondent left the flat at about 9.00 pm saying that he would be out all night at another rave. I went to bed. At about 5.00 am I woke up to find the Respondent standing at the foot of the bed holding a knife. I screamed, but he just stared at me. I asked him what he was doing and he said that voices in his head were telling him what to do. I asked him to put the knife down which he did. The Respondent then said that he felt tired and that he would sleep on the sofa. The next morning the Respondent denied all knowledge of what had happened.

8. I am very afraid of what the Respondent might do. I want him to leave the flat for the time being.

9. Because I have such a modest income I also seek an order that the Respondent should pay two-thirds of the weekly rent. I hope that the Respondent will regain his emotional and mental stability in due course and that it will be possible for us to resume our relationship and live together in the flat once more. If the rent is not paid regularly the flat will be repossessed.

10. The facts stated in this affidavit are within my own knowledge.

11. In all the circumstances I respectfully ask this Honourable Court to grant to me the relief I seek in my Notice of Application.

SWORN at the Clerkenwell County Court
at Duncan Terrace, London N1
this 21st November 1997   Before me..

                                           An officer of the Court appointed by the
                                           Judge to take affidavits

No 21: NON-MOLESTATION ORDER, OCCUPATION ORDER AND ANCILLARY ORDER, NON-ENTITLED APPLICANT AGAINST ENTITLED RESPONDENT

IN THE CLERKENWELL COUNTY COURT   No of Matter:

BETWEEN:

SUSAN WHITE

Applicant

– and –

STAN BROWN

Respondent

Date: 20th December 1997   Before District Judge Townsend

Ex Parte: No

Applicant: represented by counsel   Present: Yes

Respondent: represented by counsel   Present: Yes

Statements: of Applicant (19/11/97) of Respondent (1/12/97)

Evidence: of Applicant and of Respondent

NOTICE

Notice A:

Importnt Notice to Stan Brown

This order gives you instructions which you must follow. You should read it all carefully. If you do not understand anything in this order you should go to a solicitor, a Legal Advice Centre or a Citizens Advice Bureau.
You have a right to ask the court to change or cancel the order but you must obey it unless the court does change or cancel it.
You must obey the instructions contained in this order. If you do not, you will be guilty of contempt and you may be sent to prison.

ARREST: A power of arrest applies to paragraphs 2 and 4 hereof

IT IS ORDERED THAT:

1.   The Applicant has the right to occupy 15, De Vere Mansions, Richmond Avenue, London N5 and the Respondent shall allow the Applicant to do so;

2.   The Repsondent shall not occupy 15, De Vere Mansions from the date hereof until 19th March 1998;

3.   The Respondent shall from the date hereof until 19th March 1998 pay two-thirds of the rent for 15, De Vere Mansions;

4.   The Respondent is forbidden to use or threaten violence against the Applicant; the said order shall last until 19th March 1998;

5.   No order for costs save for legal aid taxation of both parties' costs. Certificate for counsel.

No 22: APPLICATION FOR TRANSFER OF TENANCY (FORMER COHABITANTS)

IN THE BARCHESTER COUNTY COURT   No of Matter:

In the Matter of an application under section 53 of and Schedule 7 to the Family Law Act 1996 for the transfer of a tenancy

BETWEEN:

JACQUELINE FIELDING

Applicant

– and –

NICHOLAS JONES

Respondent

TAKE NOTICE that the Applicant will apply to this court on 20th December 1997 at 10.30 a.m. for orders in the following terms:

1. that the Respondent's estate and interest in the property known as 25, Wordsworth Avenue, Barset in Barchester pursuant to a tenancy agreement dated 1st February 1996 be transferred to the Applicant;
2. that the Respondent do pay the Applicant's costs of this application.

The grounds upon which the Applicant claims to be entitled to the said order are set out in her affidavit sworn on 17th November 1997, a copy whereof is served with this application.

DATED: 20th November 1997

No 23: AFFIDAVIT IN SUPPORT OF APPLICATION AGAINST FORMER COHABITANT FOR A TRANSFER OF TENANCY ORDER

IN THE BARCHESTER COUNTY COURT   Case No:
IN THE MATTER OF AN APPLICATION UNDER
THE FAMILY LAW ACT 1996

> Affidavit No: 1
> Deponent: J. Fielding
> Date sworn: 17.11.97
> Date filed: ....

BETWEEN:

JACQUELINE FIELDING

Applicant

– and –

NICHOLAS JONES

Respondent

AFFIDAVIT OF THE APPLICANT

I, JACQUELINE FIELDING, of 25 Wordsworth Avenue, Barset in Barchester, a secretary, MAKE OATH and say as follows:

1. I am the Applicant herein and I make this affidavit in support of my application that the tenancy in relation to the aforesaid address be transferred from the joint names of the Respondent and myself to me alone.[1]

2. The Respondent and I have lived together as man and wife since 1992. He moved into my two-bedroomed council flat which I occupied with my eldest child, Kylie, who was born on 19th July 1991 and is, therefore, aged 6. After the Respondent moved in, I became pregnant with our child, Jason, who was born on 1st November 1994 and is, therefore, just over 3 years old.

3. Shortly after Jason's birth we were offered our current, three-bedroomed flat. I had been on the council waiting list for a number of years because the flat in

---

[1] See Chapter 26, paragraph 5.

which I had been living with Kylie was in a very poor condition indeed. The local authority had assured me that I was a priority case, but it took until January 1997 for suitable alternative accommodation to be found. The local authority originally offered me the tenancy of our current address in my sole name. There is produced and shown to me marked 'JF 1' a copy of a letter from the local authority dated 5th January 1997 in which the local authority make this offer. I then spoke to the Neighbourhood Office, pointed out that the Respondent would be moving with us to the new accommodation and I suggested that the tenancy should be in our joint names. The local authority agreed to this and an agreement dated 1st February 1997 was duly drawn up and signed by both of us.

4.   Within 3 weeks of our moving into the flat, the Respondent had left. He told me he could no longer stand living in a flat with 2 young children and he had decided to return to live with his mother and father. He has not seen the children since he left our home and he has made no contribution towards rent or to any other household bills.

5.   I have ensured that all rent payments have been met from my income, which comprises earnings from my part-time job as a secretary together with family credit. I have been a tenant of Barchester County Council since 1985 and I verily believe that they have never had any complaints about the way in which I have behaved as their tenant.

6.   In all the circumstances, I respectfully invite the court to transfer the tenancy of our flat to me. I should add that my financial position is not such as to enable me to offer any form of compensation payment to the Respondent[2], given my financial obligations to the 2 children and his lack of financial assistance to date.

Sworn by JACQUELINE FIELDING

At

This   day of   1997

Before me

Solicitor

---

[2] See Chapter 26, paragraph 7.

No 24: TRANSFER OF TENANCY ORDER

IN THE BARCHESTER COUNTY COURT   No of Matter:

BETWEEN:

JACQUELINE FIELDING

Applicant

– and –

NICHOLAS JONES

Respondent

UPON hearing counsel for the Applicant and for the Respondent
AND UPON reading the statements listed in the schedule hereto and taking the oral evidence of the witnesses listed in the said schedule

IT IS ORDERED THAT:
1. The estate or interest which the Respondent has in the property known as 25, Wordsworth Avenue, Barset in Barchester be with effect from 20th December 1997 by virtue of this order and without further assurance transferred to and vested in the Applicant;
2. There be no order for costs save legal aid taxation of both parties' costs.

Family Law Act 1996

CHAPTER 27
ARRANGEMENT OF SECTIONS

PART I
PRINCIPLES OF PARTS II AND III

PART II
DIVORCE AND SEPARATION

Court orders

Marital breakdown

Reflection and consideration

Orders preventing divorce

Welfare of children

Supplementary

Resolution of disputes

PART V
SUPPLEMENTAL

Schedule 3—Stay of proceedings.
Schedule 4—Provisions supplementary to sections 30 and 31.
Schedule 5—Powers of High Court and county court to remand.
Schedule 6—Amendments of Children Act 1989.
Schedule 7—Transfer of certain tenancies on divorce etc. or on separation of cohabitants.
    Part I—General.
    Part II—Orders that may be made.
    Part III—Supplementary provisions.
Schedule 8—Minor and consequential amendments.
    Part I—Amendments connected with Part II.
    Part II—Amendments connected with Part III.
    Part III—Amendments connected with Part IV.
Schedule 9—Modifications, saving and transitional.
Schedule 10—Repeals.

Family Law Act 1996

1996 CHAPTER 27

An Act to make provision with respect to: divorce and separation; legal aid in connection with mediation in disputes relating to family matters; proceedings in cases where marriages have broken down; rights of occupation of certain domestic premises; prevention of molestation; the inclusion in certain orders under the Children Act 1989 of provisions about the occupation of a dwelling-house; the transfer of tenancies between spouses and persons who have lived together as husband and wife; and for connected purposes. [4th July 1996]

BE IT ENACTED by the Queen's most Excellent Majesty, by and with the advice and consent of the Lords Spiritual and Temporal, and Commons, in this present Parliament assembled, and by the authority of the same, as follows:—

PART I
PRINCIPLES OF PARTS II AND III

1. The general principles underlying Parts II and III

The court and any person, in exercising functions under or in consequence of Parts II and III, shall have regard to the following general principles—

    (a)   that the institution of marriage is to be supported;

    (b)   that the parties to a marriage which may have broken down are to be encouraged to take all practicable steps, whether by marriage counselling or otherwise, to save the marriage;

    (c)   that a marriage which has irretrievably broken down and is being brought to an end should be brought to an end—

        (i)   with minimum distress to the parties and to the children affected;

        (ii)   with questions dealt with in a manner designed to promote as good a continuing relationship between the parties and any children affected as is possible in the circumstances; and

        (iii)   without costs being unreasonably incurred in connection with the procedures to be followed in bringing the marriage to an end; and

    (d)   that any risk to one of the parties to a marriage, and to any children, of violence from the other party should, so far as reasonably practicable, be removed or diminished.

PART II
DIVORCE AND SEPARATION

Court orders

2. Divorce and separation

(1) The court may—

(a) by making an order (to be known as a divorce order), dissolve a marriage; or

(b) by making an order (to be known as a separation order), provide for the separation of the parties to a marriage.

(2) Any such order comes into force on being made.

(3) A separation order remains in force—

(a) while the marriage continues; or

(b) until cancelled by the court on the joint application of the parties.

3. Circumstances in which orders are made

(1) If an application for a divorce order or for a separation order is made to the court under this section by one or both of the parties to a marriage, the court shall make the order applied for if (but only if)—

(a) the marriage has broken down irretrievably;

(b) the requirements of section 8 about information meetings are satisfied;

(c) the requirements of section 9 about the parties' arrangements for the future are satisfied; and

(d) the application has not been withdrawn.

(2) A divorce order may not be made if an order preventing divorce is in force under section 10.

(3) If the court is considering an application for a divorce order and an application for a separation order in respect of the same marriage it shall proceed as if it were considering only the application for a divorce order unless—

(a) an order preventing divorce is in force with respect to the marriage;

(b) the court makes an order preventing divorce; or

(c) section 7(6) or (13) applies.

4. Conversion of separation order into divorce order

(1) A separation order which is made before the second anniversary of the marriage may not be converted into a divorce order under this section until after that anniversary.

(2) A separation order may not be converted into a divorce order under this section at any time while—

(a) an order preventing divorce is in force under section 10; or

(b) subsection (4) applies.

(3) Otherwise, if a separation order is in force and an application for a divorce order—

(a) is made under this section by either or both of the parties to the marriage, and

(b) is not withdrawn,

the court shall grant the application once the requirements of section 11 have been satisfied.

(4) Subject to subsection (5), this subsection applies if—

(a)   there is a child of the family who is under the age of sixteen when the application under this section is made; or

(b)   the application under this section is made by one party and the other party applies to the court, before the end of such period as may be prescribed by rules of court, for time for further reflection.

(5)   Subsection (4)—

(a)   does not apply if, at the time when the application under this section is made, there is an occupation order or a non-molestation order in force in favour of the applicant, or of a child of the family, made against the other party;

(b)   does not apply if the court is satisfied that delaying the making of a divorce order would be significantly detrimental to the welfare of any child of the family;

(c)   ceases to apply—

(i)   at the end of the period of six months beginning with the end of the period for reflection and consideration by reference to which the separation order was made; or

(ii)   if earlier, on there ceasing to be any children of the family to whom subsection (4)(a) applied.

Marital breakdown

5.   Marital breakdown

(1)   A marriage is to be taken to have broken down irretrievably if (but only if)—

(a)   a statement has been made by one (or both) of the parties that the maker of the statement (or each of them) believes that the marriage has broken down;

(b)   the statement complies with the requirements of section 6;

(c)   the period for reflection and consideration fixed by section 7 has ended; and

(d)   the application under section 3 is accompanied by a declaration by the party making the application that—

(i)   having reflected on the breakdown, and

(ii)   having considered the requirements of this Part as to the parties' arrangements for the future,

the applicant believes that the marriage cannot be saved.

(2)   The statement and the application under section 3 do not have to be made by the same party.

(3)   An application may not be made under section 3 by reference to a particular statement if—

(a)   the parties have jointly given notice (in accordance with rules of court) withdrawing the statement; or

(b)   a period of one year ('the specified period') has passed since the end of the period for reflection and consideration.

(4)   Any period during which an order preventing divorce is in force is not to count towards the specified period mentioned in subsection (3)(b).

(5)   Subsection (6) applies if, before the end of the specified period, the parties jointly give notice to the court that they are attempting reconciliation but require additional time.

(6)   The specified period—

(a)   stops running on the day on which the notice is received by the court; but

(b)   resumes running on the day on which either of the parties gives notice to the court that the attempted reconciliation has been unsuccessful.

(7)   If the specified period is interrupted by a continuous period of more than 18 months, any application by either of the parties for a divorce order or for a separation order must be by reference to a new statement received by the court at any time after the end of the 18 months.

(8)   The Lord Chancellor may by order amend subsection (3)(b) by varying the specified period.

6.   Statement of marital breakdown

(1)   A statement under section 5(1)(a) is to be known as a statement of marital breakdown; but in this Part it is generally referred to as 'a statement'.

(2)   If a statement is made by one party it must also state that that party—

(a)   is aware of the purpose of the period for reflection and consideration as described in section 7; and

(b)   wishes to make arrangements for the future.

(3)   If a statement is made by both parties it must also state that each of them—

(a)   is aware of the purpose of the period for reflection and consideration as described in section 7; and

(b)   wishes to make arrangements for the future.

(4)   A statement must be given to the court in accordance with the requirements of rules made under section 12.

(5)   A statement must also satisfy any other requirements imposed by rules made under that section.

(6)   A statement made at a time when the circumstances of the case include any of those mentioned in subsection (7) is ineffective for the purposes of this Part.

(7)   The circumstances are—

(a)   that a statement has previously been made with respect to the marriage and it is, or will become, possible—

(i)   for an application for a divorce order, or

(ii)   for an application for a separation order,

to be made by reference to the previous statement;

(b)   that such an application has been made in relation to the marriage and has not been withdrawn;

(c)   that a separation order is in force.

Reflection and consideration

7.   Period for reflection and consideration

(1)   Where a statement has been made, a period for the parties—

(a)   to reflect on whether the marriage can be saved and to have an opportunity to effect a reconciliation, and

(b)   to consider what arrangements should be made for the future,

must pass before an application for a divorce order or for a separation order may be made by reference to that statement.

(2)   That period is to be known as the period for reflection and consideration.

(3)   The period for reflection and consideration is nine months beginning with the fourteenth day after the day on which the statement is received by the court.

(4)   Where—

(a)   the statement has been made by one party,

(b)   rules made under section 12 require the court to serve a copy of the statement on the other party, and

(c)   failure to comply with the rules causes inordinate delay in service,

the court may, on the application of that other party, extend the period for reflection and consideration.

(5)   An extension under subsection (4) may be for any period not exceeding the time between—

(a)   the beginning of the period for reflection and consideration; and

(b)   the time when service is effected.

(6)   A statement which is made before the first anniversary of the marriage to which it relates is ineffective for the purposes of any application for a divorce order.

(7)   Subsection (8) applies if, at any time during the period for reflection and consideration, the parties jointly give notice to the court that they are attempting a reconciliation but require additional time.

(8)   The period for reflection and consideration—

(a)   stops running on the day on which the notice is received by the court; but

(b)   resumes running on the day on which either of the parties gives notice to the court that the attempted reconciliation has been unsuccessful.

(9)   If the period for reflection and consideration is interrupted under subsection (8) by a continuous period of more than 18 months, any application by either of the parties for a divorce order or for a separation order must be by reference to a new statement received by the court at any time after the end of the 18 months.

(10)   Where an application for a divorce order is made by one party, subsection (13) applies if—

(a)   the other party applies to the court, within the prescribed period, for time for further reflection; and

(b)   the requirements of section 9 (except any imposed under section 9(3)) are satisfied.

(11)   Where any application for a divorce order is made, subsection (13) also applies if there is a child of the family who is under the age of sixteen when the application is made.

(12)   Subsection (13) does not apply if—

(a)   at the time when the application for a divorce order is made, there is an occupation order or a non-molestation order in force in favour of the applicant, or of a child of the family, made against the other party; or

(b)   the court is satisfied that delaying the making of a divorce order would be significantly detrimental to the welfare of any child of the family.

(13)   If this subsection applies, the period for reflection and consideration is extended by a period of six months, but—

(a)   only in relation to the application for a divorce order in respect of which the application under subsection (10) was made; and

(b)   without invalidating that application for a divorce order.

(14)   A period for reflection and consideration which is extended under subsection (13), and which has not otherwise come to an end, comes to an end on there ceasing to be any children of the family to whom subsection (11) applied.

8. Attendance at information meetings

(1) The requirements about information meetings are as follows.

(2) A party making a statement must (except in prescribed circumstances) have attended an information meeting not less than three months before making the statement.

(3) Different information meetings must be arranged with respect to different marriages.

(4) In the case of a statement made by both parties, the parties may attend separate meetings or the same meeting.

(5) Where one party has made a statement, the other party must (except in prescribed circumstances) attend an information meeting before—

   (a) making any application to the court—
      (i) with respect to a child of the family; or
      (ii) of a prescribed description relating to property or financial matters; or
   (b) contesting any such application.

(6) In this section 'information meeting' means a meeting organised, in accordance with prescribed provisions for the purpose—

   (a) of providing, in accordance with prescribed provisions, relevant information to the party or parties attending about matters which may arise in connection with the provisions of, or made under, this Part or Part III; and

   (b) of giving the party or parties attending the information meeting the opportunity of having a meeting with a marriage counsellor and of encouraging that party or those parties to attend that meeting.

(7) An information meeting must be conducted by a person who—

   (a) is qualified and appointed in accordance with prescribed provisions; and
   (b) will have no financial or other interest in any marital proceedings between the parties.

(8) Regulations made under this section may, in particular, make provision—

   (a) about the places and times at which information meetings are to be held;
   (b) for written information to be given to persons attending them;
   (c) for the giving of information to parties (otherwise than at information meetings) in cases in which the requirement to attend such meetings does not apply;
   (d) for information of a prescribed kind to be given only with the approval of the Lord Chancellor or only by a person or by persons approved by him; and
   (e) for information to be given, in prescribed circumstances, only with the approval of the Lord Chancellor or only by a person, or by persons, approved by him.

(9) Regulations made under subsection (6) must, in particular, make provision with respect to the giving of information about—

   (a) marriage counselling and other marriage support services;
   (b) the importance to be attached to the welfare, wishes and feelings of children;
   (c) how the parties may acquire a better understanding of the ways in which children can be helped to cope with the breakdown of a marriage;
   (d) the nature of the financial questions that may arise on divorce or separation, and services which are available to help the parties;
   (e) protection available against violence, and how to obtain support and assistance;
   (f) mediation;

(g)   the availability to each of the parties of independent legal advice and representation;

(h)   the principles of legal aid and where the parties can get advice about obtaining legal aid;

(i)   the divorce and separation process.

(10)   Before making any regulations under subsection (6), the Lord Chancellor must consult such persons concerned with the provision of relevant information as he considers appropriate.

(11)   A meeting with a marriage counsellor arranged under this section—

(a)   must be held in accordance with prescribed provisions; and

(b)   must be with a person qualified and appointed in accordance with prescribed provisions.

(12)   A person who would not be required to make any contribution towards mediation provided for him under Part IIIA of the Legal Aid Act 1988 shall not be required to make any contribution towards the cost of a meeting with a marriage counsellor arranged for him under this section.

(13)   In this section 'prescribed' means prescribed by regulations made by the Lord Chancellor.

9.   Arrangements for the future

(1)   The requirements as to the parties' arrangements for the future are as follows.

(2)   One of the following must be produced to the court—

(a)   a court order (made by consent or otherwise) dealing with their financial arrangements;

(b)   a negotiated agreement as to their financial arrangements;

(c)   a declaration by both parties that they have made their financial arrangements;

(d)   a declaration by one of the parties (to which no objection has been notified to the court by the other party) that—

(i)   he has no significant assets and does not intend to make an application for financial provision;

(ii)   he believes that the other party has no significant assets and does not intend to make an application for financial provision; and

(iii)   there are therefore no financial arrangements to be made.

(3)   If the parties—

(a)   were married to each other in accordance with usages of a kind mentioned in section 26(1) of the Marriage Act 1949 (marriages which may be solemnized on authority of superintendent registrar's certificate), and

(b)   are required to co-operate if the marriage is to be dissolved in accordance with those usages,

the court may, on the application of either party, direct that there must also be produced to the court a declaration by both parties that they have taken such steps as are required to dissolve the marriage in accordance with those usages.

(4)   A direction under subsection (3)—

(a)   may be given only if the court is satisfied that in all the circumstances of the case it is just and reasonable to give it; and

(b)   may be revoked by the court at any time.

(5)   The requirements of section 11 must have been satisfied.

(6)   Schedule 1 supplements the provisions of this section.

(7)   If the court is satisfied, on an application made by one of the parties after the end of the period for reflection and consideration, that the circumstances of the case are—

(a)   those set out in paragraph 1 of Schedule 1,

(b)   those set out in paragraph 2 of that Schedule,

(c)   those set out in paragraph 3 of that Schedule, or

(d)   those set out in paragraph 4 of that Schedule,

it may make a divorce order or a separation order even though the requirements of subsection (2) have not been satisfied.

(8)   If the parties' arrangements for the future include a division of pension assets or rights under section 25B of the 1973 Act or section 10 of the Family Law (Scotland) Act 1985, any declaration under subsection (2) must be a statutory declaration.

Orders preventing divorce

10.   Hardship: orders preventing divorce

(1)   If an application for a divorce order has been made by one of the parties to a marriage, the court may, on the application of the other party, order that the marriage is not to be dissolved.

(2)   Such an order (an 'order preventing divorce') may be made only if the court is satisfied—

(a)   that dissolution of the marriage would result in substantial financial or other hardship to the other party or to a child of the family; and

(b)   that it would be wrong, in all the circumstances (including the conduct of the parties and the interests of any child of the family), for the marriage to be dissolved.

(3)   If an application for the cancellation of an order preventing divorce is made by one or both of the parties, the court shall cancel the order unless it is still satisfied—

(a)   that dissolution of the marriage would result in substantial financial or other hardship to the party in whose favour the order was made or to a child of the family; and

(b)   that it would be wrong, in all the circumstances (including the conduct of the parties and the interests of any child of the family), for the marriage to be dissolved.

(4)   If an order preventing a divorce is cancelled, the court may make a divorce order in respect of the marriage only if an application is made under section 3 or 4(3) after the cancellation.

(5)   An order preventing divorce may include conditions which must be satisfied before an application for cancellation may be made under subsection (3).

(6)   In this section 'hardship' includes the loss of a chance to obtain a future benefit (as well as the loss of an existing benefit).

Welfare of children

11.   Welfare of children

(1)   In any proceedings for a divorce order or a separation order, the court shall consider—

(a)   whether there are any children of the family to whom this section applies; and

(b)   where there are any such children, whether (in the light of the arrangements which have been, or are proposed to be, made for their upbringing and welfare) it should exercise any of its powers under the Children Act 1989 with respect to any of them.

(2)   Where, in any case to which this section applies, it appears to the court that—

(a)   the circumstances of the case require it, or are likely to require it, to exercise any of its powers under the Children Act 1989 with respect to any such child,

(b)   it is not in a position to exercise the power, or (as the case may be) those powers, without giving further consideration to the case, and

(c)   there are exceptional circumstances which make it desirable in the interests of the child that the court should give a direction under this section,

it may direct that the divorce order or separation order is not to be made until the court orders otherwise.

(3)   In deciding whether the circumstances are as mentioned in subsection (2)(a), the court shall treat the welfare of the child as paramount.

(4)   In making that decision, the court shall also have particular regard, on the evidence before it, to—

(a)   the wishes and feelings of the child considered in the light of his age and understanding and the circumstances in which those wishes were expressed;

(b)   the conduct of the parties in relation to the upbringing of the child;

(c)   the general principle that, in the absence of evidence to the contrary, the welfare of the child will be best served by—

(i)   his having regular contact with those who have parental responsibility for him and with other members of his family; and

(ii)   the maintenance of as good a continuing relationship with his parents as is possible; and

(d)   any risk to the child attributable to—

(i)   where the person with whom the child will reside is living or proposes to live;

(ii)   any person with whom that person is living or with whom he proposes to live; or

(iii)   any other arrangements for his care and upbringing.

(5)   This section applies to—

(a)   any child of the family who has not reached the age of sixteen at the date when the court considers the case in accordance with the requirements of this section; and

(b)   any child of the family who has reached that age at that date and in relation to whom the court directs that this section shall apply.

Supplementary

12.   Lord Chancellor's rules

(1)   The Lord Chancellor may make rules—

(a)   as to the form in which a statement is to be made and what information must accompany it;

(b)   requiring the person making the statement to state whether or not, since satisfying the requirements of section 8, he has made any attempt at reconciliation;

(c)   as to the way in which a statement is to be given to the court;

(d)   requiring a copy of a statement made by one party to be served by the court on the other party;

    (e)   as to circumstances in which such service may be dispensed with or may be effected otherwise than by delivery to the party;

    (f)   requiring a party who has made a statement to provide the court with information about the arrangements that need to be made in consequence of the breakdown;

    (g)   as to the time, manner and (where attendance in person is required) place at which such information is to be given;

    (h)   where a statement has been made, requiring either or both of the parties—

        (i)   to prepare and produce such other documents, and

        (ii)   to attend in person at such places and for such purposes,

as may be specified;

    (i)   as to the information and assistance which is to be given to the parties and the way in which it is to be given;

    (j)   requiring the parties to be given, in such manner as may be specified, copies of such statements and other documents as may be specified.

(2)   The Lord Chancellor may make rules requiring a person who is the legal representative of a party to a marriage with respect to which a statement has been, or is proposed to be, made—

    (a)   to inform that party, at such time or times as may be specified—

        (i)   about the availability to the parties of marriage support services;

        (ii)   about the availability to them of mediation; and

        (iii)   where there are children of the family, that in relation to the arrangements to be made for any child the parties should consider the child's welfare, wishes and feelings;

    (b)   to give that party, at such time or times as may be specified, names and addresses of persons qualified to help—

        (i)   to effect a reconciliation; or

        (ii)   in connection with mediation; and

    (c)   to certify, at such time or times as may be specified—

        (i)   whether he has complied with the provision made in the rules by virtue of paragraphs (a) and (b);

        (ii)   whether he has discussed with that party any of the matters mentioned in paragraph (a) or the possibility of reconciliation; and

        (iii)   which, if any, of those matters they have discussed.

(3)   In subsections (1) and (2) 'specified' means determined under or described in the rules.

(4)   This section does not affect any power to make rules of court for the purposes of this Act.

Resolution of disputes

13. Directions with respect to mediation

(1)   After the court has received a statement, it may give a direction requiring each party to attend a meeting arranged in accordance with the direction for the purpose—

    (a)   of enabling an explanation to be given of the facilities available to the parties for mediation in relation to disputes between them; and

    (b)   of providing an opportunity for each party to agree to take advantage of those facilities.

(2)   A direction may be given at any time, including in the course of proceedings connected with the breakdown of the marriage (as to which see section 25).

(3)   A direction may be given on the application of either of the parties or on the initiative of the court.

(4)   The parties are to be required to attend the same meeting unless—

(a)   one of them asks, or both of them ask, for separate meetings; or

(b)   the court considers separate meetings to be more appropriate.

(5)   A direction shall—

(a)   specify a person chosen by the court (with that person's agreement) to arrange and conduct the meeting or meetings; and

(b)   require such person as may be specified in the direction to produce to the court, at such time as the court may direct, a report stating—

(i)   whether the parties have complied with the direction; and

(ii)   if they have, whether they have agreed to take part in any mediation.

14.   Adjournments

(1)   The court's power to adjourn any proceedings connected with the breakdown of a marriage includes power to adjourn—

(a)   for the purpose of allowing the parties to comply with a direction under section 13; or

(b)   for the purpose of enabling disputes to be resolved amicably.

(2)   In determining whether to adjourn for either purpose, the court shall have regard in particular to the need to protect the interests of any child of the family.

(3)   If the court adjourns any proceedings connected with the breakdown of a marriage for either purpose, the period of the adjournment must not exceed the maximum period prescribed by rules of court.

(4)   Unless the only purpose of the adjournment is to allow the parties to comply with a direction under section 13, the court shall order one or both of them to produce to the court a report as to—

(a)   whether they have taken part in mediation during the adjournment;

(b)   whether, as a result, any agreement has been reached between them;

(c)   the extent to which any dispute between them has been resolved as a result of any such agreement;

(d)   the need for further mediation; and

(e)   how likely it is that further mediation will be successful.

Financial provision

15.   Financial arrangements

(1)   Schedule 2 amends the 1973 Act.

(2)   The main object of Schedule 2 is—

(a)   to provide that, in the case of divorce or separation, an order about financial provision may be made under that Act before a divorce order or separation order is made; but

(b)   to retain (with minor changes) the position under that Act where marriages are annulled.

(3)   Schedule 2 also makes minor and consequential amendments of the 1973 Act connected with the changes mentioned in subsection (1).

16. Division of pension rights: England and Wales

(1) The Matrimonial Causes Act 1973 is amended as follows.

(2) In section 25B (benefits under a pension scheme on divorce, etc.), in subsection (2), after paragraph (b), insert—

'(c) in particular, where the court determines to make such an order, whether the order should provide for the accrued rights of the party with pension rights ("the pension rights") to be divided between that party and the other party in such a way as to reduce the pension rights of the party with those rights and to create pension rights for the other party.'.

(3) After subsection (7) of that section, add—

'(8) If a pensions adjustment order under subsection (2)(c) above is made, the pension rights shall be reduced and pension rights of the other party shall be created in the prescribed manner with benefits payable on prescribed conditions, except that the court shall not have the power—

(a) to require the trustees or managers of the scheme to provide benefits under their own scheme if they are able and willing to create the rights for the other party by making a transfer payment to another scheme and the trustees and managers of that other scheme are able and willing to accept such a payment and to create those rights; or

(b) to require the trustees or managers of the scheme to make a transfer to another scheme—

(i) if the scheme is an unfunded scheme (unless the trustees or managers are able and willing to make such a transfer payment); or

(ii) in prescribed circumstances.

(9) No pensions adjustment order may be made under subsection (2)(c) above—

(a) if the scheme is a scheme of a prescribed type, or

(b) in prescribed circumstances, or

(c) insofar as it would affect benefits of a prescribed type.'

(4) In section 25D (pensions: supplementary), insert—

(a) in subsection (2)—

(i) at the end of paragraph (a), the words 'or prescribe the rights of the other party under the pension scheme,'; and

(ii) after paragraph (a), the following paragraph—

'(aa) make such consequential modifications of any enactment or subordinate legislation as appear to the Lord Chancellor necessary or expedient to give effect to the provisions of section 25B; and an order under this paragraph may make provision applying generally in relation to enactments and subordinate legislation of a description specified in the order,';

(b) in subsection (4), in the appropriate place in alphabetical order, the following entries—

'"funded scheme" means a scheme under which the benefits are provided for by setting aside resources related to the value of the members' rights as they accrue (and "unfunded scheme" shall be construed accordingly);

"subordinate legislation" has the same meaning as in the Interpretation Act 1978;'; and

(c) after subsection (4), the following subsection—

'(4A) Other expressions used in section 25B above shall be construed in accordance with section 124 (interpretation of Part I) of the Pensions Act 1995.'

17. Division of pension assets: Scotland

Section 10 of the Family Law (Scotland) Act 1985 (sharing of value of matrimonial property), is amended as follows—

    (a)   in subsection (5) at the end of paragraph (b), insert ', and

       (c)   in the assets in respect of which either party has accrued rights to benefits under a pension scheme'; and

    (b)   after subsection (5) insert—

'(5A)   In the case of an unfunded pension scheme, the court may not make an order which would allow assets to be removed from the scheme earlier than would otherwise have been the case.'.

18. Grounds for financial provision orders in magistrates' courts

    (1)   In section 1 of the Domestic Proceedings and Magistrates' Courts Act 1978, omit paragraphs (c) and (d) (which provide for behaviour and desertion to be grounds on which an application for a financial provision order may be made).

    (2)   In section 7(1) of that Act (powers of magistrates' court where spouses are living apart by agreement), omit 'neither party having deserted the other'.

Jurisdiction and commencement of proceedings

19. Jurisdiction in relation to divorce and separation

    (1)   In this section 'the court's jurisdiction' means—

    (a)   the jurisdiction of the court under this Part to entertain marital proceedings; and

    (b)   any other jurisdiction conferred on the court under this Part, or any other enactment, in consequence of the making of a statement.

    (2)   The court's jurisdiction is exercisable only if—

    (a)   at least one of the parties was domiciled in England and Wales on the statement date;

    (b)   at least one of the parties was habitually resident in England and Wales throughout the period of one year ending with the statement date; or

    (c)   nullity proceedings are pending in relation to the marriage when the marital proceedings commence.

    (3)   Subsection (4) applies if—

    (a)   a separation order is in force; or

    (b)   an order preventing divorce has been cancelled.

    (4)   The court—

    (a)   continues to have jurisdiction to entertain an application made by reference to the order referred to in subsection (3); and

    (b)   may exercise any other jurisdiction which is conferred on it in consequence of such an application.

    (5)   Schedule 3 amends Schedule 1 to the Domicile and Matrimonial Proceedings Act 1973 (orders to stay proceedings where there are proceedings in other jurisdictions).

    (6)   The court's jurisdiction is exercisable subject to any order for a stay under Schedule 1 to that Act.

    (7)   In this section—

'nullity proceedings' means proceedings in respect of which the court has jurisdiction under section 5(3) of the Domicile and Matrimonial Proceedings Act 1973; and 'statement date' means the date on which the relevant statement was received by the court.

20. Time when proceedings for divorce or separation begin

(1)   The receipt by the court of a statement is to be treated as the commencement of proceedings.

(2)   The proceedings are to be known as marital proceedings.

(3)   Marital proceedings are also—

(a)   separation proceedings, if an application for a separation order has been made under section 3 by reference to the statement and not withdrawn;

(b)   divorce proceedings, if an application for a divorce order has been made under section 3 by reference to the statement and not withdrawn.

(4)   Marital proceedings are to be treated as being both divorce proceedings and separation proceedings at any time when no application by reference to the statement, either for a divorce order or for a separation order, is outstanding.

(5)   Proceedings which are commenced by the making of an application under section 4(3) are also marital proceedings and divorce proceedings.

(6)   Marital proceedings come to an end—

(a)   on the making of a separation order;

(b)   on the making of a divorce order;

(c)   on the withdrawal of the statement by a notice in accordance with section 5(3)(a);

(d)   at the end of the specified period mentioned in section 5(3)(b), if no application under section 3 by reference to the statement is outstanding;

(e)   on the withdrawal of all such applications which are outstanding at the end of that period;

(f)   on the withdrawal of an application under section 4(3).

Intestacy

21.   Intestacy: effect of separation

Where—

(a)   a separation order is in force, and

(b)   while the parties to the marriage remain separated, one of them dies intestate as respects any real or personal property,

that property devolves as if the other had died before the intestacy occurred.

Marriage support services

22.   Funding for marriage support services

(1)   The Lord Chancellor may, with the approval of the Treasury, make grants in connection with—

(a)   the provision of marriage support services;

(b)   research into the causes of marital breakdown;

(c)   research into ways of preventing marital breakdown.

(2)   Any grant under this section may be made subject to such conditions as the Lord Chancellor considers appropriate.

(3)   In exercising his power to make grants in connection with the provision of marriage support services, the Lord Chancellor is to have regard, in particular, to the desirability of services of that kind being available when they are first needed.

23.   Provision of marriage counselling

(1)   The Lord Chancellor or a person appointed by him may secure the provision, in accordance with regulations made by the Lord Chancellor, of marriage counselling.

(2)   Marriage counselling may only be provided under this section at a time when a period for reflection and consideration—

(a)   is running in relation to the marriage; or

(b)   is interrupted under section 7(8) (but not for a continuous period of more than 18 months).

(3)   Marriage counselling may only be provided under this section for persons who would not be required to make any contribution towards the cost of mediation provided for them under Part IIIA of the Legal Aid Act 1988.

(4)   Persons for whom marriage counselling is provided under this section are not to be required to make any contribution towards the cost of the counselling.

(5)   Marriage counselling is only to be provided under this section if it appears to the marriage counsellor to be suitable in all the circumstances.

(6)   Regulations under subsection (1) may—

(a)   make provision about the way in which marriage counselling is to be provided; and

(b)   prescribe circumstances in which the provision of marriage counselling is to be subject to the approval of the Lord Chancellor.

(7)   A contract entered into for the purposes of subsection (1) by a person appointed under that subsection must include such provision as the Lord Chancellor may direct.

(8)   If the person appointed under subsection (1) is the Legal Aid Board, the powers conferred on the Board by or under the Legal Aid Act 1988 shall be exercisable for the purposes of this section as they are exercisable for the purposes of that Act.

(9)   In section 15 of the Legal Aid Act 1988 (availability of, and payment for, representation under Part IV of the Act), after subsection (3H) insert—

'(3I)   A person may be refused representation for the purposes of any proceedings if—

(a)   the proceedings are marital proceedings within the meaning of Part II of the Family Law Act 1996; and

(b)   he is being provided with marriage counselling under section 23 of that Act in relation to the marriage.'

Interpretation

24.   Interpretation of Part II etc.

(1)   In this Part—

'the 1973 Act' means the Matrimonial Causes Act 1973;

'child of the family' and 'the court' have the same meaning as in the 1973 Act;

'divorce order' has the meaning given in section 2(1)(a);

'divorce proceedings' is to be read with section 20;

'marital proceedings' has the meaning given in section 20;

'non-molestation order' has the meaning given by section 42(1);

'occupation order' has the meaning given by section 39;

'order preventing divorce' has the meaning given in section 10(2);

'party', in relation to a marriage, means one of the parties to the marriage; 'period for reflection and consideration' has the meaning given in section 7;

'separation order' has the meaning given in section 2(1)(b);

'separation proceedings' is to be read with section 20;

'statement' means a statement of marital breakdown;

'statement of marital breakdown' has the meaning given in section 6(1).

(2)   For the purposes of this Part, references to the withdrawal of an application are references, in relation to an application made jointly by both parties, to its withdrawal by a notice given, in accordance with rules of court—

(a)   jointly by both parties; or

(b)   separately by each of them.

(3)   Where only one party gives such a notice of withdrawal, in relation to a joint application, the application shall be treated as if it had been made by the other party alone.

25.   Connected proceedings

(1)   For the purposes of this Part, proceedings are connected with the breakdown of a marriage if they fall within subsection (2) and, at the time of the proceedings—

(a)   a statement has been received by the court with respect to the marriage and it is or may become possible for an application for a divorce order or separation order to be made by reference to that statement;

(b)   such an application in relation to the marriage has been made and not withdrawn; or

(c)   a divorce order has been made, or a separation order is in force, in relation to the marriage.

(2)   The proceedings are any under Parts I to V of the Children Act 1989 with respect to a child of the family or any proceedings resulting from an application—

(a)   for, or for the cancellation of, an order preventing divorce in relation to the marriage;

(b)   by either party to the marriage for an order under Part IV;

(c)   for the exercise, in relation to a party to the marriage or child of the family, of any of the court's powers under Part II of the 1973 Act;

(d)   made otherwise to the court with respect to, or in connection with, any proceedings connected with the breakdown of the marriage.

PART III
LEGAL AID FOR MEDIATION IN FAMILY MATTERS

26.   Legal aid for mediation in family matters

(1)   In the Legal Aid Act 1988 insert, after section 13—

'PART IIIA
MEDIATION

13A.   Scope of this Part

(1)   This Part applies to mediation in disputes relating to family matters.

(2)   ''Family matters'' means matters which are governed by English law and in relation to which any question has arisen, or may arise—

(a)   under any provision of—

(i)   the 1973 Act;

   (ii) the Domestic Proceedings and Magistrates' Courts Act 1978;

   (iii) Parts I to V of the Children Act 1989;

   (iv) Parts II and IV of the Family Law Act 1996; or

   (v) any other enactment prescribed;

  (b) under any prescribed jurisdiction of a prescribed court or tribunal; or

  (c) under any prescribed rule of law.

 (3) Regulations may restrict this Part to mediation in disputes of any prescribed description.

 (4) The power to—

  (a) make regulations under subsection (2), or

  (b) revoke any regulations made under subsection (3),

is exercisable only with the consent of the Treasury.'

 (2) In section 2 of the 1988 Act, after subsection (3), insert—

 '(3A) "Mediation" means mediation to which Part IIIA of this Act applies; and includes steps taken by a mediator in any case—

  (a) in determining whether to embark on mediation;

  (b) in preparing for mediation; and

  (c) in making any assessment under that Part.'

 (3) In section 43 of the 1988 Act, after the definition of 'legal representative' insert—

 '"mediator" means a person with whom the Board contracts for the provision of mediation by any person.'

27. Provision and availability of mediation

After section 13A of the 1988 Act, insert—

'13B. Provision and availability of mediation

 (1) The Board may secure the provision of mediation under this Part.

 (2) If mediation is provided under this Part, it is to be available to any person whose financial resources are such as, under regulations, make him eligible for mediation.

 (3) A person is not to be granted mediation in relation to any dispute unless mediation appears to the mediator suitable to the dispute and the parties and all the circumstances.

 (4) A grant of mediation under this Part may be amended, withdrawn or revoked.

 (5) The power conferred by subsection (1) shall be exercised in accordance with any directions given by the Lord Chancellor.

 (6) Any contract entered into by the Board for the provision of mediation under this Part must require the mediator to comply with a code of practice.

 (7) The code must require the mediator to have arrangements designed to ensure—

  (a) that parties participate in mediation only if willing and not influenced by fear of violence or other harm;

  (b) that cases where either party may be influenced by fear of violence or other harm are identified as soon as possible;

  (c) that the possibility of reconciliation is kept under review throughout mediation; and

  (d) that each party is informed about the availability of independent legal advice.

(8) Where there are one or more children of the family, the code must also require the mediator to have arrangements designed to ensure that the parties are encouraged to consider—

(a) the welfare, wishes and feelings of each child; and

(b) whether and to what extent each child should be given the opportunity to express his or her wishes and feelings in the mediation.

(9) A contract entered into by the Board for the provision of mediation under this Part must also include such other provision as the Lord Chancellor may direct the Board to include.

(10) Directions under this section may apply generally to contracts, or to contracts of any description, entered into by the Board, but shall not be made with respect to any particular contract.'

28. Payment for mediation

(1) After section 13B of the 1988 Act, insert—

'13C. Payment for mediation under this Part

(1) Except as provided by this section, the legally assisted person is not to be required to pay for mediation provided under this Part.

(2) Subsection (3) applies if the financial resources of a legally assisted person are such as, under regulations, make him liable to make a contribution.

(3) The legally assisted person is to pay to the Board in respect of the costs of providing the mediation, a contribution of such amount as is determined or fixed by or under the regulations.

(4) If the total contribution made by a person in respect of any mediation exceeds the Board's liability on his account, the excess shall be repaid to him.

(5) Regulations may provide that, where—

(a) mediation under this Part is made available to a legally assisted person, and

(b) property is recovered or preserved for the legally assisted person as a result of the mediation,

a sum equal to the Board's liability on the legally assisted person's account is, except so far as the regulations otherwise provide, to be a first charge on the property in favour of the Board.

(6) Regulations under subsection (5) may, in particular, make provision—

(a) as to circumstances in which property is to be taken to have been, or not to have been, recovered or preserved; and

(b) as to circumstances in which the recovery or preservation of property is to be taken to be, or not to be, the result of any mediation.

(7) For the purposes of subsection (5), the nature of the property and where it is situated is immaterial.

(8) The power to make regulations under section 34(2)(f) and (8) is exercisable in relation to any charge created under subsection (5) as it is exercisable in relation to the charge created by section 16.

(9) For the purposes of subsections (4) and (5), the Board's liability on any person's account in relation to any mediation is the aggregate amount of—

(a) the sums paid or payable by the Board on his account for the mediation, determined in accordance with subsection (10);

(b) any sums paid or payable in respect of its net liability on his account, determined in accordance with subsection (11) and the regulations—

(i)   in respect of any proceedings, and

(ii)   for any advice or assistance under Part III in connection with the proceedings or any matter to which the proceedings relate,

so far as the proceedings relate to any matter to which the mediation relates; and

(c)   any sums paid or payable in respect of its net liability on his account, determined in accordance with the regulations, for any other advice or assistance under Part III in connection with the mediation or any matter to which the mediation relates.

(10)   For the purposes of subsection (9)(a), the sums paid or payable by the Board on any person's account for any mediation are—

(a)   sums determined under the contract between the Board and the mediator as payable by the Board on that person's account for the mediation; or

(b)   if the contract does not differentiate between such sums and sums payable on any other person's account or for any other mediation, such part of the remuneration payable under the contract as may be specified in writing by the Board.

(11)   For the purposes of subsection (9)(b), the Board's net liability on any person's account in relation to any proceedings is its net liability on his account under section 16(9)(a) and (b) in relation to the proceedings.'

(2)   In section 16(9), after paragraph (b) insert "and

"(c)   if and to the extent that regulations so provide, any sums paid or payable in respect of the Board's liability on the legally assisted person's account in relation to any mediation in connection with any matter to which those proceedings relate."

(3)   At the end of section 16, insert—

'(11)   For the purposes of subsection (9)(c) above, the Board's liability on any person's account in relation to any mediation is its liability on his account under section 13C(9)(a) and (c) above in relation to the mediation.'

29.   Mediation and civil legal aid

In section 15 of the 1988 Act, after subsection (3E) insert—

'(3F)   A person shall not be granted representation for the purposes of proceedings relating to family matters, unless he has attended a meeting with a mediator—

(a)   to determine—

(i)   whether mediation appears suitable to the dispute and the parties and all the circumstances, and

(ii)   in particular, whether mediation could take place without either party being influenced by fear of violence or other harm; and

(b)   if mediation does appear suitable, to help the person applying for representation to decide whether instead to apply for mediation.

(3G)   Subsection (3F) does not apply—

(a)   in relation to proceedings under—

(i)   Part IV of the Family Law Act 1996;

(ii)   section 37 of the Matrimonial Causes Act 1973;

(iii) Part IV or V of the Children Act 1989;

(b)   in relation to proceedings of any other description that may be prescribed; or

(c)   in such circumstances as may be prescribed.

(3H)   So far as proceedings relate to family matters, the Board, in determining under subsection (3)(a) whether, in relation to the proceedings, it is reasonable that a person should be granted representation under this Part—

(a)   must have regard to whether and to what extent recourse to mediation would be a suitable alternative to taking the proceedings; and

(b)   must for that purpose have regard to the outcome of the meeting held under subsection (3F) and to any assessment made for the purposes of section 13B(3).'

PART IV
FAMILY HOMES AND DOMESTIC VIOLENCE

Rights to occupy matrimonial home

30.   Rights concerning matrimonial home where one spouse has no estate, etc.

(1)   This section applies if—

(a)   one spouse is entitled to occupy a dwelling-house by virtue of—

(i)   a beneficial estate or interest or contract; or

(ii)   any enactment giving that spouse the right to remain in occupation; and

(b)   the other spouse is not so entitled.

(2)   Subject to the provisions of this Part, the spouse not so entitled has the following rights ('matrimonial home rights')—

(a)   if in occupation, a right not to be evicted or excluded from the dwelling-house or any part of it by the other spouse except with the leave of the court given by an order under section 33;

(b)   if not in occupation, a right with the leave of the court so given to enter into and occupy the dwelling-house.

(3)   If a spouse is entitled under this section to occupy a dwelling-house or any part of a dwelling-house, any payment or tender made or other thing done by that spouse in or towards satisfaction of any liability of the other spouse in respect of rent, mortgage payments or other outgoings affecting the dwelling-house is, whether or not it is made or done in pursuance of an order under section 40, as good as if made or done by the other spouse.

(4)   A spouse's occupation by virtue of this section—

(a)   is to be treated, for the purposes of the Rent (Agriculture) Act 1976 and the Rent Act 1977 (other than Part V and sections 103 to 106 of that Act), as occupation by the other spouse as the other spouse's residence, and

(b)   if the spouse occupies the dwelling-house as that spouse's only or principal home, is to be treated, for the purposes of the Housing Act 1985 and Part I of the Housing Act 1988, as occupation by the other spouse as the other spouse's only or principal home.

(5)   If a spouse ('the first spouse')—

(a)   is entitled under this section to occupy a dwelling-house or any part of a dwelling-house, and

(b)   makes any payment in or towards satisfaction of any liability of the other spouse ('the second spouse') in respect of mortgage payments affecting the dwelling-house,

the person to whom the payment is made may treat it as having been made by the second spouse, but the fact that that person has treated any such payment as having been so made does not affect any claim of the first spouse against the second spouse to an interest in the dwelling-house by virtue of the payment.

(6) If a spouse is entitled under this section to occupy a dwelling-house or part of a dwelling-house by reason of an interest of the other spouse under a trust, all the provisions of subsections (3) to (5) apply in relation to the trustees as they apply in relation to the other spouse.

(7) This section does not apply to a dwelling-house which has at no time been, and which was at no time intended by the spouses to be, a matrimonial home of theirs.

(8) A spouse's matrimonial home rights continue—

(a) only so long as the marriage subsists, except to the extent that an order under section 33(5) otherwise provides; and

(b) only so long as the other spouse is entitled as mentioned in subsection (1) to occupy the dwelling-house, except where provision is made by section 31 for those rights to be a charge on an estate or interest in the dwelling-house.

(9) It is hereby declared that a spouse—

(a) who has an equitable interest in a dwelling-house or in its proceeds of sale, but

(b) is not a spouse in whom there is vested (whether solely or as joint tenant) a legal estate in fee simple or a legal term of years absolute in the dwelling-house,

is to be treated, only for the purpose of determining whether he has matrimonial home rights, as not being entitled to occupy the dwelling-house by virtue of that interest.

31. Effect of matrimonial home rights as charge on dwelling-house

(1) Subsections (2) and (3) apply if, at any time during a marriage, one spouse is entitled to occupy a dwelling-house by virtue of a beneficial estate or interest.

(2) The other spouse's matrimonial home rights are a charge on the estate or interest.

(3) The charge created by subsection (2) has the same priority as if it were an equitable interest created at whichever is the latest of the following dates—

(a) the date on which the spouse so entitled acquires the estate or interest;

(b) the date of the marriage; and

(c) 1st January 1968 (the commencement date of the Matrimonial Homes Act 1967).

(4) Subsections (5) and (6) apply if, at any time when a spouse's matrimonial home rights are a charge on an interest of the other spouse under a trust, there are, apart from either of the spouses, no persons, living or unborn, who are or could become beneficiaries under the trust.

(5) The rights are a charge also on the estate or interest of the trustees for the other spouse.

(6) The charge created by subsection (5) has the same priority as if it were an equitable interest created (under powers overriding the trusts) on the date when it arises.

(7) In determining for the purposes of subsection (4) whether there are any persons who are not, but could become, beneficiaries under the trust, there is to be disregarded any potential exercise of a general power of appointment exercisable by either or both of the spouses alone (whether or not the exercise of it requires the consent of another person).

(8) Even though a spouse's matrimonial home rights are a charge on an estate or interest in the dwelling-house, those rights are brought to an end by—

(a)   the death of the other spouse, or

(b)   the termination (otherwise than by death) of the marriage, unless the court directs otherwise by an order made under section 33(5).

(9)   If—

(a)   a spouse's matrimonial home rights are a charge on an estate or interest in the dwelling-house, and

(b)   that estate or interest is surrendered to merge in some other estate or interest expectant on it in such circumstances that, but for the merger, the person taking the estate or interest would be bound by the charge,

the surrender has effect subject to the charge and the persons thereafter entitled to the other estate or interest are, for so long as the estate or interest surrendered would have endured if not so surrendered, to be treated for all purposes of this Part as deriving title to the other estate or interest under the other spouse or, as the case may be, under the trustees for the other spouse, by virtue of the surrender.

(10)   If the title to the legal estate by virtue of which a spouse is entitled to occupy a dwelling-house (including any legal estate held by trustees for that spouse) is registered under the Land Registration Act 1925 or any enactment replaced by that Act—

(a)   registration of a land charge affecting the dwelling-house by virtue of this Part is to be effected by registering a notice under that Act; and

(b)   a spouse's matrimonial home rights are not an overriding interest within the meaning of that Act affecting the dwelling-house even though the spouse is in actual occupation of the dwelling-house.

(11)   A spouse's matrimonial home rights (whether or not constituting a charge) do not entitle that spouse to lodge a caution under section 54 of the Land Registration Act 1925.

(12)   If—

(a)   a spouse's matrimonial home rights are a charge on the estate of the other spouse or of trustees of the other spouse, and

(b)   that estate is the subject of a mortgage,

then if, after the date of the creation of the mortgage ('the first mortgage'), the charge is registered under section 2 of the Land Charges Act 1972, the charge is, for the purposes of section 94 of the Law of Property Act 1925 (which regulates the rights of mortgagees to make further advances ranking in priority to subsequent mortgages), to be deemed to be a mortgage subsequent in date to the first mortgage.

(13)   It is hereby declared that a charge under subsection (2) or (5) is not registrable under subsection (10) or under section 2 of the Land Charges Act 1972 unless it is a charge on a legal estate.

32.   Further provisions relating to matrimonial home rights

Schedule 4 re-enacts with consequential amendments and minor modifications provisions of the Matrimonial Homes Act 1983.

Occupation orders

33.   Occupation orders where applicant has estate or interest etc. or has matrimonial home rights

(1)   If—

(a)   a person ('the person entitled')—

　　　　(i)　　is entitled to occupy a dwelling-house by virtue of a beneficial estate or interest or contract or by virtue of any enactment giving him the right to remain in occupation, or

　　　　(ii)　　has matrimonial home rights in relation to a dwelling-house, and

　　(b)　the dwelling-house—

　　　　(i)　　is or at any time has been the home of the person entitled and of another person with whom he is associated, or

　　　　(ii)　　was at any time intended by the person entitled and any such other person to be their home,

the person entitled may apply to the court for an order containing any of the provisions specified in subsections (3), (4) and (5).

(2)　If an agreement to marry is terminated, no application under this section may be made by virtue of section 62(3)(e) by reference to that agreement after the end of the period of three years beginning with the day on which it is terminated.

(3)　An order under this section may—

　　(a)　enforce the applicant's entitlement to remain in occupation as against the other person ('the respondent');

　　(b)　require the respondent to permit the applicant to enter and remain in the dwelling-house or part of the dwelling-house;

　　(c)　regulate the occupation of the dwelling-house by either or both parties;

　　(d)　if the respondent is entitled as mentioned in subsection (1)(a)(i), prohibit, suspend or restrict the exercise by him of his right to occupy the dwelling-house;

　　(e)　if the respondent has matrimonial home rights in relation to the dwelling-house and the applicant is the other spouse, restrict or terminate those rights;

　　(f)　require the respondent to leave the dwelling-house or part of the dwelling-house; or

　　(g)　exclude the respondent from a defined area in which the dwelling-house is included.

(4)　An order under this section may declare that the applicant is entitled as mentioned in subsection (1)(a)(i) or has matrimonial home rights.

(5)　If the applicant has matrimonial home rights and the respondent is the other spouse, an order under this section made during the marriage may provide that those rights are not brought to an end by—

　　(a)　the death of the other spouse; or

　　(b)　the termination (otherwise than by death) of the marriage.

(6)　In deciding whether to exercise its powers under subsection (3) and (if so) in what manner, the court shall have regard to all the circumstances including—

　　(a)　the housing needs and housing resources of each of the parties and of any relevant child;

　　(b)　the financial resources of each of the parties;

　　(c)　the likely effect of any order, or of any decision by the court not to exercise its powers under subsection (3), on the health, safety or well-being of the parties and of any relevant child; and

　　(d)　the conduct of the parties in relation to each other and otherwise.

(7)　If it appears to the court that the applicant or any relevant child is likely to suffer significant harm attributable to conduct of the respondent if an order under this section containing one or more of the provisions mentioned in subsection (3) is not made, the court shall make the order unless it appears to it that—

    (a)   the respondent or any relevant child is likely to suffer significant harm if the order is made; and

    (b)   the harm likely to be suffered by the respondent or child in that event is as great as, or greater than, the harm attributable to conduct of the respondent which is likely to be suffered by the applicant or child if the order is not made.

    (8)   The court may exercise its powers under subsection (5) in any case where it considers that in all the circumstances it is just and reasonable to do so.

    (9)   An order under this section—

    (a)   may not be made after the death of either of the parties mentioned in subsection (1); and

    (b)   except in the case of an order made by virtue of subsection (5)(a), ceases to have effect on the death of either party.

    (10)   An order under this section may, in so far as it has continuing effect, be made for a specified period, until the occurrence of a specified event or until further order.

34.   Effect of order under s. 33 where rights are charge on dwelling-house

    (1)   If a spouse's matrimonial home rights are a charge on the estate or interest of the other spouse or of trustees for the other spouse—

    (a)   an order under section 33 against the other spouse has, except so far as a contrary intention appears, the same effect against persons deriving title under the other spouse or under the trustees and affected by the charge, and

    (b)   sections 33(1), (3), (4) and (10) and 30(3) to (6) apply in relation to any person deriving title under the other spouse or under the trustees and affected by the charge as they apply in relation to the other spouse.

    (2)   The court may make an order under section 33 by virtue of subsection (1)(b) if it considers that in all the circumstances it is just and reasonable to do so.

35.   One former spouse with no existing right to occupy

    (1)   This section applies if—

    (a)   one former spouse is entitled to occupy a dwelling-house by virtue of a beneficial estate or interest or contract, or by virtue of any enactment giving him the right to remain in occupation;

    (b)   the other former spouse is not so entitled; and

    (c)   the dwelling-house was at any time their matrimonial home or was at any time intended by them to be their matrimonial home.

    (2)   The former spouse not so entitled may apply to the court for an order under this section against the other former spouse ('the respondent').

    (3)   If the applicant is in occupation, an order under this section must contain provision— (a) giving the applicant the right not to be evicted or excluded from the dwelling-house or any part of it by the respondent for the period specified in the order; and

    (b)   prohibiting the respondent from evicting or excluding the applicant during that period.

    (4)   If the applicant is not in occupation, an order under this section must contain provision—

    (a)   giving the applicant the right to enter into and occupy the dwelling-house for the period specified in the order; and

(b) requiring the respondent to permit the exercise of that right.

(5) An order under this section may also—

(a) regulate the occupation of the dwelling-house by either or both of the parties;

(b) prohibit, suspend or restrict the exercise by the respondent of his right to occupy the dwelling-house;

(c) require the respondent to leave the dwelling-house or part of the dwelling-house; or

(d) exclude the respondent from a defined area in which the dwelling-house is included.

(6) In deciding whether to make an order under this section containing provision of the kind mentioned in subsection (3) or (4) and (if so) in what manner, the court shall have regard to all the circumstances including—

(a) the housing needs and housing resources of each of the parties and of any relevant child;

(b) the financial resources of each of the parties;

(c) the likely effect of any order, or of any decision by the court not to exercise its powers under subsection (3) or (4), on the health, safety or well-being of the parties and of any relevant child;

(d) the conduct of the parties in relation to each other and otherwise;

(e) the length of time that has elapsed since the parties ceased to live together;

(f) the length of time that has elapsed since the marriage was dissolved or annulled; and

(g) the existence of any pending proceedings between the parties—

(i) for an order under section 23A or 24 of the Matrimonial Causes Act 1973 (property adjustment orders in connection with divorce proceedings etc.);

(ii) for an order under paragraph 1(2)(d) or (e) of Schedule 1 to the Children Act 1989 (orders for financial relief against parents); or

(iii) relating to the legal or beneficial ownership of the dwelling-house.

(7) In deciding whether to exercise its power to include one or more of the provisions referred to in subsection (5) ('a subsection (5) provision') and (if so) in what manner, the court shall have regard to all the circumstances including the matters mentioned in subsection (6)(a) to (e).

(8) If the court decides to make an order under this section and it appears to it that, if the order does not include a subsection (5) provision, the applicant or any relevant child is likely to suffer significant harm attributable to conduct of the respondent, the court shall include the subsection (5) provision in the order unless it appears to the court that—

(a) the respondent or any relevant child is likely to suffer significant harm if the provision is included in the order; and

(b) the harm likely to be suffered by the respondent or child in that event is as great as or greater than the harm attributable to conduct of the respondent which is likely to be suffered by the applicant or child if the provision is not included.

(9) An order under this section—

(a) may not be made after the death of either of the former spouses; and

(b) ceases to have effect on the death of either of them.

(10) An order under this section must be limited so as to have effect for a specified period not exceeding six months, but may be extended on one or more occasions for a further specified period not exceeding six months.

(11)   A former spouse who has an equitable interest in the dwelling-house or in the proceeds of sale of the dwelling-house but in whom there is not vested (whether solely or as joint tenant) a legal estate in fee simple or a legal term of years absolute in the dwelling-house is to be treated (but only for the purpose of determining whether he is eligible to apply under this section) as not being entitled to occupy the dwelling-house by virtue of that interest.

(12)   Subsection (11) does not prejudice any right of such a former spouse to apply for an order under section 33.

(13)   So long as an order under this section remains in force, subsections (3) to (6) of section 30 apply in relation to the applicant—

(a)   as if he were the spouse entitled to occupy the dwelling-house by virtue of that section; and

(b)   as if the respondent were the other spouse.

36.   One cohabitant or former cohabitant with no existing right to occupy

(1)   This section applies if—

(a)   one cohabitant or former cohabitant is entitled to occupy a dwelling-house by virtue of a beneficial estate or interest or contract or by virtue of any enactment giving him the right to remain in occupation;

(b)   the other cohabitant or former cohabitant is not so entitled; and

(c)   that dwelling-house is the home in which they live together as husband and wife or a home in which they at any time so lived together or intended so to live together.

(2)   The cohabitant or former cohabitant not so entitled may apply to the court for an order under this section against the other cohabitant or former cohabitant ('the respondent').

(3)   If the applicant is in occupation, an order under this section must contain provision—

(a)   giving the applicant the right not to be evicted or excluded from the dwelling-house or any part of it by the respondent for the period specified in the order; and

(b)   prohibiting the respondent from evicting or excluding the applicant during that period.

(4)   If the applicant is not in occupation, an order under this section must contain provision—

(a)   giving the applicant the right to enter into and occupy the dwelling-house for the period specified in the order; and

(b)   requiring the respondent to permit the exercise of that right.

(5)   An order under this section may also—

(a)   regulate the occupation of the dwelling-house by either or both of the parties;

(b)   prohibit, suspend or restrict the exercise by the respondent of his right to occupy the dwelling-house;

(c)   require the respondent to leave the dwelling-house or part of the dwelling-house; or

(d)   exclude the respondent from a defined area in which the dwelling-house is included.

(6)   In deciding whether to make an order under this section containing provision of the kind mentioned in subsection (3) or (4) and (if so) in what manner, the court shall have regard to all the circumstances including—

(a)   the housing needs and housing resources of each of the parties and of any relevant child;

(b)   the financial resources of each of the parties;

(c)   the likely effect of any order, or of any decision by the court not to exercise its powers under subsection (3) or (4), on the health, safety or well-being of the parties and of any relevant child;

(d)   the conduct of the parties in relation to each other and otherwise;

(e)   the nature of the parties' relationship;

(f)   the length of time during which they have lived together as husband and wife;

(g)   whether there are or have been any children who are children of both parties or for whom both parties have or have had parental responsibility;

(h)   the length of time that has elapsed since the parties ceased to live together; and

(i)   the existence of any pending proceedings between the parties—

(i)   for an order under paragraph 1(2)(d) or (e) of Schedule 1 to the Children Act 1989 (orders for financial relief against parents); or

(ii)   relating to the legal or beneficial ownership of the dwelling-house.

(7)   In deciding whether to exercise its powers to include one or more of the provisions referred to in subsection (5) ('a subsection (5) provision') and (if so) in what manner, the court shall have regard to all the circumstances including—

(a)   the matters mentioned in subsection (6)(a) to (d); and

(b)   the questions mentioned in subsection (8).

(8)   The questions are—

(a)   whether the applicant or any relevant child is likely to suffer significant harm attributable to conduct of the respondent if the subsection (5) provision is not included in the order; and

(b)   whether the harm likely to be suffered by the respondent or child if the provision is included is as great as or greater than the harm attributable to conduct of the respondent which is likely to be suffered by the applicant or child if the provision is not included.

(9)   An order under this section—

(a)   may not be made after the death of either of the parties; and

(b)   ceases to have effect on the death of either of them.

(10)   An order under this section must be limited so as to have effect for a specified period not exceeding six months, but may be extended on one occasion for a further specified period not exceeding six months.

(11)   A person who has an equitable interest in the dwelling-house or in the proceeds of sale of the dwelling-house but in whom there is not vested (whether solely or as joint tenant) a legal estate in fee simple or a legal term of years absolute in the dwelling-house is to be treated (but only for the purpose of determining whether he is eligible to apply under this section) as not being entitled to occupy the dwelling-house by virtue of that interest.

(12)   Subsection (11) does not prejudice any right of such a person to apply for an order under section 33.

(13)   So long as the order remains in force, subsections (3) to (6) of section 30 apply in relation to the applicant—

(a)   as if he were a spouse entitled to occupy the dwelling-house by virtue of that section; and

(b)   as if the respondent were the other spouse.

37.   Neither spouse entitled to occupy

(1)   This section applies if—

(a)   one spouse or former spouse and the other spouse or former spouse occupy a dwelling-house which is or was the matrimonial home; but

(b)   neither of them is entitled to remain in occupation—

(i)   by virtue of a beneficial estate or interest or contract; or

(ii)   by virtue of any enactment giving him the right to remain in occupation.

(2)   Either of the parties may apply to the court for an order against the other under this section.

(3)   An order under this section may—

(a)   require the respondent to permit the applicant to enter and remain in the dwelling-house or part of the dwelling-house;

(b)   regulate the occupation of the dwelling-house by either or both of the spouses;

(c)   require the respondent to leave the dwelling-house or part of the dwelling-house; or

(d)   exclude the respondent from a defined area in which the dwelling-house is included.

(4)   Subsections (6) and (7) of section 33 apply to the exercise by the court of its powers under this section as they apply to the exercise by the court of its powers under subsection (3) of that section.

(5)   An order under this section must be limited so as to have effect for a specified period not exceeding six months, but may be extended on one or more occasions for a further specified period not exceeding six months.

38.   Neither cohabitant or former cohabitant entitled to occupy

(1)   This section applies if—

(a)   one cohabitant or former cohabitant and the other cohabitant or former cohabitant occupy a dwelling-house which is the home in which they live or lived together as husband and wife; but

(b)   neither of them is entitled to remain in occupation—

(i)   by virtue of a beneficial estate or interest or contract; or

(ii)   by virtue of any enactment giving him the right to remain in occupation.

(2)   Either of the parties may apply to the court for an order against the other under this section.

(3)   An order under this section may—

(a)   require the respondent to permit the applicant to enter and remain in the dwelling-house or part of the dwelling-house;

(b)   regulate the occupation of the dwelling-house by either or both of the parties;

(c)   require the respondent to leave the dwelling-house or part of the dwelling-house; or

(d)   exclude the respondent from a defined area in which the dwelling-house is included.

(4)   In deciding whether to exercise its powers to include one or more of the provisions referred to in subsection (3) ('a subsection (3) provision') and (if so) in what manner, the court shall have regard to all the circumstances including—

(a)   the housing needs and housing resources of each of the parties and of any relevant child;

(b)   the financial resources of each of the parties;

(c)   the likely effect of any order, or of any decision by the court not to exercise its powers under subsection (3), on the health, safety or well-being of the parties and of any relevant child;

(d)   the conduct of the parties in relation to each other and otherwise; and

(e)   the questions mentioned in subsection (5).

(5)   The questions are—

(a)   whether the applicant or any relevant child is likely to suffer significant harm attributable to conduct of the respondent if the subsection (3) provision is not included in the order; and

(b)   whether the harm likely to be suffered by the respondent or child if the provision is included is as great as or greater than the harm attributable to conduct of the respondent which is likely to be suffered by the applicant or child if the provision is not included.

(6)   An order under this section shall be limited so as to have effect for a specified period not exceeding six months, but may be extended on one occasion for a further specified period not exceeding six months.

39.   Supplementary provisions

(1)   In this Part an 'occupation order' means an order under section 33, 35, 36, 37 or 38.

(2)   An application for an occupation order may be made in other family proceedings or without any other family proceedings being instituted.

(3)   If—

(a)   an application for an occupation order is made under section 33, 35, 36, 37 or 38, and

(b)   the court considers that it has no power to make the order under the section concerned, but that it has power to make an order under one of the other sections, the court may make an order under that other section.

(4)   The fact that a person has applied for an occupation order under sections 35 to 38, or that an occupation order has been made, does not affect the right of any person to claim a legal or equitable interest in any property in any subsequent proceedings (including subsequent proceedings under this Part).

40.   Additional provisions that may be included in certain occupation orders

(1)   The court may on, or at any time after, making an occupation order under section 33, 35 or 36—

(a)   impose on either party obligations as to—

(i)   the repair and maintenance of the dwelling-house; or

(ii)   the discharge of rent, mortgage payments or other outgoings affecting the dwelling-house;

(b)   order a party occupying the dwelling-house or any part of it (including a party who is entitled to do so by virtue of a beneficial estate or interest or contract or by virtue of any enactment giving him the right to remain in occupation) to make periodical payments to the other party in respect of the accommodation, if the other party would (but for the order) be entitled to occupy the dwelling-house by virtue of a beneficial estate or interest or contract or by virtue of any such enactment;

(c)   grant either party possession or use of furniture or other contents of the dwelling-house;

(d)   order either party to take reasonable care of any furniture or other contents of the dwelling-house;

(e)   order either party to take reasonable steps to keep the dwelling-house and any furniture or other contents secure.

(2)   In deciding whether and, if so, how to exercise its powers under this section, the court shall have regard to all the circumstances of the case including—

(a)   the financial needs and financial resources of the parties; and

(b)   the financial obligations which they have, or are likely to have in the foreseeable future, including financial obligations to each other and to any relevant child.

(3)   An order under this section ceases to have effect when the occupation order to which it relates ceases to have effect.

41.   Additional considerations if parties are cohabitants or former cohabitants

(1)   This section applies if the parties are cohabitants or former cohabitants.

(2)   Where the court is required to consider the nature of the parties' relationship, it is to have regard to the fact that they have not given each other the commitment involved in marriage.

Non-molestation orders

42.   Mon-molestation orders

(1)   In this Part a 'non-molestation order' means an order containing either or both of the following provisions—

(a)   provision prohibiting a person ('the respondent') from molesting another person who is associated with the respondent;

(b)   provision prohibiting the respondent from molesting a relevant child.

(2)   The court may make a non-molestation order—

(a)   if an application for the order has been made (whether in other family proceedings or without any other family proceedings being instituted) by a person who is associated with the respondent; or

(b)   if in any family proceedings to which the respondent is a party the court considers that the order should be made for the benefit of any other party to the proceedings or any relevant child even though no such application has been made.

(3)   In subsection (2) 'family proceedings' includes proceedings in which the court has made an emergency protection order under section 44 of the Children Act 1989 which includes an exclusion requirement (as defined in section 44A(3) of that Act).

(4)   Where an agreement to marry is terminated, no application under subsection (2)(a) may be made by virtue of section 62(3)(e) by reference to that agreement after the end of the period of three years beginning with the day on which it is terminated.

(5)   In deciding whether to exercise its powers under this section and, if so, in what manner, the court shall have regard to all the circumstances including the need to secure the health, safety and well-being—

(a)   of the applicant or, in a case falling within subsection (2)(b), the person for whose benefit the order would be made; and

(b)   of any relevant child.

(6)   A non-molestation order may be expressed so as to refer to molestation in general, to particular acts of molestation, or to both.

(7)   A non-molestation order may be made for a specified period or until further order.

(8)   A non-molestation order which is made in other family proceedings ceases to have effect if those proceedings are withdrawn or dismissed.

Further provisions relating to occupation and non-molestation orders

43.   Leave of court required for applications by children under sixteen

(1)   A child under the age of sixteen may not apply for an occupation order or a non-molestation order except with the leave of the court.

(2)   The court may grant leave for the purposes of subsection (1) only if it is satisfied that the child has sufficient understanding to make the proposed application for the occupation order or non-molestation order.

44.   Evidence of agreement to marry

(1)   Subject to subsection (2), the court shall not make an order under section 33 or 42 by virtue of section 62(3)(e) unless there is produced to it evidence in writing of the existence of the agreement to marry.

(2)   Subsection (1) does not apply if the court is satisfied that the agreement to marry was evidenced by—

(a)   the gift of an engagement ring by one party to the agreement to the other in contemplation of their marriage, or

(b)   a ceremony entered into by the parties in the presence of one or more other persons assembled for the purpose of witnessing the ceremony.

45.   Ex parte orders

(1)   The court may, in any case where it considers that it is just and convenient to do so, make an occupation order or a non-molestation order even though the respondent has not been given such notice of the proceedings as would otherwise be required by rules of court.

(2)   In determining whether to exercise its powers under subsection (1), the court shall have regard to all the circumstances including—

(a)   any risk of significant harm to the applicant or a relevant child, attributable to conduct of the respondent, if the order is not made immediately;

(b)   whether it is likely that the applicant will be deterred or prevented from pursuing the application if an order is not made immediately; and

(c)   whether there is reason to believe that the respondent is aware of the proceedings but is deliberately evading service and that the applicant or a relevant child will be seriously prejudiced by the delay involved—

(i)   where the court is a magistrates' court, in effecting service of proceedings; or

(ii)   in any other case, in effecting substituted service.

(3)   If the court makes an order by virtue of subsection (1) it must afford the respondent an opportunity to make representations relating to the order as soon as just and convenient at a full hearing.

(4)   If, at a full hearing, the court makes an occupation order ('the full order'), then—

(a)   for the purposes of calculating the maximum period for which the full order may be made to have effect, the relevant section is to apply as if the period for which the full order will have effect began on the date on which the initial order first had effect; and

(b)   the provisions of section 36(10) or 38(6) as to the extension of orders are to apply as if the full order and the initial order were a single order.

(5)   In this section—

'full hearing' means a hearing of which notice has been given to all the parties in accordance with rules of court;

'initial order' means an occupation order made by virtue of subsection (1); and

'relevant section' means section 33(10), 35(10), 36(10), 37(5) or 38(6).

46.   Undertakings

(1)   In any case where the court has power to make an occupation order or non-molestation order, the court may accept an undertaking from any party to the proceedings.

(2)   No power of arrest may be attached to any undertaking given under subsection (1).

(3)   The court shall not accept an undertaking under subsection (1) in any case where apart from this section a power of arrest would be attached to the order.

(4)   An undertaking given to a court under subsection (1) is enforceable as if it were an order of the court.

(5)   This section has effect without prejudice to the powers of the High Court and the county court apart from this section.

47.   Arrest for breach of order

(1)   In this section 'a relevant order' means an occupation order or a non-molestation order.

(2)   If—

(a)   the court makes a relevant order; and

(b)   it appears to the court that the respondent has used or threatened violence against the applicant or a relevant child,

it shall attach a power of arrest to one or more provisions of the order unless satisfied that in all the circumstances of the case the applicant or child will be adequately protected without such a power of arrest.

(3)   Subsection (2) does not apply in any case where the relevant order is made by virtue of section 45(1), but in such a case the court may attach a power of arrest to one or more provisions of the order if it appears to it—

(a)   that the respondent has used or threatened violence against the applicant or a relevant child; and

(b)   that there is a risk of significant harm to the applicant or child, attributable to conduct of the respondent, if the power of arrest is not attached to those provisions immediately.

(4)   If, by virtue of subsection (3), the court attaches a power of arrest to any provisions of a relevant order, it may provide that the power of arrest is to have effect for a shorter period than the other provisions of the order.

(5)   Any period specified for the purposes of subsection (4) may be extended by the court (on one or more occasions) on an application to vary or discharge the relevant order.

(6)   If, by virtue of subsection (2) or (3), a power of arrest is attached to certain provisions of an order, a constable may arrest without warrant a person whom he has reasonable cause for suspecting to be in breach of any such provision.

(7)   If a power of arrest is attached under subsection (2) or (3) to certain provisions of the order and the respondent is arrested under subsection (6)—

(a)   he must be brought before the relevant judicial authority within the period of 24 hours beginning at the time of his arrest; and

(b)   if the matter is not then disposed of forthwith, the relevant judicial authority before whom he is brought may remand him.

In reckoning for the purposes of this subsection any period of 24 hours, no account is to be taken of Christmas Day, Good Friday or any Sunday.

(8)   If the court has made a relevant order but—

(a)   has not attached a power of arrest under subsection (2) or (3) to any provisions of the order, or

(b)   has attached that power only to certain provisions of the order,

then, if at any time the applicant considers that the respondent has failed to comply with the order, he may apply to the relevant judicial authority for the issue of a warrant for the arrest of the respondent.

(9)   The relevant judicial authority shall not issue a warrant on an application under subsection (8) unless—

(a)   the application is substantiated on oath; and

(b)   the relevant judicial authority has reasonable grounds for believing that the respondent has failed to comply with the order.

(10)   If a person is brought before a court by virtue of a warrant issued under subsection (9) and the court does not dispose of the matter forthwith, the court may remand him.

(11)   Schedule 5 (which makes provision corresponding to that applying in magistrates' courts in civil cases under sections 128 and 129 of the Magistrates' Courts Act 1980) has effect in relation to the powers of the High Court and a county court to remand a person by virtue of this section.

(12)   If a person remanded under this section is granted bail (whether in the High Court or a county court under Schedule 5 or in a magistrates' court under section 128 or 129 of the Magistrates' Courts Act 1980), he may be required by the relevant judicial authority to comply, before release on bail or later, with such requirements as appear to that authority to be necessary to secure that he does not interfere with witnesses or otherwise obstruct the course of justice.

48.   Remand for medical examination and report

(1)   If the relevant judicial authority has reason to consider that a medical report will be required, any power to remand a person under section 47(7)(b) or (10) may be exercised for the purpose of enabling a medical examination and report to be made.

(2)   If such a power is so exercised, the adjournment must not be for more than 4 weeks at a time unless the relevant judicial authority remands the accused in custody.

(3)   If the relevant judicial authority so remands the accused, the adjournment must not be for more than 3 weeks at a time.

(4)   If there is reason to suspect that a person who has been arrested—
    (a)   under section 47(6), or
    (b)   under a warrant issued on an application made under section 47(8),
is suffering from mental illness or severe mental impairment, the relevant judicial authority has the same power to make an order under section 35 of the Mental Health Act 1983 (remand for report on accused's mental condition) as the Crown Court has under section 35 of the Act of 1983 in the case of an accused person within the meaning of that section.

49.   Variation and discharge of orders
(1)   An occupation order or non-molestation order may be varied or discharged by the court on an application by—
    (a)   the respondent, or
    (b)   the person on whose application the order was made.
(2)   In the case of a non-molestation order made by virtue of section 42(2)(b), the order may be varied or discharged by the court even though no such application has been made.
(3)   If a spouse's matrimonial home rights are a charge on the estate or interest of the other spouse or of trustees for the other spouse, an order under section 33 against the other spouse may also be varied or discharged by the court on an application by any person deriving title under the other spouse or under the trustees and affected by the charge.
(4)   If, by virtue of section 47(3), a power of arrest has been attached to certain provisions of an occupation order or non-molestation order, the court may vary or discharge the order under subsection (1) in so far as it confers a power of arrest (whether or not any application has been made to vary or discharge any other provision of the order).

Enforcement powers of magistrates' courts

50.   Power of magistrates' court to suspend execution of committal order
(1)   If, under section 63(3) of the Magistrates' Courts Act 1980, a magistrates' court has power to commit a person to custody for breach of a relevant requirement, the court may by order direct that the execution of the order of committal is to be suspended for such period or on such terms and conditions as it may specify.
(2)   In subsection (1) 'a relevant requirement' means—
    (a)   an occupation order or non-molestation order;
    (b)   an exclusion requirement included by virtue of section 38A of the Children Act 1989 in an interim care order made under section 38 of that Act, or
    (c)   an exclusion requirement included by virtue of section 44A of the Children Act 1989 in an emergency protection order under section 44 of that Act.

51.   Power of magistrates' court to order hospital admission or guardianship
(1)   A magistrates' court has the same power to make a hospital order or guardianship order under section 37 of the Mental Health Act 1983 or an interim hospital order under section 38 of that Act in the case of a person suffering from mental illness or severe mental impairment who could otherwise be committed to custody for breach of a relevant requirement as a magistrates' court has under those sections in the case of a person convicted of an offence punishable on summary conviction with imprisonment.

(2)   In subsection (1) 'a relevant requirement' has the meaning given by section 50(2).

Interim care orders and emergency protection orders

52.   Amendments of Children Act 1989
Schedule 6 makes amendments of the provisions of the Children Act 1989 relating to interim care orders and emergency protection orders.

Transfer of tenancies

53.   Transfer of certain tenancies
Schedule 7 makes provision in relation to the transfer of certain tenancies on divorce etc. or on separation of cohabitants.

Dwelling-house subject to mortgage

54.   Dwelling-house subject to mortgage
(1)   In determining for the purposes of this Part whether a person is entitled to occupy a dwelling-house by virtue of an estate or interest, any right to possession of the dwelling-house conferred on a mortgagee of the dwelling-house under or by virtue of his mortgage is to be disregarded.

(2)   Subsection (1) applies whether or not the mortgagee is in possession.

(3)   Where a person ('A') is entitled to occupy a dwelling-house by virtue of an estate or interest, a connected person does not by virtue of—

(a)   any matrimonial home rights conferred by section 30, or

(b)   any rights conferred by an order under section 35 or 36,

have any larger right against the mortgagee to occupy the dwelling-house than A has by virtue of his estate or interest and of any contract with the mortgagee.

(4)   Subsection (3) does not apply, in the case of matrimonial home rights, if under section 31 those rights are a charge, affecting the mortgagee, on the estate or interest mortgaged.

(5)   In this section 'connected person', in relation to any person, means that person's spouse, former spouse, cohabitant or former cohabitant.

55.   Actions by mortgagees: joining connected persons as parties
(1)   This section applies if a mortgagee of land which consists of or includes a dwelling-house brings an action in any court for the enforcement of his security.

(2)   A connected person who is not already a party to the action is entitled to be made a party in the circumstances mentioned in subsection (3).

(3)   The circumstances are that—

(a)   the connected person is enabled by section 30(3) or (6) (or by section 30(3) or (6) as applied by section 35(13) or 36(13)), to meet the mortgagor's liabilities under the mortgage;

(b)   he has applied to the court before the action is finally disposed of in that court; and

(c)   the court sees no special reason against his being made a party to the action and is satisfied—

(i)   that he may be expected to make such payments or do such other things in or towards satisfaction of the mortgagor's liabilities or obligations as might affect the outcome of the proceedings; or

(ii)   that the expectation of it should be considered under section 36 of the Administration of Justice Act 1970.

(4)   In this section 'connected person' has the same meaning as in section 54.

56.   Actions by mortgagees: service of notice on certain persons

(1)   This section applies if a mortgagee of land which consists, or substantially consists, of a dwelling-house brings an action for the enforcement of his security, and at the relevant time there is—

(a)   in the case of unregistered land, a land charge of Class F registered against the person who is the estate owner at the relevant time or any person who, where the estate owner is a trustee, preceded him as trustee during the subsistence of the mortgage; or

(b)   in the case of registered land, a subsisting registration of—

(i)   a notice under section 31(10);

(ii)   a notice under section 2(8) of the Matrimonial Homes Act 1983; or

(iii)   a notice or caution under section 2(7) of the Matrimonial Homes Act 1967.

(2)   If the person on whose behalf—

(a)   the land charge is registered, or

(b)   the notice or caution is entered,

is not a party to the action, the mortgagee must serve notice of the action on him.

(3)   If—

(a)   an official search has been made on behalf of the mortgagee which would disclose any land charge of Class F, notice or caution within subsection (1)(a) or (b),

(b)   a certificate of the result of the search has been issued, and

(c)   the action is commenced within the priority period,

the relevant time is the date of the certificate.

(4)   In any other case the relevant time is the time when the action is commenced.

(5)   The priority period is, for both registered and unregistered land, the period for which, in accordance with section 1 1(5) and (6) of the Land Charges Act 1972, a certificate on an official search operates in favour of a purchaser.

Jurisdiction and procedure etc.

57.   Jurisdiction of courts

(1)   For the purposes of this Part 'the court' means the High Court, a county court or a magistrates' court.

(2)   Subsection (1) is subject to the provision made by or under the following provisions of this section, to section 59 and to any express provision as to the jurisdiction of any court made by any other provision of this Part.

(3)   The Lord Chancellor may by order specify proceedings under this Part which may only be commenced in—

(a)   a specified level of court;

(b)   a court which falls within a specified class of court; or

(c)   a particular court determined in accordance with, or specified in, the order.

(4)   The Lord Chancellor may by order specify circumstances in which specified proceedings under this Part may only be commenced in—

(a)   a specified level of court;

(b)   a court which falls within a specified class of court; or

(c)   a particular court determined in accordance with, or specified in, the order.

(5)   The Lord Chancellor may by order provide that in specified circumstances the whole, or any specified part of any specified proceedings under this Part is to be transferred to—

(a)   a specified level of court;

(b)   a court which falls within a specified class of court; or

(c)   a particular court determined in accordance with, or specified in, the order.

(6)   An order under subsection (5) may provide for the transfer to be made at any stage, or specified stage, of the proceedings and whether or not the proceedings, or any part of them, have already been transferred.

(7)   An order under subsection (5) may make such provision as the Lord Chancellor thinks appropriate for excluding specified proceedings from the operation of section 38 or 39 of the Matrimonial and Family Proceedings Act 1984 (transfer of family proceedings) or any other enactment which would otherwise govern the transfer of those proceedings, or any part of them.

(8)   For the purposes of subsections (3), (4) and (5), there are three levels of court—

(a)   the High Court;

(b)   any county court; and

(c)   any magistrates' court.

(9)   The Lord Chancellor may by order make provision for the principal registry of the Family Division of the High Court to be treated as if it were a county court for specified purposes of this Part, or of any provision made under this Part.

(10)   Any order under subsection (9) may make such provision as the Lord Chancellor thinks expedient for the purpose of applying (with or without modifications) provisions which apply in relation to the procedure in county courts to the principal registry when it acts as if it were a county court.

(11)   In this section 'specified' means specified by an order under this section.

58.   Contempt proceedings

The powers of the court in relation to contempt of court arising out of a person's failure to comply with an order under this Part may be exercised by the relevant judicial authority.

59.   Magistrates' courts

(1)   A magistrates' court shall not be competent to entertain any application, or make any order, involving any disputed question as to a party's entitlement to occupy any property by virtue of a beneficial estate or interest or contract or by virtue of any enactment giving him the right to remain in occupation, unless it is unnecessary to determine the question in order to deal with the application or make the order.

(2)   A magistrates' court may decline jurisdiction in any proceedings under this Part if it considers that the case can more conveniently be dealt with by another court.

(3)   The powers of a magistrates' court under section 63(2) of the Magistrates' Courts Act 1980 to suspend or rescind orders shall not apply in relation to any order made under this Part.

60.   Provision for third parties to act on behalf of victims of domestic violence

(1)   Rules of court may provide for a prescribed person, or any person in a prescribed category, ('a representative') to act on behalf of another in relation to proceedings to which this Part applies.

(2)   Rules made under this section may, in particular, authorise a representative to apply for an occupation order or for a non-molestation order for which the person on whose behalf the representative is acting could have applied.

(3)   Rules made under this section may prescribe—

(a)   conditions to be satisfied before a representative may make an application to the court on behalf of another; and

(b)   considerations to be taken into account by the court in determining whether, and if so how, to exercise any of its powers under this Part when a representative is acting on behalf of another.

(4)   Any rules made under this section may be made so as to have effect for a specified period and may make consequential or transitional provision with respect to the expiry of the specified period.

(5)   Any such rules may be replaced by further rules made under this section.

61.   Appeals

(1)   An appeal shall lie to the High Court against–

(a)   the making by a magistrates' court of any order under this Part, or

(b)   any refusal by a magistrates' court to make such an order,

but no appeal shall lie against any exercise by a magistrates' court of the power conferred by section 59(2).

(2)   On an appeal under this section, the High Court may make such orders as may be necessary to give effect to its determination of the appeal.

(3)   Where an order is made under subsection (2), the High Court may also make such incidental or consequential orders as appear to it to be just.

(4)   Any order of the High Court made on an appeal under this section (other than one directing that an application be re-heard by a magistrates' court) shall, for the purposes—

(a)   of the enforcement of the order, and

(b)   of any power to vary, revive or discharge orders,

be treated as if it were an order of the magistrates' court from which the appeal was brought and not an order of the High Court.

(5)   The Lord Chancellor may by order make provision as to the circumstances in which appeals may be made against decisions taken by courts on questions arising in connection with the transfer, or proposed transfer, of proceedings by virtue of any order under section 57(5).

(6)   Except to the extent provided for in any order made under subsection (5), no appeal may be made against any decision of a kind mentioned in that subsection.

General

62.   Meaning of 'cohabitants', 'relevant child' and 'associated persons'

(1)   For the purposes of this Part—

(a)   'cohabitants' are a man and a woman who, although not married to each other, are living together as husband and wife; and

(b)   'former cohabitants' is to be read accordingly, but does not include cohabitants who have subsequently married each other.

(2)   In this Part, 'relevant child', in relation to any proceedings under this Part, means—

(a)   any child who is living with or might reasonably be expected to live with either party to the proceedings;

(b)   any child in relation to whom an order under the Adoption Act 1976 or the Children Act 1989 is in question in the proceedings; and

(c)   any other child whose interests the court considers relevant.

(3)   For the purposes of this Part, a person is associated with another person if—

(a)   they are or have been married to each other;

(b)   they are cohabitants or former cohabitants;

(c)   they live or have lived in the same household, otherwise than merely by reason of one of them being the other's employee, tenant, lodger or boarder;

(d)   they are relatives;

(e)   they have agreed to marry one another (whether or not that agreement has been terminated);

(f)   in relation to any child, they are both persons falling within subsection (4); or

(g)   they are parties to the same family proceedings (other than proceedings under this Part).

(4)   A person falls within this subsection in relation to a child if—

(a)   he is a parent of the child; or

(b)   he has or has had parental responsibility for the child.

(5)   If a child has been adopted or has been freed for adoption by virtue of any of the enactments mentioned in section 16(1) of the Adoption Act 1976, two persons are also associated with each other for the purposes of this Part if—

(a)   one is a natural parent of the child or a parent of such a natural parent; and

(b)   the other is the child or any person—

(i)   who has become a parent of the child by virtue of an adoption order or has applied for an adoption order, or

(ii)   with whom the child has at any time been placed for adoption.

(6)   A body corporate and another person are not, by virtue of subsection (3)(f) or (g), to be regarded for the purposes of this Part as associated with each other.

63.   Interpretation of Part IV

(1)   In this Part—

'adoption order' has the meaning given by section 72(1) of the Adoption Act 1976;

'associated', in relation to a person, is to be read with section 62(3) to (6);

'child' means a person under the age of eighteen years;

'cohabitant' and 'former cohabitant' have the meaning given by section 62(1);

'the court' is to be read with section 57;

'development' means physical, intellectual, emotional, social or behavioural development;

'dwelling-house' includes (subject to subsection (4))—

(a)   any building or part of a building which is occupied as a dwelling,

(b)   any caravan, house-boat or structure which is occupied as a dwelling,

and any yard, garden, garage or outhouse belonging to it and occupied with it;

'family proceedings' means any proceedings—

(a)   under the inherent jurisdiction of the High Court in relation to children; or

(b)   under the enactments mentioned in subsection (2);

'harm'—

(a)   in relation to a person who has reached the age of eighteen years, means ill-treatment or the impairment of health; and

(b) in relation to a child, means ill-treatment or the impairment of health or development;

'health' includes physical or mental health;

'ill-treatment' includes forms of ill-treatment which are not physical and, in relation to a child, includes sexual abuse;

'matrimonial home rights' has the meaning given by section 30;

'mortgage', 'mortgagor' and 'mortgagee' have the same meaning as in the Law of Property Act 1925;

'mortgage payments' includes any payments which, under the terms of the mortgage, the mortgagor is required to make to any person;

'non-molestation order' has the meaning given by section 42(1);

'occupation order' has the meaning given by section 39;

'parental responsibility' has the same meaning as in the Children Act 1989;

'relative', in relation to a person, means—

(a) the father, mother, stepfather, stepmother, son, daughter, stepson, stepdaughter, grandmother, grandfather, grandson or granddaughter of that person or of that person's spouse or former spouse, or

(b) the brother, sister, uncle, aunt, niece or nephew (whether of the full blood or of the half blood or by affinity) of that person or of that person's spouse or former spouse,

and includes, in relation to a person who is living or has lived with another person as husband and wife, any person who would fall within paragraph (a) or (b) if the parties were married to each other;

'relevant child', in relation to any proceedings under this Part, has the meaning given by section 62(2);

'the relevant judicial authority', in relation to any order under this Part, means—

(a) where the order was made by the High Court, a judge of that court;

(b) where the order was made by a county court, a judge or district judge of that or any other county court; or

(c) where the order was made by a magistrates' court, any magistrates' court.

(2) The enactments referred to in the definition of 'family proceedings' are—

(a) Part II;

(b) this Part;

(c) the Matrimonial Causes Act 1973;

(d) the Adoption Act 1976;

(e) the Domestic Proceedings and Magistrates' Courts Act 1978;

(f) Part III of the Matrimonial and Family Proceedings Act 1984;

(g) Parts I, II and IV of the Children Act 1989;

(h) section 30 of the Human Fertilisation and Embryology Act 1990.

(3) Where the question of whether harm suffered by a child is significant turns on the child's health or development, his health or development shall be compared with that which could reasonably be expected of a similar child.

(4) For the purposes of sections 31, 32, 53 and 54 and such other provisions of this Part (if any) as may be prescribed, this Part is to have effect as if paragraph (b) of the definition of 'dwelling-house' were omitted.

(5) It is hereby declared that this Part applies as between the parties to a marriage even though either of them is, or has at any time during the marriage been, married to more than one person.

PART V
SUPPLEMENTAL

64. Provision for separate representation for children

(1)   The Lord Chancellor may by regulations provide for the separate representation of children in proceedings in England and Wales which relate to any matter in
respect of which a question has arisen, or may arise, under—

    (a)   Part II;

    (b)   Part IV;

    (c)   the 1973 Act; or

    (d)   the Domestic Proceedings and Magistrates' Courts Act 1978.

(2)   The regulations may provide for such representation only in specified
circumstances.

65. Rules, regulations and orders

(1)   Any power to make rules, orders or regulations which is conferred by this
Act is exercisable by statutory instrument.

(2)   Any statutory instrument made under this Act may—

    (a)   contain such incidental, supplemental, consequential and transitional
provision as the Lord Chancellor considers appropriate; and

    (b)   make different provision for different purposes.

(3)   Any statutory instrument containing an order, rules or regulations made
under this Act, other than an order made under section 5(8) or 67(3), shall be subject
to annulment by a resolution of either House of Parliament.

(4)   No order shall be made under section 5(8) unless a draft of the order has been
laid before, and approved by a resolution of, each House of Parliament.

(5)   This section does not apply to rules of court made, or any power to make rules
of court, for the purposes of this Act.

66. Consequential amendments, transitional provisions and repeals

(1)   Schedule 8 makes minor and consequential amendments.

(2)   Schedule 9 provides for the making of other modifications consequential on
provisions of this Act, makes transitional provisions and provides for savings.

(3)   Schedule 10 repeals certain enactments.

67. Short title, commencement and extent

(1)   This Act may be cited as the Family Law Act 1996.

(2)   Section 65 and this section come into force on the passing of this Act.

(3)   The other provisions of this Act come into force on such day as the Lord
Chancellor may by order appoint; and different days may be appointed for different
purposes.

(4)   This Act, other than section 17, extends only to England and Wales, except
that—

    (a)   in Schedule 8—

        (i)   the amendments of section 38 of the Family Law Act 1986 extend also
to Northern Ireland;

        (ii)   the amendments of the Judicial Proceedings (Regulation of Reports)
Act 1926 extend also to Scotland; and

        (iii) the amendments of the Maintenance Orders Act 1950, the Civil
Jurisdiction and Judgments Act 1982, the Finance Act 1985 and sections 42 and

51 of the Family Law Act 1986 extend also to both Northern Ireland and Scotland; and

(b)   in Schedule 10, the repeal of section 2(1)(b) of the Domestic and Appellate Proceedings (Restriction of Publicity) Act 1968 extends also to Scotland.

SCHEDULES

Section 9(6)

SCHEDULE 1
ARRANGEMENTS FOR THE FUTURE

The first exemption

1.   The circumstances referred to in section 9(7)(a) are that—

(a)   the requirements of section 11 have been satisfied;

(b)   the applicant has, during the period for reflection and consideration, taken such steps as are reasonably practicable to try to reach agreement about the parties' financial arrangements; and

(c)   the applicant has made an application to the court for financial relief and has complied with all requirements of the court in relation to proceedings for financial relief but—

(i)   the other party has delayed in complying with requirements of the court or has otherwise been obstructive; or

(ii)   for reasons which are beyond the control of the applicant, or of the other party, the court has been prevented from obtaining the information which it requires to determine the financial position of the parties.

The second exemption

2.   The circumstances referred to in section 9(7)(b) are that—

(a)   the requirements of section 11 have been satisfied;

(b)   the applicant has, during the period for reflection and consideration, taken such steps as are reasonably practicable to try to reach agreement about the parties' financial arrangements;

(c)   because of—

(i)   the ill health or disability of the applicant, the other party or a child of the family (whether physical or mental), or

(ii)   an injury suffered by the applicant, the other party or a child of the family,

the applicant has not been able to reach agreement with the other party about those arrangements and is unlikely to be able to do so in the foreseeable future; and

(d)   a delay in making the order applied for under section 3—

(i)   would be significantly detrimental to the welfare of any child of the family; or

(ii)   would be seriously prejudicial to the applicant.

The third exemption

3.   The circumstances referred to in section 9(7)(c) are that—

(a)   the requirements of section 11 have been satisfied;

(b)   the applicant has found it impossible to contact the other party; and

(c)   as a result, it has been impossible for the applicant to reach agreement with the other party about their financial arrangements.

The fourth exemption

4. The circumstances referred to in section 9(7)(d) are that—

(a) the requirements of section 11 have been satisfied;

(b) an occupation order or a non-molestation order is in force in favour of the applicant or a child of the family, made against the other party;

(c) the applicant has, during the period for reflection and consideration, taken such steps as are reasonably practicable to try to reach agreement about the parties' financial arrangements;

(d) the applicant has not been able to reach agreement with the other party about those arrangements and is unlikely to be able to do so in the foreseeable future; and

(e) a delay in making the order applied for under section 3—

(i) would be significantly detrimental to the welfare of any child of the family; or

(ii) would be seriously prejudicial to the applicant.

Court orders and agreements

5.—(1) Section 9 is not to be read as requiring any order or agreement to have been carried into effect at the time when the court is considering whether arrangements for the future have been made by the parties.

(2) The fact that an appeal is pending against an order of the kind mentioned in section 9(2)(a) is to be disregarded.

Financial arrangements

6. In section 9 and this Schedule 'financial arrangements' has the same meaning as in section 34(2) of the 1973 Act.

Negotiated agreements

7. In section 9(2)(b) 'negotiated agreement' means a written agreement between the parties as to future arrangements—

(a) which has been reached as the result of mediation or any other form of negotiation involving a third party; and

(b) which satisfies such requirements as may be imposed by rules of court.

Declarations

8.—(1) Any declaration of a kind mentioned in section 9—

(a) must be in a prescribed form;

(b) must, in prescribed cases, be accompanied by such documents as may be prescribed; and

(c) must, in prescribed cases, satisfy such other requirements as may be prescribed.

(2) The validity of a divorce order or separation order made by reference to such a declaration is not to be affected by any inaccuracy in the declaration.

Interpretation

9. In this Schedule—

"financial relief" has such meaning as may be prescribed; and

"prescribed" means prescribed by rules of court.

Section 15 SCHEDULE 2
FINANCIAL PROVISION

Introductory

1.   Part II of the 1973 Act (financial provision and property adjustment orders) is amended as follows.

The orders

2.   For section 21 (definitions) substitute—

'21.   Financial provision and property adjustment orders
   (1)   For the purposes of this Act, a financial provision order is—
      (a)   an order that a party must make in favour of another person such periodical payments, for such term, as may be specified (a ''periodical payments order'');
      (b)   an order that a party must, to the satisfaction of the court, secure in favour of another person such periodical payments, for such term, as may be specified (a ''secured periodical payments order'');
      (c)   an order that a party must make a payment in favour of another person of such lump sum or sums as may be specified (an ''order for the payment of a lump sum'').
   (2)   For the purposes of this Act, a property adjustment order is—
      (a)   an order that a party must transfer such of his or her property as may be specified in favour of the other party or a child of the family;
      (b) an order that a settlement of such property of a party as may be specified must be made, to the satisfaction of the court, for the benefit of the other party and of the children of the family, or either or any of them;
      (c)   an order varying, for the benefit of the parties and of the children of the family, or either or any of them, any marriage settlement;
      (d) an order extinguishing or reducing the interest of either of the parties under any marriage settlement.
   (3)   Subject to section 40 below, where an order of the court under this Part of this Act requires a party to make or secure a payment in favour of another person or to transfer property in favour of any person, that payment must be made or secured or that property transferred—
      (a)   if that other person is the other party to the marriage, to that other party; and
      (b)   if that other person is a child of the family, according to the terms of the order—
         (i)   to the child; or
         (ii)   to such other person as may be specified, for the benefit of that child.
   (4)   References in this section to the property of a party are references to any property to which that party is entitled either in possession or in reversion.
   (5)   Any power of the court under this Part of this Act to make such an order as is mentioned in subsection (2)(b) to (d) above is exercisable even though there are no children of the family.
   (6)   In this section—
''marriage settlement'' means an ante-nuptial or post-nuptial settlement made on the parties (including one made by will or codicil);

''party'' means a party to a marriage; and
''specified'' means specified in the order in question.'

Financial provision: divorce and separation

3.   Insert, before section 23—

'22A.   Financial provision orders: divorce and separation
(1)   On an application made under this section, the court may at the appropriate time make one or more financial provision orders in favour of—
(a)   a party to the marriage to which the application relates; or
(b)   any of the children of the family.
(2)   The ''appropriate time'' is any time—
(a)   after a statement of marital breakdown has been received by the court and before any application for a divorce order or for a separation order is made to the court by reference to that statement;
(b)   when an application for a divorce order or separation order has been made under section 3 of the 1996 Act and has not been withdrawn;
(c)   when an application for a divorce order has been made under section 4 of the 1996 Act and has not been withdrawn;
(d)   after a divorce order has been made;
(e)   when a separation order is in force.
(3)   The court may make—
(a)   a combined order against the parties on one occasion,
(b)   separate orders on different occasions,
(c)   different orders in favour of different children,
(d)   different orders from time to time in favour of the same child,
but may not make, in favour of the same party, more than one periodical payments order, or more than one order for payment of a lump sum, in relation to any marital proceedings, whether in the course of the proceedings or by reference to a divorce order or separation order made in the proceedings.
(4)   If it would not otherwise be in a position to make a financial provision order in favour of a party or child of the family, the court may make an interim periodical payments order, an interim order for the payment of a lump sum or a series of such orders, in favour of that party or child.
(5)   Any order for the payment of a lump sum made under this section may—
(a)   provide for the payment of the lump sum by instalments of such amounts as may be specified in the order; and
(b)   require the payment of the instalments to be secured to the satisfaction of the court.
(6)   Nothing in subsection (5) above affects—
(a)   the power of the court under this section to make an order for the payment of a lump sum; or
(b)   the provisions of this Part of this Act as to the beginning of the term specified in any periodical payments order or secured periodical payments order.
(7)   Subsection (8) below applies where the court—
(a)   makes an order under this section (''the main order'') for the payment of a lump sum; and
(b)   directs—

(i)   that payment of that sum, or any part of it, is to be deferred; or

(ii)   that that sum, or any part of it, is to be paid by instalments.

(8)   In such a case, the court may, on or at any time after making the main order, make an order (''the order for interest'') for the amount deferred, or the instalments, to carry interest (at such rate as may be specified in the order for interest)—

(a)   from such date, not earlier than the date of the main order, as may be so specified;

(b)   until the date when the payment is due.

(9)   This section is to be read subject to any restrictions imposed by this Act and to section 19 of the 1996 Act.

22B.   Restrictions affecting section 22A

(1)   No financial provision order, other than an interim order, may be made under section 22A above so as to take effect before the making of a divorce order or separation order in relation to the marriage, unless the court is satisfied—

(a)   that the circumstances of the case are exceptional; and

(b)   that it would be just and reasonable for the order to be so made.

(2)   Except in the case of an interim periodical payments order, the court may not make a financial provision order under section 22A above at any time while the period for reflection and consideration is interrupted under section 7(8) of the 1996 Act.

(3)   No financial provision order may be made under section 22A above by reference to the making of a statement of marital breakdown if, by virtue of section 5(3) or 7(9) of the 1996 Act (lapse of divorce or separation process), it has ceased to be possible—

(a)   for an application to be made by reference to that statement; or

(b)   for an order to be made on such an application.

(4)   No financial provision order may be made under section 22A after a divorce order has been made, or while a separation order is in force, except—

(a)   in response to an application made before the divorce order or separation order was made; or

(b)   on a subsequent application made with the leave of the court.'

(5)   In this section, ''period for reflection and consideration'' means the period fixed by section 7 of the 1996 Act.'

Financial provision: nullity of marriage

4.   For section 23 substitute—

'23.   Financial provision orders: nullity

(1)   On or after granting a decree of nullity of marriage (whether before or after the decree is made absolute), the court may, on an application made under this section, make one or more financial provision orders in favour of—

(a)   either party to the marriage; or

(b)   any child of the family.

(2)   Before granting a decree in any proceedings for nullity of marriage, the court may make against either or each of the parties to the marriage—

(a)   an interim periodical payments order, an interim order for the payment of a lump sum, or a series of such orders, in favour of the other party;

(b)   an interim periodical payments order, an interim order for the payment of a lump sum, a series of such orders or any one or more other financial provision orders in favour of each child of the family.

(3)   Where any such proceedings are dismissed, the court may (either immediately or within a reasonable period after the dismissal) make any one or more financial provision orders in favour of each child of the family.

(4)   An order under this section that a party to a marriage must pay a lump sum to the other party may be made for the purpose of enabling that other party to meet any liabilities or expenses reasonably incurred by him or her in maintaining himself or herself or any child of the family before making an application for an order under this section in his or her favour.

(5)   An order under this section for the payment of a lump sum to or for the benefit of a child of the family may be made for the purpose of enabling any liabilities or expenses reasonably incurred by or for the benefit of that child before the making of an application for an order under this section in his favour to be met.

(6)   An order under this section for the payment of a lump sum may—

(a)   provide for the payment of that sum by instalments of such amount as may be specified in the order; and

(b)   require the payment of the instalments to be secured to the satisfaction of the court.

(7)   Nothing in subsections (4) to (6) above affects—

(a)   the power under subsection (1) above to make an order for the payment of a lump sum; or

(b)   the provisions of this Act as to the beginning of the term specified in any periodical payments order or secured periodical payments order.

(8)   The powers of the court under this section to make one or more financial provision orders are exercisable against each party to the marriage by the making of—

(a)   a combined order on one occasion, or

(b)   separate orders on different occasions,

but the court may not make more than one periodical payments order, or more than one order for payment of a lump sum, in favour of the same party.

(9)   The powers of the court under this section so far as they consist in power to make one or more orders in favour of the children of the family—

(a)   may be exercised differently in favour of different children; and

(b)   except in the case of the power conferred by subsection (3) above, may be exercised from time to time in favour of the same child; and

(c)   in the case of the power conferred by that subsection, if it is exercised by the making of a financial provision order of any kind in favour of a child, shall include power to make, from time to time, further financial provision orders of that or any other kind in favour of that child.

(10)   Where an order is made under subsection (1) above in favour of a party to the marriage on or after the granting of a decree of nullity of marriage, neither the order nor any settlement made in pursuance of the order takes effect unless the decree has been made absolute.

(11)   Subsection (10) above does not affect the power to give a direction under section 30 below for the settlement of an instrument by conveyancing counsel.

(12)   Where the court—

(a)   makes an order under this section ("the main order") for the payment of a lump sum; and

(b)   directs—

    (i)   that payment of that sum or any part of it is to be deferred; or

    (ii)   that that sum or any part of it is to be paid by instalments,

it may, on or at any time after making the main order, make an order ("the order for interest") for the amount deferred or the instalments to carry interest at such rate as may be specified by the order for interest from such date, not earlier than the date of the main order, as may be so specified, until the date when payment of it is due.

(13)   This section is to be read subject to any restrictions imposed by this Act.'

Property adjustment orders: divorce and separation

5.   Insert, before section 24—

'23A.   Property adjustment orders: divorce and separation

(1)   On an application made under this section, the court may, at any time mentioned in section 22A(2) above, make one or more property adjustment orders.

(2)   If the court makes, in favour of the same party to the marriage, more than one property adjustment order in relation to any marital proceedings, whether in the course of the proceedings or by reference to a divorce order or separation order made in the proceedings, each order must fall within a different paragraph of section 21(2) above.

(3)   The court shall exercise its powers under this section, so far as is practicable, by making on one occasion all such provision as can be made by way of one or more property adjustment orders in relation to the marriage as it thinks fit.

(4)   Subsection (3) above does not affect section 31 or 31A below.

(5)   This section is to be read subject to any restrictions imposed by this Act and to section 19 of the 1996 Act.

23B.   Restrictions affecting section 23A

(1)   No property adjustment order may be made under section 23A above so as to take effect before the making of a divorce order or separation order in relation to the marriage unless the court is satisfied—

(a)   that the circumstances of the case are exceptional; and

(b)   that it would be just and reasonable for the order to be so made.

(2)   The court may not make a property adjustment order under section 23A above at any time while the period for reflection and consideration is interrupted under section 7(8) of the 1996 Act.

(3)   No property adjustment order may be made under section 23A above by virtue of the making of a statement of marital breakdown if, by virtue of section 5(3) or 7(5) of the 1996 Act (lapse of divorce or separation process), it has ceased to be possible—

(a)   for an application to be made by reference to that statement; or

(b)   for an order to be made on such an application.

(4)   No property adjustment order may be made under section 23A above after a divorce order has been made, or while a separation order is in force, except—

(a)   in response to an application made before the divorce order or separation order was made; or

(b)   on a subsequent application made with the leave of the court.

(5)   In this section, "period for reflection and consideration" means the period fixed by section 7 of the 1996 Act.'

Property adjustment orders: nullity

6.   For section 24, substitute—

'24.   Property adjustment orders: nullity of marriage

(1)   On or after granting a decree of nullity of marriage adjustment (whether before or after the decree is made absolute), the court may, on an application made under this section, make one or more property adjustment orders in relation to the marriage.

(2)   The court shall exercise its powers under this section, so far as is practicable, by making on one occasion all such provision as can be made by way of one or more property adjustment orders in relation to the marriage as it thinks fit.

(3)   Subsection (2) above does not affect section 31 or 31A below.

(4)   Where a property adjustment order is made under this section on or after the granting of a decree of nullity of marriage, neither the order nor any settlement made in pursuance of the order is to take effect unless the decree has been made absolute.

(5)   That does not affect the power to give a direction under section 30 below for the settlement of an instrument by conveyancing counsel.

(6)   This section is to be read subject to any restrictions imposed by this Act.'

Period of secured and unsecured payments orders

7.—(1)   In section 28(1) (duration of a continuing financial provision order in favour of a party to a marriage), for paragraphs (a) and (b) substitute—

'(a)   a term specified in the order which is to begin before the making of the order shall begin no earlier—

(i)   where the order is made by virtue of section 22A(2)(a) or (b) above, unless sub-paragraph (ii) below applies, than the beginning of the day on which the statement of marital breakdown in question was received by the court;

(ii)   where the order is made by virtue of section 22A(2)(b) above and the application for the divorce order was made following cancellation of an order preventing divorce under section 10 of the 1996 Act, than the date of the making of that application;

(iii)   where the order is made by virtue of section 22A(2)(c) above, than the date of the making of the application for the divorce order; or

(iv)   in any other case, than the date of the making of the application on which the order is made;

(b)   a term specified in a periodical payments order or secured periodical payments order shall be so defined as not to extend beyond—

(i)   in the case of a periodical payments order, the death of the party by whom the payments are to be made; or

(ii)   in either case, the death of the party in whose favour the order was made or the remarriage of that party following the making of a divorce order or decree of nullity.'

(2)   In section 29 (duration of continuing financial provision order in favour of a child of the family) insert after subsection (1)—

'(1A)   The term specified in a periodical payments order or secured periodical payments order made in favour of a child shall be such term as the court thinks fit.

(1B)   If that term is to begin before the making of the order, it may do so no earlier than—

(a)   in the case of an order made by virtue of section 22A(2)(a) or (b) above, except where paragraph (b) below applies, the beginning of the day on which the statement of marital breakdown in question was received by the court;

(b)   in the case of an order made by virtue of section 22A(2)(b) above where the application for the divorce order was made following cancellation of an order preventing divorce under section 10 of the 1996 Act, the date of the making of that application;

(c)   in the case of an order made by virtue of section 22A(2)(c) above, the date of the making of the application for the divorce order; or

(d)   in any other case, the date of the making of the application on which the order is made.'

Variations etc. following reconciliations

8.   Insert after section 31—

'31A.   Variation etc. following reconciliations

(1)   Where, at a time before the making of a divorce order—

(a)   an order ("a paragraph (a) order") for the payment of a lump sum has been made under section 22A above in favour of a party,

(b)   such an order has been made in favour of a child of the family but the payment has not yet been made, or

(c)   a property adjustment order ("a paragraph (c) order") has been made under section 23A above,

the court may, on an application made jointly by the parties to the marriage, vary or discharge the order.

(2)   Where the court varies or discharges a paragraph (a) order, it may order the repayment of an amount equal to the whole or any part of the lump sum.

(3)   Where the court varies or discharges a paragraph (c) order, it may (if the order has taken effect)—

(a)   order any person to whom property was transferred in pursuance of the paragraph (c) order to transfer—

(i)   the whole or any part of that property, or

(ii)   the whole or any part of any property appearing to the court to represent that property,

in favour of a party to the marriage or a child of the family; or

(b)   vary any settlement to which the order relates in favour of any person or extinguish or reduce any person's interest under that settlement.

(4)   Where the court acts under subsection (3) it may make such supplemental provision (including a further property adjustment order or an order for the payment of a lump sum) as it thinks appropriate in consequence of any transfer, variation, extinguishment or reduction to be made under paragraph (a) or (b) of that subsection.

(5)   Sections 24A and 30 above apply for the purposes of this section as they apply where the court makes a property adjustment order under section 23A or 24 above.

(6)   The court shall not make an order under subsection (2), (3) or (4) above unless it appears to it that there has been a reconciliation between the parties to the marriage.

(7)   The court shall also not make an order under subsection (3) or (4) above unless it appears to it that the order will not prejudice the interests of—

(a)   any child of the family; or

(b)   any person who has acquired any right or interest in consequence of the paragraph (c) order and is not a party to the marriage or a child of the family.'

Section 19(5)   SCHEDULE 3
                                      STAY OF PROCEEDINGS

Introductory

1.   Schedule 1 to the Domicile and Matrimonial Proceedings Act 1973 (which relates to the staying of matrimonial proceedings) is amended as follows.

Interpretation

2.   In paragraph 1, for 'The following five paragraphs' substitute 'Paragraphs 2 to 6 below'.

3.   For paragraph 2 substitute—

'2.—(1)   ''Matrimonial proceedings'' means—

(a)   marital proceedings;

(b)   proceedings for nullity of marriage;

(c)   proceedings for a declaration as to the validity of a marriage of the petitioner; or

(d)   proceedings for a declaration as to the subsistence of such a marriage.

(2)   ''Marital proceedings'' has the meaning given by section 20 of the Family Law Act 1996.

(3)   ''Divorce proceedings'' means marital proceedings that are divorce proceedings by virtue of that section.'

4.   Insert, after paragraph 4—

'4A.—(1)   ''Statement of marital breakdown'' has the same meaning as in the Family Law Act 1996.

(2)   ''Relevant statement'' in relation to any marital proceedings, means—

(a)   the statement of marital breakdown with which the proceedings commenced; or

(b)   if the proceedings are for the conversion of a separation order into a divorce order under section 4 of the Family Law Act 1996, the statement of marital breakdown by reference to which the separation order was made.'

Duty to furnish particulars of concurrent proceedings

5.   For paragraph 7 substitute—

'7.—(1)   While marital proceedings are pending in the court with respect to a marriage, this paragraph applies—

(a)   to the party or parties to the marriage who made the relevant statement; and

(b)   in prescribed circumstances where the statement was made by only one party, to the other party.

(2)   While matrimonial proceedings of any other kind are pending in the court with respect to a marriage and the trial or first trial in those proceedings has not begun, this paragraph applies—

(a)   to the petitioner; and

(b)   if the respondent has included a prayer for relief in his answer, to the respondent.

(3)   A person to whom this paragraph applies must give prescribed information about any proceedings which—

(a)   he knows to be continuing in another jurisdiction; and

(b)   are in respect of the marriage or capable of affecting its validity or subsistence.

(4)   The information must be given in such manner, to such persons and on such occasions as may be prescribed.'

Obligatory stays in divorce cases

6.—(1)   Paragraph 8 is amended as follows.

(2)   For the words before paragraph (a) of sub-paragraph (1) substitute—

'(1)   This paragraph applies where divorce proceedings are continuing in the court with respect to a marriage.

(2)   Where it appears to the court, on the application of a party to the marriage—'.

(3)   In sub-paragraph (1), in the words after paragraph (d), for 'proceedings' substitute 'divorce proceedings'.

(4)   For sub-paragraph (2) substitute—

'(3)   The effect of such an order is that, while it is in force—

(a)   no application for a divorce order in relation to the marriage may be made either by reference to the relevant statement or by reference to any subsequent statement of marital breakdown; and

(b)   if such an application has been made, no divorce order may be made on that application.'

Discretionary stays

7.—(1)   Paragraph 9 is amended as follows.

(2)   For sub-paragraph (1), substitute—

'(1)   Sub-paragraph (1A) below applies where—

(a)   marital proceedings are continuing in the court; or

(b)   matrimonial proceedings of any other kind are continuing in the court, if the trial or first trial in the proceedings has not begun.

(1A)   The court may make an order staying the proceedings if it appears to the court—

(a)   that proceedings in respect of the marriage, or capable of affecting its validity or subsistence, are continuing in another jurisdiction; and

(b)   that the balance of fairness (including convenience) as between the parties to the marriage is such that it is appropriate for proceedings in that jurisdiction to be disposed of before further steps are taken in the proceedings to which the order relates.'

(3)   For sub-paragraph (3) substitute—

'(3)   Where an application for a stay is pending under paragraph 8 above, the court shall not make an order under sub-paragraph (1A) staying marital proceedings in relation to the marriage.'

(4)   In sub-paragraph 4, after 'pending in the court,' insert 'other than marital proceedings,'.

(5)   After sub-paragraph (4), insert—

'(5)   The effect of an order under sub-paragraph (1A) for a stay of marital proceedings is that, while it is in force—

(a)   no application for a divorce order or separation order in relation to the marriage may be made either by reference to the relevant statement or by reference to any subsequent statement of marital breakdown; and

(b)   if such an application has been made, no divorce order or separation order shall be made on that application.'

Discharge of orders

8.   In paragraph 10, for sub-paragraph (2), substitute—

'(1A)   Where the court discharges an order staying any proceedings, it may direct that the whole or a specified part of any period while the order has been in force—

(a)   is not to count towards any period specified in section 5(3) or 7(9) of the Family Law Act 1996; or

(b)   is to count towards any such period only for specified purposes.

(2)   Where the court discharges an order under paragraph 8 above, it shall not again make such an order in relation to the marriage except in a case where the obligation to do so arises under that paragraph following receipt by the court of a statement of marital breakdown after the discharge of the order.'

Ancillary matters

9.—(1)   Paragraph 11 is amended as follows.

(2)   For sub-paragraph (1) substitute—

'(1)   Sub-paragraphs (2) and (3) below apply where a stay of marital proceedings or proceedings for nullity of marriage—

(a)   has been imposed by reference to proceedings in a related jurisdiction for divorce, separation or nullity of marriage, and

(b)   is in force.

(1A)   In this paragraph—

''lump sum order'', in relation to a stay, means an order—

(a)   under section 22A or 23, 31 or 31A of the Matrimonial Causes Act 1973 which is an order for the payment of a lump sum for the purposes of Part II of that Act, or

(b)   made in any equivalent circumstances under Schedule 1 to the Children Act 1989 and of a kind mentioned in paragraph 1(2)(a) or (b) of that Schedule,

so far as it satisfies the condition mentioned in sub-paragraph (1C) below;

''the other proceedings'', in relation to a stay, means the proceedings in another jurisdiction by reference to which the stay was imposed;

''relevant order'', in relation to a stay, means—

(a)   any financial provision order (including an interim order), other than a lump sum order;

(b)   any order made in equivalent circumstances under Schedule 1 to the Children Act 1989 and of a kind mentioned in paragraph 1(2)(a) or (b) of that Schedule;

(c)   any section 8 order under the Act of 1989; and

(d)   except for the purposes of sub-paragraph (3) below, any order restraining a person from removing a child out of England and Wales or out of the care of another person,

so far as it satisfies the condition mentioned in sub-paragraph (1C) below.

(1C)   The condition is that the order is, or (apart from this paragraph) could be, made in connection with the proceedings to which the stay applies.'

(3)   In sub-paragraph (2)—

(a)   for 'any proceedings are stayed' substitute 'this paragraph applies in relation to a stay';

(b)   in paragraph (a), and in the first place in paragraph (c), omit 'in connection with the stayed proceedings'; and

(c)   in paragraphs (b) and (c), for 'made in connection with the stayed proceedings' substitute 'already made'.

(4)   In sub-paragraph (3)—

(a)   for 'any proceedings are stayed' substitute 'this paragraph applies in relation to a stay';

(b)   in paragraph (a), for 'made in connection with the stayed proceedings' substitute 'already made';

(c)   in paragraphs (b) and (c), omit 'in connection with the stayed proceedings'.

(5)   In sub-paragraph (3A), for the words before 'any order made' substitute—
'Where a secured periodical payments order within the meaning of the Matrimonial Causes Act 1973—

(a)   has been made under section 22A(1)(b) or 23(1)(b) or (2)(b) of that Act, but

(b)   ceases to have effect by virtue of sub-paragraph (2) or (3) above,'.

(6)   For sub-paragraph (4), substitute—
'(4)   Nothing in sub-paragraphs (2) and (3) above affects any relevant order or lump sum order or any power to make such an order in so far as—

(a)   where the stay applies to matrimonial proceedings other than marital proceedings, the order has been made or the power may be exercised following the receipt by the court of a statement of marital breakdown;

(b)   where the stay is of marital proceedings, the order has been made or the power may be exercised in matrimonial proceedings of any other kind; or

(c)   where the stay is of divorce proceedings only, the order has been made or the power may be exercised—

(i)   in matrimonial proceedings which are not marital proceedings, or

(ii)   in marital proceedings in which an application has been made for a separation order.'

(7)   In sub-paragraph (5)(c), for the words from 'in connection' onwards substitute 'where a stay no longer applies'.

Section 32   SCHEDULE 4
        PROVISIONS SUPPLEMENTARY TO SECTIONS 30 AND 31

Interpretation

1.—(1)   In this Schedule—

(a)   any reference to a solicitor includes a reference to a licensed conveyancer or a recognised body, and

(b)   any reference to a person's solicitor includes a reference to a licensed conveyancer or recognised body acting for that person.

(2)   In sub-paragraph (1)—

'licensed conveyancer' has the meaning given by section 11(2) of the Administration of Justice Act 1985;

'recognised body' means a body corporate for the time being recognised under section 9 (incorporated practices) or section 32 (provision of conveyancing by recognised bodies) of that Act.

Restriction on registration where spouse entitled to more than one charge

2.   Where one spouse is entitled by virtue of section 31 to a registrable charge in respect of each of two or more dwelling-houses, only one of the charges to which that spouse is so entitled shall be registered under section 31(10) or under section 2 of the Land Charges Act 1972 at any one time, and if any of those charges is registered under either of those provisions the Chief Land Registrar, on being satisfied that any other of them is so registered, shall cancel the registration of the charge first registered.

Contract for sale of house affected by registered charge to include term requiring cancellation of registration before completion

3.—(1)   Where one spouse is entitled by virtue of section 31 to a charge on an estate in a dwelling-house and the charge is registered under section 31(10) or section 2 of the Land Charges Act 1972, it shall be a term of any contract for the sale of that estate whereby the vendor agrees to give vacant possession of the dwelling-house on completion of the contract that the vendor will before such completion procure the cancellation of the registration of the charge at his expense.

(2)   Sub-paragraph (1) shall not apply to any such contract made by a vendor who is entitled to sell the estate in the dwelling-house freed from any such charge.

(3)   If, on the completion of such a contract as is referred to in sub-paragraph (1), there is delivered to the purchaser or his solicitor an application by the spouse entitled to the charge for the cancellation of the registration of that charge, the term of the contract for which sub-paragraph (1) provides shall be deemed to have been performed.

(4)   This paragraph applies only if and so far as a contrary intention is not expressed in the contract.

(5)   This paragraph shall apply to a contract for exchange as it applies to a contract for sale.

(6)   This paragraph shall, with the necessary modifications, apply to a contract for the grant of a lease or underlease of a dwelling-house as it applies to a contract for the sale of an estate in a dwelling-house.

Cancellation of registration after termination of marriage, etc.

4.—(1)   Where a spouse's matrimonial home rights are a charge on an estate in the dwelling-house and the charge is registered under section 31(10) or under section 2 of the Land Charges Act 1972, the Chief Land Registrar shall, subject to sub-paragraph (2), cancel the registration of the charge if he is satisfied—

(a)   by the production of a certificate or other sufficient evidence, that either spouse is dead, or

(b)   by the production of an official copy of a decree or order of a court, that the marriage in question has been terminated otherwise than by death, or

(c)   by the production of an order of the court, that the spouse's matrimonial home rights constituting the charge have been terminated by the order.

(2)   Where—

(a)   the marriage in question has been terminated by the death of the spouse entitled to an estate in the dwelling-house or otherwise than by death, and

(b)   an order affecting the charge of the spouse not so entitled had been made under section 33(5),

then if, after the making of the order, registration of the charge was renewed or the charge registered in pursuance of sub-paragraph (3), the Chief Land Registrar shall not cancel the registration of the charge in accordance with sub-paragraph (1) unless he is also satisfied that the order has ceased to have effect.

(3)   Where such an order has been made, then, for the purposes of sub-paragraph (2), the spouse entitled to the charge affected by the order may—

(a)   if before the date of the order the charge was registered under section 31(10) or under section 2 of the Land Charges Act 1972, renew the registration of the charge, and

(b)   if before the said date the charge was not so registered, register the charge under section 31(10) or under section 2 of the Land Charges Act 1972.

(4)   Renewal of the registration of a charge in pursuance of sub-paragraph (3) shall be effected in such manner as may be prescribed, and an application for such renewal or for registration of a charge in pursuance of that sub-paragraph shall contain such particulars of any order affecting the charge made under section 33(5) as may be prescribed.

(5)   The renewal in pursuance of sub-paragraph (3) of the registration of a charge shall not affect the priority of the charge.

(6)   In this paragraph 'prescribed' means prescribed by rules made under section 16 of the Land Charges Act 1972 or section 144 of the Land Registration Act 1925, as the circumstances of the case require.

Release of matrimonial home rights

5.—(1)   A spouse entitled to matrimonial home rights may by a release in writing release those rights or release them as respects part only of the dwelling-house affected by them.

(2)   Where a contract is made for the sale of an estate or interest in a dwelling-house, or for the grant of a lease or underlease of a dwelling-house, being (in either case) a dwelling-house affected by a charge registered under section 31(10) or under section 2 of the Land Charges Act 1972, then, without prejudice to sub-paragraph (1), the matrimonial home rights constituting the charge shall be

deemed to have been released on the happening of whichever of the following events first occurs—

(a)   the delivery to the purchaser or lessee, as the case may be, or his solicitor on completion of the contract of an application by the spouse entitled to the charge for the cancellation of the registration of the charge; or

(b)   the lodging of such an application at Her Majesty's Land Registry.

Postponement of priority of charge

6.   A spouse entitled by virtue of section 31 to a charge on an estate or interest may agree in writing that any other charge on, or interest in, that estate or interest shall rank in priority to the charge to which that spouse is so entitled.

Section 47(11)   SCHEDULE 5
POWERS OF HIGH COURT AND COUNTY COURT TO REMAND

Interpretation

1.   In this Schedule 'the court' means the High Court or a county court and includes—

(a)   in relation to the High Court, a judge of that court, and

(b)   in relation to a county court, a judge or district judge of that court.

Remand in custody or on bail

2.—(1)   Where a court has power to remand a person under section 47, the court may—

(a)   remand him in custody, that is to say, commit him to custody to be brought before the court at the end of the period of remand or at such earlier time as the court may require, or

(b)   remand him on bail—

(i)   by taking from him a recognizance (with or without sureties) conditioned as provided in sub-paragraph (3), or

(ii)   by fixing the amount of the recognizances with a view to their being taken subsequently in accordance with paragraph 4 and in the meantime committing the person to custody in accordance with paragraph (a).

(2)   Where a person is brought before the court after remand, the court may further remand him.

(3)   Where a person is remanded on bail under sub-paragraph (1), the court may direct that his recognizance be conditioned for his appearance—

(a)   before that court at the end of the period of remand, or

(b)   at every time and place to which during the course of the proceedings the hearing may from time to time be adjourned.

(4)   Where a recognizance is conditioned for a person's appearance in accordance with sub-paragraph (1)(b), the fixing of any time for him next to appear shall be deemed to be a remand; but nothing in this sub-paragraph or sub-paragraph (3) shall deprive the court of power at any subsequent hearing to remand him afresh.

(5)   Subject to paragraph 3, the court shall not remand a person under this paragraph for a period exceeding 8 clear days, except that—

(a)   if the court remands him on bail, it may remand him for a longer period if he and the other party consent, and

(b)   if the court adjourns a case under section 48(1), the court may remand him for the period of the adjournment.

(6)   Where the court has power under this paragraph to remand a person in custody it may, if the remand is for a period not exceeding 3 clear days, commit him to the custody of a constable.

Further remand

3.—(1)   If the court is satisfied that any person who has been remanded under paragraph 2 is unable by reason of illness or accident to appear or be brought before the court at the expiration of the period for which he was remanded, the court may, in his absence, remand him for a further time; and paragraph 2(5) shall not apply.

(2)   Notwithstanding anything in paragraph 2(1), the power of the court under sub-paragraph (1) to remand a person on bail for a further time may be exercised by enlarging his recognizance and those of any sureties for him to a later time.

(3)   Where a person remanded on bail under paragraph 2 is bound to appear before the court at any time and the court has no power to remand him under sub-paragraph (1), the court may in his absence enlarge his recognizance and those of any sureties for him to a later time; and the enlargement of his recognizance shall be deemed to be a further remand.

Postponement of taking of recognizance

4.   Where under paragraph 2(1)(b)(ii) the court fixes the amount in which the principal and his sureties, if any, are to be bound, the recognizance may thereafter be taken by such person as may be prescribed by rules of court, and the same consequences shall follow as if it had been entered into before the court.

SCHEDULE 6
AMENDMENTS OF CHILDREN ACT 1989

1.   After section 38 of the Children Act 1989 insert—

'38A.   Power to include exclusion requirement in interim care order
     (1)   Where—
         (a)   on being satisfied that there are reasonable grounds for believing that the circumstances with respect to a child are as mentioned in section 31(2)(a) and (b)(i), the court makes an interim care order with respect to a child, and
         (b)   the conditions mentioned in subsection (2) are satisfied,
the court may include an exclusion requirement in the interim care order.
     (2)   The conditions are—
         (a)   that there is reasonable cause to believe that, if a person (''the relevant person'') is excluded from a dwelling-house in which the child lives, the child will cease to suffer, or cease to be likely to suffer, significant harm, and
         (b)   that another person living in the dwelling-house (whether a parent of the child or some other person)—
             (i)   is able and willing to give to the child the care which it would be reasonable to expect a parent to give him, and
             (ii)   consents to the inclusion of the exclusion requirement.
     (3)   For the purposes of this section an exclusion requirement is any one or more of the following—

(a) a provision requiring the relevant person to leave a dwelling-house in which he is living with the child,

(b) a provision prohibiting the relevant person from entering a dwelling-house in which the child lives, and

(c) a provision excluding the relevant person from a defined area in which a dwelling-house in which the child lives is situated.

(4) The court may provide that the exclusion requirement is to have effect for a shorter period than the other provisions of the interim care order.

(5) Where the court makes an interim care order containing an exclusion requirement, the court may attach a power of arrest to the exclusion requirement.

(6) Where the court attaches a power of arrest to an exclusion requirement of an interim care order, it may provide that the power of arrest is to have effect for a shorter period than the exclusion requirement.

(7) Any period specified for the purposes of subsection (4) or (6) may be extended by the court (on one or more occasions) on an application to vary or discharge the interim care order.

(8) Where a power of arrest is attached to an exclusion requirement of an interim care order by virtue of subsection (5), a constable may arrest without warrant any person whom he has reasonable cause to believe to be in breach of the requirement.

(9) Sections 47(7), (11) and (12) and 48 of, and Schedule 5 to, the Family Law Act 1996 shall have effect in relation to a person arrested under subsection (8) of this section as they have effect in relation to a person arrested under section 47(6) of that Act.

(10) If, while an interim care order containing an exclusion requirement is in force, the local authority have removed the child from the dwelling-house from which the relevant person is excluded to other accommodation for a continuous period of more than 24 hours, the interim care order shall cease to have effect in so far as it imposes the exclusion requirement.

38B. Undertakings relating to interim care orders

(1) In any case where the court has power to include an exclusion requirement in an interim care order, the court may accept an undertaking from the relevant person.

(2) No power of arrest may be attached to any undertaking given under subsection (1).

(3) An undertaking given to a court under subsection (1)—

(a) shall be enforceable as if it were an order of the court, and

(b) shall cease to have effect if, while it is in force, the local authority have removed the child from the dwelling-house from which the relevant person is excluded to other accommodation for a continuous period of more than 24 hours.

(4) This section has effect without prejudice to the powers of the High Court and county court apart from this section.

(5) In this section ''exclusion requirement'' and ''relevant person'' have the same meaning as in section 38A.'

2. In section 39 of the Children Act 1989 (discharge and variation etc. of care orders and supervision orders) after subsection (3) insert—

'(3A)   On the application of a person who is not entitled to apply for the order to be discharged, but who is a person to whom an exclusion requirement contained in the order applies, an interim care order may be varied or discharged by the court in so far as it imposes the exclusion requirement.

(3B)   Where a power of arrest has been attached to an exclusion requirement of an interim care order, the court may, on the application of any person entitled to apply for the discharge of the order so far as it imposes the exclusion requirement, vary or discharge the order in so far as it confers a power of arrest (whether or not any application has been made to vary or discharge any other provision of the order).'

3.   After section 44 of the Children Act 1989 insert—

'44A.   Power to include exclusion requirement in emergency protection order

(1)   Where—

(a)   on being satisfied as mentioned in section 44(1)(a), (b) or (c), the court makes an emergency protection order with respect to a child, and

(b)   the conditions mentioned in subsection (2) are satisfied,

the court may include an exclusion requirement in the emergency protection order.

(2)   The conditions are—

(a)   that there is reasonable cause to believe that, if a person ("the relevant person") is excluded from a dwelling-house in which the child lives, then—

(i)   in the case of an order made on the ground mentioned in section 44(1)(a), the child will not be likely to suffer significant harm, even though the child is not removed as mentioned in section 44(1)(a)(i) or does not remain as mentioned in section 44(1)(a)(ii), or

(ii)   in the case of an order made on the ground mentioned in paragraph (b) or (c) of section 44(1), the enquiries referred to in that paragraph will cease to be frustrated, and

(b)   that another person living in the dwelling-house (whether a parent of the child or some other person)—

(i)   is able and willing to give to the child the care which it would be reasonable to expect a parent to give him, and

(ii)   consents to the inclusion of the exclusion requirement.

(3)   For the purposes of this section an exclusion requirement is any one or more of the following—

(a)   a provision requiring the relevant person to leave a dwelling-house in which he is living with the child,

(b)   a provision prohibiting the relevant person from entering a dwelling-house in which the child lives, and

(c)   a provision excluding the relevant person from a defined area in which a dwelling-house in which the child lives is situated.

(4)   The court may provide that the exclusion requirement is to have effect for a shorter period than the other provisions of the order.

(5)   Where the court makes an emergency protection order containing an exclusion requirement, the court may attach a power of arrest to the exclusion requirement.

(6)   Where the court attaches a power of arrest to an exclusion requirement of an emergency protection order, it may provide that the power of arrest is to have effect for a shorter period than the exclusion requirement.

(7)   Any period specified for the purposes of subsection (4) or (6) may be extended by the court (on one or more occasions) on an application to vary or discharge the emergency protection order.

(8)   Where a power of arrest is attached to an exclusion requirement of an emergency protection order by virtue of subsection (5), a constable may arrest without warrant any person whom he has reasonable cause to believe to be in breach of the requirement.

(9)   Sections 47(7), (11) and (12) and 48 of, and Schedule 5 to, the Family Law Act 1996 shall have effect in relation to a person arrested under subsection (8) of this section as they have effect in relation to a person arrested under section 47(6) of that Act.

(10)   If, while an emergency protection order containing an exclusion requirement is in force, the applicant has removed the child from the dwelling-house from which the relevant person is excluded to other accommodation for a continuous period of more than 24 hours, the order shall cease to have effect in so far as it imposes the exclusion requirement.

44b.   Undertakings relating to emergency protection orders

(1)   In any case where the court has power to include an exclusion requirement in an emergency protection order, the court may accept an undertaking from the relevant person.

(2)   No power of arrest may be attached to any undertaking given under subsection (1).

(3)   An undertaking given to a court under subsection (1)—

(a)   shall be enforceable as if it were an order of the court, and

(b)   shall cease to have effect if, while it is in force, the applicant has removed the child from the dwelling-house from which the relevant person is excluded to other accommodation for a continuous period of more than 24 hours.

(4)   This section has effect without prejudice to the powers of the High Court and county court apart from this section.

(5)   In this section ''exclusion requirement'' and ''relevant person'' have the same meaning as in section 44A.'

4.   In section 45 of the Children Act 1989 (duration of emergency protection orders and other supplemental provisions), insert after subsection (8)—

'(8A)   On the application of a person who is not entitled to apply for the order to be discharged, but who is a person to whom an exclusion requirement contained in the order applies, an emergency protection order may be varied or discharged by the court in so far as it imposes the exclusion requirement.

(8B)   Where a power of arrest has been attached to an exclusion requirement of an emergency protection order, the court may, on the application of any person entitled to apply for the discharge of the order so far as it imposes the exclusion requirement, vary or discharge the order in so far as it confers a power of arrest (whether or not any application has been made to vary or discharge any other provision of the order).'

5.   In section 105(1) of the Children Act 1989 (interpretation), after the definition of 'domestic premises', insert—

'dwelling-house' includes—
- (a)   any building or part of a building which is occupied as a dwelling;
- (b)   any caravan, house-boat or structure which is occupied as a dwelling;

and any yard, garden, garage or outhouse belonging to it and occupied with it;'.

Section 53   SCHEDULE 7
TRANSFER OF CERTAIN TENANCIES ON DIVORCE ETC. OR ON
SEPARATION OF COHABITANTS

PART I
GENERAL

Interpretation

1.   In this Schedule—

'cohabitant', except in paragraph 3, includes (where the context requires) former cohabitant;

'the court' does not include a magistrates' court,

'landlord' includes—
- (a)   any person from time to time deriving title under the original landlord; and
- (b)   in relation to any dwelling-house, any person other than the tenant who is, or (but for Part VII of the Rent Act 1977 or Part II of the Rent (Agriculture) Act 1976) would be, entitled to possession of the dwelling-house;

'Part II order' means an order under Part II of this Schedule;

'a relevant tenancy' means—
- (a)   a protected tenancy or statutory tenancy within the meaning of the Rent Act 1977;
- (b)   a statutory tenancy within the meaning of the Rent (Agriculture) Act 1976;
- (c)   a secure tenancy within the meaning of section 79 of the Housing Act 1985; or
- (d)   an assured tenancy or assured agricultural occupancy within the meaning of Part I of the Housing Act 1988;

'spouse', except in paragraph 2, includes (where the context requires) former spouse; and

'tenancy' includes sub-tenancy.

Cases in which the court may make an order

2.—(1)   This paragraph applies if one spouse is entitled, either in his own right or jointly with the other spouse, to occupy a dwelling-house by virtue of a relevant tenancy.

(2)   At any time when it has power to make a property adjustment order under section 23A (divorce or separation) or 24 (nullity) of the Matrimonial Causes Act 1973 with respect to the marriage, the court may make a Part II order.

3.—(1)   This paragraph applies if one cohabitant is entitled, either in his own right or jointly with the other cohabitant, to occupy a dwelling-house by virtue of a relevant tenancy.

(2)   If the cohabitants cease to live together as husband and wife, the court may make a Part II order.

4. The court shall not make a Part II order unless the dwelling-house is or was—

    (a)   in the case of spouses, a matrimonial home; or

    (b)   in the case of cohabitants, a home in which they lived together as husband and wife.

Matters to which the court must have regard

5.   In determining whether to exercise its powers under Part II of this Schedule and, if so, in what manner, the court shall have regard to all the circumstances of the case including—

    (a)   the circumstances in which the tenancy was granted to either or both of the spouses or cohabitants or, as the case requires, the circumstances in which either or both of them became tenant under the tenancy;

    (b)   the matters mentioned in section 33(6)(a), (b) and (c) and, where the parties are cohabitants and only one of them is entitled to occupy the dwelling-house by virtue of the relevant tenancy, the further matters mentioned in section 36(6)(e), (f), (g) and (h); and

    (c)   the suitability of the parties as tenants.

PART II
ORDERS THAT MAY BE MADE

References to entitlement to occupy

6.   References in this Part of this Schedule to a spouse or a cohabitant being entitled to occupy a dwelling-house by virtue of a relevant tenancy apply whether that entitlement is in his own right or jointly with the other spouse or cohabitant.

Protected, secure or assured tenancy or assured agricultural occupancy

7.—(1)   If a spouse or cohabitant is entitled to occupy the dwelling-house by virtue of a protected tenancy within the meaning of the Rent Act 1977, a secure tenancy within the meaning of the Housing Act 1985 or an assured tenancy or assured agricultural occupancy within the meaning of Part I of the Housing Act 1988, the court may by order direct that, as from such date as may be specified in the order, there shall, by virtue of the order and without further assurance, be transferred to, and vested in, the other spouse or cohabitant—

    (a)   the estate or interest which the spouse or cohabitant so entitled had in the dwelling-house immediately before that date by virtue of the lease or agreement creating the tenancy and any assignment of that lease or agreement, with all rights, privileges and appurtenances attaching to that estate or interest but subject to all covenants, obligations, liabilities and incumbrances to which it is subject; and

    (b)   where the spouse or cohabitant so entitled is an assignee of such lease or agreement, the liability of that spouse or cohabitant under any covenant of indemnity by the assignee express or implied in the assignment of the lease or agreement to that spouse or cohabitant.

    (2)   If an order is made under this paragraph, any liability or obligation to which the spouse or cohabitant so entitled is subject under any covenant having reference to the dwelling-house in the lease or agreement, being a liability or obligation falling due to be discharged or performed on or after the date so specified, shall not be enforceable against that spouse or cohabitant.

(3) If the spouse so entitled is a successor within the meaning of Part IV of the Housing Act 1985, his former spouse or former cohabitant (or, if a separation order is in force, his spouse) shall be deemed also to be a successor within the meaning of that Part.

(4) If the spouse or cohabitant so entitled is for the purpose of section 17 of the Housing Act 1988 a successor in relation to the tenancy or occupancy, his former spouse or former cohabitant (or, if a separation order is in force, his spouse) is to be deemed to be a successor in relation to the tenancy or occupancy for the purposes of that section.

(5) If the transfer under sub-paragraph (1) is of an assured agricultural occupancy, then, for the purposes of Chapter III of Part I of the Housing Act 1988—

(a) the agricultural worker condition is fulfilled with respect to the dwelling-house while the spouse or cohabitant to whom the assured agricultural occupancy is transferred continues to be the occupier under that occupancy, and

(b) that condition is to be treated as so fulfilled by virtue of the same paragraph of Schedule 3 to the Housing Act 1988 as was applicable before the transfer.

(6) In this paragraph, references to a separation order being in force include references to there being a judicial separation in force.

Statutory tenancy within the meaning of the Rent Act 1977

8.—(1) This paragraph applies if the spouse or cohabitant is entitled to occupy the dwelling-house by virtue of a statutory tenancy within the meaning of the Rent Act 1977.

(2) The court may by order direct that, as from the date specified in the order—

(a) that spouse or cohabitant is to cease to be entitled to occupy the dwelling-house; and

(b) the other spouse or cohabitant is to be deemed to be the tenant or, as the case may be, the sole tenant under that statutory tenancy.

(3) The question whether the provisions of paragraphs 1 to 3, or (as the case may be) paragraphs 5 to 7 of Schedule 1 to the Rent Act 1977, as to the succession by the surviving spouse of a deceased tenant, or by a member of the deceased tenant's family, to the right to retain possession are capable of having effect in the event of the death of the person deemed by an order under this paragraph to be the tenant or sole tenant under the statutory tenancy is to be determined according as those provisions have or have not already had effect in relation to the statutory tenancy.

Statutory tenancy within the meaning of the Rent (Agriculture) Act 1976

9.—(1) This paragraph applies if the spouse or cohabitant is entitled to occupy the dwelling-house by virtue of a statutory tenancy within the meaning of the Rent (Agriculture) Act 1976.

(2) The court may by order direct that, as from such date as may be specified in the order—

(a) that spouse or cohabitant is to cease to be entitled to occupy the dwelling-house; and

(b) the other spouse or cohabitant is to be deemed to be the tenant or, as the case may be, the sole tenant under that statutory tenancy.

(3) A spouse or cohabitant who is deemed under this paragraph to be the tenant under a statutory tenancy is (within the meaning of that Act) a statutory tenant in his

own right, or a statutory tenant by succession, according as the other spouse or cohabitant was a statutory tenant in his own right or a statutory tenant by succession.

PART III
SUPPLEMENTARY PROVISIONS

Compensation

10.—(1)   If the court makes a Part II order, it may by the order direct the making of a payment by the spouse or cohabitant to whom the tenancy is transferred ('the transferee') to the other spouse or cohabitant ('the transferor').

(2)   Without prejudice to that, the court may, on making an order by virtue of sub-paragraph (1) for the payment of a sum—

    (a)   direct that payment of that sum or any part of it is to be deferred until a specified date or until the occurrence of a specified event, or

    (b)   direct that that sum or any part of it is to be paid by instalments.

(3)   Where an order has been made by virtue of sub-paragraph (1), the court may, on the application of the transferee or the transferor—

    (a)   exercise its powers under sub-paragraph (2), or

    (b)   vary any direction previously given under that sub-paragraph,

at any time before the sum whose payment is required by the order is paid in full.

(4)   In deciding whether to exercise its powers under this paragraph and, if so, in what manner, the court shall have regard to all the circumstances including—

    (a)   the financial loss that would otherwise be suffered by the transferor as a result of the order;

    (b)   the financial needs and financial resources of the parties; and

    (c)   the financial obligations which the parties have, or are likely to have in the foreseeable future, including financial obligations to each other and to any relevant child.

(5)   The court shall not give any direction under sub-paragraph (2) unless it appears to it that immediate payment of the sum required by the order would cause the transferee financial hardship which is greater than any financial hardship that would be caused to the transferor if the direction were given.

Liabilities and obligations in respect of the dwelling-house

11.—(1)   If the court makes a Part II order, it may by the order direct that both spouses or cohabitants are to be jointly and severally liable to discharge or perform any or all of the liabilities and obligations in respect of the dwelling-house (whether arising under the tenancy or otherwise) which—

    (a)   have at the date of the order fallen due to be discharged or performed by one only of them; or

    (b)   but for the direction, would before the date specified as the date on which the order is to take effect fall due to be discharged or performed by one only of them.

(2)   If the court gives such a direction, it may further direct that either spouse or cohabitant is to be liable to indemnify the other in whole or in part against any payment made or expenses incurred by the other in discharging or performing any such liability or obligation.

Date when order made between spouses is to take effect

12.—(1)   In the case of a decree of nullity of marriage, the date specified in a Part II order as the date on which the order is to take effect must not be earlier than the date on which the decree is made absolute.

(2)   In the case of divorce proceedings or separation proceedings, the date specified in a Part II order as the date on which the order is to take effect is to be determined as if the court were making a property adjustment order under section 23A of the Matrimonial Causes Act 1973 (regard being had to the restrictions imposed by section 23B of that Act).

Remarriage of either spouse

13.—(1)   If after the making of a divorce order or the grant of a decree annulling a marriage either spouse remarries, that spouse is not entitled to apply, by reference to the making of that order or the grant of that decree, for a Part II order.

(2)   For the avoidance of doubt it is hereby declared that the reference in sub-paragraph (1) to remarriage includes a reference to a marriage which is by law void or voidable.

Rules of court

14.—(1)   Rules of court shall be made requiring the court, before it makes an order under this Schedule, to give the landlord of the dwelling-house to which the order will relate an opportunity of being heard.

(2)   Rules of court may provide that an application for a Part II order by reference to an order or decree may not, without the leave of the court by which that order was made or decree was granted, be made after the expiration of such period from the order or grant as may be prescribed by the rules.

Saving for other provisions of Act

15.—(1)   If a spouse is entitled to occupy a dwelling-house by virtue of a tenancy, this Schedule does not affect the operation of sections 30 and 31 in relation to the other spouse's matrimonial home rights.

(2)   If a spouse or cohabitant is entitled to occupy a dwelling-house by virtue of a tenancy, the court's powers to make orders under this Schedule are additional to those conferred by sections 33, 35 and 36.

Section 66(1)   SCHEDULE 8
                   MINOR AND CONSEQUENTIAL AMENDMENTS

PART I
AMENDMENTS CONNECTED WITH PART II

The Wills Act 1837 (c. 26)

1.   In section 18A(1) of the Wills Act 1837 (effect of dissolution or annulment of marriage on wills), for 'a decree' substitute 'an order or decree'.

The Judicial Proceedings (Regulation of Reports) Act 1926 (c. 61)

2.   In section 1(1)(b) of the Judicial Proceedings (Regulation of Reports) Act 1926 (restriction on reporting) after 'in relation to' insert 'any proceedings under Part II of the Family Law Act 1996 or otherwise in relation to'.

The Maintenance Orders Act 1950 (c. 37)

3.   In section 16 of the Maintenance Orders Act 1950 (orders to which Part II of that Act applies)—
   (a)   in subsection (2)(a)(i), for '23(1), (2) and (4)' substitute '22A, 23'; and
   (b)   in subsection (2)(c)(v), after 'Matrimonial Causes Act 1973' insert '(as that Act had effect immediately before the passing of the Family Law Act 1996)'.

The Matrimonial Causes Act 1973 (c. 18)

4.   The 1973 Act is amended as follows.
5.   In section 8 (intervention of Queen's Proctor)—
   (a)   for 'a petition for divorce' substitute 'proceedings for a divorce order';
   (b)   in subsection (1)(b), omit 'or before the decree nisi is made absolute'; and
   (c)   in subsection (2), for 'a decree nisi in any proceedings for divorce' substitute 'the making of a divorce order'.
6.   For section 15 (application of provisions relating to divorce to nullity proceedings) substitute—

'15.   Decrees of nullity to be decrees nisi
Every decree of nullity of marriage shall in the first instance be a decree nisi and shall not be made absolute before the end of six weeks from its grant unless—
      (a)   the High Court by general order from time to time fixes a shorter period;
or
      (b)   in any particular case, the court in which the proceedings are for the time being pending from time to time by special order fixes a shorter period than the period otherwise applicable for the time being by virtue of this section.

15A.   Intervention of Queen's Proctor
   (1)   In the case of a petition for nullity of marriage—
      (a)   the court may, if it thinks fit, direct all necessary papers in the matter to be sent to the Queen's Proctor, who shall under the directions of the Attorney-General instruct counsel to argue before the court any question in relation to the matter which the court considers it necessary or expedient to have fully argued;
      (b)   any person may at any time during the progress of the proceedings or before the decree nisi is made absolute give information to the Queen's Proctor on any matter material to the due decision of the case, and the Queen's Proctor may thereupon take such steps as the Attorney-General considers necessary or expedient.
   (2)   If the Queen's Proctor intervenes or shows cause against a decree nisi in any proceedings for nullity of marriage, the court may make such order as may be just as to the payment by other parties to the proceedings of the costs incurred by him in so doing or as to the payment by him of any costs incurred by any of those parties by reason of his so doing.
   (3)   Subsection (3) of section 8 above applies in relation to this section as it applies in relation to that section.

15B.   Proceedings after decree nisi: general powers of court
   (1)   Where a decree of nullity of marriage has been granted under this Act but not made absolute, then, without prejudice to section 15A above, any person (excluding a party to the proceedings other than the Queen's Proctor) may show

cause why the decree should not be made absolute by reason of material facts not having been brought before the court; and in such a case the court may—

    (a)   notwithstanding anything in section 15 above (but subject to section 41 below) make the decree absolute; or

    (b)   rescind the decree; or

    (c)   require further inquiry; or

    (d)   otherwise deal with the case as it thinks fit.

    (2)   Where a decree of nullity of marriage has been granted under this Act and no application for it to be made absolute has been made by the party to whom it was granted, then, at any time after the expiration of three months from the earliest date on which that party could have made such an application, the party against whom it was granted may make an application to the court, and on that application the court may exercise any of the powers mentioned in paragraphs (a) to (d) of subsection (1) above.'

7.   In section 19(4) (application of provisions relating to divorce to proceedings under section 19)—

    (a)   for '1(5), 8 and 9' substitute '15, 15A and 15B'; and

    (b)   for 'divorce' in both places substitute 'nullity of marriage'.

8.   In section 24A(1) (orders for sale of property), for 'section 23 or 24 of this Act' substitute 'any of sections 22A to 24 above'.

9.—(1)   Section 25 (matters to which the court is to have regard) is amended as follows.

    (2)   In subsection (1), for 'section 23, 24 or 24A' substitute 'any of sections 22A to 24A'.

    (3)   In subsection (2)—

    (a)   for 'section 23(1)(a), (b) or (c)' substitute 'section 22A or 23 above to make a financial provision order in favour of a party to a marriage or the exercise of its powers under section 23A,';

    (b)   in paragraph (g), after 'parties' insert ', whatever the nature of the conduct and whether it occurred during the marriage or after the separation of the parties or (as the case may be) dissolution or annulment of the marriage,'; and

    (c)   in paragraph (h), omit 'in the case of proceedings for divorce or nullity of marriage,'.

    (4)   In subsection (3), for 'section 23(1)(d), (e) or (f), (2) or (4)' substitute 'section 22A or 23 above to make a financial provision order in favour of a child of the family or the exercise of its powers under section 23A,'.

    (5)   In subsection (4), for 'section 23(1)(d), (e) or (f), (2) or (4), 24 or 24A' substitute 'any of sections 22A to 24A'.

    (6)   After subsection (4) insert—

    '(5)   In relation to any power of the court to make an interim periodical payments order or an interim order for the payment of a lump sum, the preceding provisions of this section, in imposing any obligation on the court with respect to the matters to which it is to have regard, shall not require the court to do anything which would cause such a delay as would, in the opinion of the court, be inappropriate having regard—

    (a)   to any immediate need for an interim order;

    (b)   to the matters in relation to which it is practicable for the court to inquire before making an interim order; and

(c) to the ability of the court to have regard to any matter and to make appropriate adjustments when subsequently making a financial provision order which is not interim.'

10.—(1) Section 25A (requirement to consider need to provide for 'a clean break') is amended as follows.

(2) In subsection (1), for the words from the beginning to 'the marriage' substitute—

'If the court decides to exercise any of its powers under any of sections 22A to 24A above in favour of a party to a marriage (other than its power to make an interim periodical payments order or an interim order for the payment of a lump sum)'.

(3) In subsection (1), for 'the decree' substitute 'a divorce order or decree of nullity'.

(4) For subsection (3) substitute—

'(3) If the court—

(a) would have power under section 22A or 23 above to make a financial provision order in favour of a party to a marriage ("the first party"), but

(b) considers that no continuing obligation should be imposed on the other party to the marriage ("the second party") to make or secure periodical payments in favour of the first party,

it may direct that the first party may not at any time after the direction takes effect, apply to the court for the making against the second party of any periodical payments order or secured periodical payments order and, if the first party has already applied to the court for the making of such an order, it may dismiss the application.

(3A) If the court—

(a) exercises, or has exercised, its power under section 22A at any time before making a divorce order, and

(b) gives a direction under subsection (3) above in respect of a periodical payments order or a secured periodical payments order,

it shall provide for the direction not to take effect until a divorce order is made.'

11. In each of sections 25B(2) and (3), 25C(1) and (3) and 25D (1)(a), (2)(a), (c) and (e) (benefits under a pension scheme on divorce, etc.) for 'section 23' substitute 'section 22A or 23'.

12. In section 26(1) (commencement of proceedings for ancillary relief), for the words from the beginning to '22 above' substitute—

'(1) If a petition for nullity of marriage has been presented, then, subject to subsection (2) below, proceedings'.

13.—(1) Section 27 (financial provision orders etc. in case of failure to provide proper maintenance) is amended as follows.

(2) In subsection (5)—

(a) after 'an order requiring the respondent' insert '—

(a)'; and

(b) at the end insert ', or

(b) to pay to the applicant such lump sum or sums as the court thinks reasonable.'

(3) For subsection (6) substitute—

'(6) Subject to the restrictions imposed by the following provisions of this Act, if on an application under this section the applicant satisfies the court of any ground mentioned in subsection (1) above, the court may make one or more financial provision orders against the respondent in favour of the applicant or a child of the family.'

(4)   In subsection (7), for '(6)(c) or (f)' substitute '(6)'.

14.—(1)   Section 28 (duration of continuing financial provision order in favour of a party to a marriage) is amended as follows.

(2)   In subsection (1A), for the words from the beginning to 'nullity of marriage' substitute—

'(1A)   At any time when—

(a)   the court exercises, or has exercised, its power under section 22A or 23 above to make a financial provision order in favour of a party to a marriage,

(b)   but for having exercised that power, the court would have power under one of those sections to make such an order, and

(c)   an application for a divorce order or a petition for a decree of nullity of marriage is outstanding or has been granted in relation to the marriage,'.

(3)   Insert, after subsection (1A)—

'(1B)   If the court—

(a)   exercises, or has exercised, its power under section 22A at any time before making a divorce order, and

(b)   gives a direction under subsection (1A) above in respect of a periodical payments order or a secured periodical payments order,

it shall provide for the direction not to take effect until a divorce order is made.'

(4)   In subsection (2), for the words from 'on or after' to 'nullity of marriage' substitute 'at such a time as is mentioned in subsection (1A)(c) above'.

(5)   In subsection (3)—

(a)   for 'a decree' substitute 'an order or decree'; and

(b)   for 'that decree' substitute 'that order or decree'.

15.   In section 29(1) (duration of a continuing financial provision order in favour of a child of the family), for 'under section 24(1)(a)' substitute 'such as is mentioned in section 21(2)(a)'.

16.—(1)   Section 31 (variation etc. of orders) is amended as follows.

(2)   In subsection (2)—

(a)   after 'following orders' insert 'under this Part of this Act';

(b)   for paragraph (d) substitute—

'(d)   an order for the payment of a lump sum in a case in which the payment is to be by instalments;';

(c)   in paragraph (dd), for '23(1)(c)' substitute '21(1)(c)';

(d)   after paragraph (dd) insert—

'(de)   any other order for the payment of a lump sum, if it is made at a time when no divorce order has been made, and no separation order is in force, in relation to the marriage;';

(e)   for paragraph (e) substitute—

'(e)   any order under section 23A of a kind referred to in section 21(2)(b),(c) or (d) which is made on or after the making of a separation order;

(ea)   any order under section 23A which is made at a time when no divorce order has been made, and no separation order is in force, in relation to the marriage;'.

(3)   In subsection (4)—

(a) for the words from 'for a settlement' to '24(1)(c) or (d)', substitute 'referred to in subsection (2)(e)'; and

(b) for paragraphs (a) and (b) substitute 'on an application for a divorce order in relation to the marriage'.

(4) After subsection (4) insert—

'(4A) In relation to an order which falls within subsection (2)(de) or (ea) above ("the subsection (2) order")—

(a) the powers conferred by this section may be exercised—

(i)   only on an application made before the subsection (2) order has or, but for paragraph (b) below, would have taken effect; and

(ii)   only if, at the time when the application is made, no divorce order has been made in relation to the marriage and no separation order has been so made since the subsection (2) order was made; and

(b) an application made in accordance with paragraph (a) above prevents the subsection (2) order from taking effect before the application has been dealt with.

(4B) No variation—

(a) of a financial provision order made under section 22A above, other than an interim order, or

(b) of a property adjustment order made under section 23A above,
shall be made so as to take effect before the making of a divorce order or separation order in relation to the marriage, unless the court is satisfied that the circumstances of the case are exceptional, and that it would be just and reasonable for the variation to be so made.'

(5) In subsection (5)—

(a)   insert, at the beginning, 'Subject to subsections (7A) to (7F) below and without prejudice to any power exercisable by virtue of subsection (2)(d),(dd) or (e) above or otherwise than by virtue of this section,'; and

(b)   for 'section 23', in each place, substitute 'section 22A or 23'.

(6) In subsection (7)(a)—

(a)   for 'on or after' to 'consider' substitute 'in favour of a party to a marriage, the court shall, if the marriage has been dissolved or annulled, consider'; and

(b)   after 'sufficient' insert '(in the light of any proposed exercise by the court, where the marriage has been dissolved, of its powers under subsection (7B) below)'.

(7) After subsection (7), insert—

'(7A) Subsection (7B) below applies where, after the dissolution of a marriage, the court—

(a) discharges a periodical payments order or secured periodical payments order made in favour of a party to the marriage; or

(b) varies such an order so that payments under the order are required to be made or secured only for such further period as is determined by the court.

(7B) The court has power, in addition to any power it has apart from this subsection, to make supplemental provision consisting of any of—

(a)   an order for the payment of a lump sum in favour of a party to the marriage;

(b)   one or more property adjustment orders in favour of a party to the marriage;

(c)   a direction that the party in whose favour the original order discharged or varied was made is not entitled to make any further application for—

(i)   a periodical payments or secured periodical payments order, or

(ii)   an extension of the period to which the original order is limited by any variation made by the court.

(7C)   An order for the payment of a lump sum made under subsection (7B) above may—

(a)   provide for the payment of that sum by instalments of such amount as may be specified in the order; and

(b)   require the payment of the instalments to be secured to the satisfaction of the court.

(7D)   Subsections (7) and (8) of section 22A above apply where the court makes an order for the payment of a lump sum under subsection (7B) above as they apply where it makes such an order under section 22A above.

(7E)   If under subsection (7B) above the court makes more than one property adjustment order in favour of the same party to the marriage, each of those orders must fall within a different paragraph of section 21(2) above.

(7F)   Sections 24A and 30 above apply where the court makes a property adjustment order under subsection (7B) above as they apply where it makes such an order under section 23A above.'

17.   In section 32(1) (payment of certain arrears to be unenforceable), for the words from 'an order' to 'financial provision order' substitute 'any financial provision order under this Part of this Act or any interim order for maintenance'.

18.   For section 33(2) (repayment of sums paid under certain orders) substitute—

'(2)   This section applies to the following orders under this Part of this Act—

(a)   any periodical payments order;

(b)   any secured periodical payments order; and

(c)   any interim order for maintenance, so far as it requires the making of periodical payments.'

19.—(1)   Section 33A (consent orders) is amended as follows.

(2)   In subsection (2), after 'applies', in the first place, insert '(subject, in the case of the powers of the court under section 31A above, to subsections (6) and (7) of that section)'.

(3)   In subsection (3), in the definition of 'order for financial relief', for 'an order under any of sections 23, 24, 24A or 27 above' substitute 'any of the following orders under this Part of this Act, that is to say, any financial provision order, any property adjustment order, any order for the sale of property or any interim order for maintenance'.

20.   In section 35 (alteration of maintenance agreements), after subsection (6), insert—

'(7)   Subject to subsection (5) above, references in this Act to any such order as is mentioned in section 21 above shall not include references to any order under this section.'

21.   In section 37(1) (avoidance of transactions intended to prevent or reduce financial relief), for '22, 23, 24, 27, 31 (except subsection (6))' substitute '22A to 24, 27, 31 (except subsection (6)), 31A'.

22.   In section 47(2) (relief in cases of polygamous marriages)—

(a)   in paragraph (a), after 'any' insert the words 'divorce order, any separation order under the 1996 Act or any'; and

(b)   in paragraph (d), after 'this Act' insert 'or the 1996 Act' and for 'such decree or order' substitute 'a statement of marital breakdown or any such order or decree'.

23.   Omit section 49 (under which a person who is alleged to have committed adultery with a party to a marriage is required to be made a party to certain proceedings).

24.—(1)   Section 52(1) (interpretation) is amended as follows.

(2)   After 'In this Act', insert—

'"the 1996 Act" means the Family Law Act 1996;'.

(3)   After the definition of 'maintenance assessment' insert—

'"statement of marital breakdown" has the same meaning as in the Family Law Act 1996.'

25.   In section 52(2)(a), for 'with section 21 above' substitute '(subject to section 35(7) above) with section 21 above and—

(i)   in the case of a financial provision order or periodical payments order, as including (except where the context otherwise requires) references to an interim periodical payments order under section 22A or 23 above; and

(ii)   in the case of a financial provision order or order for the payment of a lump sum, as including (except where the context otherwise requires) references to an interim order for the payment of a lump sum under section 22A or 23 above;'.

The Domicile and Matrimonial Proceedings Act 1973 (c. 45)

26.   For section 5(5) of the Domicile and Matrimonial Proceedings Act 1973 (jurisdiction in cases of change of domicile or habitual residence) substitute—

'(5)   The court shall have jurisdiction to entertain proceedings for nullity of marriage (even though it would not otherwise have jurisdiction) at any time when marital proceedings, as defined by section 20 of the Family Law Act 1996, are pending in relation to the marriage.'

The Inheritance (Provision for Family and Dependants) Act 1975 (c. 63)

27.—(1)   The Inheritance (Provision for Family and Dependants) Act 1975 (meaning of reasonable financial provision) is amended as follows.

(2)   In section 1(2)(a), for the words from 'the marriage' to 'in force' substitute ', at the date of death, a separation order under the Family Law Act 1996 was in force in relation to the marriage'.

(3)   In section 3(2) (matters to which the court is to have regard)—

(a)   for 'decree of judicial separation' substitute 'separation order under the Family Law Act 1996'; and

(b)   for 'a decree of divorce' substitute 'a divorce order'.

(4)   In section 14 (provision where no financial relief was granted on divorce)—

(a)   in subsection (1), for the words from 'a decree' to first 'granted' substitute 'a divorce order or separation order has been made under the Family Law Act 1996 in relation to a marriage or a decree of nullity of marriage has been made absolute';

(b)   in subsection (1)(a), for 'section 23' and 'section 24' substitute respectively, 'section 22A or 23' and 'section 23A or 24';

(c)   after paragraph (b), for the words from 'the decree of divorce' to the end substitute ', as the case may be, the divorce order or separation order had not been made or the decree of nullity had not been made absolute'; and

(d) in subsection (2), for 'decree of judicial separation' and 'the decree' substitute, respectively, 'separation order' and 'the order'.

(5) In section 15(1) (restriction imposed in divorce proceedings on applications under that Act), for the words from the beginning to 'thereafter' substitute—

'At any time when the court—

(a) has jurisdiction under section 23A or 24 of the Matrimonial Causes Act 1973 to make a property adjustment order in relation to a marriage; or

(b) would have such jurisdiction if either the jurisdiction had not already been exercised or an application for such an order were made with the leave of the court,'.

(6) In section 15, for subsections (2) to (4) substitute—

'(2) An order made under subsection (1) above with respect to any party to a marriage has effect in accordance with subsection (3) below at any time—

(a) after the marriage has been dissolved;

(b) after a decree of nullity has been made absolute in relation to the marriage; and

(c) while a separation order under the Family Law Act 1996 is in force in relation to the marriage and the separation is continuing.

(3) If at any time when an order made under subsection (1) above with respect to any party to a marriage has effect the other party to the marriage dies, the court shall not entertain any application made by the surviving party to the marriage for an order under section 2 of this Act.'

(7) In section 19(2)(b) (effect and duration of certain orders), for the words from 'the marriage' to 'in force' substitute ', at the date of death, a separation order under the Family Law Act 1996 was in force in relation to the marriage with the deceased'.

(8) In section 25 (interpretation), in the definition of 'former wife' and 'former husband', for 'a decree', in the first place, substitute 'an order or decree'.

The Domestic Proceedings and Magistrates' Courts Act 1978 (c. 22)

28.—(1) Section 28(1) of the Domestic Proceedings and Magistrates' Courts Act 1978 (powers of High Court in respect of orders under Part I) is amended as follows.

(2) After 'this Act' insert—

'(a) a statement of marital breakdown under section 5 of the Family Law Act 1996 with respect to the marriage has been received by the court but no application has been made under that Act by reference to that statement, or

(b)'

(3) For the words from 'then' to 'lump sum' substitute 'then, except in the case of an order for the payment of a lump sum, any court to which an application may be made under that Act by reference to that statement or, as the case may be,'.

The Housing Act 1980 (c. 51)

29. In section 54(2) of the Housing Act 1980 (prohibition of assignment of shorthold tenancy under that section) for 'section 24' substitute 'sections 23A or 24'.

The Supreme Court Act 1981 (c. 54)

30. In section 18 of the Supreme Court Act 1981 (restrictions on appeals to Court of Appeal), in paragraph (d) of subsection (1) omit 'divorce or' and after that paragraph insert—

'(dd)   from a divorce order;'.

The Civil Jurisdiction and Judgments Act 1982 (c. 27)

31.   In section 18(6)(a) of the Civil Jurisdiction and Judgments Act 1982 (decrees of judicial separation), for 'a decree' substitute 'an order or decree'.

The Matrimonial and Family Proceedings Act 1984 (c. 42)

32.—(1)   The Matrimonial and Family Proceedings Act 1984 is amended as follows.

(2)   In section 17(1) (financial relief in the case of overseas divorces etc.), for the words from 'any' where it first occurs to the end substitute 'one or more orders each of which would, within the meaning of Part II of the 1973 Act, be a financial provision order in favour of a party to the marriage or child of the family or a property adjustment order in relation to the marriage.'

(3)   For section 21(a) (provisions of the 1973 Act applied for the purposes of the powers to give relief in the case of overseas divorces etc.) substitute—

'(a)   section 22A(5) (provisions about lump sums in relation to divorce or separation);

(aa)   section 23(4), (5) and (6) (provisions about lump sums in relation to annulment);'.

(4)   In section 27 (interpretation), for the definition of 'property adjustment order', substitute—

''property adjustment order'' and ''secured periodical payments order'' mean any order which would be a property adjustment order or, as the case may be, secured periodical payments order within the meaning of Part II of the 1973 Act;'

(5)   In section 32 (meaning of 'family business'), for the definition of 'matrimonial cause' substitute—

''matrimonial cause'' means an action for nullity of marriage or any marital proceedings under the Family Law Act 1996;'.

The Finance Act 1985 (c. 54)

33.   In section 83(1) of the Finance Act 1985 (stamp duty for transfers of property in connection with divorce etc.)—

(a)   after paragraph (b), insert—

'(bb)   is executed in pursuance of an order of a court which is made at any time under section 22A, 23A or 24A of the Matrimonial Causes Act 1973, or'; and

(b)   in paragraph (c), for 'or their judicial separation' substitute ', their judicial separation or the making of a separation order in respect of them'.

The Housing Act 1985 (c.68)

34.   In each of sections 39(1)(c), 88(2), 89(3), 90(3)(a), 91(3)(b), 99B(2)(e), 101(3)(c), 160(1)(c), 171B(4)(b)(i) of, and paragraph 1(2)(c) to, Schedule 6A of the Housing Act 1985 (which refers to the 1973 Act), for 'section 24' substitute 'section 23A or 24'.

The Housing Associations Act 1985 (c.69)

35.   In paragraph 5(1)(c) of Schedule 2 to the Housing Associations Act 1985 (which refers to the 1973 Act), for 'section 24' substitute 'section 23A or 24'.

The Agricultural Holdings Act 1986 (c.5)

36. In paragraph 1(3) of Schedule 6 to the Agricultural Holdings Act 1986 (spouse of close relative not to be treated as such when marriage subject to decree nisi etc.), for the words from 'when' to the end substitute 'when a separation order or a divorce order under the Family Law Act 1996 is in force in relation to the relative's marriage or that marriage is the subject of a decree nisi of nullity.'

The Family Law Act 1986 (c.55)

37.—(1) The Family Law Act 1986 is amended as follows.

(2) For section 2(1) and (2) (jurisdiction to make orders under section 1) substitute—

'(1) A court in England and Wales shall not have jurisdiction to make a section 1(1)(a) order with respect to a child unless—

(a) the case falls within section 2A below; or

(b) in any other case, the condition in section 3 below is satisfied.'

(3) For section 2A(1) (jurisdiction in or in connection with matrimonial proceedings), substitute—

'(1) Subject to subsections (2) to (4) below, a case falls within this section for the purposes of the making of a section 1(1)(a) order if that order is made—

(a) at a time when—

(i) a statement of marital breakdown under section 5 of the Family Law Act 1996 with respect to the marriage of the parents of the child concerned has been received by the court; and

(ii) it is or may become possible for an application for a divorce order or for a separation order to be made by reference to that statement; or

(b) at a time when an application in relation to that marriage for a divorce order, or for a separation order under the Act of 1996, has been made and not withdrawn.

(1A) A case also falls within this section for the purposes of the making of a section 1(1)(a) order if that order is made in or in connection with any proceedings for the nullity of the marriage of the parents of the child concerned and—

(a) those proceedings are continuing; or

(b) the order is made—

(i) immediately on the dismissal, after the beginning of the trial, of the proceedings; and

(ii) on an application made before the dismissal.'

(4) In section 2A(2), for the words from the beginning to 'judicial separation' substitute 'A case does not fall within this section if a separation order under the Family Law Act 1996 is in force in relation to the marriage of the parents of the child concerned if,'.

(5) In section 2A(3), for 'in which the other proceedings there referred to' substitute 'in Scotland, Northern Ireland or a specified dependent territory in which the proceedings for divorce or nullity'.

(6) In section 2A(4)—

(a) for 'in or in connection with matrimonial proceedings' substitute 'by virtue of the case falling within this section'; and

(b) for 'in or in connection with those proceedings' substitute 'by virtue of section 2(1)(a) of this Act'.

(7) In section 3 (child habitually resident or present in England and Wales), for 'section 2(2)' substitute 'section 2(1)(b)'.

(8) In section 6 (duration and variation of Part I orders), for subsections (3A) and (3B) substitute—

'(3A) Subsection (3) above does not apply if the Part I order was made in a case falling within section 2A of this Act.'

(9) In section 38 (restriction on removal of wards of court from the jurisdiction), insert after subsection (3)—

'(4) The reference in subsection (2) above to a time when proceedings for divorce or judicial separation are continuing in respect of a marriage in another part of the United Kingdom includes, in relation to any case in which England and Wales would be another part of the United Kingdom, any time when—

(a) a statement of marital breakdown under section 5 of the Family Law Act 1996 with respect to that marriage has been received by the court and it is or may become possible for an application for a divorce order or for a separation order to be made by reference to that statement; or

(b) an application in relation to that marriage for a divorce order, or for a separation order under the Act of 1996, has been made and not withdrawn.'

(10) In section 42(2) (times when divorce etc. proceedings are to be treated as continuing for the purposes of certain restrictions on the removal of children from the jurisdiction), for the words from 'unless' to the end substitute 'be treated as continuing (irrespective of whether a divorce order, separation order or decree of nullity has been made)—

(a) from the time when a statement of marital breakdown under section 5 of the Family Law Act 1996 with respect to the marriage is received by the court in England and Wales until such time as the court may designate or, if earlier, until the time when—

(i)   the child concerned attains the age of eighteen; or

(ii) it ceases, by virtue of section 5(3) or 7(9) of that Act (lapse of divorce or separation process) to be possible for an application for a divorce order, or for a separation order, to be made by reference to that statement; and

(b) from the time when a petition for nullity is presented in relation to the marriage in England and Wales or a petition for divorce, judicial separation or nullity is presented in relation to the marriage in Northern Ireland or a specified dependent territory, until the time when—

(i)   the child concerned attains the age of eighteen; or

(ii) if earlier, proceedings on the petition are dismissed.'

(11) In section 51(4) (definitions), after the definition of 'the relevant date' insert—

'"judicial separation" includes a separation order under the Family Law Act 1996;'.

The Landlord and Tenant Act 1987 (c. 31)

38. In section 4(2)(c) of the Landlord and Tenant Act 1987 (which refers to the 1973 Act), for 'section 24' substitute 'section 23A, 24'.

The Legal Aid Act 1988 (c. 34)

39.　In paragraph 5A of Part II of Schedule 2 to the Legal Aid Act 1988 (excepted proceedings)—

　　(a)　for 'decree of divorce or judicial separation' substitute 'a divorce order or a separation order'; and

　　(b)　in sub-paragraph (b) of that paragraph, for 'petition' substitute 'application'.

The Housing Act 1988 (c. 50)

40.　In paragraph 4(1)(c) of Schedule 11 (which refers to the 1973 Act), for 'section 24' substitute 'section 23A or 24'.

The Children Act 1989 (c. 41)

41.—(1)　The Children Act 1989 is amended as follows.

(2)　In section 6(3A) (revocation or appointment of guardian) for paragraph (a) substitute—

　　'(a)　a court of civil jurisdiction in England and Wales by order dissolves, or by decree annuls, a marriage, or'.

(3)　In section 8(3) after 'means' insert '(subject to subsection (5))'.

(4)　In section 8, insert after subsection (4)—

　　'(5)　For the purposes of any reference in this Act to family proceedings, powers which under this Act are exercisable in family proceedings shall also be exercisable in relation to a child, without any such proceedings having been commenced or any application having been made to the court under this Act, if—

　　(a)　a statement of marital breakdown under section 5 of the Family Law Act 1996 with respect to the marriage in relation to which that child is a child of the family has been received by the court; and

　　(b)　it may, in due course, become possible for an application for a divorce order or for a separation order to be made by reference to that statement.'

The Local Government and Housing Act 1989 (c. 42)

42.　In section 124(3)(c) of the Local Government and Housing Act 1989 (which refers to the 1973 Act), for 'section 24' substitute 'section 23A or 24'.

Pensions Act 1995 (c. 26)

43.　In section 166(4) of the Pensions Act 1995 (jurisdiction of the court under the Matrimonial Causes Act 1973 in respect of pensions to which that section applies) for 'section 23' substitute 'section 22A or 23'.

PART II
AMENDMENTS CONNECTED WITH PART III

The Legal Aid Act 1988 (c. 34)

44.—(1)　The 1988 Act is amended as follows.

(2)　In section 1, after 'III' insert 'IIIA'.

(3)　In sections 1, 2(11), 3(2), 4(1), (2) and (4), 5(1) and (6), 6(2)(a) and (3)(a), 34(2)(c) and (d) and (11), 38(1) and (6) and 39(1) and (4)(a), after 'assistance', in each place, insert ', mediation'.

(4) In section 3(9), after paragraph (a) insert—
'(aa) the provision of mediation;'.
(5) In section 6, after subsection (3)(c) insert—
'(ca) any sum which is to be paid out of property on which it is charged under regulations under section 13C(5) below'.
(6) In section 15—
(a) in subsection (1), after '(3D)' insert 'and (3F)'; and
(b) in subsection (3D), after '(3)' insert 'and (3F)'.
(7) In section 16(9), leave out 'and' at the end of paragraph (a).
(8) In section 38—
(a) in subsection (1)(f), after 'legal representatives' insert 'or mediators'; and
(b) in subsection (6), after 'legal representative' insert 'or mediator'.
(9) In section 43—
(a) after '"assistance"' insert ', "mediation"';
(b) after '(3)' insert ', (3A)'; and
(c) after the definition of 'financial resources' insert—
'"family matters" has the meaning assigned by section 13A(2);'.

PART III
AMENDMENTS CONNECTED WITH PART IV

The Land Registration Act 1925 (c. 21)

45.   In section 64 of the Land Registration Act 1925 (certificates to be produced and noted on dealings) in subsection (5) for 'section 2(8) of the Matrimonial Homes Act 1983' substitute 'section 31 (10) of the Family Law Act 1996 and for "rights of occupation" substitute "matrimonial home rights"'.

The Land Charges Act 1972 (c. 61)

46.   In section 1(6A) of the Land Charges Act 1972 (cases where county court has jurisdiction to vacate registration) in paragraph (d)—
(a) after 'section 1 of the Matrimonial Homes Act 1983' insert 'or section 33 of the Family Law Act 1996'; and
(b) for 'that section' substitute 'either of those sections'.
47.   In section 2(7) of that Act (Class F land charge) for 'Matrimonial Homes Act 1983' substitute 'Part IV of the Family Law Act 1996'.

The Land Compensation Act 1973 (c. 26)

48.—(1)   Section 29A of the Land Compensation Act 1973 (spouses having statutory rights of occupation) is amended as follows.
(2)   In subsection (1), for 'rights of occupation (within the meaning of the Matrimonial Homes Act 1983)' substitute 'matrimonial home rights (within the meaning of Part IV of the Family Law Act 1996)'.
(3)   In subsection (2)(a), for 'rights of occupation' substitute 'matrimonial home rights'.

The Magistrates' Courts Act 1980 (c. 43)

49.   In section 65(1) of the Magistrates' Courts Act 1980 (meaning of family proceedings) after paragraph (o) insert—

'(p)   Part IV of the Family Law Act 1996;'.

The Contempt of Court Act 1981 (c. 49)

50.   In Schedule 3 to the Contempt of Court Act 1981 (application of Magistrates' Courts Act 1980 to civil contempt proceedings), in paragraph 3 for the words from ''or, having been arrested'' onwards substitute—
"or, having been arrested under section 47 of the Family Law Act 1996 in connection with the matter of the complaint, is at large after being remanded under subsection (7)(b) or (10) of that section.'''

The Supreme Court Act 1981 (c. 54)

51.   In Schedule 1 to the Supreme Court Act 1981 (distribution of business in High Court), in paragraph 3 (Family Division)—
(a)   in paragraph (d), after 'matrimonial proceedings' insert 'or proceedings under Part IV of the Family Law Act 1996', and
(b)   in paragraph (f)(i), for 'Domestic Violence and Matrimonial Proceedings Act 1976' substitute 'Part IV of the Family Law Act 1996'.

The Matrimonial and Family Proceedings Act 1984 (c. 42)

52.   For section 22 of the Matrimonial and Family Proceedings Act 1984 substitute—

'22.   Powers of court in relation to certain tenancies of dwelling-houses
(1)   This section applies if—
(a)   an application is made by a party to a marriage for an order for financial relief; and
(b)   one of the parties is entitled, either in his own right or jointly with the other party, to occupy a dwelling-house situated in England or Wales by virtue of a tenancy which is a relevant tenancy within the meaning of Schedule 7 to the Family Law Act 1996 (certain statutory tenancies).
(2)   The court may make in relation to that dwelling-house any order which it could make under Part II of that Schedule if—
(a)   a divorce order,
(b)   a separation order, or
(c)   a decree of nullity of marriage,
had been made or granted in England and Wales in respect of the marriage.
(3)   The provisions of paragraphs 10, 11 and 14(1) in Part III of that Schedule apply in relation to any order under this section as they apply to any order under Part II of that Schedule.'

The Housing Act 1985 (c. 68)

53.—(1)   Section 85 of the Housing Act 1985 (extended discretion of court in certain proceedings for possession) is amended as follows.
(2)   In subsection (5)—
(a)   in paragraph (a), for 'rights of occupation under the Matrimonial Homes Act 1983' substitute 'matrimonial home rights under Part IV of the Family Law Act 1996'; and
(b)   for 'those rights of occupation' substitute 'those matrimonial home rights'.

(3) After subsection (5) insert—

'(5A) If proceedings are brought for possession of a dwelling-house which is let under a secure tenancy and—

(a) an order is in force under section 35 of the Family Law Act 1996 conferring rights on the former spouse of the tenant or an order is in force under section 36 of that Act conferring rights on a cohabitant or former cohabitant (within the meaning of that Act) of the tenant,

(b) the former spouse, cohabitant or former cohabitant is then in occupation of the dwelling-house, and

(c) the tenancy is terminated as a result of those proceedings,

the former spouse, cohabitant or former cohabitant shall, so long as he or she remains in occupation, have the same rights in relation to, or in connection with, any adjournment, stay, suspension or postponement in pursuance of this section as he or she would have if the rights conferred by the order referred to in paragraph (a) were not affected by the termination of the tenancy.'

54. In section 99B of that Act (persons qualifying for compensation for improvements) in subsection (2) for paragraph (f) substitute—

'(f) a spouse, former spouse, cohabitant or former cohabitant of the improving tenant to whom the tenancy has been transferred by an order made under Schedule 1 to the Matrimonial Homes Act 1983 or Schedule 7 to the Family Law Act 1996.'

55. In section 101 of that Act (rent not to be increased on account of tenant's improvements) in subsection (3) for paragraph (d) substitute—

'(d) a spouse, former spouse, cohabitant or former cohabitant of the tenant to whom the tenancy has been transferred by an order made under Schedule 1 to the Matrimonial Homes Act 1983 or Schedule 7 to the Family Law Act 1996.'

56. In section 171B of that Act (extent of preserved right to buy: qualifying persons and dwelling-houses) in subsection (4)(b)(ii) after 'Schedule 1 to the Matrimonial Homes Act 1983' insert 'or Schedule 7 to the Family Law Act 1996'.

The Insolvency Act 1986 (c. 45)

57.—(1) Section 336 of the Insolvency Act 1986 (rights of occupation etc. of bankrupt's spouse) is amended as follows.

(2) In subsection (1), for 'rights of occupation under the Matrimonial Homes Act 1983' substitute 'matrimonial home rights under Part IV of the Family Law Act 1996'.

(3) In subsection (2)—

(a) for 'rights of occupation under the Act of 1983' substitute 'matrimonial home rights under the Act of 1996', and

(b) in paragraph (b), for 'under section 1 of that Act' substitute 'under section 33 of that Act'.

(4) In subsection (4), for 'section 1 of the Act of 1983' substitute 'section 33 of the Act of 1996'.

58.—(1) Section 337 of that Act is amended as follows.

(2) In subsection (2), for 'rights of occupation under the Matrimonial Homes Act 1983' substitute 'matrimonial home rights under Part IV of the Family Law Act 1996'.

(3) For subsection (3) substitute—

'(3)   The Act of 1996 has effect, with the necessary modifications, as if—

(a)   the rights conferred by paragraph (a) of subsection (2) were matrimonial home rights under that Act,

(b)   any application for such leave as is mentioned in that paragraph were an application for an order under section 33 of that Act, and

(c)   any charge under paragraph (b) of that subsection on the estate or interest of the trustee were a charge under that Act on the estate or interest of a spouse.'

(4)   In subsections (4) and (5) for 'section 1 of the Act of 1983' substitute 'section 33 of the Act of 1996'.

The Housing Act 1988 (c. 50)

59.—(1)   Section 9 of the Housing Act 1988 (extended discretion of court in possession claims) is amended as follows.

(2)   In subsection (5)—

(a)   in paragraph (a), for 'rights of occupation under the Matrimonial Homes Act 1983' substitute 'matrimonial home rights under Part IV of the Family Law Act 1996', and

(b)   for 'those rights of occupation' substitute 'those matrimonial home rights'.

(3)   After subsection (5) insert—

'(5A)   In any case where—

(a)   at a time when proceedings are brought for possession of a dwelling-house let on an assured tenancy—

(i)   an order is in force under section 35 of the Family Law Act 1996 conferring rights on the former spouse of the tenant, or

(ii)   an order is in force under section 36 of that Act conferring rights on a cohabitant or former cohabitant (within the meaning of that Act) of the tenant,

(b)   that cohabitant, former cohabitant or former spouse is then in occupation of the dwelling-house, and

(c)   the assured tenancy is terminated as a result of those proceedings,

the cohabitant, former cohabitant or former spouse shall have the same rights in relation to, or in connection with, any such adjournment as is referred to in subsection (1) above or any such stay, suspension or postponement as is referred to in subsection (2) above as he or she would have if the rights conferred by the order referred to in paragraph (a) above were not affected by the termination of the tenancy.'

The Children Act 1989 (c. 41)

60.—(1)   In section 8(4) of the Children Act 1989 (meaning of 'family proceedings' for purposes of that Act), omit paragraphs (c) and (f) and after paragraph (g) insert—

'(h)   the Family Law Act 1996.'

(2)   In Schedule 11 to that Act, in paragraph 6(a) (amendment of the Domestic Proceedings and Magistrates' Courts Act 1978), for 'sections 16(5)(c) and' substitute 'section'.

The Courts and Legal Services Act 1990 (c. 41)

61.   In section 58 of the Courts and Legal Services Act 1990 (conditional fee agreements) in subsection (10), omit paragraphs (b) and (e) and immediately before the 'or' following paragraph (g) insert—

'(gg)   Part IV of the Family Law Act 1996'.

Section 66(2)   SCHEDULE 9
                    MODIFICATIONS, SAVING AND TRANSITIONAL

Transitional arrangements for those who have been living apart

1.—(1)   The Lord Chancellor may by order provide for the application of Part II
to marital proceedings which—
   (a)   are begun during the transitional period, and
   (b)   relate to parties to a marriage who immediately before the beginning of
that period were living apart,
subject to such modifications (which may include omissions) as may be prescribed.
   (2)   An order made under this paragraph may, in particular, make provision as to
the evidence which a party who claims to have been living apart from the other party
immediately before the beginning of the transitional period must produce to the court.
   (3)   In this paragraph—
'marital proceedings' has the same meaning as in section 24;
'prescribed' means prescribed by the order; and
'transitional period' means the period of two years beginning with the day on
which section 3 is brought into force.'

Modifications of enactments etc.

2.—(1)   The Lord Chancellor may by order make such consequential modifications of any enactment or subordinate legislation as appear to him necessary or
expedient in consequence of Part II in respect of any reference (in whatever terms)
to—
   (a)   a petition;
   (b)   the presentation of a petition;
   (c)   the petitioner or respondent in proceedings on a petition;
   (d)   proceedings on a petition;
   (e)   proceedings in connection with any proceedings on a petition;
   (f)   any other matrimonial proceedings;
   (g)   a decree; or
   (h)   findings of adultery in any proceedings.
   (2)   An order under sub-paragraph (1) may, in particular—
   (a)   make provision applying generally in relation to enactments and subordinate legislation of a description specified in the order;
   (b)   modify the effect of sub-paragraph (3) in relation to documents and
agreements of a description so specified.
   (3)   Otherwise a reference (in whatever terms) in any instrument or agreement to
the presentation of a petition or to a decree has effect, in relation to any time after the
coming into force of this paragraph—
   (a)   in the case of a reference to the presentation of a petition, as if it included
a reference to the making of a statement; and
   (b)   in the case of a reference to a decree, as if it included a reference to a
divorce order or (as the case may be) a separation order.
   3.   If an Act or subordinate legislation—
   (a)   refers to an enactment repealed or amended by or under this Act, and

(b)   was passed or made before the repeal or amendment came into force, the Lord Chancellor may by order make such consequential modifications of any provision contained in the Act or subordinate legislation as appears to him necessary or expedient in respect of the reference.

Expressions used in paragraphs 2 and 3

4.   In paragraphs 2 and 3—

'decree' means a decree of divorce (whether a decree nisi or a decree which has been made absolute) or a decree of judicial separation;

'instrument' includes any deed, will or other instrument or document

'petition' means a petition for a decree of divorce or a petition for a decree of judicial separation; and

'subordinate legislation' has the same meaning as in the Interpretation Act 1978.

Proceedings under way

5.—(1)   Except for paragraph 6 of this Schedule, nothing in any provision of Part II, Part I of Schedule 8 or Schedule 10—

    (a)   applies to, or affects—

        (i)   any decree granted before the coming into force of the provision;

        (ii)   any proceedings begun, by petition or otherwise, before that time; or

        (iii)   any decree granted in any such proceedings;

    (b)   affects the operation of—

        (i)   the 1973 Act,

        (ii)   any other enactment, or

        (iii)   any subordinate legislation,

in relation to any such proceedings or decree or to any proceedings in connection with any such proceedings or decree; or

    (c)   without prejudice to paragraph (b), affects any transitional provision having effect under Schedule 1 to the 1973 Act.

(2)   In this paragraph, 'subordinate legislation' has the same meaning as in the Interpretation Act 1978.

6.—(1)   Section 31 of the 1973 Act has effect as amended by this Act in relation to any order under Part II of the 1973 Act made after the coming into force of the amendments.

(2)   Subsections (7) to (7F) of that section also have effect as amended by this Act in relation to any order made before the coming into force of the amendments.

Interpretation

7.   In paragraphs 8 to 15 'the 1983 Act' means the Matrimonial Homes Act 1983.

Pending applications for orders relating to occupation and molestation

8.—(1)   In this paragraph and paragraph 10 'the existing enactments' means—

    (a)   the Domestic Violence and Matrimonial Proceedings Act 1976;

    (b)   sections 16 to 18 of the Domestic Proceedings and Magistrates' Courts Act 1978; and

    (c)   sections 1 and 9 of the 1983 Act.

(2)   Nothing in Part IV, Part III of Schedule 8 or Schedule 10 affects any application for an order or injunction under any of the existing enactments which is pending immediately before the commencement of the repeal of that enactment.

Pending applications under Schedule 1 to the Matrimonial Homes Act 1983

9. Nothing in Part IV, Part III of Schedule 8 or Schedule 10 affects any application for an order under Schedule 1 to the 1983 Act which is pending immediately before the commencement of the repeal of that Schedule.

Existing orders relating to occupation and molestation

10.—(1) In this paragraph 'an existing order' means any order or injunction under any of the existing enactments which—

(a) is in force immediately before the commencement of the repeal of that enactment; or

(b) was made or granted after that commencement in proceedings brought before that commencement.

(2) Subject to sub-paragraphs (3) and (4), nothing in Part IV, Part III of Schedule 8 or Schedule 10—

(a) prevents an existing order from remaining in force; or

(b) affects the enforcement of an existing order.

(3) Nothing in Part IV, Part III of Schedule 8 or Schedule 10 affects any application to extend, vary or discharge an existing order, but the court may, if it thinks it just and reasonable to do so, treat the application as an application for an order under Part IV.

(4) The making of an order under Part IV between parties with respect to whom an existing order is in force discharges the existing order.

Matrimonial home rights

11.—(1) Any reference (however expressed) in any enactment, instrument or document (whether passed or made before or after the passing of this Act) to rights of occupation under, or within the meaning of, the 1983 Act shall be construed, so far as is required for continuing the effect of the instrument or document, as being or as the case requires including a reference to matrimonial home rights under, or within the meaning of, Part IV.

(2) Any reference (however expressed) in this Act or in any other enactment, instrument or document (including any enactment amended by Schedule 8) to matrimonial home rights under, or within the meaning of, Part IV shall be construed as including, in relation to times, circumstances and purposes before the commencement of sections 30 to 32, a reference to rights of occupation under, or within the meaning of, the 1983 Act.

12.—(1) Any reference (however expressed) in any enactment, instrument or document (whether passed or made before or after the passing of this Act) to registration under section 2(8) of the 1983 Act shall, in relation to any time after the commencement of sections 30 to 32, be construed as being or as the case requires including a reference to registration under section 31(10).

(2) Any reference (however expressed) in this Act or in any other enactment, instrument or document (including any enactment amended by Schedule 8) to registration under section 31(10) shall be construed as including a reference to—

(a) registration under section 2(7) of the Matrimonial Homes Act 1967 or section 2(8) of the 1983 Act, and

(b)   registration by caution duly lodged under section 2(7) of the Matrimonial Homes Act 1967 before 14th February 1983 (the date of the commencement of section 4(2) of the Matrimonial Homes and Property Act 1981).

13.   In sections 30 and 31 and Schedule 4—

(a)   any reference to an order made under section 33 shall be construed as including a reference to an order made under section 1 of the 1983 Act, and

(b)   any reference to an order made under section 33(5) shall be construed as including a reference to an order made under section 1 of the 1983 Act by virtue of section 2(4) of that Act.

14.   Neither section 31(11) nor the repeal by the Matrimonial Homes and Property Act 1981 of the words 'or caution' in section 2(7) of the Matrimonial Homes Act 1967, affects any caution duly lodged as respects any estate or interest before 14th February 1983.

15.   Nothing in this Schedule is to be taken to prejudice the operation of sections 16 and 17 of the Interpretation Act 1978 (which relate to the effect of repeals).

Section 66(3)   SCHEDULE 10
                                                 REPEALS

Chapter	Short title	Extent of repeal
1968 c. 63.	The Domestic and Appellate Proceedings (Restriction of Publicity) Act 1968.	Section 2(1)(b).
1973 c. 18.	The Matrimonial Causes Act 1973.	Sections 1 to 7. In section 8(1)(b), the words 'or before the decree nisi is made absolute'. Sections 9 and 10. Sections 17 and 18. Section 20. Section 22. In section 24A(3), the words 'divorce or'. In section 25(2)(h), the words 'in the case of proceedings for divorce or nullity of marriage,'. In section 28(1), the words from 'in', in the first place where it occurs, to 'nullity of marriage' in the first place where those words occur. In section 29(2), the words from 'may begin' to 'but'.

Chapter	Short title	Extent of repeal
		In section 30, the words 'divorce' and 'or judicial separation'. In section 31, in subsection (2)(a), the words 'order for maintenance pending suit and any'. In section 41, in subsection (1) the words 'divorce or' and 'or a decree of judicial separation' and in subsection (2) the words 'divorce or' and 'or that the decree of judicial separation is not to be granted'. Section 49. In section 52(2)(b), the words 'to orders for maintenance pending suit and', 'respectively' and 'section 22 and'. In Schedule 1, paragraph 8.
1973 c. 45.	The Domicile and Matrimonial Proceedings Act 1973.	In Section 5, in subsection (1), the words 'subject to section 6(3) and (4) of this Act' and, in paragraph (a), 'divorce, judicial separation or' and subsection (2). Section 6(3) and (4). In Schedule 1, in paragraph 11, in sub-paragraph (2)(a), in sub-paragraph (2)(c), in the first place where they occur, and in sub-paragraph (3)(b) and (c), the words 'in connection with the stayed proceedings'.
1976 c. 50.	The Domestic Violence and Matrimonial Proceedings Act 1976.	The whole Act.

Chapter	Short title	Extent of repeal
1978 c. 22.	The Domestic Proceedings and Magistrates' Courts Act 1978.	In section 1, paragraphs (c) and (d) and the word 'or' preceding paragraph (c). In section 7(1), the words 'neither party having deserted the other'. Sections 16 to 18. Section 28(2). Section 63(3). In Schedule 2, paragraphs 38 and 53.
1980 c. 43.	The Magistrates' Courts Act 1980.	In Schedule 7, paragraph 159.
1981 c. 54.	The Supreme Court Act 1981.	In section 18(1)(d), the words 'divorce or'.
1982 c. 53.	The Administration of Justice Act 1982.	Section 16.
1983 c. 19.	The Matrimonial Homes Act 1983.	The whole Act.
1984 c. 42.	The Matrimonial and Family Proceedings Act 1984.	Section 1. In section 21(f) the words 'except subsection (2)(e) and subsection (4)'. In section 27, the definition of 'secured periodical payments order'. In Schedule 1, paragraph 10.
1985 c. 61.	The Administration of Justice Act 1985.	In section 34(2), paragraph (f) and the word 'and' immediately preceding it. In Schedule 2, in paragraph 37, paragraph (e) and the word 'and' immediately preceding it.
1985 c. 71.	The Housing (Consequential Provisions) Act 1985.	In Schedule 2, paragraph 56.
1986 c. 53.	The Building Societies Act 1986.	In Schedule 21, paragraph 9(f).
1986 c. 55.	The Family Law Act 1986.	In Schedule 1, paragraph 27.

Chapter	Short title	Extent of repeal
1988 c. 34.	The Legal Aid Act 1988.	In section 16(9), the word 'and' at the end of paragraph (a).
1988 c. 50.	The Housing Act 1988.	In Schedule 17, paragraphs 33 and 34.
1989 c. 41.	The Children Act 1989.	Section 8(4)(c) and (f). In Schedule 11, paragraph 6(b). In Schedule 13, paragraphs 33(1) and 65(1).
1990 c. 41.	The Courts and Legal Services Act 1990.	Section 58(10)(b) and (e). In Schedule 18, paragraph 21.
1995 c. 42.	The Private International Law (Miscellaneous Provisions) Act 1995.	In the Schedule, paragraph 3.

Index